Praise for *What Have They Done with Jesus?*

"Ben Witherington does a great job of cutting through the fluff and fuss around modern thinking about Jesus. He shows that much of this isn't really 'thinking' after all. Here is in-depth, faithful scholarship made accessible for all of the rest of us. Here is orthodox, traditional Christianity not only defended but also made delightful."

—Bishop William H. Willimon

"In this accessible, yet scholarly book, Ben Witherington is absolutely right to focus on the people who were closest to Jesus. We know a lot about them, enough to know that they knew a lot about Jesus. As Witherington shows, to know the real Jesus, we don't have to resort to late and unreliable sources. The best sources are the ones we've always known about."

—Richard Bauckham, Professor of New Testament Studies, University of St. Andrews, Scotland

"Witherington insightfully critiques today's plethora of speculations about the evolution of earliest Christianity, rightly pointing us away from misinterpretations of Gnostic and other late documents and back to the earliest sources."

—Craig S. Keener, Professor of New Testament, Eastern University, and author of three commentaries on the Gospels

"Witherington brings sanity into those areas of the historical Jesus debate where it has been lacking, even as he presents what can and can't be known about the first, closest followers of Jesus and what their testimony demonstrates about Jesus himself."

—Craig L. Blomberg, Distinguished Professor of New Testament, Denver Seminary

"The question Jesus asked about himself long ago, "Who do folks say that I am?" just won't go away. Ben Witherington gauges the plausibility of some of the recent answers and presents a new portrait of the Jesus of history who emerges as a believable, compelling figure still to be reckoned with. A superb read by one of our finest scholars of Christian origins."

—Timothy George, Dean of Beeson Divinity School, Samford University, and an executive editor of *Christianity Today*

"Ben Witherington III is respected in the academy and honored in the Church. This book shows why: it is candid, it is fair-minded, and it tells the truth: nonsense is nonsense. Very few can get to the heart of historical issues as Ben Witherington can."

—Scot McKnight, Karl A. Olsson Professor in Religious Studies, North Park University

"A fresh, bracing approach, pursued with both rigor and real verve: to discover Jesus through the records we have of those closest to him, whether before his death or after it. The Marys, Peter, the Beloved Disciple, the brothers of Jesus—all come out of the shadows in this book; and so does Jesus himself."

—Robin Griffith-Jones, author of *The Four Witnesses* and Master of the Temple Church, London

WHAT HAVE THEY DONE WITH JESUS?

Beyond Strange Theories and Bad History— Why We Can Trust the Bible

BEN WITHERINGTON III

HarperSanFrancisco

A Division of HarperCollinsPublishers

HarperCollins Web site: http://www.harpercollins.com
HarperCollins®, ☰®, and HarperSanFrancisco™ are
trademarks of HarperCollins Publishers.

FIRST EDITION
Designed by Joseph Rutt

Library of Congress Cataloging-in-Publication Data
Witherington, Ben
What have they done with Jesus? : beyond strange theories and bad history —
why we can trust the bible / Ben Witherington III.
p. cm.
Includes bibliographical references and index.
ISBN-13: 978-0-06-112001-5
ISBN-10: 0-06-112001-4
1. Jesus Christ—Historicity. 2. Jesus Christ—Biography—Sources. 3. Jesus Christ—
History of doctrines. 4. Jesus Christ—Friends and associates—Biography.
5. Bible. N.T. Gospels—Biography. 6. Christianity—Historiography. I. Title.
BT303.2.W58   2006
232.9—dc22   2006041226

06 07 08 09 10 RRD (H) 10 9 8 7 6 5 4 3 2 1

To all my friends at CBS—
Miguel, Maureen, Shoshanah, John, Dustin, and Issah—
it was wonderful to work with you in the lands of the Bible.

In no case can any distinct separation be achieved between the genuine words of Jesus and constructions of the community. We do not escape the fact that we know Jesus only as the disciples remembered him. Whoever thinks that the disciples completely misunderstood their Master or even consciously falsified his picture may give fantasy free rein. From a purely scientific point of view, however, it is logical to assume that the Master can be known through his disciples' words about him and their historical influence.

—Nils Dahl,
Jesus the Christ:
The Historical Origins of
Christological Doctrine[1]

The Resurrection of Jesus is the central fact of Christian devotion and the ground of all Christian thinking. The Resurrection was not a solitary occurrence, a prodigious miracle, but an event within a framework of Jewish history, and it brought into being a new community, the church. Christianity enters history not only as a message but as a communal life, a society.... The intellectual effort of the early church was at the service of a much loftier goal than giving conceptual form to Christian belief. Its mission was to win the hearts and minds of men and women and to change their lives. Christian thinkers appealed to a much deeper level of human experience than had the religious institutions of society or the doctrines of philosophers.... It narrated a history that reached back into antiquity even to the beginning of the world, it was filled with stories of unforgettable men and women (not all admirable) who were actual historical persons rather than mythical figures.... The faithful of one generation were united to the faithful of former times, not by a set of ideas or teachings (though this was assumed) but by the community that remembered their names.... They trailed their thoughts after the lives of others ... so there was no Christian thinking without the church.

—Robert L. Wilken,
The Spirit of Early Christian Thought[2]

Contents

Contents

The Origins of the Specious

THE JESUS WE NEVER KNEW AND THE FOLLOWERS HE NEVER HAD

Why is it that we are hearing so many new things about Jesus and his earliest followers these days? Has someone struck the mother lode and found all kinds of new information about Jesus and first-century Christians? Have archaeologists dug up previously unknown documents that provide shocking new credible evidence that Jesus was married to Mary Magdalene, or his mother Mary was a supporter of revolutionaries in Galilee, or James was a hard-line Judaizer, or Paul was a renegade Zealot, or Peter went to Iraq (known then as Babylon) and wrote a letter from there? Are there really recently recovered first-century documents that tell a very unfamiliar tale about the life of Jesus and the origins of Christianity, providing evidence so compelling that it eclipses and corrects what we have long heard about these subjects?

Right from the beginning of this study I must say, *Caveat emptor!* Readers should beware of shocking new claims about Jesus or his earliest followers based on flimsy evidence. They need to read the fine print on the bottle of so-called truth serum before swallowing the contents in a single gulp. A perfect illustration of my point is the long-ballyhooed "secret" Gospel of Mark supposedly discovered by Morton Smith in 1958, which included a "value-added" story about Jesus having an encounter with a naked youth who ran off from the posse in the Garden of Gethsemane. It looks now as if we were being scammed by Professor Smith: his fraud has been thoroughly exposed to the light of day.[1]

But some people maintain that the major fraud was perpetrated in a more "orthodox" direction. They claim we've been snookered into thinking that earliest Christianity was far more uniform than it in fact was. Relying on "secret teachings" showing that Jesus was closer to later Gnostics than to earlier Jewish sages, they believe that there was at least one

Jesus community that simply meditated on Jesus's sayings (ignoring his death and resurrection). Are those folks right—are there really "lost Christianities" that can trace their pedigree all the way back to the first century, communities of faith that were suppressed by the church and only now are getting their proper due? Was earliest Christianity really like dueling banjos playing competing and discordant tunes?

The news media are all abuzz with these sorts of questions, and network after network is running specials that address such issues. Recently I did an interview with a major network for a Christmas show on Mary and the virginal conception, and the first question out of the chute was, Could Mary have been a temple prostitute in the Jerusalem Temple who was raped by someone there? It was suggested that this is why Luke, in his gospel, has Jesus say, "Didn't you know I had to be in my Father's house?" (2:41–52) when Jesus visited there as a twelve-year-old. Inquiring minds want to know: Have we been duped about Jesus and his earliest followers?

Perhaps a better set of questions might be, What is it about our culture that makes us prone to listen to sensational claims about Jesus and his earliest followers, even when there is little or no hard evidence to support such conjectures? Why are we especially prone to this when it comes to the origins of Christianity? Why would a poorly researched but readable thriller like *The Da Vinci Code*, which claims to reveal startling new truths about Jesus and his life, create such a sensation in our culture? Let's pause and reflect for a moment on the religious character of our own culture.

TAKE A CULTURE, A RELIGIOUS CULTURE: GULLIBLE'S TRAVELS

In America we live in a Jesus-haunted culture that is biblically illiterate. Jesus is a household name, and yet only a distinct minority of Americans have studied an English translation of the original documents that tell us about Jesus, much less read them in the original Greek. In this sort of environment, almost any wild theory about Jesus or his earliest followers can pass for knowledge with some audiences, because so few people actually know the primary sources, the relevant texts, or the historical context with which we should be concerned. In our soap opera culture, perhaps it was inevitable that someone would turn the story of Jesus into a soap opera. The problem is, some people are naive enough to believe it. Maybe we need to heed the old saying of my grandmother: "Don't be so open-minded that your brains fall out." It's still good advice. But there are other factors than just gullibility that are in play as well.

There are a large number of people in America whose spiritual birth certificate comes from the state of Missouri: they say, "Show me." In other words, they've been burned enough by bad experiences in the church or by extravagant claims by preachers selling snake oil or simply promoting themselves that they position themselves resolutely at the other end of the spectrum from gullible—they're profoundly skeptical, particularly of traditional answers. Strange as it may seem, while these skeptical folks won't listen patiently to old answers they've heard before (maybe even heard in church), they will gladly listen to new theories, even when there is little or no solid evidence to support them.

Another characteristic of our culture is that we have bought into the essential sales pitch which drives our economy. All too often we get caught up in the myth that the latest is the greatest; we buy into the "new is true" phenomenon. But frankly, historical truth can as often, if not more often, be found in old sources and old traditions than in new ones. In fact, I would say that historical truths are far more likely to be found in older sources that have stood close critical scrutiny and the test of time.

It is one of the primary principles of good historical inquiry that, all other things being equal, the sources written closest to a particular event—that is, the sources most in touch with eyewitnesses—are more likely to give us clear insights into the origins of that particular historical phenomenon. This is not always the case, of course; but in general, historians agree that later sources require more critical scrutiny than earlier ones precisely because later ones lack the check and balance of being corrected by those who were present at the events recorded. It is especially crucial in the case of Jesus that we go back to the original inner circle of his followers—men and women who knew Jesus or, in the case of Paul, who had contact with an array of others who knew Jesus personally.

We need to understand that the documents we find in the New Testament—including the gospels, the book of Acts, and Paul's letters, to mention a few—are our earliest and best sources for understanding the character of Jesus and the rise of Christianity. They are not products of revisionist history of a later, non-eyewitness generation, nor were they written in response to some other, even earlier "lost Christianity," such that we could claim that early Christian history was written by the "winners."[2]

To the contrary, our earliest documents were written by members of a tiny minority sect that was rather tightly knit ideologically and had good social networks among its communities in the eastern end of the Roman Empire. Insofar as it was engaged in a religious struggle, it was struggling in the main with the larger pagan culture and with its mother religion, Judaism, to survive. This is a very different matter than suggesting it was engaged largely in family feuds in the first century. We have no good evidence that the earliest Christians were in pitched battles with rival forms of early Christianity or that there were parallel streams of early Christianity all flowing out of the Christ event, streams that only occasionally crossed each other's paths. As a careful study of the inner circle of Jesus will show, these folks all knew each other, worked with each other, and (when they disagreed, as they sometimes did vociferously) worked out concordats such as we see in Acts 15 so that they could continue to be a basically unified movement in the empire.

There is yet another reason why American culture is all abuzz about "lost" or alternate Christianities. It's what I call the "flamin' fundy factor." What I mean by this is that a disproportionate number of fundamentalists manage to get on TV, and they don't do Jesus or authentic Christianity any real service. Many scholars whose area is the Bible or early Christianity watch fundamentalists passing them in the fast lane, garnering way too much attention. This causes the scholars to see red, and they react by trying to present Christianity in a way that is as distant as possible from what they see fundamentalists teaching; they offer ideas and theories that they find more personally congenial. I do understand this reaction (or, better said, overreaction). Such scholars are correct that arrogance and ignorance are a lethal combination, especially when a person is dealing with an important historical subject, and these vices are paraded all too frequently on TV and elsewhere when the subject is Jesus or his earliest followers.

One such scholar who overreacted to the fundamentalist element in our culture, and in fact was one of the founders of the now famous (or infamous) Jesus Seminar, came right out and said that part of his mission was to deconstruct the "Sunday school Jesus."[3] This is hardly what one would call an objective historical agenda. But the story of Robert Funk is hardly an isolated one in our culture. In fact, there are numerous tales of scholars in America who came out of conservative churches like men and women fleeing burning buildings. Having lost some or all of their traditional Christian faith, they have set out to rewrite the history of Jesus and/or early Christianity. In some cases they have looked down the well of history and seen their own reflection in the face of Jesus or his earliest followers. I understand this narcissistic spiritual pilgrimage, though I can't identify with it.

It is true, unfortunately, that the church is often the worst witness to Jesus and the early Christian movement. That's because when you consistently do historical work out of your own personal experience, whatever that experience may be, you are bound to skew the historical data some. Revisionist history writing is often done with the goal of making that history more appealing and interesting to the writers as they try to reclaim fragments of the past they still find user-friendly.

The scholarly world also has to contend with what I call the "justification by doubt" factor. Some scholars think they must prove (to themselves and/or others) that they are good critical scholars by showing how much of the Jesus tradition or the New Testament in general they can discount, explain away, or discredit. This supposedly demonstrates that they are objective. At most, all it shows is that they are capable of critical thinking. Oddly, these same scholars often fail to apply the same critical rigor and skepticism to their own pet extracanonical texts or pet theories. If such scholars would reflect diligently on why the four canonical gospels have stood the test of time and other apocryphal gospels and texts have not, they might well conclude that it's because the canonical gospels are our earliest gospels and have actual historical substance, while the later gospels have little or none. It's not because of later political maneuvering in the church of the fourth or fifth century that the earliest gospels are our best historical sources; it's because they were written by honest, believing persons who were themselves eyewitnesses or who heard direct eyewitness testimony about Jesus and his first followers. The later gospels of Mary or Philip or Judas or even Thomas were not written by such well-informed persons.

Finally, there are presuppositional issues that come into play in our American culture. Some modern scholars, including historians, simply assume that miracles *cannot* happen and therefore *do not* happen. This is a faith assumption actually, since no human being has exhaustive knowledge of present reality, never mind the past. Such folks seem to assume that the rest of human experience is identical to their own: if they themselves have not experienced a miracle, neither has anyone else. This is called *solipsism,* or making the mistake of generalizing from the part to the whole.

Even some contemporary Bible scholars assume that miracles must be left out of account if we are going to do "scholarly" work like "other *critical* historians." This is a carryover from the anti-supernatural bias of many Enlightenment historians, but it seems a very odd presupposition today. Our postmodern world is experiencing a newfound openness to miracles, magic, the supernatural, the spiritual, or whatever you want to call it. Our culture is Harry Pottering around at this juncture, and is happy to do so.

It's a shame that the academy thinks it an unscholarly enterprise to ask whether there might be something remarkable and real generating this sea change in the culture. As a historian, I am ashamed to say that historical scholars are often the last ones to figure out what's going on in their own culture, perhaps because they live in their minds and their minds are fixated on the past.

Perhaps current science is giving us a wake-up call. We hear one scientist after another professing Christian faith or Jewish faith and arguing that the empirical data we have about the space-time continuum cannot rule out the possibility of miracles, not least because it cannot declare the space-time continuum a fixed or a closed system, subject only to "known" natural laws.[4]

These then are just some of the factors in play in our culture, and in the scholarly subculture, which have led to the expositing of new theories about Jesus and his earliest followers, the widespread belief in some of these theories, and the press's eagerness to publicize such theories. After all, it is only what's "new" that's news—right? But what would our intellectual world look like if we didn't listen to the siren song of our own culture, the song claiming that the "latest is the greatest" or that "there is secret knowledge to be had about truths long suppressed"?

Right at Easter time, just as the dandelions are starting to appear in my yard, a new crop of theories about Jesus and the Gospels usually pops up as well, often rushed into the Easter market. Clearly the appropriate amount of fertilizer has been applied to these supposed "new revelations" to make such hothouse theories grow, seemingly overnight. This Easter is no different: we have (1) Bart Ehrman's *Misquoting Jesus* climbing up the *New York Times* best seller list; (2) the *National Geographic* special on the "Gospel of Judas," which is supposed to rock our worldviews when it comes to the relationship of Jesus and Judas; (3) Michael Baigent's *The Jesus Papers*, which revives the "swoon theory" in regard to Jesus's death, a theory thoroughly discredited when it first was noised about in the book *The Passover Plot*; and (4) James Tabor's *The Jesus Dynasty*, which presents us once more with a Schweitzerian Jesus, Jesus the messianic prophet who got the timing of the end of the world wrong and failed to bring in the kingdom he promised would supplant the Romans.

In my judgment only the last of these "revelations" deserves extended critique as it really does present a theory about Jesus and the origins of Christianity that attempts to grapple with the hard historical, archaeological, and literary data from the first century that is of relevance to the discussion. Accordingly we will critique this work at length in an appendix to this study, but here we must say a few things about the other three works.

Baigent's work is the easiest to deal with, as it requires that Baigent explain away all the evidence we have from Paul (our earliest New Testament writer), from the canonical gospels, from Josephus, and from Roman sources (such as Tacitus and later Suetonius) that Jesus suffered the extreme penalty and died from crucifixion under and at the hands of Pontius Pilate. Not many people are taking seriously Baigent's attempts at revisionist history. It goes against every shred of first-century evidence, Christian or otherwise, that we have about Jesus's demise.

Bart Ehrman's work deserves more serious attention, but in my judgment he has done what the British call "over-egging the pudding." By this I mean his conclusions far outstrip his evidence for them. Textual variants in manuscripts of New Testament books are many and varied to be sure, but it is simply a myth to take the variants Ehrman deals with in his books as evidence that some essential Christian belief was cooked up after the fact and retrojected into the text of New Testament documents by overzealous and less than scrupulous scribes. There is no hard evidence in any of the variants he treats either in *The Orthodox Corruption of Scripture* or his more recent *Misquoting Jesus* that in any way demonstrates that ideas like the virginal conception, crucifixion, bodily resurrection of Jesus, or even the Trinity were ideas later added to copies of New Testament documents to make them more "orthodox." This is simply false.

What is the case is that we have evidence of such ideas being amplified or clarified by overzealous scribes in a text like 1 John 5:7b. That is the most that sober historical judgment will allow in regard to such variants. There is a reason that both Ehrman's mentor in text criticism and mine, Bruce Metzger, has said that there is nothing in these variants that really challenges any essential Christian belief: they don't. I would add that other experts in text criticism, such as Gordon Fee, have been equally emphatic about the flawed nature of Ehrman's analysis of the significance of such textual variants.[5]

This brings us to the "Gospel of Judas," now touted as a document that can shake the faith of Christians worldwide due to its revelation that Jesus put Judas up to betraying him. Unfortunately, this is hype, not history. The Gospel of Judas is a document carbon-dated to the beginning of the fourth century and bearing all the earmarks of a Gnostic theology that did not exist before the second half of the second century. Judas, for example, is quoted as telling Jesus he will help him slough off the flesh and so get into the spiritual realm and condition more quickly if Judas will just betray him to the authorities. This sort of flesh/spirit dualism certainly characterizes much of later Gnosticism, but it in no way comports with the historical Jesus's view, for he was a proponent of a very different form of eternal life—life in a resurrection body.

The document is written in Coptic, not in Greek, and its relationship to a document of this name mentioned by Irenaeus about 180 needs to be established, not assumed, since the content that Irenaeus mentions for the document of this name does not match up very well with the content of this later and Coptic Gospel of Judas. It is possible that the Coptic Gospel of Judas is based on and expands upon the earlier Judas document, but since we don't have the latter, we cannot be sure. We need hard evidence that there was a Greek Gospel of Judas. Thus far, this evidence is lacking. Even if it was to surface, such a document would only be of value for reconstructing the Gnostic theology of the second through fourth centuries, not for reconstructing what happened to the historical Jesus or Judas. In other words, it can illumine the church historical discussion of the period in which Gnosticism thrived, but it can't tell us anything about the first century, since we have no evidence at all that this document can be traced back to a first-century author. To say otherwise is an argument entirely from silence, not from hard evidence.

When I asked my friend Dr. A. J. Levine, who was on the team of scholars involved with the unveiling of the Gospel of Judas, whether she thought anything in the Gospel of Judas tells us anything about the historical Jesus or historical Judas she was emphatic—it tells us nothing about them. She was equally clear that she didn't see anything in these documents that could or should shake the faith of modern Christians, because of course this document is not a first-century document written by anyone who knew Jesus or Judas.

Furthermore, in the case of the Gospel of Judas we are dealing with a practice called "pseudonymity"—the false attribution of a document to a notable figure of an earlier era. The reason for this practice is simple: the actual author of the document does not have the authority of an apostolic or eyewitness, and so he attributes the document to someone who is known to have existed during the time of Jesus. It needs to be stressed that this practice, while not rare, was not an accepted literary practice of the era in question. Indeed it was considered morally reprehensible when detected.

I have demonstrated at length in another work that this practice was roundly condemned not only by church fathers in the second century, but also by various Greco-Roman writers who wrote between the second century B.C. and the second century A.D.[6] The Gospel of Judas is such a document, and like all other such documents it is intended to deceive the reader into thinking it is authored by a person of an earlier historical period. Such practices do not comport with the high standards of truth and honesty that Jesus and his first followers upheld.

THE POINT OF DEPARTURE, THE RULES OF THE GAME

How does a new religion actually start? The traditional wisdom is that it requires a compelling and charismatic figure who impresses people by saying and doing things that are dramatic and noble and above all inspiring and memorable. That charismatic leader model doesn't seem to adequately explain the Jesus movement, however. Jesus died an ignominious death by crucifixion, the "extreme punishment" of the overlords in that era, suggesting that he generated as many foes as friends, as many adversaries as advocates. His ministry was fraught with peril in the midst of perilous times in a land that was occupied territory—a Roman province, in fact.

Since Jesus did not leave us a written legacy ("the Jesus papers"), we must look for indirect evidence for how Christianity got started. As New Testament scholar James Dunn has stressed, what we have in the New Testament and elsewhere is Jesus remembered.[7] But remembered by whom? Was there an inner circle of Jesus's followers who were the bearers of the story of Jesus to all future generations? And if so, who were these persons, and what were their stories? These questions get at the heart of the matter.

It was New Testament scholar Alfred Loisy who said that Jesus preached the kingdom but it was the church that showed up. Yes, that's part of the truth. Since it is so, perhaps it would be easier to understand the rise of Christianity if we focused on the impact crater that we do know about and have a record of. Taking that stance, this book looks at the impact Jesus made on his earliest followers, the so-called inner circle. We could quibble about who should be included in that inner circle, but I would urge that the following is a reasonable short list: Mary, James, and Jude from Jesus's own physical family; Peter, the Beloved Disciple, Mary Magdalene, Joanna, and Paul from outside his immediate family.

There are other figures we might include in such a study, of course. For instance, we might include the sons of Zebedee, especially if his son John was also the Beloved Disciple. But this is far from clear from a historical point of view. In fact, it is very unlikely that the Beloved Disciple is *that* John, since the stories that mention the Zebedees—such as the story of the

raising of Jairus's daughter and the story of the transfiguration—are found
in the synoptic gospels but not in the Fourth Gospel. We would expect
these stories to be in the Fourth Gospel if it was written by a Zebedee.

We might even want to include the man we now call Doubting
Thomas, in view of the great interest today in the so-called Gospel of
Thomas, but unfortunately we know nothing substantive about Thomas
after the Easter period, nor do we have any firm or clear evidence that this
Thomas is the author of the Gospel of Thomas. The Gospel of John tells
us that Thomas was of a rather fatalistic bent and that he was not present
when Jesus first appeared to his male disciples on Easter. Hearing of that
appearance, Thomas demanded tactile proof of Jesus's return from death.
Jesus is said to have appeared to the male disciples again a week after Easter, this time with Thomas present, and the disciple was exhorted to stop
disbelieving (the Greek doesn't say *doubting*) and instead do the opposite.
He then offered the greatest confession of who Jesus is in the whole of the
Fourth Gospel ("My Lord and my God," John 20:28). It is interesting that
the text does not say that he took Jesus up on his offer to put his fingers
in Jesus's wounds.

Later we find Thomas back in Galilee with six other disciples when Jesus
appeared to them once more. After that the trail grows cold, however.
Thomas is not mentioned in the book of Acts or in any other document of
the first century, unless of course one believes that the Gospel of Thomas
was written by this Thomas. Alas, this would be a decidedly minority opinion among scholars worldwide. Most scholars of whatever theological
persuasion (or none) are convinced that the Gospel of Thomas is a second-
century document based on earlier gospel (and Pauline) texts and that it
certainly was not authored by one of the original inner circle of Jesus's disciples. But I will say more about this matter in due course.

I have decided to stick with the very short list of eyewitnesses already
mentioned, with Paul being the odd man out because he seems not to
have had a personal relationship with the historical Jesus. Nonetheless, he
is a very crucial link for the transition of the Jesus movement from Jewish
sect to world religion. If it is true in any sense that Peter stands behind the
Gospel of Mark (as is often argued) and that Paul was a sometime companion and mentor of the author of the Gospel of Luke, then my short list
could be said to account for at least three of the gospels (that is, all but
Matthew), the book of Acts, the Pauline corpus, the Johannine letters, the
Petrine letters, and the sermons/letters of James and Jude. In short, it
could be said to account for almost all of our earliest written witnesses
about early Christianity.

In the following chapters I intend to draw a portrait of each of these people, based on a critical analysis of our earliest and best sources, commenting on their relationship with Jesus and other relevant topics. Even Paul—the *ek troma,* or "one born out of due season," as he puts it himself in dramatic fashion (1 Cor. 15:8)—made bold to claim to be an eyewitness of the risen Lord, by no small miracle on the road to Damascus. And at the end of the day it is this fact, having seen the risen Lord, that binds all these persons together, cementing their place in the family of faith, centered on Jesus. Without that fact, none of these men and women would have been founding figures of early Christianity. But with that fact, even outsiders like Paul and disbelievers like James and Jude could become insiders almost overnight.

In other words, I am claiming that after the crucifixion, it took a miracle to generate the church—indeed, even to generate the inner circle of Jesus's followers. Our earliest sources, by their own confession, are clear that almost the entire inner circle of male disciples denied, deserted, or betrayed Jesus, while the women watched him die and then went to lay a wreath, as it were, on the tomb. It is the historical event we call Easter that reversed this drastic trend, without which the story of Jesus would have been left in the dustbin of history.

But what do we know about these original witnesses of Jesus and his resurrection? What are their stories? What were their contributions to Christianity? We will explore these sorts of questions in the following chapters, in an effort to understand earliest Christianity better. I believe that this focus on specific historical persons is more likely to help us understand our subject than abstract analysis of social or anthropological or even historical factors could do, though we cannot ignore such factors. Nor do I think that a history-of-ideas approach to this subject in the end could do it full justice. Christianity was not in the first instance a movement generated by texts, but rather one generated by oral proclamation in a largely oral culture and by the making of personal contacts and the building of personal relationships—the creating of community, as historian Robert Wilkens has so rightly stressed (see this book's epigraph).

To the reader I would urge the following at the outset: read all of these chapters together and evaluate the cumulative impact of the material. By learning about Jesus's inner circle you will indirectly learn about Jesus, since you can discern a lot about a person by evaluating the company he keeps. The ordering of this book is simple. I will deal first with those who played an important role in the life or ministry of the historical Jesus as well as in the church, and then I will deal with those (James, Jude, Paul) whose main if not sole contribution to the Jesus movement came after the death and resurrection of Jesus. This amounts to studying these figures in chronological order of their contact with Jesus, roughly speaking.

There will, I promise, be some surprises along the way, but this investigation won't entail resurrecting the ghosts of lost Christianities—movements that came into being as offshoots of mainstream Christianity in the second through fourth centuries, well after the apostolic era. No, as it turns out, there are quite enough surprises and interesting possibilities and permutations to be ferreted out of our earliest and best sources, which are found in the New Testament. We don't need to look to later and more dubious material to learn something new about Jesus and his inner circle.

PART ONE

THE WOMEN IN JESUS'S LIFE

ONE

Joanna and Mary Magdalene: Female Disciples from the Seashore of Galilee

It cannot have been easy for women of Jesus's locale and time. The Maccabean struggles had led to only a brief period of independence, and then once more Jews were thrust under the onerous system of corrupt client kings or, as was the case in Judea, the even greater indignity of direct rule by Rome. Furthermore, the rulers were both literally and figuratively taxing the people. Herod Antipas, the ruler of Galilee, of Idumean or Edomite descent, was not really a Jew. He was an Idumean—that is, a descendent of the Edomites, Israel's bitter rivals for many centuries. He modeled himself on Hellenistic rulers. Due to that background and to his sly and predatory character, Jesus called him "that fox" (Luke 13:31–32). A ruler so insensitive to Jewish religious ardor that he would build a capital city, Tiberias, on a Jewish graveyard and then try to cajole people into living in that unclean spot cannot have been well thought of by Torah-true Jews.[8]

Furthermore, people growing up in the region of Galilee, by the shores of its large lake, would have encountered commerce and traffic from various directions and various neighboring cultures, most of it not very (or not at all) Jewish. The fishing trade, the economic foundation of the region, took the men away for days at a time, leaving the women behind to hold things together, keep the family going, cultivate the garden, and keep so busy that they could not cultivate their minds or spirits to their full potential.

So far as we can tell, women were not disciples of early Jewish teachers before Jesus's time. Prophetesses such as Miriam were distant memories, even though our Mary Magdalene was likely named after her. It is not a surprise that deeply spiritual and bright women might have leaped at the chance to dabble in foreign religions from nearby Gentile territory or jump on the bandwagon of a radical rabbi from Nazareth when he offered them a chance to fish for followers. This must have seemed like a big step up from gutting fish and sweeping dirt floors, though these women continued to serve the traveling band of disciples either by patronage or by actually provisioning and cooking for them ("helping to support them out of their own means," Luke 8:3). What then can we say about these remarkable women who seem to have dropped everything to follow Jesus? We will examine the stories of two of the more prominent female disciples, Joanna and Mary Magdalene, and see what their tales reveal.

JOANNA/JUNIA: FOLLOWER OF JESUS, APOSTLE OF CHRIST

Jesus, it can be said, had an entourage, and that entourage, according to the Gospel of Luke, included several women of substance. Luke tells us that as Jesus traveled through the cities and villages of Galilee, "proclaiming and bringing the good news of the kingdom of God," he was accompanied by the Twelve as well as by "some women who had been cured of evil spirits and infirmities: Mary, called Magdalene, from whom seven demons had gone out, and Joanna, the wife of Herod's steward Chuza, and Susanna and many others, who provided for them out of their resources" (Luke 8:1–3). We will focus first on the second-named woman: the wife of Herod Antipas's steward.

Herod Antipas, a son of King Herod the Great, ruled over Galilee and Perea (the desert region south of Galilee and east of the Jordan River and the Dead Sea). As the wife of his steward, Joanna was no peasant. Rather, she would have been a middle- or even high-status woman apparently able to travel on her own or with friends without fear of reprisal. Her traveling, then, is no surprise. What *is* surprising is who she traveled with. Women in early Jewish culture were not supposed to fraternize with men they weren't related to, never mind travel around Galilee with them.

And yet Joanna not only followed a controversial man named Jesus around Galilee; she supported him financially. Joanna apparently had access to her husband's material wealth and used it, as the earlier quote tells us, to become one of Jesus's patronesses.[9] Her funds helped Jesus, the Twelve, and the women disciples travel, eat, and minister together.

Joanna's support of Jesus is especially surprising because of her husband's employment. After all, Herod Antipas was the infamous beheader of John the Baptist. He cannot have been pleased that his steward's wife was running after Jesus, a radical sage and a relative of John the Baptist. It surely didn't help Chuza's situation that Jesus, as noted earlier, had called Herod "that fox."

That Joanna would nevertheless leave her home and put her husband's career at risk to follow Jesus shows how very attractive the ministry of Jesus must have been to women and how brave (or foolhardy) Joanna was. But there were good reasons to follow Jesus. He did not treat women as if they were made unclean periodically by menstruation; he saw God's grace as having overruled such conditions and the rules they entailed. This open attitude allowed women to become his close and constant disciples without fear of contaminating others in the circle. Second, Jesus apparently dismissed contemporary taboos against men talking with women who were not their relatives (cf., e.g., John 4:27).[10] This was a radical step in a highly patriarchal culture like that of Galilee. Indeed, it would be a radical step in most Middle Eastern cultures today.

When Jesus traveled to Jerusalem for the Passover festival, his unusual entourage of women and men accompanied him. This, too, is extraordinary. Normally women went to such festivals with their own families, but Joanna and several other Galilean women broke the cultural norm to be with Jesus. These women were likewise present at the crucifixion. Luke tells us, "All his acquaintances, including the women who had followed him from Galilee, stood at a distance, watching these things" (23:49). According to Luke, Joanna and other women not only witnessed the death, but followed Joseph of Arimathea to the tomb. When they saw where Jesus had been laid, they went to someone's house and prepared burial spices and ointment, returning to the tomb once the Sabbath was over to anoint and cleanse Jesus's body and to wrap spices in the burial shroud to retard the odor.[11]

But when the women—Luke later identifies them as "Mary Magdalene, Joanna, Mary the mother of James, and the other women" (Luke 24:10)—arrived at the tomb on Easter morning, "they found the stone rolled away from the tomb.... When they went in, they did not find the body" (Luke 24:3). Two angels—"men in dazzling clothes"—approached the women and asked them, "Why do you look for the living among the dead? He is not here, but has risen. Remember how he told you, while he was still in Galilee, that the Son of Man must be handed over to sinners, and be crucified, and on the third day rise again?" The text continues: "Then they remembered his [Jesus's] words, and returning from the tomb they told all this to the eleven and to all the rest."

Notice the repetition of the word "remember." With that literary device the author is telling us that the women had, when Jesus was still alive, received teaching from him about his coming death and resurrection. It was not just the Twelve who had been taught these things at Caesarea Philippi, as we might have assumed based on that story in Luke 9:18–27. To the contrary, the women had also been instructed in the crucial coming events in Jesus's life. They too were intended to play a role in these matters.

The men apparently thought that the women's tale of a risen Jesus was nonsense, "an idle tale," and "they did not believe them" (Luke 24:11). This is not surprising: women in that culture were generally considered too emotional or too illiterate to be valid witnesses. For this reason, it is all the more striking that women were the key witnesses to the heart of the later Christian creed, for they were last at the cross, first at the tomb, first to hear the Easter message, first to see the risen Lord, and first to proclaim the Easter message. We may assume that Joanna, like Mary Magdalene, is alluded to in Acts 1:14, where we learn that "certain women" prayed with the disciples, but it would appear that Joanna's story ends in that scene in the upper room. Or does it?

In Romans 16 Paul mentions several church leaders and workers who are in Rome or will be traveling to Rome, and he asks the locals to treat them well. The list includes a handful of women, including one Junia and her husband, Andronicus, mentioned at Romans 16:7. The Latin name Junia is in fact equivalent to the Hebrew Joanna. In Paul's day, Galilee and Judea were territories within the Roman Empire. In order to survive, many Jews, especially the elite, adopted Roman customs, conventions, and even names. It is no accident that Herod Antipas, a client king of Rome, named his capital Tiberias after the Roman emperor. Even the Sea of Galilee came to be known as Lake Tiberias in this period.

As a steward or estate agent responsible for managing and buying the king's land, Chuza undoubtedly moved in circles where he would have had close contact with Romans and the Jewish royal family. It is quite possible that he and his wife adopted Latin names. Might Paul's Junia be the woman Luke calls Joanna? On first glance this seems unlikely, since Junia is said to be married to a man named Andronicus, which is not equivalent to the Hebrew Chuza. Yet the name Andronicus could be a nickname, meaning no more than "conqueror of men."

There are several clues in Romans 16:7 that suggest another verdict. Paul writes: "Greet Andronicus and Junia, my kinsmen who were in prison with me; they are notable among the apostles, and they were in Christ before I was." First Paul tells us, by calling Junia his "kin," that she is Jewish, not Roman. Second, Paul reveals that he knows this couple intimately:

they had done time together, apparently imprisoned because of their work as ministers and missionaries. This is actually quite unusual. Criminal women were generally not jailed but were put under house arrest, unless they had done something notorious to offend a city's officials. Paul appears to be suggesting that Junia and her husband were, as he was, ring-leaders of the "notorious" Christian sect that was causing so much trouble throughout the empire.

Third, Paul notes that Junia and Andronicus were in Christ *before* him. Paul was converted only two or three years after Jesus died, which would mean that Junia and Andronicus numbered among Jesus's earliest followers. But where might they have been, that they were "in Christ" before Paul? Surely they would have had to be part of the Jerusalem church that Paul himself persecuted when he was Saul the Pharisee!

Finally, and most importantly, the couple are said to be "*notable* [or, depending on the translation, *prominent* or *outstanding*] among the apostles." The Greek word *episemoi* can mean any of these things but in all cases is a superlative of some sort. Whether we call them prominent or notable or outstanding apostles, Paul clearly thinks highly of them.

The Greek phrase has sometimes been taken to mean "notable to the apostles" or even "noted by the apostles," but the Greek preposition *en* here surely has its normal meaning of "in" or "among," as Origen and John Chrysostom, the earliest Greek commentators on this verse, admit. Some scholars have tried to minimize the importance of this statement, suggesting that Paul is using the term "apostle" to refer to an emissary of a local church, as he seems to do in 2 Corinthians 8:23 and perhaps Philippians 2:25. But in both of those texts the word "apostle" is qualified in such a way that it is clear he is talking about a local church emissary. There is no such qualification in our text; rather, the context suggests that by "apostle" Paul means the same thing here that he means when he applies the term to himself, since he is describing itinerant missionaries who did time with him courtesy of the Roman system of jurisprudence.[12]

Paul's letter to the Romans, written around A.D. 57–58, predates the earliest gospel (Mark) by at least ten to twelve years, which means that Romans 16:7 is the first New Testament reference to a woman as an apostle. This is impressive, especially when we remember that when Paul uses the term "apostle" this way (without any qualification), he means an Apostle with a capital A—that is, someone who has seen the risen Lord, has been commissioned by Jesus, and now serves as a missionary.[13] In sum, Paul is writing about a Jewish woman called Junia (but presumably named Joanna in Hebrew) who was an early, close, and prominent follower of

Jesus, who witnessed Jesus's resurrection, and who then boldly spread the gospel. Might she be the Joanna of Luke's gospel?

I believe she is. One could ask, "But what happened to Chuza?" I suspect that he divorced Joanna and she then remarried a Christian named Andronicus, with whom she undertook missionary work that took her to the heart of the empire (and, at least once, to jail). It's easy to see why Chuza would have divorced a woman who was using his money to chase after a radical prophet who had insulted his boss. In the honor-and-shame culture in which they lived, Herod Antipas would hardly have retained Chuza as an estate agent if Chuza had retained Joanna as a wife! The divorce might also explain why Joanna was free to follow Jesus to Jerusalem for Passover in the year 30.

As historians continue to learn about the social context in which women operated in the first-century world, and as small points of language and linguistics become clear, fresh insights into scripture are made possible.[14] I admit it takes a certain amount of detective work to connect Joanna with Junia. Nevertheless, the links are plausible. They are strengthened by the fact that Junia *must* have been part of the original circle of followers of Jesus in Jerusalem if indeed she was "in Christ" before Paul's conversion in A.D. 34–35. This was before there was a mission outside of Israel, never mind a mission to Gentiles. Furthermore, Luke presents Joanna as a bold and prominent disciple, and Paul's Junia is similarly characterized.

Whether they are two women or, as I believe, one, the two depictions provide an unusual glimpse into the life of an unusual woman in the early church.[15] Here indeed we have a profile in courage and great faith. The question this raises is, What manner of man could inspire this sort of loyalty, courage, and devotion? The biblical facts of Joanna's life offer a remarkable though indirect witness to the towering figure Joanna believed Jesus to be. We will say more about this after considering one of Joanna's more famous female cohorts in ministry, Mary Magdalene.

THE TALE OF MIRIAM OF MIGDAL: A RECOVERING SPIRITUALIST

We do not know nearly as much as we would like to about the women who followed Jesus. Our clues are partial and piecemeal at best, and we must rely on our general knowledge of the social and religious milieu to help us fill in the gaps. One of the things we do know about socially and spiritually oppressive situations (such as that of Jewish women in Jesus's time and place) is that the marginalized often frantically look for help in strange places—dabbling in darkness, necromancy, shadowy spirits. We may remember the tale of the medium of Endor whom King Saul consulted in his desperation, seeking to call up the shade of Samuel the prophet and get some answers and direction (1 Sam. 28). Desperate times often lead to desperate measures, whether they call for them or not.

We need to clear up a few facts first. No, Magdalene was not Mary's last name; rather, it identified her as coming from the tiny village of Migdal, along the northwestern Galilean shore. Her first name was probably actually Miriam, after the sister of Moses.

Miriam of Migdal was possessed by demons before she met Jesus, according to Luke 8:2. In fact, she endured a particularly malignant form of possession: seven demons had a death grip on her. (Seven, in the Jewish way of thinking, was a complete set, perhaps not as severe as the "Legion" in the Gadarene demoniac story of Mark 5, but nonetheless a very severe case.) For whatever reason, Miriam had dabbled one time too many with the dark powers and perhaps also the spirits of the dead, and instead of being able to manipulate them, they came to control, indeed to possess, her. Tales of demonic possession and exorcism are well known throughout the last two thousand years and from many different cultures, of course, and such stories continue to be told even today. Sometimes modern and even postmodern people have assumed that such references are simply about people who suffer fits due to a mental illness or epilepsy. While that is perhaps true in some cases, there is considerable and credible cross-cultural testimony to the reality of evil spirits and the practice of exorcism over many centuries, including our own. The reality is that occult and astrological practices existed in Jesus's day and have continued in every century since then, and it is precisely these sorts of practices that have often led to spiritual problems in the life of the practitioners. Miriam may well have been such a practitioner. Thus it will not do to simply dismiss the possibility that Jesus addressed some spiritual malady in the life of the woman from Migdal.

Among the types of miracles that Jesus performed, exorcism is one of the most (if not the most) frequently reported in our earliest-written gospel (Mark), though not many scholars have wanted to highlight this fact in the modern era. Exorcism made Jesus a very controversial figure in his day, as the debate in Mark 3 over Jesus being in league with Beelzebul or Satan shows.[16] In fact, it made Jesus too controversial for some: the Gospel of John, for example, reports no exorcisms performed by Jesus.

From a Jewish viewpoint, demons not only degraded a person, they defiled a person, and so they were called "unclean spirits." A person who was unclean was not to participate in group gatherings, such as worship in the synagogue, for fear of contamination of others. This in turn suggests that Miriam of Migdal, by dabbling with the darker forces, had managed to cut herself off from spiritual nurture and training in her own village or in the nearby fishing villages. Unlike physical uncleanness, spiritual uncleanness was harder to shed.

Then a controversial healer and preacher from Nazareth somehow crossed paths with Miriam, perhaps when he was preaching along the northwest shore of the Sea of Galilee, and he exorcised the demons from her.[17] This is the very first thing we learn about this woman in Luke 8:2, in an almost parenthetical comment by Luke. She too must have been rather notorious, something of a *cause célèbre* because of this remarkable event in her life; otherwise, Luke would hardly have introduced her this way.

We need to be clear here that "spiritual pollution" was not seen as the same thing as immorality in early Judaism, though sometimes it could be caused by or lead to immoral behavior. Later readers have sometimes assumed immorality on the part of Miriam, confusing her with other biblical characters, but that is the result of misreading scripture. The anonymous sinner mentioned in Luke 7:36–50 as having anointed Jesus's feet in the house of Simon the Pharisee, for example, has often been assumed to be Miriam of Migdal. This serious mistake became possible only once manuscripts of the New Testament began to have the separation of words, sentences, paragraphs, chapters, and verses, which first happened in the early Middle Ages.

Let me explain. The culture into which Luke wrote his gospel was overwhelmingly an oral culture, and documents were just aids and tools of oral communication. Luke's gospel was not likely part of a culture of texts or published and public literature; rather, it was intended to educate a high-status new Christian named Theophilus (see Luke 1 and Acts 1). Without the separation of the gospel into stories, there was no real way to skip ahead in the narrative and learn more about a character who was mentioned but not named. Put another way, Luke was a careful historian and narrator: if he had wanted Theophilus—who would be hearing this document read in all likelihood, rather than reading it himself—to think that Miriam of Migdal was the sinner woman of Luke 7, he would have had to name her in that first mention of the woman in the narrative. Otherwise, no one would ever have guessed this was the case, since she is not mentioned in Luke 1–6, even obliquely. Had Miriam of Migdal been the same woman as the anonymous person mentioned in Luke 7:36–50 as a "sinner," Luke would simply have introduced Miriam's name at Luke 7:36, not at Luke 8:2.

Even less plausible is the attempt to identify Miriam of Migdal with the anonymous woman caught in adultery in John 7:53–8:11. Miriam does not show up in John's gospel until the cross in John 19, and once again the woman caught in adultery is not named.[18]

But there is much more to say about Miriam. Almost always named first when a list of women disciples is given in the gospels, she seems to have been as much of a risk taker as her Master. As noted earlier, Jesus seems to have been the first early Jewish teacher to have women disciples. Furthermore, these were women not related to him or to the Twelve, *and* they were traveling with him in Galilee. This would surely have been surprising if not shocking to many in traditional Galilee. Luke takes the trouble to mention three women by name, though he adds that there were "many others" as well (8:3), so presumably we are meant to see these women as representative of the entire group of women disciples. If so they must have been a diverse lot.

It is out of the ordinary that *any* women were named. Usually in such a patriarchal culture, women, even honorable ones, were "anonymous" in the stories of the day (see, for example, Luke 7:36–50; Luke 8:43–56; John 7:53–8:11; Mark 14:3–9), especially women with some sort of social liability—for example, a disease, demon possession, or connections with a despised or immoral ruler or leader. What is most interesting, then, about the three named women is that the first two who are mentioned had significant social liabilities.[19] Mary Magdalene was plagued by demons until Jesus exorcised them, and Joanna was the wife of Herod Antipas's estate manager. Despite their liabilities, these women and others were patronesses and provisioners of Jesus's traveling entourage, practicing the sort of hospitality Jesus had told the disciples to rely on when they traveled from town to town.

The next place we hear of Miriam is in the story of Jesus's final days in Jerusalem, as told by Matthew. We do not know what Miriam did during the time between when she was converted and first traveled with Jesus in Galilee and this last week of Jesus's life in April of the year 30, other than that Mark 15:41 says she was one of the disciples traveling *in* Galilee. What Matthew 27:55 tells us is that several women, including our Miriam, traveled with Jesus and the Twelve up to Jerusalem from Galilee for the Passover celebration.

This is a helpful reminder of a couple of things. It shows us that Jesus continued to associate with and travel with women as well as men throughout his ministry, even if this scandalized the more conservative Galilean and Judean Jews when he went up to Jerusalem. It also shows just how devoted Miriam and others were to Jesus, and how devout she had become, making the long trek up to Jerusalem for the Passover celebration. Neither she nor the others could have realized that dramatic events were about to happen to Jesus, changing their world and worldview.

According to Mark 15:40–41 a group of women watched the crucifixion from afar. The first person mentioned in Mark's list is Miriam of Migdal. We are reminded again in 15:41 that she and other women had followed Jesus while in Galilee and had provided for him. Here we have a somewhat more specific reference to attending to Jesus and his needs, but it likely means no more than the reference in Luke 8:3. While the male disciples had all denied, deserted, or betrayed Jesus, the same could not be said about the female disciples, or at least these three (Salome and Miriam the mother of James and Joses are also mentioned). They were allowed to remain at the cross, presumably because the Romans did not expect women to try to take Jesus down from the cross. (In fact, though, that sort of behavior did happen from time to time, when a watchman was not placed on the site where the execution took place.) In any case, these women were there until the bitter end and are mentioned only after the narrative concludes the discussion of Jesus's death.

Again at Mark 15:47 we are told that the two Miriams saw where Jesus was buried in Joseph of Arimathea's tomb. Immediately thereafter we have the brief reference at Mark 16:1 to their coming to the tomb on Easter morning, apparently fully expecting to anoint the body and change the linens during the period of mourning. What they found instead was the empty tomb. Mark recounts an encounter with an angel at the tomb, always a sign of divine activity, but he does not, in the present form of the ending of Mark, tell the story of the appearance of Jesus to these women. That story appears in truncated fashion in Matthew 28:8–10 and in much fuller form in the famous account in John 20, to which we must devote the rest of our time.

New Testament scholar C. H. Dodd once said that the story of Mary Magdalene in John 20 was the most self-authenticating of all the Easter narratives, because who would make up the notion that Jesus appeared first to a little-known woman from Migdal?[20] It is still a pertinent question. The scene reads like a narrative of the progress of a soul going from grief to euphoria. But there is much more to the scene. The story, as John tells it, makes it apparent that Miriam, like the other disciples, was not really anticipating encountering a risen Jesus. His appearance came as a total shock. This was no dream or wish-projection of an overheated imagination. This was a profound encounter that changed a person's mental outlook totally.

Part of the transformation that John stresses is that Miriam can no longer cling to the old Jesus, whom she tellingly calls *rabbouni,* "my teacher" or "my master" (not, for instance, "my beloved" or "my husband"!). There was a teacher-disciple relationship between these two persons.[21] Miriam seems to assume that things will return to the way they were before. Jesus's command to her is not "Touch me not," as some have rendered it, but rather "Don't cling to me." She is being warned not to hold on to the Jesus of the past, the Jesus one could touch. Rather, she is to go forward into the future, proclaiming that Jesus had risen and had appeared to her. One church father called Miriam at this juncture in her life the apostle to the apostles (a matter we will address in the next chapter). It is Jesus who commissioned Miriam to tell the male disciples where he was going now that he had risen. It is not surprising that many in the Jesus movement thereafter saw this as a sufficient, though remarkable, precedent for women to proclaim the gospel. In fact, John's gospel depicts Miriam as not only the first to see the risen Jesus but the first to proclaim the Easter message. But even this is not quite the end of the story. According to Luke's second volume, "the women" disciples were present in the upper room praying when the new member of the Twelve was selected (Acts 1:14). We may assume then that they, including Miriam of Migdal, were present at Pentecost as well.

The New Testament tells us nothing more of the story of Miriam. She disappears into the sands of time. We will deal shortly with later conjectures about her that seem to have very little (or no) historical basis. But we have more than enough material in the New Testament to say that a strong case can be made that she was an important early disciple of and witness for Jesus, self-sacrificially serving him; and we can say with equal certainty that there is absolutely no early, particularly no first-century, historical evidence that Miriam's relationship with Jesus was anything other than that of a disciple to her master-teacher. We can also conclude that it is crucial that the risen Jesus commissioned her to be the first person to proclaim the Easter message, even to proclaim it to the inner circle of male disciples. This provided a remarkable precedent for women to be involved in the Jesus movement from then on.

TWO

The Mary Magdalene of Myth and Legend

Revisionist history is all the rage these days. Not satisfied with what our earliest and best witnesses have to say about the life of Mary Magdalene, various scholars have dredged up later data that has no strong claim to be based in first-century evidence and have used it to rewrite the story of Mary Magdalene. In order to understand what happened to the traditions about Mary Magdalene in the second century and on into the Middle Ages, we need to have a rather clear understanding of the nature, character, and origins of the Nag Hammadi texts, the primary source of alternative accounts. A more general discussion is required to put the Mary traditions found in some of those documents, discovered in the desert sands of Egypt at a place called Nag Hammadi in the late 1940s, into a proper context and perspective. Though what follows may seem to be a digression from the subject of Mary Magdalene, it in fact is not. The Gnostic documents discussed below are the source of most of today's misunderstandings about Mary and her relationship with Jesus.

DOUBTING THOMAS

There is no doubting that the Gospel of Thomas, perhaps the most famous Nag Hammadi text, is an interesting document, but almost everything else about this gospel is debatable and debated, including whether it is a first- or second-century document. The majority of scholars think, for various reasons, that it is a second-century document, though it contains some early Jesus traditions that we also find in the canonical gospels. This gospel was touted by Gnostic scholar Elaine Pagels many years ago as a Gnostic gospel, but today even she is doubtful that this is a good way to characterize it.[22] (In my view, her original assessment is probably more accurate than her recent retrenchment.) What I would stress about this gospel is that its "character"—particularly its sayings, which are distinctive to this gospel—makes it quite different from the canonical gospels. This suggests that it was written after, and on the basis of, not only the canonical gospels but also several of Paul's letters and other New Testament documents.

If I am right in this assessment, the Gospel of Thomas probably adds very little that's new about the historical Jesus or the historical Mary Magdalene or the various forms of Christianity that existed in the early or middle first century during what can be called the *apostolic* and *formative* era. This is an important conclusion because it makes it all the less likely that we can learn anything new at all about Jesus or his inner circle from apocryphal gospels written even later. If even the Gospel of Thomas does not provide a new window on Jesus and the earliest Christian period, we should surely abandon hope about documents written long after the age of the apostles and the eyewitnesses.

The tone is set in the Gospel of Thomas right from its outset. It claims to be offering us "the secret wisdom sayings" of Jesus. In other words, it purports to give us esoteric or insider knowledge about Jesus's in-house teaching, and indeed in-house knowledge that goes back to one of the original disciples: Didymus Judas Thomas. The esoteric character of the document becomes immediately apparent not only from the incipit (or introductory passage), which uses the phrase mentioned above, but also from the first saying, which sounds nothing like the historical Jesus as he is depicted in the canonical gospels. It reads, "Whoever discovers the interpretation of these sayings will not taste death." In other words, one must become a scribe or a scholar to be able to ferret out the meaning of secret sayings if one wants to have everlasting life.

This puts salvation on a whole different footing than what we find in either the authentic parables or the aphorisms of Jesus. Salvation is a matter of what you know and how well you understand these secret sayings. Furthermore, since salvation is dependent on an individual's ability to interpret these sayings, we are dealing with *self*-salvation, and presumably salvation for the literate or even the learned. It is not a surprise that some scholars find this vision of salvation appealing. This is not salvation for the least, the last, the lost, and the illiterate, and it is certainly not offered on the basis of grace through faith.

Further proof that it is salvation only for the elite and the worthy is found in saying 62: "Jesus said, 'I disclose my mysteries to those [who are worthy] of [my] mysteries.'" One gets the sense that salvation comes to those who persevere through the maze of interpretation, ponder the sayings deeply, and then have an "aha" moment. Listen to the second saying in this gospel: "Jesus said, 'Those who seek should not stop seeking until they find. When they find, they will be disturbed. When they are disturbed, they will marvel, and will reign over all.'" This sounds like a form of revelation that can be received only by those who have far too much time on their hands—a scribe or a scholar, say. Like Jacob wrestling the angel, readers have to wrestle with the saying until they get a blessing. The focus is clearly on the inner workings of the mind.

And those inner workings are potent. Saying 3 insists that the Father's kingdom is "within you," though it also is said to be "outside of you."[23] Saying 70 takes that one step further, clinching the fact that we are dealing with a gospel of self-salvation: "If you bring forth what is within you, what you have will save you."

Next in Thomas, we are given a Socratic twist. Saying 3b says, "When you know yourselves, then you will be known." The search must be within yourself, at least initially. This is a gospel for narcissists. There is nothing here about knowing God being the key to understanding yourself. The *I* becomes the *Thou*—or at least the *Thou* is believed to be found in the first instance within the *I*.

Unlike the synoptic teachings of Jesus, which can sometimes be enigmatic in order to tease the mind of the audience into active thought about God's divine saving activity, this gospel offers up conundrums or riddles for their own sake. Consider saying 7, which suggests, "Lucky is the lion that the human will eat, so that the lion becomes human. And foul is the human that the lion will eat, and the lion still will become human." Or consider saying 19: "Congratulations to the one who came into being before coming into being. If you become my disciples and pay attention to my sayings, these stones will serve you." No wonder Matthew, as quoted in this gospel, says Jesus is like a wise philosopher (saying 13), and Jesus warns in saying 21, "Let there be a person among you who understands." This is not a gospel for the slow of understanding!

The lion saying seems to relate in some way to saying 11b, which reads, "The dead are not alive, and the living will not die. During the days when you ate what is dead, you made it come alive." Clearly the author of this document is fascinated by what happens when a living being eats another creature that was alive. What these sayings probably reflect is the pagan notion that the life force can be transferred from a lesser being to a greater one (even to a god) by the greater being sacrificing or consuming or even strangling (and so squeezing the life breath out of) the lesser being.

What is the character of the person or community that generated this document in the second century? We get a clue in saying 12, where the disciples ask about who should lead them when Jesus departs. He responds, "No matter where you are you are to go to James the Just, for whose sake heaven and earth came into being."

Now no one in the New Testament documents refers to James the brother of Jesus in this way. James the Just is what he was called by those outside the community (Josephus, for example, and later Christian sources such as Eusebius, the father of church history, writing around the turn of the fourth century).[24] It is a phrase used only after James got a reputation for exhibiting a certain sort of piety in Jerusalem, *well after the death of Jesus.* Thus this saying does not go back to the historical Jesus; rather, it is used to legitimate a later tradition, reflecting a later view of James, and indeed a view of James that Jesus himself would never have endorsed, especially during his ministry when his brothers didn't yet believe in him (John 7:3–5). Jesus actually spoke of persons other than his physical family being his own family of faith (see Mark 3:21, 31–35), as we will see in later chapters.

And if we were not puzzled enough, when we get to saying 22 we are confronted with the following:

> When you make the two into one, and when you make the inner like the outer and the outer like the inner, and the upper like the lower, and when you make male and female into a single one, so that the male will not be male nor the female be female, when you make eyes in place of an eye, a hand in place of a hand, a foot in place of a foot, an image in place of an image, then you will enter [the kingdom].

It is frankly hard to keep a straight face and say that this sounds anything like the historical Jesus we find in the Q sayings—those sayings from various New Testament texts that seem to come from a single, earlier, imagined source that historians call Q (from the German *Quelle,* or source)—or in Mark or even in the Gospel of John. The person who wrote this was a wordsmith, someone who liked to play with words and phrases with puzzling meanings.

Unlike the other gospels, the Gospel of Thomas lacks a future eschatological focus. In fact, when the disciples ask how their end will come, Jesus asks them if they have found their beginning. Their end is said to be found when they find their beginning (saying 18). This is just being obscure for obscurity's sake! Or even more clearly we can compare saying 51:

His disciples said to him, "When will the rest for the dead take place, and when will the new world come?" He said to them, "What you are looking forward to has come, but you don't know it."

The disciples are called by this gospel to extreme asceticism, to abandon even clothing! Listen to saying 37:

When you strip without being ashamed, and you take your clothes and put them under your feet like little children and trample them, then [you] will see the son of the living one and you will not be afraid.

This comports with saying 64b, which says buyers and merchants will not enter the places of the Father.

You may well ask what happened to the Jesus who was known as the friend of tax collectors and sinners, the man who was accused of being a glutton and a wine-bibber. And can it really be said that the following (saying 30) sounds even remotely like the monotheistic Jewish Jesus of the early first century?

Jesus said, "Where there are three deities, they are divine. Where there are two or one, I am with that one."

To this we may add the infamous saying 77:

Jesus said, "I am the light that is over all things. I am all: from me all came forth, and to me all attained. Split a piece of wood; I am there. Lift up the stone, and you will find me there."

This certainly sounds like pantheistic thought.

We also have misogynistic material at the end of the collection in saying 114, which reads:

Simon Peter said to them, "Make Mary leave us, for females don't deserve life." Jesus said, "Look, I will guide her to make her male, so that she too may become a living spirit resembling you males. For every female who makes herself male will enter the kingdom of Heaven."

What is especially interesting about this saying, besides its misogyny, is that it recognizes Mary Magdalene as part of the inner circle of disciples.

It hints at a rivalry between Peter and Mary, or between disciples like Peter and those like Mary. This theme is developed further in later Gnostic literature.

Some scholars have tried to soften the impact of saying 77 by suggesting it was later added to the collection,[25] but alas, where is the textual basis for this conjecture? Do we have manuscripts that don't include this saying? Well no, we don't. This conjecture is a ploy of desperation meant to salvage the Gospel of Thomas from appearing to be what it is—a mishmash of some authentic sayings of Jesus found in earlier canonical gospels coupled with later pantheistic sayings, ascetical sayings, Gnostic sayings, philosophical sayings, and even misogynistic sayings. It is the *distinctive* sayings of Thomas, highlighted above, that indicate just how far removed this gospel is in its portrayal of Jesus from the Jewish eschatological non-ascetical Jesus we find in the Q sayings and in general in the synoptic gospels. Even the authentic sayings of Jesus that we do find in this gospel in various places are de-eschatologized in the service of the larger agenda of the author.

Careful examinations of the Gospel of Thomas by Klyne Snodgrass and C. M. Tuckett have shown that this text reflects not only a knowledge of all four canonical gospels but also familiarity with the editorial work of all the evangelists, including John, the so-called Fourth Evangelist.[26] Thomas also reflects a knowledge of the editorial work of Matthew and Luke even in the Greek version of Thomas.[27] It also reflects a knowledge of various of Paul's letters, Hebrews, 1 John, and perhaps even Revelation. One has to ask, Who could the author of this document have been, and when could he have written to know all these sources in detail? The answer is surely that he is someone who lived in the second century and had an admiration especially for James, who was martyred in A.D. 62.

This is why James Dunn and others have rightly drawn the conclusion that Thomas postdates all the canonical documents, as do all the other Nag Hammadi texts. Listen to Dunn: "The more obvious interpretation of the Nag Hammadi documents is that they are all typically syncretistic: they draw bits and pieces of tradition from a wide range of religious influences in the ancient world, including Judaism and Christianity, but including others as well. As such they are totally explainable in terms of what we now know about second and third-century Gnosticism."[28] Just so, and as such this material is miles from the character of the canonical gospels. Dunn rightly includes the Gospel of Thomas in this description. The attempt to de-Gnosticize Thomas in order to rescue it and make it a genuine first-century gospel will not work (witness how this Gospel is now portrayed as the crown jewel of the Gnostic Society Library)[29]—and in any case, whenever it was written, its distinctive sayings are miles from the Jewish and eschatological and intelligible character of Jesus's actual aphorisms, proverbs, and the like.

In the end, the Gospel of Thomas should never have been called a gospel, for it has no narrative about the life or death of Jesus, no recounting of miracles, and no prophetic signs. It simply serves up Jesus the talking head. What Thomas's Jesus really wants to accomplish is to be a facilitator so that persons of discernment who are worthy can know themselves, can look deep within themselves, and can thus save themselves by obtaining esoteric knowledge while engaging in ascetical practices. *Notice, however, that these are not Jewish ritual practices like circumcision, which is disavowed in Thomas and contrasted with the more valuable "spiritual circumcision."* Soteriology (that is, salvation theology) is indeed reduced to anthropology, and salvation becomes a human self-help program in this gospel. Therein lie two reasons for this gospel's appeal in America, where we love self-help programs and where our theme song is generally "I Did It My Way" or even "It's All about Me."

What is truly strange is that no one is talking about the fact that this gospel has several sayings (quoted above) which suggest that this document was not compiled by a committed monotheist—which is to say, it was not compiled by someone who was either a faithful early Jew or a Christian. Rather, the distinctive sayings in Thomas, those that reveal the most about the author, show us a person who is:

- Trying to fit Jesus into a larger syncretistic religious model

- Holding up a program of asceticism as a means to prepare for gaining (or actually gaining) spiritual knowledge, using James as an exemplar

- Offering more of a sapiential philosophy of life by which people can save themselves than an opportunity for following Jesus

- Declining to befriend women, including Mary Magdalene

Given these sorts of views, it is no surprise that we have no evidence that this gospel was ever seriously considered for inclusion in the New Testament. It violates the Jewish and eschatological character of the teachings of Jesus. It violates the adherence to monotheism which was the hallmark of early Judaism and its early Christian offshoot. Finally, it violates the inclusivity of

Jesus, revealing its patriarchal character and bias against women in the climactic sayings of the collection, which are probably original.

But what of some of the later extracanonical documents—what about the famous Gospel of Mary or the Gospel of Philip, for example? Could they reveal to us a Jesus who was more like later Gnostics, and perhaps was even married to Mary Magdalene?

NAUGHTY GNOSTIC GOSPELS?

Thus far we have been talking about the most famous of the Nag Hammadi documents, the Gospel of Thomas. Before we turn to several others, perhaps I should say something about the Nag Hammadi finds in general.[30] Though it may be fashionable to suggest that we should be gracious and include the Gnostic texts along with the New Testament as equally valid sources of the truth about early Christianity, the truth is that *both* sources cannot be correct about the historical Jesus, or about the nature of the movement he set in motion, or about the people he consorted with, such as Mary Magdalene.

I should stress that I quite agree that these Nag Hammadi documents deserve a close and fair reading; at least the same historical critical scrutiny should be applied to them as to the canon of the New Testament. In fact one could make a case for more critical scrutiny being applied to texts, the further removed in time they are from the subjects they are written about. But when you actually undertake such a scholarly enterprise, you realize pretty quickly that the Gnostic documents do not reveal anything about the historical Jesus that could not be deduced from the canonical material itself, and in the places they disagree with the canonical material, they are surely not more authentic witnesses to Jesus and his movement than the New Testament documents. Let us consider these Gnostic texts a bit further, and consider the work of two scholars, Elaine Pagels and Karen King, on these texts.

The Nag Hammadi documents found in a storage jar in 1945 by two brothers digging for nitrate soil to use as fertilizer are currently housed in the Coptic Museum in Cairo. Their journey to this museum was circuitous. When the brothers first took these documents home, their mother promptly used some of the papyrus to stoke the fire of her bread oven! The rest of the pages were rescued and eventually found their way through the hands of dealers and collectors into the aforementioned museum.

While these Nag Hammadi documents may have been deliberately hidden from the public eye at some juncture in a storage jar, they are now open secrets: anyone who has the time and patience can study them. Indeed, since they have all been translated into English, one can read them without benefit of learning Coptic or Greek or any other such ancient language. Elaine Pagels's *The Gnostic Gospels* has become something of a popular reference text about the Gnostic texts we are most concerned with, but she does not present us with the actual texts intact; rather, she analyzes them at some length. The Nag Hammadi library, as it is best called, included a wide array of differing kinds of documents. It included even a portion of Plato's *Republic*! One must always be cautious about judging documents that are part of a library. I would hardly want someone to judge my own theology on the basis of some of the books currently found in the Asbury Seminary library. Nevertheless, close scrutiny of many of these documents is very revealing when it comes to shedding light on Gnosticism.

Let us consider first the contents of the thirteen codices (the ancient equivalents of books) that contain these Nag Hammadi documents. Shown below is a table of contents, and what immediately jumps out at you is that not a single Old or New Testament book is included! If the community that generated these documents had the Bible as we know it, these codices do not show it. However, it is plausible that these works were selections deliberately hidden from view, perhaps in the fourth or fifth centuries, when we know that certain works deemed heretical were ferreted out and done away with.

Table of Contents

I,*1*   The Prayer of the Apostle Paul (colophon)
I,*2*   The Apocryphon of James
I,*3*   The Gospel of Truth
I,*4*   The Treatise on the Resurrection
I,*5*   The Tripartite Tractate

II,*1*   The Apocryphon of John
II,*2*   The Gospel of Thomas
II,*3*   The Gospel of Philip
II,*4*   The Hypostasis of the Archons
II,*5*   On the Origin of the World
II,*6*   The Exegesis on the Soul
II,*7*   The Book of Thomas the Contender (colophon)

III,*1*   The Apocryphon of John
III,*2*   The Gospel of the Egyptians
III,*3*   Eugnostos the Blessed

III,4   The Sophia of Jesus Christ
III,5   The Dialogue of the Savior

IV,1   The Apocryphon of John
IV,2   The Gospel of the Egyptians

V,1   Eugnostos the Blessed
V,2   The Apocalypse of Paul
V,3   The (First) Apocalypse of James
V,4   The (Second) Apocalypse of James
V,5   The Apocalypse of Adam

VI,1   The Acts of Peter and the Twelve Apostles
VI,2   The Thunder: Perfect Mind
VI,3   Authoritative Teaching
VI,4   The Concept of Our Great Power
VI,5   Plato, Republic 588b–589b
VI,6   The Discourse on the Eighth and Ninth
VI,7   The Prayer of Thanksgiving (scribal note)
VI,8   Asclepius 21–29

VII,1   The Paraphrase of Shem
VII,2   The Second Treatise of the Great Seth
VII,3   The Apocalypse of Peter
VII,4   The Teachings of Silvanus (colophon)
VII,5   The Three Steles of Seth (colophon)

VIII,1   Zostrianos (cryptogram)
VIII,2   The Letter of Peter to Philip

IX,1   Melchizedek
IX,2   The Thought of Norea
IX,3   The Testimony of Truth

X,1   Marsanes

XI,1   The Interpretation of Knowledge
XI,2   A Valentinian Exposition
XI,3   Allogenes
XI,4   Hypsiphrone

XII,1   The Sentences of Sextus
XII,2   The Gospel of Truth
XII,3   Fragments

XIII,*1* Trimorphic Protennoia
XIII,*2* On the Origin of the World

Several factors indicate that these documents came not out of a church community, but out of a rather isolated monastery in the Egyptian desert. For one thing, these documents were found at the base of a mountain where there is also evidence of a Byzantine-era grave area, including caves that were used for graves. One of these caves has an inscription in Coptic with lines from some Psalms texts. Scholars have suggested that these documents actually came from a nearby monastery but were buried several miles away because the content of these books had come under suspicion. In other words, we do *not* have clear evidence from these documents that there existed a separate Gnostic community.

These documents seem to have come from a Christian monastery—we know that there were several nearby—where a certain amount of speculation and open philosophical discussion was permitted. This theory of the origins of these documents is supported by the fact that the carton that came with Codex VII also contained fragments of a biblical codex, a homily, and a letter from one Pachomius, perhaps the Pachomius for whom the nearby Basilica of St. Pachomius is named. Furthermore, some of the scribal notes in some of the manuscripts show that the texts were studied by Christians. These readers inscribed pious Christian prayers in the colophons (that is, the appendices) to documents from several of the codices (I, II, and VII). Scriptoriums of monasteries were of course the main places book-copying took place in the early Middle Ages, and the monks frequently would copy all sorts of documents, without by any means necessarily endorsing all the content. We know, in fact, that the monk who was Pachomius's successor, Theodore, undertook a purging of heretical books in A.D. 367 in response to a letter of Athanasius in that year. Possibly the Nag Hammadi codices were hastily buried by monks who objected to their destruction. This is just a plausible conjecture, however. We really don't know what happened.

It has been suggested that these Nag Hammadi documents were not in fact in use for very long. There is material in Codex VII which shows that it was produced after A.D. 348, giving us a potential starting date, and the codices were probably placed in their storage jar somewhere in the fourth or fifth century, judging by dating of its lid. The content likewise offers clues that place the collection in that time period, particularly a document that calls itself a Valentinian exposition and several others that come from that strain of Gnosticism.

Valentinus is certainly one of the most prominent names associated with Gnosticism. He began as an orthodox monk in the second century, lost an election to be bishop, and thereafter pursued a Gnostic direction which Tertullian, a contemporary, called a lapse into heresy. His real influence came in the last third of the second century, and there is no evidence that his offshoot of early Christianity existed before the second half of that century. After his death there followed perhaps a couple of centuries of development of his line of thought before it was officially repudiated, but it is clear enough from Tertullian and Irenaeus that it was already deemed heretical by major figures in the second century.[31] The fact that the Gnostics and their literature were allowed to have a hearing for a long time before the works were condemned by a widespread consensus of Christian leaders tells us something about the flexibility and fairness of early Christianity.

There are some fifty-two documents in the Nag Hammadi collection, but five are duplicates. Every one of these documents appears to be a Coptic translation of a Greek document, which suggests that they are translations from an earlier period, perhaps some of them going back to the second century. We can say this with some assurance in regard to the Gospel of Thomas, because earlier Greek fragments of this document have also been found. This is of course also true of Plato's *Republic,* the Sentences of Sextus, and one other document.

One of the more crucial conclusions that has resulted from the more than half century of scholarly study of these documents is that they are not a library from a single sect or religious group of people. While most of the texts are Gnostic in their theological and philosophical leanings, not all of them can be labeled Gnostic. Instead, what unites them is their ascetical piety. Presumably they were collected to provide support and guidance for the ascetical lifestyle of monks.

Even among the documents that are clearly Gnostic there is variety. As noted earlier, some reflect Valentinian thought, the best-known form of Gnosticism. Among the documents that come from this school of thought are the Prayer of Paul, the Gospel of Truth, and most importantly for our purposes the Gospel of Philip. It is probable that the Gospel of Mary comes from this strain of Gnosticism as well, though it was not part of the Nag Hammadi collection. It first came to light in 1896 in Cairo.

Other Nag Hammadi documents subscribe to the Sethian brand of Gnosticism and the particular mythological system associated with it—namely, that Adam had a son named Seth who was the spiritual father of a Gnostic race of Sethians. Seth is portrayed as a revealer figure in this literature, which includes the Apocryphon of John, the Hypostasis of Archons, the Gospel of the Egyptians, the Apocalypse of Adam, the Three Steles of Seth, Zostrianos, Melchizedek, the Thought of Norea, Marsanes, Allogenes, and Trimorphic Protennoia.

While none of the Gnostic documents we are mainly concerned with (the gospels of Philip, Mary, and Thomas) reflect this brand of thought, these Sethian documents reveal two things important to our study: first, that Gnostic thought could be highly speculative in character, and second that it focused more on philosophical ideas than on historical events or persons. This is not a surprise since Gnosticism does not really want to underscore the importance of mundane events or processes or persons when it comes to knowledge and the consequent salvation that comes from it.

It is difficult to talk about any of these documents without giving a taste of them so that readers can see how different in character they are from the canonical gospels. Included below are a few representative samplings from various gospels (primarily Valentinian) that will give you a feel for how the texts read without narratives about the deeds of Jesus and without detailed commentary.

These documents I'll quote from, like other Gnostic documents, see self-knowledge as the essence of salvation, and indeed even appear to urge the worship of human beings. The Gospel of Philip 85:1–4, for example, says, "God created man and man created God. So it is in the world. Men make gods and they worship their creations. It would be fitting for gods to worship men."[32] This is not, in fact, a critique of idolatry. It is the divine within human beings that seems to be the ultimate object of worship. Furthermore, the flaws that exist in creation are blamed on some malignant deity—perhaps the so-called Demiurge, which is a lesser god who made the tainted material realm. Human sin is not to blame for the tainted character of creation. Not surprisingly, in this system of thinking it is ignorance, not sin, that is the ultimate human dilemma.

Showing how very different Gnosticism as presented in the Gospel of Philip is from the claims of the canonical gospels is not difficult. Consider, for example, the following quote from the Gospel of Philip:

> Some said, "Mary conceived by the Holy Spirit." They are in error. They do not know what they are saying. When did a woman ever conceive by a woman? Mary is the virgin whom no power defiled. She is a great anathema to the Hebrews, who are the apostles and

the apostolic men. This virgin whom no power defiled […] the powers defile themselves. And the Lord would not have said "My Father
who is in Heaven" [a text paralleled in Matt. 16:17] unless he had
had another father, but he would have said simply "My father."

This quote identifies the Holy Spirit as a woman and implies that Jesus
had a human father. It also shows the anti-Semitic flavor that permeates
these documents. Being a Hebrew was not seen as a good thing. Notice as
well an allusion to Mary being a perpetual virgin. This document clearly
reflects knowledge of what the canonical gospels and later traditions
claim, but its author is not afraid to contradict those sources in various
important ways. For example, in regard to the resurrection of Jesus we
hear: "Those who say that the Lord died first and [then] rose up are in
error, for he rose up first and [then] died. If one does not first attain the
resurrection, he will not die. As God lives, he would […]." This passage
affirms the idea of preexistence, not only of Christ but of other humans.
The putting on of flesh referred to here is what took place when one
became a human being. Resurrection in the flesh is redefined as human
conception leading to physical birth.

Consider, too, the Gospel of Philip:

Some are afraid lest they rise naked. Because of this they wish to
rise in the flesh, and they do not know that it is those who wear the
flesh who are naked. It is those who […] unclothe themselves who
are not naked. "Flesh and blood shall not inherit the kingdom of
God" [1 Cor. 15:50]. What is this which will not inherit? This which
is on us. But what is this, too, which will inherit? It is that which
belongs to Jesus and his blood. Because of this he said, "He who
shall not eat my flesh and drink my blood has not life in him" [John
6:53]. What is it? His flesh is the word, and his blood is the Holy
Spirit. He who has received these has food and he has drink and
clothing.

Notice that this passage includes a quote from Paul and from the Gospel
of John. There are also quotations from Matthew's gospel and from the
extracanonical Gospel of Thomas. Clearly this document was written later
than New Testament times.

More telling for our purposes is the following quote, which refers to
Mary Magdalene:

For it is by a kiss that the perfect conceive and give birth. For this reason we also kiss one another. We receive conception from the grace which is in one another.

There were three who always walked with the Lord: Mary, his mother, and her sister, and Magdalene, the one who was called his companion. His sister and his mother and his companion were each a Mary.

This passage is followed by another, the Gospel of Philip 63:32–36, which has gained notoriety in Dan Brown's bestselling novel *The Da Vinci Code*.

As for the Wisdom who is called "the barren," she is the mother of the angels. And the companion of the […] Mary Magdalene. […] loved her more than [all] the disciples, and [used to] kiss her often on her […]. The rest of the disciples […]. They said to him, "Why do you love her more than all of us?" The Savior answered and said to them, "Why do I not love you like her? When a blind man and one who sees are both together in darkness, they are no different from one another. When the light comes, then he who sees will see the light, and he who is blind will remain in darkness."

What needs to be said about this text can be summarized quickly:

- It says nothing about Jesus having been married to Mary Magdalene. We have here the Greek word *koinonos,* which means "companion" and can be applied to the relationship between any two people who are close to each other—friends, cousins, and spouses as well. The important thing is that it is not a technical term for "spouse"; something else in the context would have to suggest marriage for it to mean such a thing in this text, and there is no such clue—not even in the larger context.

- This text is in a highly ascetical document. It is hardly likely that the author would want to suggest or even hint that Jesus was married.

- The kissing referred to was a strange ritual that was believed to convey esoteric knowledge from one person to another. A form of holy kissing, it has nothing to do with romance.

- The text has holes in it, as indicated by the dots and brackets. We are not certain what goes in the gaps. One could say that if one's theory that Jesus was married to Mary Magdalene is based largely or solely on this text, that theory is as full of holes as the papyrus in question!

The Gnostics believed that, since creation is a fallen enterprise from the outset, normal human forms of relating, such as marriage and intercourse, are seen as inherently defiling, as the Gospel of Philip makes evident.

No one can know when the husband and the wife have intercourse with one another, except the two of them. Indeed, marriage in the world is a mystery for those who have taken a wife. If there is a hidden quality to the marriage of defilement, how much more is the undefiled marriage a true mystery! It is not fleshly, but pure. It belongs not to desire, but to the will. It belongs not to the darkness or the night, but to the day and the light. If a marriage is open to the public, it has become prostitution, and the bride plays the harlot not only when she is impregnated by another man, but even if she slips out of her bedroom and is seen.

As we have stressed, salvation in this system of thinking is a matter of knowing the right things, as is clear in the Gospel of Philip:

He who has knowledge of the truth is a free man, but the free man does not sin, for "He who sins is the slave of sin" [John 8:34]. Truth is the mother, knowledge the father. Those who think that sinning does not apply to them are called "free" by the world. Knowledge of the truth merely makes such people arrogant, which is what the words "it makes them free" mean. It even gives them a sense of superiority over the whole world. But "Love builds up" [1 Cor. 8:1]. In fact, he who is really free, through knowledge, is a slave, because of love for those who have not yet been able to attain to the freedom of knowledge. Knowledge makes them capable of becoming free.

Before I comment on any of these texts in more detail, let's look at a sampling of material from the Gospel of Mary as well. This document has been more difficult to piece together because there are two different Greek recensions, and in fact the text is in poor condition.[33] There is also the problem that the Coptic and Greek versions don't match up. The Coptic version has Mary's reaction to Peter's rejection of her revelation (18:1–5); the Greek does not. P. Perkins, suggests, I think rightly, that this gospel was composed toward the end of the second century A.D., as was the Gospel of Philip, based on the fact that the Greek version is from the third century. Once again there is absolutely no historical evidence that this text, and its special interests, has its origins in the first century. Rather, it is the product of the Gnostic movement that arose in the second century.

Like various other Gnostic texts, such as the Apocryphon of John and the Sophia of Jesus Christ, the Gospel of Mary centers on the motif of the risen Jesus instructing the disciples in the esoteric and secret Gnostic teachings. Like so much of this literature, it proposes a strong rejection of the goodness of the material realm. Whatever has a material origin, the document claims, is subject to passion, disease, decay, death, and evil. The Gnostic believer, by contrast, has a spiritual point of origin and thus is not to participate in physical passions (7:1–8:10). The male disciples are commissioned, in this account, to spread the Gnostic version of the gospel, but they give way to despair because of the fear of suffering.

Mary Magdalene shames them, reminding them of God's grace and protection. They already have the true Gnostic identity, she says. That process is defined in the Gospel of Philip as "putting on the perfect man," but the Gospel of Mary says, "He has prepared us and made us into men," a phrase that harks back to the Gospel of Thomas 114, which we discussed earlier in this chapter. Notice that Mary says she too has been made into a man. Lest we think these texts are somehow feminist-friendly, this phrase reminds us that this is not so. There seems to be an assumption, however, that men have more difficulty struggling with physical passions, and so women can sometimes be better examples of the true ascetic and thus the true Gnostic.

Mary, in this account, is asked by Peter to recount the vision or revelation she has received. This section of the manuscript is mutilated, and so we do not have it all. But what we do have entails a teaching about the mind being the intermediary between the soul and spirit to receive the Gnostic revelation, and it speaks of how the soul ascends past the cosmic powers on its way to heaven, the place of rest (15:1–17:9). Hence Mary has insight into the destiny of the soul enlightened by Gnostic wisdom. When Peter objects to this teaching, Levi rebukes him. There is a similar defense of Mary's revelation in the Gospel of Philip, as we have seen, as well as in Pistis Sophia.

What are we to make of this material? Should we see such texts as an indirect testimony to women teachers in Gnostic circles? This is possible. Should we see Peter as representing orthodox Christianity's voice, which objected to such Gnostic revelations? Perhaps so.

But what this text does not suggest is that Peter objected to the fact of Mary having some kind of revelation. The issue here is the substance of her teaching. In other words, it is doubtful that these texts attest to the banning of women teachers within orthodox Christianity. In the first place, these documents arose at the same time as we have clear testimony to women playing prominent roles in early Christianity, including being exemplary martyrs. The famous story of the martyrdom of Perpetua (told in the Acts of Perpetua and Felicitas) under the reign of Septimus Severus when there was a great persecution (A.D. 303–312) comes to mind. These events and their recounting came after or about the same time that these Gnostic documents were written.

It is of course true that there was opposition to women assuming teaching and preaching roles during and after the second century A.D., both inside and outside the orthodox churches. In the story of Paul and Thecla (from the second century), Thecla must in essence renounce her gendered identity and commit herself to absolute chastity to do ministry, but *the same thing can be said of the women discussed in these Gnostic documents*.

Not only are these Gnostic books not likely sources for the theory that Mary Magdalene was married, they are not very useful sources for the modern feminist agenda, because they do not attest to the equality of women and men in Gnostic circles. As we saw, women had to become "perfect men" to be accepted, and this entailed renouncing their physical identity. In other words, Gnostics were no less patriarchal in the way they thought about perfection than non-Gnostics were. Its just that they were not prepared to affirm the goodness of any created or fleshly identity!

Gnostic scholar Karen King seeks to make a case for Mary Magdalene being identified with Wisdom in the Gospel of Philip, which would imply that Mary is the mother of angels and the spiritual sister of Jesus, and indeed his female counterpart. However, that theory doesn't seem to be supported by either canonical scripture or the Gospel of Mary. Wisdom in the canonical gospels is something Jesus is said to embody, and in the Old Testament it is a personified attribute of God, Yahweh (Prov. 3, 8, 9). In the Gospel of Mary, Mary Magdalene, though clearly privy to a special revelation from God, is not divinized or touted as some sort of female deity named Sophia. No, in that Gnostic account Mary as a female disciple puts the male disciples to shame; and they, having been shamed, go out and evangelize as good male apostles were supposed to do. In other words, Mary is used as a shaming device, perhaps to exhort male Gnostic ascetics to get on with the Great Commission—only in this case Gnostic Wisdom is the Gospel they are to spread.

At the end of the day, Gnostic literature is no friend to women in the Christian tradition. Why then have the more radical feminist scholars gravitated toward it, rather than toward the New Testament itself? The latter affirms a variety of roles for women, including teaching and prophesying (see, for example, Acts 18, with its description of Priscilla, and 1 Cor. 11).[34] The answer in part is given in a moment of candor by Elaine Pagels when she says that her study of Gnostic literature has helped her "clarify what I cannot love: the tendency to identify Christianity with a single authorized set of beliefs however these actually vary from church to church—coupled with the conviction that Christian belief alone offers access to God."[35]

This amazing remark is highly ironic. When you read the Gnostic documents, you discover that these folks are just as dogmatic as any of the orthodox Christians—indeed, often more so! They insist that you must have the Gnostic wisdom or your soul will not ascend to heaven. They are not early advocates of modern religious pluralism, and they should not be made the poster children for such a modern crusade. When it comes to Gnostics and Christians, we are dealing with dueling versions of the truth about God, creation, revelation, salvation, and a host of other subjects. Even in the Gospel of Thomas we find not a parallel to modern religious pluralism (which is a sort of *Live and let live* philosophy), but rather a syncretism of Jewish, Christian, and pagan ideas as if all were equally valid and valuable sources of truth, an attitude that early Jews and Christians of the New Testament did not share.

Both the Christians and the Gnostics saw themselves as serving up mutually exclusive truth claims, and both thought they offered the one way to salvation and the true knowledge of God. *They were right about the issue of mutual exclusivity:* both of these belief systems could be false, but both could not be true, nor could both be meaningfully or accurately called Christian. According to our earliest sources—that is, the New Testament documents—being Christian entails affirming the goodness of creation, of the incarnation of God in Jesus, of the death and bodily resurrection of Jesus, and of salvation by grace through faith in the atoning death of Jesus, with salvation being for everyone, not just the intellectuals; it's more a matter of whom you trust than how much you know.

Instead of listening to Elaine Pagels or Karen King about this complex and confusing Gnostic literature, we would do better to heed the Eastern Orthodox scholar Frederica Matthewes-Green. She stresses that the rebuttal of orthodox Christians to the Gnostics was that the latter were playing fast and loose with the historical record about early Christianity, and in fact were letting their philosophical speculations lead them to engage in revisionist history as well as revisionist theology.

> The problem wasn't the insistence that we can directly experience God. It was that Gnostics' schemes of how to do this were so *wacky*. Preposterous stories about creation, angels, demons, and spiritual hierarchies multiplied like mushrooms.... The version attributed to Valentinus, the best known Gnostic, is typical. Valentinus supposedly taught a hierarchy of spiritual beings called 'aeons'. One of the lowest aeons, Sophia, fell and gave birth to the Demiurge, the God of the Hebrew Scriptures. This evil Demiurge created the visible world, which was a bad thing, because now we pure spirits are all tangled up in fleshy bodies. Christ was an aeon who took possession of the body of the human Jesus, and came to free us from the prison of materiality. 'Us' by the way did not mean everybody. Not all people have a divine spark within, just intellectuals: 'gnosis', by definition, concerns what you know. Some few who are able to grasp these insights could be initiated into deeper mysteries. Ordinary Christians, who lacked sufficient brainpower, could only attain the Demiurge's middle realm. Everyone else was doomed. Under Gnosticism, there was no hope of salvation for most of the human race.[36]

This is hardly literature that might or should comfort the marginalized or the oppressed. To the contrary, it is intellectually arrogant and elitist to the core. Furthermore, it hardly differs in dogmatism from the Christianity Pagels complains about, and as we saw earlier it is tainted by occasionally blatant anti-Semitism. At times, like that other second-century heretic Marcion and his writings, it repudiates both the God of the Hebrew scriptures and those scriptures themselves. But Gnosticism's most egregious flaw lies in the notion that salvation is a human self-help program or an exercise in which one pursues self-knowledge and self-awareness. Gnosticism repudiates the Christian belief that history, not just esoteric knowledge, matters, and that salvation was wrought outside of human musings and machinations, in the person of Jesus of Nazareth, through his death and bodily resurrection. Gnostic literature attests just how far wrong one can go when one untethers one's theological reflections from their grounding in historical events and persons. In fact, one can go all the way to pantheism if one pursues the earliest form of the Gnostic agenda far enough—the notion that there is a little bit of the divine in all things and persons.

In light of the evidence of the primary sources themselves, it is puzzling why scholars such as Elaine Pagels, Karen King, Stephen Patterson, Marvin Meyer, and James Robinson would find this material so exciting. None of them are actually ascetics like the original Gnostics, nor have they withdrawn from the world and anathematized the goodness of things material. Frankly, the Old Gnostics would have repudiated the new ones, and would even have rejected their revisionist take on Christian history, seeing it as an unnecessary enterprise. Focusing on real history and real events in space and time would not have been spiritual or philosophical enough for the old Gnostics; it would have been a good example of failing to transcend the material realm that nurtures and supports us all.

These scholars seem to be engaged in creating a new myth of origins, one that better suits their own more anthropocentric approaches to religion. This is only conjecture, but it makes some sense of why certain scholars would so strongly embrace literature that is not in accord with their personal agendas or consonant with their personal lifestyles. It is a tragic form of grasping at straws, because these scholars are left with no viable alternative than to reject the whole of early Christianity and its history, lock, stock, and barrel. They're throwing all that away for nothing, because only an argument from silence can suggest that these later Gnostic variants from early Christianity were actually extant in the first century. There is no hard evidence to support such a claim unless Thomas provides it; and as we have seen, Thomas is most likely a second-century document reflecting back on the literature of the apostolic era.

It is striking to me that scholars who try to rewrite the history of early Christianity by privileging later documents and marginalizing earlier ones often ignore altogether such early Christian documents as the Didache, 1 Clement, the Epistle of Barnabas, Hermas, and even the letters of Ignatius, all of which come from the late first or early second century. Why? Precisely because these documents pursue the historical and theological trajectories found within the earlier documents—which is to say, the documents we now find in the New Testament. Barnabas is a profoundly Jewish document, 1 Clement echoes Paul's 1 Corinthians, Hermas continues in the tradition of Revelation's Jewish-Christian apocalypticism, and so on.

These noncanonical documents do not offer up wild and outlandish philosophy as an attempt to de-Judaize and de-eschatologize the early Jesus tradition or syncretize it with later pagan and ascetical notions. In short, these extracanonical documents do not support the notion that earliest Christianity was as intellectually broad-minded as these revisionist historians would like us to think. There were boundaries of belief and behavior even in the first century, boundaries beyond which Jesus's followers knew they should not go; and the Gnostic documents clearly crossed those boundaries in various ways. As it turns out, the lost Christianities so often touted today were not so much lost as abandoned for good reasons. They were not suppressed because they offered an alternative, earlier, and truer version of Christian origins; they were tried and found wanting because they betrayed the essentially Jewish monotheistic, eschatological character of Jesus and his movement.

So should we despair of learning anything new about Jesus or his earliest followers these days? I would say no. The actual original mother lode, found in the New Testament, still has not been mined for all its worth. This study seeks to begin to unearth that great treasure. There is, however, one more set of traditions about Mary Magdalene of a non-Gnostic nature from an even later period that deserves our attention.

THE LEGENDARY MARY MAGDALENE

Last but not least, there are a surprising number of medieval stories about Mary Magdalene, some of which have a little basis in the New Testament and others of which have none whatsoever. For example, in the *Golden Legend* (1.374–83) from the eighth century, Mary is called the first apostle—indeed, the "apostle to the apostles." She is said to be the beautiful, long-haired daughter of wealthy parents and the sister of Martha and Lazarus. Another story has her betrothed to John the Evangelist, but she loses him to the service of Jesus; after she is healed of her diseases, she also joins Jesus's service. As a quasi-apostle she then undertakes a career in missionary work, going first to Ephesus and then to Marseilles, where she preaches the faith along with Martha and Lazarus. The *Golden Legend* goes on to have Lazarus become the bishop of that city after Mary Magdalene converts the local pagan ruler and his wife and enables them to conceive a child.

This tradition varies greatly from another medieval tradition about Mary Magdalene. In that version she spends thirty years doing penance near Marseilles as one of the seventy-two disciples who went with her to convert pagans in that region. According to this tradition Mary dies there after receiving final Communion from angels. She is then interred at Vezelay in Burgundy, where her shrine and her corpse become a prime source of relics. The twelfth-century Basilica of "la Madeleine" has long been a popular pilgrimage center.

Once again, unfortunately, in these traditions Mary Magdalene's story is amalgamated with the story of the sinner woman of Luke 7:36–50 or

John 7:53–8:11 (or both), as in Mel Gibson's recent movie *The Passion of the Christ*.[37]

The unbelievable and unhistorical nature of many of these traditions does not mean that none of them has any basis in fact; but clearly such later traditions have to be examined with an extremely critical eye, especially when they do not seem to have any analogues or precursors in traditions that go back as far as the second century. We can say that to the extent that such traditions highlight what is already present in our earliest witnesses to the life of Mary Magdalene in the canonical texts, they have some basis in truth. For example, Mary certainly was the first proclaimer of the Easter gospel, the "Good News." But to the extent that they depart from our earliest witnesses, they are not to be trusted. They should be seen as hagiography at best, and as a tendentious misuse of the Mary traditions to further certain later agendas at worst.

WHAT WE'VE LEARNED AND WHAT THAT KNOWLEDGE TELLS US ABOUT JESUS

We have examined two remarkable women and their legacy in this section of our book. The first of them, Joanna, was actually called an apostle in her lifetime. The second was later described as such by church fathers. While the biblical Joanna did not spawn later legends, the Mary Magdalene tradition clearly did so, chiefly because of John 20—a text that presents us with the woman who was the first person to encounter the risen Jesus on Easter. The remarkable nature of these women as witnesses is in no way diminished by the fact that we learn nothing historical or substantive about them, or about their relationship with Jesus or the inner circle of disciples, from the later Gnostic or medieval materials. But those later materials do confirm what we already knew about Mary Magdalene from the New Testament: she was important as a woman who witnessed and proclaimed the Good News.

Joanna and Mary Magdalene were important because they were among the first female disciples of any Jewish sage in early Judaism; because of the sacrifices they made to bear witness to the gospel message, despite rejection and even imprisonment in the case of Joanna/Junia, and because they remind us that the inner circle of Jesus did not involve just men, much less just the Twelve. Jesus's inner circle was an odd collection of family and non-family members, both men and women. Lastly, these women are important because they set a remarkable precedent for women after them to discover the Good News and learn how to share it despite dispute and rejection and suffering. This in itself is more than enough to celebrate. We do not need the later Gnostic myths and medieval legends to gild these lilies. Joanna and Mary were already courageous saints in their own day.

But what does this fascinating material tell us about Jesus himself? First, it affirms the resurrection story as told in the New Testament. When these women, caught up in grief and in the rituals of burial, went to the tomb on Easter Sunday morning, the last thing they expected to see was a risen Jesus! They went to anoint the body, not worship the Lord. The most reasonable explanation for the stories we have in the gospels and other faith documents about these women having seen the risen Lord is that they *did* in fact see him, and that experience caused a revolution in their thinking and in the direction of their lives. Before they had been devoted followers of Jesus; now they were commissioned to be leaders and proclaimers of the Easter news, first to the Twelve and then to the wider world. It was Jesus himself who commissioned them for this, and indeed it was the appearances of the risen Jesus that made possible their transition from follower to leader.

As noted earlier, in a patriarchal culture like that of the early Jewish and Greco-Roman world, no one would have made up a story about a hero who appeared after death to *some grieving women* and use it as the basis of a new religious movement, unless one is pressed to do so by the witness of history. No, the stories run that way because that's how it happened: Joanna and Mary Magdalene believed they saw and even touched the risen Jesus, and thus I believe he actually appeared to them and was alive and tangible. From the very beginnings of the post-Easter Jesus movement, there was a profound conviction that Jesus was indeed the risen Lord—a conviction that grew because he clearly, convincingly, and in various places and ways and to various persons presented himself in the flesh. Certainly neither Mary nor Joanna would have continued to be a disciple of Jesus if something had not happened after the crucifixion, nor would either have become an "apostle to the apostles." This in turn has consequences for what we think about the historical Jesus and earliest Christianity.

The Easter experience of Joanna and Mary refutes attempts to create a gap between the historical Jesus and the risen Christ of faith, perhaps even a gap of many years. Such attempts simply will not work, historically speaking. The people who were in the inner circle of Jesus are the very people who were the earliest eyewitnesses of the risen Lord. They weren't all victims of mass amnesia or hallucination after the crucifixion. To the contrary, they had clarifying experiences that *confirmed* and indeed *amplified* what they had already believed about Jesus before Golgotha. They had faith in Jesus before he died, and they continued to have faith in him thereafter—no disconnect there. They did not exchange one set of beliefs for another, but expanded their understanding of the original things they believed about Jesus. Paul tells us that these same Aramaic-speaking followers prayed to Jesus after he ascended, using the Aramaic phrase *"Marana tha"*—"Come, O Lord" (1 Cor. 16:22). They would not have prayed *to* a deceased rabbi to come back, though they might have hoped for his resurrection in due course. But believing that Jesus was the divine Lord, they prayed to him to come once more.

These remarkable messianic beliefs about Jesus, uttered first by Mary and Joanna and then shared with other monotheistic Jews—beliefs about Jesus being both human and more than human, someone who rightly could be worshipped and prayed to—did not arise out of thin air or wishful thinking on the part of postapostolic Christians of a later era. These beliefs, or at least some form and aspect of them, already existed in the inner circle of Jesus at least as early as Easter if not before.

The second thing these stories tell us is that the witnesses to the risen Jesus, both women and men, were not just watchers on Easter, confirming their own faith in Jesus; they believed they were commissioned to bear witness about these things. In other words, just as Jesus had sent his disciples out in pairs to bear witness during his ministry, so also did he spread the news about himself after the crucifixion. What sort of Jewish person would do this in a tradition-bound culture—a profoundly monotheistic culture at that? The options are only two: an extreme megalomaniac (and thus someone demented), or someone who had an exalted self-understanding and sense of importance. Jesus was the latter: he acknowledged that he was the Jewish messiah and king before he died, he was crucified for that treasonous acknowledgment, and he presented himself as the risen Lord thereafter.

If you recognize the genuineness of the testimony of Mary and Joanna, and realize that they became apostles, bearing witness to the risen Jesus, you have to recognize certain facts about the historical Jesus. He did not just present himself as a great teacher, a wise sage, a miracle worker, an exorcist. This inner circle knew better than that, and they were faithful to say so after the fact. The Jesus about whom the earliest disciples bore witness was and is the real Jesus of history and faith. The impact crater in the lives of these disciples, male and female, matches up with the impression Jesus deliberately left on these persons, as we will see in more detail as we turn now to Peter.

PART TWO

PETER: THE PRINCIPAL SHEPHERD

THREE

Fishing for Followers: For Pete's Sake

Familiarity breeds contempt, it has sometimes been said, but in the case of Peter it seems to have bred adoration and a glossing over of his faults and the real role he played in the early church. In the gospel of Matthew, Jesus says to him, "You are Peter, and upon this rock I will build my church" (16:18). Based primarily on that text, an early tradition grew up that Peter was the first pope of the Christian church. Despite our best efforts, however, historians have been unable to verify that he was either the first pope or the bishop of Rome or even the primary apostle in Rome when he finally got there, perhaps sometime in the 60s. The evidence of the New Testament strongly suggests that the church in Rome had existed for quite some time before Peter ever darkened its doors. He isn't mentioned in either Romans 16 or Hebrews, for example.

When Peter arrived in Rome, he ranked himself with the Christian elders and the other apostolic witnesses (see 1 Pet., 5:1), many of whom had apparently been there since long before he arrived. However, if due to his long relationship with Jesus he became *primus inter partes* in Rome, the first among many, that exalted role is not depicted in his letters. In fact, 1 Peter depicts him exercising his authority over those who lived outside "Babylon"—that is, outside Rome. As for the Gospel of Mark, which was likely written in Rome about A.D. 68–70, perhaps in part based on Peter's own testimony, it does not provide us with the material we find in Matthew 16 about Peter's special role in relationship to the church anywhere, much less in Rome. We must therefore be cautious about later claims that Peter was the first bishop or pope of Rome. He was in fact unlikely to have been even the first apostle to reach Rome. Paul seems to have gotten there first, courtesy of Roman imperial hospitality and his ongoing trial. What then can we say about Peter, the chief of Jesus's chosen fishermen?

Fishing has always been an iffy proposition. Sometimes people try for hours and catch nothing. Other times they make a big catch almost immediately. When Jesus reeled in Peter, there were no immediate signs that he had caught a big fish. Yet if the measure of a person's importance is shown by the frequency with which others talk about him, Peter was definitely a big fish. He is the only one of the Twelve for whom we have anything like a life history, and he is the only one who is a major player in all four gospels and in the first half of Acts. Furthermore, he is mentioned as a "pillar" apostle in Paul's correspondence, and there are two letters in the canon named after him. Certainly, quite a few people in the early church thought Peter was a big fish. As a result of all this, a huge body of scholarly and popular literature has been written about the man, even if we count only the last hundred years' worth of spilled ink.[38] And the debate about Peter shows no signs of abating.

While our chronologically earliest sources about Peter are Paul's letters (particularly Galatians and 1 Corinthians), it is necessary to examine the gospels critically to assess his beginnings and learn about the relationship between Peter and Jesus. That secondhand material will be the focus of the current chapter. I will then suggest in the next chapter that we also have firsthand information in 1 Peter, as well as Peter's own testimony to the transfiguration in 2 Peter (though the latter is a composite document from the end of the New Testament era). For the most part, however, that firsthand information in fact deals with post-Easter matters.

SIMON PETER: THE ROCK

Though Shakespeare suggested to us that there's not much in a name, and modern Western folks tend to see names as simply labels, this was certainly not the case in the world of Judaism in the first century and before. Properly speaking, the name of the person under consideration here is Simon, Simon bar Jonah. He was named after one of the Maccabean heroes, Simon; and his father was named after that most reluctant of all Old Testament exilic prophets, Jonah, with "bar" indicating "son of." This name suggests that Simon's family sympathized with or supported the Zealots (a sect of Judaism that militantly opposed domination by the Romans) or at least longed for the days when Jews controlled their own land. With this background it is not entirely surprising that Simon would sign on with a messianic operation that was based in the town of Capernaum, where he settled—a place that still resonates with his presence in the site known as the House of Peter (or, better said, of his mother-in-law).[39]

So why would the site be called the House of *Peter* when his name was Simon? According to the gospels and Paul's letters, this man also had a nickname, Cephas, which came to be rendered in Greek as Petros, or as we would say, Peter. *Cephas* is an Aramaic word that means "rock," and as such it is highly ironic. Perhaps Simon was sometimes solid as a rock, but his faith journey also had its rocky moments, its moments of fear, flight, and denial. It is not entirely inappropriate to say that his real name when he was involved with Jesus was Rocky Jonahson. It has a ring to it!

Our earliest accounts of Simon meeting Jesus come from two gospel sources, Mark and John. We will consider the Markan story first. Mark 1:16–20 tells us that Jesus was strolling along the Sea of Galilee when he saw Simon and his brother Andrew fishing. He urged them to follow him, promising that he would make them fishers of human beings. He then called James and John, sons of Zebedee, who were likewise fishermen. The four men weren't called upon to repent and believe, but rather to leave their nets and follow. The primary task in this scene seems to have been recruitment of disciples for new tasks, not (or at least not primarily) the conversion of the lost. However, by so recruiting and training followers, Jesus *de facto* established a new social entity, a new community.

Though we are accustomed to thinking of these men as poor, the social indicators in the text suggest otherwise. The Zebedees, for example, could afford to have both a boat and a hired man. Furthermore, we know that fishermen were indeed the regular targets of tax collectors, since they had to sell their product quickly and thus more often dealt in money rather than relying on the barter system. If it is true that the Sea of Galilee was teeming with fish, fishing was probably a reasonably prosperous business.

The social situation described in this recruitment scene is typical, for in both cases we are dealing with family businesses—in the case of the Zebedees involving not only hired help but also two generations working together. Peter and Andrew would seem to have had a more modest business, as they are not said to have had a boat, but rather were using a circular net with weighted edges to trap fish near the shore. As Ched Myers has noted, "The fishing trade is accurately represented: we see an independent artisan class, distinct from day laborers, whom they could afford to hire (1:20)."[40]

Jesus's call is quoted only once in Mark's brief passage, and in essence the call is to "fall in line" behind Jesus (the word *opiso* is used in verses 16 and 20). These are marching orders. The recruits are called to break ties with the past, but also to take up a new trade that is analogous to their old one. This is a call for total dedication to the mission. It is significant that though the men respond to the call here, they do not fully take up the tasks entailed for some time. They must first be "made" fishers of human beings—shaped and molded and trained in the requisite skills. And of course, human beings are a hard species of creature to catch.

The text says that the fishermen responded "immediately" to the summons. Commentators have often speculated whether this suggests the authoritativeness of Jesus's summons,[41] or whether, as John 3–4 may suggest, they had known something of Jesus's message and methods prior to this summons. There is a brief indication of the degree of sacrifice involved—namely, the Zebedees left father, boat, hired man, and nets behind and got in line behind Jesus. As Myers observes, "The point here is that following Jesus requires not just assent of the heart, but a fundamental reordering of socio-economic relationship.... This is not a call 'out of the world', but into an alternative social practice."[42] But the renunciation does not seem to be absolute, for we find the disciples back in their own homes soon thereafter, reminding us that it is likely that there was a home base for the disciples (apparently Capernaum) from which they regularly went with Jesus to various parts of the region. After all, one could get to Nazareth and then back to Capernaum in a day on foot if one was able-bodied.

There is no evidence that the early church generally referred to missionary work as fishing. We don't hear this usage in Paul's or Peter's letters or in Acts, for example. It's something distinctive that comes from Jesus the wordsmith. When Luke uses the metaphor of fishing in 5:10, he uses the verb *zogron,* which literally means "to catch or take alive." This suggests a rescue operation. Back in Mark, just before his account of Jesus's recruitment of the four fishermen, the message of John the Baptist is repeated by Jesus—"Repent, and believe in the good news" (1:15)—suggesting that this rescue had to do with rescuing people from the wrath to come, seeking and saving the lost before it was too late.

There is some Old Testament background to the fishing metaphor that we need to consider at this juncture.[43] There is a series of Old Testament texts that, taken together, suggest an ominous overtone to this language of Jesus. Jeremiah 16:16 and Ezekiel 29:4–5 in particular suggest the connotation of catching people in wickedness and for judgment, with either God or God's agent doing the catching. We need to bear in mind that for land-hugging peoples like Jews, water was associated with chaos and danger, and even demons and spirits or ghosts were thought to dwell in large bodies of water (cf., e.g., Ps. 74:13; Matt. 14:26). In this context, to fish for a human being was to rescue that person from drowning in the dangerous waters of chaos. Jesus envisions the rescuing of lost Jews, in all likelihood. After all, this was a mission that someone named Simon who knew his Maccabean history was eager to sign on for. Jesus believed he was working against time to prevent the end of Israel's world as they knew it. Thus we have here not just a call to discipleship and learning, but a call to a mission, and Simon is apparently the first to sign up.

In the Markan ordering of things Jesus first calls Simon and then, later in the same chapter, heals his mother-in-law (Mark 1:38–39), which means Simon was already married when he was called. Luke has the reverse of this order, and he has a much fuller version of the calling of Simon in Luke 5:1–11. That account includes Jesus teaching from Simon's boat, a miraculous catch of fish after a night of no results, and a request by Simon, once he has seen this huge catch of fish, for Jesus to leave him, "for I am a sinful man." Jesus responds that Simon should not be afraid, because from that point on he wouldn't need to bother with fish, but instead would catch human beings—an even more slippery prey. Presumably, we are meant to think that Simon saw himself as unworthy and too much of a sinner to be in the presence of such a holy man.

In the Gospel of John, Simon is introduced at the outset in a telegraphic fashion. At John 1:43–44 we are told that Andrew, who had heard what John the Baptist had said about Jesus and was already following him, found Simon his brother and told him, "We have found the messiah"; then he led Simon to a place where he could meet Jesus. In this narrative the first words Jesus is said to have spoken to Simon are "You are Simon son of John; you shall be called Cephas." It is likely that the Fourth Evangelist, in order to introduce his *dramatis personae* up front, has moved this tradition to this spot, for Simon received this nickname much later in the ministry, according to the synoptics.[44] (I will have much more to say about the nickname when we get to the Caesarea Philippi story, below.)

In listings of the Twelve, Simon is always named first. In addition, when we hear stories that involve an inner circle of the Twelve, Peter is always included coupled with the Zebedee brothers, and he often features prominently as the spokesman for the Twelve. He seems to be a sort of lightning rod, reflecting the mind or mood of the Twelve. In the Gethsemane story as told in Mark 14:32–42, it is clear that Jesus expects more of Simon than he does of the others, in terms of keeping watch and praying while Jesus is praying. And sometimes, of course, Jesus gets more out of Simon than he does the other disciples. It was only Simon who attempted to walk on water as Jesus had done, according to Matthew 14:28–30;[45] and it was he who protested most vehemently in Mark 14:27–31 that he would never deny or desert Jesus, despite being told he would deny him three times (a protestation that led to the threefold restoration scene in John 21, which we'll address below).

It is remarkable in the wake of all this that we have no record in the gospels of the story of the resurrected Jesus appearing to Simon, even though we have clear mention in Luke 24:34 and elsewhere of the tradition that Jesus did so. In fact, the earliest record, found in 1 Corinthians 15:5, suggests that of the Twelve, it was Simon to whom Jesus appeared first.

SIMON SAYS: A SUMMIT ON THE SUMMIT (MATT. 16:13–28)

Hardly any story from Jesus's ministry is more familiar than the one about Simon Peter's confession at Caesarea Philippi, north of Antipas's territory of Galilee, found in full at Matthew 16:13–28.[46] Let's consider the first seven verses:

> Now when Jesus came into the district of Caesarea Philippi, he asked his disciples, "Who do people say that the Son of Man is?" And they said, "Some say John the Baptist, but others Elijah, and still others Jeremiah or one of the prophets." He said to them, "But who do you say that I am?" Simon Peter answered, "You are the Messiah, the Son of the living God." And Jesus answered him, "Blessed are you, Simon bar Jonah! For flesh and blood has not revealed this to you, but my Father in heaven. And I tell you, you are Peter, and on this rock I will build my church, and the gates of Hades will not prevail against it. I will give you the keys of the kingdom of heaven [or the Dominion], and whatever you bind on earth will be bound in heaven, and whatever you loose on earth will be loosed in heaven."

This story draws upon Mark 8:27–30, with only minor alterations, and on special Petrine traditions. The story occurs in the middle of the narrative about Jesus's Galilean ministry, after the disciples have gone out two by two and evangelized the region, bringing back with them the polling data on what the people were saying about Jesus and who they thought he was.

The setting of this confession is surely important. Philip's Caesarea— or, as the Greeks had previously called it, Panyas, named after the Greek god Pan—had been a center of various sorts of pagan worship since the

Hellenistic age; and in Jesus's day it was also a center for emperor worship, hence the renaming of the city.

The discussion was prompted by Jesus himself: the disciples didn't volunteer the fact that Jesus was the Jewish messiah or God's unique son. The question Jesus asked first was a personal one: "Who do people say that I am?" In a culture where names gave clues to a person's nature and character (as we saw in the case of Simon bar Jonah), the way people named Jesus would have been revealing of what they thought of him. The disciples responded that people saw him as John the Baptist, Elijah, Jeremiah, or one of the prophets. Despite Jesus's miracles, apparently people didn't see Jesus as the messiah, although in the north there was the tradition about Elijah and miracles, and there had been some suggestion that John the Baptist was an Elijah figure after whom would come a greater one.

However, Jesus did not play out the messianic script along Davidic (or warrior) lines, and that confused various people. One of the more interesting things about this story is that human beings and mere human logic weren't adequate to come up with the right answer about the identity of Jesus—it required a revelation from above. This being the case, ordinary people—whether Jewish or not, whether well informed about Judaism or not—could not be faulted for lacking a full understanding of Jesus. It was not immediately evident who Jesus was from his words and deeds, however remarkable, and apparently Jesus wanted it that way. Only by his revealing himself in his own way and on his own terms, or by God's revelation, could even the disciples come to understand the mystery that was Jesus.

Both the incident at Caesarea Philippi and the subsequent transfiguration involved revelation to a select group. While Caesarea Philippi involved the Twelve, the transfiguration involved only three disciples. There was good reason for Jesus to reveal himself only to his inner circle: they would be able to interpret such a revelation in the larger context of the ongoing relationship they had with Jesus and their knowledge of what he had been saying and doing over a considerable period of time, which included hearing him ask and answer questions about his identity.

After Jesus sampled the opinions of the general public, which suggested that he was likely some sort of prophetic figure, he then turned and asked the disciples who they said Jesus was. Notice the emphatic position of the word "you" in this verse—"but *you* [plural], who do *you* say that I am?" Peter—let's call him by that name now—as so often, responds as the representative and leader of the inner circle, and he confesses Jesus to be the messiah. As far as the synoptic accounts go, only in Matthew do we have the additional phrase of acclamation "the Son of the living God" (and John's gospel does not record the Caesarea episode at all).

The phrase "Son of the living God" is especially apt considering the setting, because from a Jewish point of view, Caesarea Philippi was a place where various "dead" gods or non-gods were worshipped. Alternatively, this phrase could be the Evangelist's parenthetical further explanation of the meaning of the acclamation. "Son of God" was certainly already a known title for the messiah in this era, and it meant God's vice-regent, the second in command. The supplemental phrase "the living God" comes up elsewhere in Matthew and is grounded in the Old Testament.[47] That phrase at a minimum implies a special relationship between the person so designated and the one true God, conveying more significance in Judaism than the comparable phrase "son of the gods" would have in a polytheistic context.

We learn that Peter's confession comes from the prompting of a revelation of God, not from a flash of human ingenuity or Sherlock Holmes-like deduction. What then follows is the unique commissioning of Peter, which material is not found in the First Evangelist's Markan source, so it must have come to him from his special Matthean source. (The so-called First Evangelist was the compiler of Matthew's gospel. Matthew himself was only one of the sources of material in this gospel, albeit the most famous one.) It must be borne in mind, lest too much be made of what is said here, that the powers bestowed on Peter are also bestowed on the community of Jesus's followers in Matthew, so Peter may simply represent the group again. Matthew 18:18–20 says clearly enough that the power of binding and loosing is bestowed on all those to whom Jesus is speaking; and furthermore, that when two or three of them agree in prayer on anything, they have the immediate ear of the Father.

Down through the centuries there have been various attempts, especially by Protestants, to explain Matthew 16:17–19 and its echo in Matthew 18:18–20 in such a fashion so as to explain them away, or on the other hand to make so much of them that a whole theory of church hierarchy, apostolicity, and the like is derived from them.[48] Does Matthew 16:17–19 have to do with some sort of authority invested in Peter alone as an individual, or is it more about him as a representative of a group, or should we focus on Peter's faith or confession as the foundation of Jesus's *ekklesia* (a term that here need mean no more than the gathered community of Jesus)?

Let's go back and consider the play on words—first *petros* and then *petra*, Greek for "rock"—found in Matthew 16:18. I know of no evidence of Petros (or the Aramaic original, Cephas) being used as a man's name prior to this usage. A close reading of the text reveals that Jesus bestowed the name because of the rightness of Peter's confession. The wordplay would have been rendered inept if the two words—*petros* and *petra*—did not refer to the same object. Notice that we do not find the two forms of the nickname juxtaposed: the disciple may be called Simon Peter but not Cephas Peter. We are not then dealing with a double name like John Mark, but rather a name and a nickname.

The tense of the verbs in this narrative is also of importance. *Oikodomeso*, meaning "I will build [my church]," and indeed the following verbs are in the future tense. (In Aramaic this would likely have meant some form of the imperfect, indicating action that was not yet complete or finished.) What the Greek rendering of this saying suggests is that Jesus did not found his own community during his ministry, but rather that would happen later, a conclusion that seems supported by the larger context— for example, 16:21. It was only after the death and resurrection of Jesus that his community was properly founded. Thus this passage suggests that Peter would play an important role later, in addition to the role he played during the ministry of Jesus.

The image of building something on a rock has plenty of Jewish precedent; indeed, it even has precedent in the teaching of Jesus. For example, the rock on which the holy Temple in Jerusalem was built was thought of as sealing the gateway to Sheol, the underworld, and the Temple itself was seen as the gateway to heaven. If Jesus is alluding to that Temple, then he is suggesting that he will build a different sort of temple on a different sort of rock. The problem with this conclusion is that the term "temple" does not come up here.

The setting of the saying in Caesarea Philippi also works against that interpretation. At Caesarea Philippi there was an underground stream that surfaced and can still be seen today. Tradition held that this was one of the gates to the underworld and the river Styx. Both the saying of Peter and the saying of Jesus take on special relevance if they were in fact given in the locale where there were shrines to other sons of the gods, and next to the river that was thought to go into Hades/Sheol.

In affirming that "the gates of Hades will not prevail against [my church]," Jesus is saying that his community, once founded on the confessing Peter, will never die out. Despite the reference to the underworld, this saying is probably not about spiritual struggles between the church and the devil. Death rather than the devil is the focus: Jesus is referring to the gates of death and the land of the dead (as several Old Testament writers do), not the gates of hell. The message is that death will not eliminate this community; indeed, it will help perpetuate it.

The next point of importance is that Jesus calls this community "*my* church." This is important not least because in the Old Testament the community of faith is said to belong to God, not to the messiah. This saying, then, may well imply something important about Jesus's self-understanding as one who fulfills a divine role. At 16:19 we hear of the keys of the Dominion, and again the verb tense ("I will give") is future. Having talked of the gates of death, Jesus now talks about the gates of life—in other words, the entrance into God's Dominion.

Very likely Isaiah 22:15–25 lies in the background here. That passage is addressed to a steward who has hewn a habitation or tomb for himself in the rock—that is, he has bought a one-way ticket to the gates of Sheol. This steward, Shebna, is to be deposed because of that act and replaced with Eliakim, who is said to be a father to the "house" of Judah and to Jerusalem. To him will be given the "key of the house of David," which he may open and no one can shut, and he shall shut and no one shall open. Later Christian interpretation of that passage and Matthew 16's parallel "key" and "bind/loose" language saw the key(s) as fitting the pearly gates, allowing access into heaven. But if the focus of Jesus's saying in Matthew was intended to be eschatological, it would not have referred to any authority that Peter had before the end-times; in other words, it would have nothing to do with any authority Peter might have had over who got into the community of Jesus, which was distinctly on earth rather than in heaven.[49] And yet both Matthew 16 and Matthew 18 speak of Peter's having such power on earth—power that is confirmed in heaven. Probably, then, the keys are a symbol of Peter's authority in general, allowing him to make binding decisions about what is and is not permitted of the followers of Jesus.

The problem with an earthly, ecclesiastical reading of this text is that Peter does not seem to have historically exercised such authority after Easter. As noted earlier, he was certainly not the head of the early church in Jerusalem when the important council described in Acts 15 took place (more on that council in a later chapter), and Galatians 2 suggests that he wasn't before then either. Perhaps one could argue that he was in charge for a time, until he departed Jerusalem, leaving the church in the hands of James. However, Acts 11.2 tells us that he was called on the carpet over the baptizing of Cornelius and his household, and Galatians 2 suggests that Peter acted on the basis of what he thought James wanted of him. He was, as Paul calls him in Galatians 1–2, one of the pillar apostles in Jerusalem, but he is only one of the three. He was not the sole founder of this church.[50]

Peter may have been one of the first real "overseers" (*episcopoi*) in Rome in the 50s or 60s, but in 1 Peter 5:1 he speaks of himself as one of a *group* of fellow elders, though the others are in a different location. In 1 Peter 1:1 he presents himself as one apostle of Jesus Christ, using the same terminology as Paul. Tradition aside, then, there is nothing in Matthew or 1 Peter or Acts to suggest that Peter was the first pope. Thus there is still a possibility that Jesus is referring to the eschatological role Peter will play when God's Dominion comes finally and fully on earth. John 21 suggests that Peter would tend Jesus's flock, and 1 Peter suggests he accomplished that task. If Acts 10 is to be taken seriously, with its account of the baptism of Cornelius, a case could be made that Peter pioneered or opened the door to the mission to Gentiles, though Paul became known as the quintessential apostle to the Gentiles. In addition, it's clear from Galatians 2 that Peter was assigned the task of evangelizing Jews.

Matthew 16 brings a reassuring note, for Jesus builds his community on the basis of ordinary, flawed, and vacillating persons like Peter. He authorizes and equips them to serve, giving them the power and authority to determine what is and is not allowed in that community. We hear nothing of any apostolic succession of persons, a later idea in any case. But it is people like Simon whom God enables to make the good confession about Jesus. There is a rather complex theology of community and leadership developed here, deriving from the acts and power and authority of Jesus himself. The First Evangelist would have us realize that it is precisely because Jesus is the origin of his community of faith—the messiah who died and rose again—that it will never die out, no matter how low an ebb it may reach; there shall always be his community, his people, his Dominion.

The First Evangelist places his first Passion prediction immediately after the incident at Caesarea Philippi. "From that time on Jesus began to show his disciples that he must go to Jerusalem and undergo great suffering..., and be killed..., and on the third day be raised" (16:21). This may explain Jesus's strong response to Peter's rebuke. Peter was acting the part of Satan and tempting Jesus to go against the specific divine will that Jesus must go the route of the cross. As New Testament scholar Susan Garrett points out, "The severity of Jesus' rebuke of Peter in Mark 8:33 [and Matt. 16:23] corresponds to the magnitude of Jesus' temptation here: the rebuke is sharp because the temptation is profound. Although Jesus knows where God's path for him leads—through suffering, rejection, death, and resurrection... he is sorely tempted to follow Peter in departing from this path. Jesus perseveres on the straight and narrow in spite of temptation, but one senses that his endurance is hard-won."[51]

The above-quoted verse indicates that Jesus began to explain the issue of the Passion to his disciples. We should perhaps envision him breaking it to them gradually. But Peter's response in the next verse indicates that he understands quite well what Jesus is saying; and he doesn't like it. He takes Jesus aside and says, "God forbid it, Lord. This shall never happen to you!" He could hardly be more emphatic. As Peter had rebuked Jesus, so Jesus turns to Peter and rebukes him, saying, "Get behind me, Satan" (presumably meaning, "Take the proper place of a disciple and follow me and my example"). Jesus implies that Peter, far from protesting Jesus's destiny and getting in the way of the trip up to Jerusalem, ought to take up his cross and follow him. It is, of course, possible to see the use of the term "Satan" here as generic, meaning "adversary," but the apocalyptic character of the narrative suggests a stronger reading. While Peter is not possessed, he is influenced by the forces of darkness to think in a merely human manner about the future of Jesus.

So Peter unwittingly serves as Satan's tool here, ironically at the precise moment when he also has gained a partial insight into Jesus's identity. Jesus's response suggests, as noted earlier, that Jesus was tempted not to go the direction he had just predicted; that he was tempted to bypass such an experience is confirmed later in the Garden of Gethsemane—though he chose to acquiesce to divine will. Peter likewise has a choice: he can either heed Satan and be a hindrance whom Jesus must leave behind on the way to the cross, or he can be a true follower of Jesus and prepare for suffering as Jesus is doing.

After rebuking Peter, Jesus extends the call of discipleship and cross-bearing to *all* the disciples: "If any want to become my followers, let them deny themselves and take up their cross and follow me" (v. 24). As Plutarch reminds us, "Every criminal who is executed carries his own cross."[52] In other words, the cost of discipleship may involve great shame, and all disciples must be prepared to bear that cost. If the reference to the cross is indeed part of the original wording of this saying, there is no reason why Jesus could not have meant this remark rather literally—in effect, "Be prepared to die a shameful death by public execution if you want to be my follower." The phrase "Take up your cross and follow me" would not have sounded like a flowery metaphor to first-century persons. Rather, since crucifixion was reserved for the most hardened criminals and those committing treason against the state, it would have been seen as an invitation to martyrdom. While Jesus did not inculcate a martyrdom complex, he did insist that his followers deny themselves and be prepared to die *if that should be required to remain true to their faith in and following of Jesus.*

SIMON SEES: ANOTHER MOUNTAINTOP EXPERIENCE (MATT. 17:1–13)

Hardly any narrative in Matthew's gospel is more mysterious than the transfiguration account in 17:1–13. Jesus takes Peter, James, and John up an unnamed mountain (traditionally thought to be Mt. Tabor, but possibly Mt. Hermon), where they have a visionary encounter with Moses and Elijah and see that Jesus is as glorious as those earlier heroes were thought to be—indeed, more glorious than either the representative of the Law (Moses) or the representative of the prophets (Elijah).

What exactly was going on when the four men paid a visit to a "high mountain"? The story is not simply about portraying Jesus as the new Moses or the new Elijah. For one thing, the disciples are exhorted to listen just to Jesus, not to Moses or Elijah. So why are Moses and Elijah even there? Do they represent the Law and the prophets—that is, the attestation of the whole Hebrew canon—to Jesus? This would certainly suit the First Evangelist's theology. Another possibility is that Moses and Elijah were there in fulfillment of eschatological traditions in early Judaism about these two figures returning together at the end of the age.

The First Evangelist is careful to call this a "vision," a term from apocalyptic discourse. A vision often involves an inward or subjective experience, though the ancients all believed that visions had an objective origin.[53] But if the appearance of Moses and Elijah was in fact a vision, it must have been a *group* visionary experience. Peter reacts as if the three in the cloud are real enough, but the text makes clear that only Jesus is present before, during, and after the vision. In other words, he is not part of the vision. Whatever its exact nature, the point of the experience was to inform the disciples about an aspect of Jesus's nature.

Notice that this story follows Peter's confession, the commission, and the prediction of Jesus's death and resurrection. Perhaps the transfiguration was intended to offset the shock of the prediction of the Passion, reassuring the disciples that Jesus should still be seen as God's Son, even if he was going to be killed. If traditional messianic hopes had to be shattered, then new and better hopes could be confirmed with the mountaintop experience. But the transfiguration could be seen as a time of confirmation for Jesus as well, for Moses and Elijah speak only to Jesus. Possibly they are present, as Luke's account seems to stress, because they had already had an extraordinary exodus from life. Here, then, the disciples get a sort of sneak preview of Jesus in glory after the ascension.

Here in Matthew for the first time there is mention of the inner circle of the three whom Jesus takes with him up the mountain. They are seen as the representatives of the Twelve. Jesus takes charge here, choosing them deliberately and then leading them up the mountain. Matthew stresses that Jesus takes them up privately. This may suggest that what was revealed to them was not a public matter, at least at this juncture.

In the presence of the three disciples, Jesus either changed or appeared to change visibly. (The verb *metamorpheo* can refer to either a change in appearance or a change in essence, a purely inward and spiritual change.) In Matthew Jesus's face is said to shine like the sun, and his garment is white as light, though Mark offers a more mundane description. The First Evangelist's order of things suggests that Moses and Elijah appeared suddenly after Jesus had undergone metamorphosis.

Peter, awed by the changed Jesus and the sight of Moses and Elijah, exclaims, "Lord, it is good for us to be here; if you wish, I will make three dwellings here, one for you, one for Moses, and one for Elijah." Peter's suggestion that he build shelters may relate to the Feast of Booths, an occasion of messianic and national celebration, the first day of which involved the setting up of the booths. The word used in Matthew, *skene*, actually means tent rather than booth, which may mean that we are not to associate Peter's comment with the Feast of Booths. In any case, Peter apparently thinks it is incumbent on him to honor the revered guests. The First Evangelist's version of Peter's words ("It is good that we are here") differs a little from the Markan version, which paints Peter and the other disciples in a more negative light (adding that neither Peter nor the others understood what was meant). There can be little doubt that the First Evangelist wanted to portray the disciples (and particularly Peter) in a more positive light than we find in Mark, our earliest gospel.

While Peter was speaking, "a bright cloud overshadowed them, and from the cloud a voice said, 'This is my Son, the Beloved; with him I am well pleased; listen to him!'" The words of God in Matthew are identical to those at the baptism. The point again is to confirm Jesus's identity as God's Son—this time to the three rather than to Jesus. The story indicates an attitude of fear on the part of the listeners, or less possibly worship. The disciples hear the voice, fall prostrate, and "fear greatly." When they look up, they see only Jesus. This aspect of the story, like the vision of Moses, Elijah, and the transfigured Jesus, could be an attempt to encourage the disciples after their shock at the Passion prediction and get them to look beyond it to the glorious future for Jesus and God's people.

We learn much about Simon Peter from a close reading of these stories in Matthew 16–17. We will have occasion in the next chapter to consider at length Peter's own later reflections on the transfiguration event. But now we must turn to another side of his great confession—namely, the prediction of his denial, his vehement denial that he would deny, his inability to watch with Jesus, and finally his renunciation and desertion of Jesus.

SIMON RECANTS: THE THREEFOLD DENIAL (MATT. 26: 30–75)

In Matthew 26:31, which brings us closer to the crucifixion, Jesus tells his disciples, "You will all become deserters because of me this night; for it is written, 'I will strike the shepherd, and the sheep of the flock will be scattered.'" The story is a sordid one, because the disciples, despite loud protestations and promises on their part, go on to do exactly what Jesus predicted. The prophetic scripture Jesus quotes is from Zechariah: "Strike down the shepherd and the sheep will be scattered" (13:7). Notice the difference: here in Matthew the passage as Jesus quotes it is, "*I* will strike the shepherd," stressing that it is by God's design and action that the unfolding events are happening to Jesus.

Jesus goes on, in verse 32, to say, "But after I am raised up, I will go ahead of you to Galilee." This is an exceedingly important verse from the point of view of Matthean theology, because it points to a positive conclusion beyond the cross. The desertion of the disciples will not mean the end of their following of Jesus, he assures them. They will be regathered as a group, and God in the end will be vindicated.

As was true in Matthew 16, Peter fixates on the part of Jesus's prediction that refers to the coming desertions and the death of Jesus, rather than on the promise of resurrection and regathering. Peter strongly affirms that though all others may desert him, Peter himself will not do so. Peter's remark in Matthew provokes a dark rejoinder, as was the case in Matthew 16. Jesus tells him that that very night Peter will deny him three times before the cock crows.[54] Peter offers an equally strong rebuttal: "Even if I must die with you, I will never disown you" (v. 35). (The verb that we translate "disown" means to divest oneself of an association that one had previously.) All the other disciples chimed in at this juncture, affirming the same thing. But of course all of them, including Peter, will do just the opposite of what they say. Very few of us know what we are capable of when it's midnight in the garden of evil, and it is to that story that we now turn.

In Matthew 26:36 we are told that Jesus and the disciples went to a place called Gethsemane, which means "oil press," and thus presumably into a grove of olive trees. (It is only John's account that calls Gethsemane a garden.) Jesus first tells the disciples to sit at a particular place while he goes "over there" to pray, but he takes Peter and the two sons of Zebedee with him. Then, taking on the role of the righteous sufferer of the Psalms, Jesus says, "My spirit is sorrowful unto death."[55] He is so sad he could simply die of a broken heart, not least because of how badly he knows the disciples are going to fail him. He urges the three men to stay and keep watch with him while he goes a little distance away and throws himself face down on the ground (a gesture suggesting utter supplication and submission). He prays, "My Father, if it is possible, may this cup be taken away from me. Yet not as I will but as you will." There are several apparent echoes of the Lord's Prayer in this prayer: the Father address, the stress on God's will being done, and the post-prayer stress on the disciples not falling into temptation. Perhaps the First Evangelist wanted us to see the Lord's Prayer, as given in Matthew 6, as indeed Jesus's own prayer, one he not only gives to his disciples but also prays himself.

Jesus prays three times to God, as was customary for Jews in distress. After each prayer he returns to the three waiting disciples, and each time he finds them asleep. This parallel to Peter's threefold denial shows the lack of readiness of these disciples for what is about to transpire. They should have stayed awake and prayed not to fall into temptation. Peter is chided directly in verse 40 the first time Jesus returns and finds them sleeping, urging him to "stay awake and pray that you may not come into the time of trial; the spirit indeed is willing, but the flesh is weak" (v. 41). Falling asleep is not the temptation Jesus is referring to; giving way to some evil, such as deserting Jesus or responding to his arrest inappropriately, is the real temptation. The "spirit" that is willing is the Holy Spirit, which is literally eager/ready (*prothumon*) to help, despite the weakness of human flesh.[56] Notice that Jesus is concerned for the disciples and their testing, even in the hour of his own greatest trial.

When Jesus returns to the disciples the third time he asks them, "Are you still sleeping and resting?" (v. 45). There is no more time for cajoling or pleading with the disciples, or even for warnings, because "the hour is at hand." This is typical of the apocalyptic language Jesus tended to use, with "the hour" being one appointed and determined by God; indeed, the phrase usually refers to the hour of the consummation of God's final judgment.[57] It is time, Jesus says, for the Son of Man to be betrayed into the hands of "sinners," which could mean Gentiles, or possibly bad Jews and Gentiles. In either case it is a negative comment on those he is handed over to, and it may allude to Isaiah 53.

Jesus then rouses the disciples, announcing the arrival of his betrayer. Judas shows up, leading a posse carrying swords and clubs, and identifies

Jesus for the arresters. One of the disciples—the First Evangelist does not tell us which one—reacts with violence to the seizure of Jesus, cutting off the ear of a servant of the high priest. The Fourth Evangelist tells us it was Peter (see John 18:10), a tradition we can well believe to be true, not only because Peter was the leader of the Twelve and was impetuous, but also because the Beloved Disciple (according to the Fourth Gospel) had a close relationship with Peter. The Fourth Gospel gives the servant's name but the First Evangelist does not, perhaps in an attempt to soften the portrayal of Peter. Nor are we told in Matthew that Jesus heals the injury. The First Evangelist simply focuses on this incident's lesson about nonviolence when it comes to the cause of Jesus. The crucial element in the teaching comes in the words of Jesus: "All those who draw the sword will perish by it" (v. 52). In Matthew 5:39-42 Jesus had enunciated a teaching on nonviolence, and here in this section he is seen to live out his credo. The resistance of the disciples and Peter in particular amounts to resistance to God's will, for God willed the Passion events to happen.

Peter follows Jesus after his arrest to see how things will end, and thus begins the tale of Peter's threefold denial. The account of Jesus's trial is sandwiched in between the two halves of the account of Peter's demise, with one story commenting on the other. Jesus's faithfulness and truthfulness to the end are contrasted with Peter's unfaithfulness and dishonesty. We are dealing with a heavily ironic situation, for just as Jesus is being denounced as a false prophet, his prophecy about Peter's denials is coming true! The Matthean account of Jesus's reaction and testimony is clearly meant to be contrasted with the witness—or, better said, the lack thereof—of Peter, who under insignificant pressure from a slave girl denies Jesus as the disciple waits in the courtyard. It is truly a sad contrast.

Matthew clearly portrays Peter the pilgrim's regress, both physically and morally. First he is in the courtyard of the house, then at its gate, then outside. He seems to be steadily retreating. Initially he feigns not to understand what people are saying to him (maybe claiming he doesn't understand their accent). When further pressed, having been recognized by his Galilean dialect, he claims under oath not to know Jesus. Then he curses either Jesus or himself and says yet again that he does not know Jesus.

But no sooner has Peter finished swearing that he doesn't know Jesus than the cock crows, and he goes out and weeps bitterly. For all his protestations, Peter could not escape the truth that Jesus had foreseen for his life. Even in his denials he fulfilled the words of Jesus, thus vindicating Jesus. It was a bitter pill to swallow, letting himself and his Master down so grievously. It was an awful thing, after all, to swear to God that he did not know God's Son. Paradoxically, while Peter was busy denying he knew Jesus, Jesus was affirming his own identity.

SIMON RESTORED: THE RETURN TO THE SEASHORE (JOHN 21:1–19)

In the synoptic gospels there is no account of the restoration of Peter in particular, but in John 21:1–19 there is. We turn to that poignant post-Easter story now as we bring this chapter to a close.

We are not told when this story actually transpires, but clearly enough various disciples have come back to Galilee, including Simon and some other members of the Twelve, and also the Beloved Disciple. It is interesting that the Fourth Gospel is not much interested in the story of Peter prior to Jesus's resurrection and subsequent appearances—but then, the Fourth Gospel spends little time on the Twelve as the inner circle of Jesus in general. This, then, is the only story in John about Peter being a fisherman. It has some interesting resonances with the story of the miraculous catch in Luke 5. In fact, some scholars have (mistakenly, in my view) thought this story to be a variant of that one, or vice versa.[58]

This story, like so many others in the Fourth Gospel, is highly symbolic. Its main focal point is the restoration of Peter, so that he can be a main shepherd or overseer of Jesus's flock. The story begins in earnest by telling us that Peter decides to go fishing, and various others, including the Beloved Disciple, decide to go with him. They fish all night and catch nothing. When sunrise comes, a man standing on the shore suggests that they cast the net out one more time on the right side of the boat. They do—and suddenly there is a miraculous catch of fish.

It is the Beloved Disciple who recognizes that the speaker is Jesus. Impetuous Peter then immediately dives overboard and swims toward shore. While the other disciples are left in the lurch, struggling to get the boat ashore, Peter is swimming to Jesus. When the boat finally reaches shore and Jesus asks the fishermen to bring him some of the fish they just caught, it is Peter who goes back on the boat and drags the whole net of fish—some 153—up to Jesus. Clearly Peter is anxious to please Jesus and to obey any dictate Jesus gives him, perhaps to make amends for his denials, and at least in this account he's obviously got the physical strength to do it. There is some evidence that ancient peoples believed that there were some 153 or 157 different kinds of fish in the sea.[59] This haul of 153, then, could be seen as a symbolic catch, suggesting the universal scope or mandate of the gospel call to fish for followers. Some scholars have also made much about how the net, seen to be a symbol of the church, does not tear, but can hold all these different kinds of fish. If this is in the Fourth Evangelist's mind, however, he does not make anything of it.

Instead, John focuses on the restoration of Peter, including some minute details that are important. For example, the text refers to a charcoal fire burning its welcome on the beach. This is only the second such reference in this gospel, the first being the fire where Peter warmed his hands just before his denials. John has the threefold restoration take place in a setting similar to where the threefold denial did. It's like revisiting the scene of the crime, only this time getting it right. Some New Testament texts, such as Luke 24:34, suggest that this restoration of Peter transpired when Jesus first appeared to Peter after his resurrection—but did Jesus first appear to Peter in Galilee or Judea? In any case, this story does appear to be a first-appearance sort of account: in verse 12 the disciples are on pins and needles, afraid to ask Jesus who he really is.

After a meal of fresh-caught fish and bread, Jesus begins the inquiry that restores Peter. The question Jesus raises repeatedly is about love: Does Peter really love Jesus? He starts this questioning by going back to Peter's birth name: Simon son of Jonah. In other words, he is starting over from scratch with Simon. The first question differs a little from the second two. It probably means, "Do you love me more than you love these other friends?" though it is just possible it means, "Do you love me more than they love me?" or even (the least likely, grammatically speaking) "Do you love me more than you love these things" (that is, fishing!)? The question, then, addresses where Peter's ultimate love priority lies.

Scholars continue to debate whether the use of two different words for love in these questions is significant. I have changed my mind on this, and now think it is. In the first two questions Jesus asks about *agape* and Peter replies with *phileo*. But the third time, Jesus's and Peter's words match up, and the term is *phileo*. Thus the questioning goes as follows:

1. Jesus asks if Peter loves him with an unconditional God-given love, and Peter replies that he loves him like a brother.

2. The second interchange is the same.

3. The third time, however, Jesus merely asks, Do you at least love me like a brother? Peter, becoming distraught, says with all his heart that he loves Jesus like a true brother.

This, then, should be seen as a narrative about Jesus's gracious conde-scension to the level that Peter was prepared to respond at this juncture. Even with Peter's inadequate response, there is a threefold commission-ing, which seems to be incrementally more involved with each step. After each question, Jesus assigns Peter a task: first he is to feed the little lambs; then he is to tend Jesus's sheep; finally he is to feed the adult sheep. The text does not rule out others becoming shepherds of Jesus's flock, but Peter in particular is commissioned to be an overseer and a teacher of the flock. He takes on this role in earnest after Easter, though he becomes an evangelist as well, seeking new Christians in addition to discipling mem-bers of the faith family.

It had been a difficult road back for Peter, but now he was recommis-sioned and had sworn his love to Jesus once more. This did not mean he was perfect, of course. Far from it, for in the very next part of the story he is chided for comparing himself to the Beloved Disciple! I will reserve my comments on that passage for the end of the next chapter. It is now time to sum up what we have discovered in this chapter.

WHAT WE'VE LEARNED AND WHAT THAT KNOWLEDGE TELLS US ABOUT JESUS

The story of Peter is painted in vivid hues, especially in Matthew's gospel. There can be no doubt whatsoever that Peter was part of the inner circle of Jesus and indeed played the most crucial role within that circle. That is why his perfidy was so shameful and why there needed to be a public res-toration in the presence of some of the other disciples. Accountability for wrongdoing is a good thing, especially amongst the disciples of Jesus.

Peter was a fisherman, and he was trained by Jesus to do a new sort of fishing. The training was extensive and intensive, transpiring over a period of no more than three years and perhaps as few as one, to judge from the Markan outline. But it was not just what he was explicitly taught that instructed him; it was also the experiences he had with Jesus. He was the disciple to first confess who Jesus truly was and the first to receive an eschatological commission—in other words, to be promised a role not only in the community of Jesus now but at the eschaton, judging the tribes of Israel.

Was Jesus indeed building his community on so variable and shaky a foundation as Peter? Apparently he was, though it must be remembered that Jesus talks of that building on the Rock right after Peter made his good confession. Presumably, in light of Matthew 18, Jesus meant that he would build the community on Peter *and others who made a similar good confession.* Jesus also bequeathed to Peter the power of binding and loosing, of obligation and accountability; at the same time he is held accountable for his own behavior. This seems to be especially critical for leaders in Jesus's community, for as Chaucer once said, "If gold rusts, what then will iron do?"

We have seen Peter's ups and downs in these gospel stories, in snapshots that are sometimes painfully honest. As Peter himself said when Jesus first sat in his boat, he was a sinner like the rest of us, especially when compared to Jesus. As we move on in the next chapter to Peter's post-Easter ministry and life, we will see hints of the same quixotic nature, but on the whole he seems a much more confident and accomplished leader of Jesus's followers in his later days.

Something crucial happens when we look at Jesus through the eyes of Peter: we see the radical implications of our declarations of faith. Scripture certainly gives the impression that Peter would not have been promised a prominent role in the community of Jesus if he had not first confessed Jesus to be the Christ. His later role reflects what he earlier, perhaps earliest of all the disciples, believed about Jesus—specifically, what he believed before the crucifixion. This is extremely important. Peter, the most prominent disciple, was prepared to say that this same Jesus whom he saw risen from the dead was the one whom he himself had confessed as the Christ, the Son of the living God, during Jesus's ministry. Thus in the person of Peter and what he knew and believed we find a continuity of Christology between the Jesus of history, who accepted Peter's confession, and the Christ of faith.

Peter is without question one of the people I would most like to interview about Jesus and the faith of the earliest Christians, precisely because he was there from the beginning and continued on beyond the end of Jesus's life and ministry. He was a living witness to how Jesus presented himself, to what Jesus would become after Easter, and to what would later be believed about Jesus. It is a telling thing that Galatians 1–2 suggests that Paul's beliefs about Jesus must have passed muster with Peter himself, with whom Paul spent important time in Jerusalem after his conversion. Peter, James, and John must have believed that Paul was proclaiming the same kind of message about Jesus as they were, or else they would never have given him the imprimatur to preach to the Gentiles. These stories about interconnections within the inner circle must make some sense, and they bear a telling witness to the fact that Jesus was seen and confessed as a messianic figure both before and after his death on a cross. No one knew this better than Peter, and no one would have been more vehement in rebuttal of the suggestion that Jesus had not presented himself in an exalted and messianic light during his ministry. He became a shepherd of Jesus's flock for a good reason: he knew the Story, he believed in the Christ, and he accepted his commission. In the next chapter we will see what the post-Easter Peter has to say to us about these things.

FOUR

Peter:
Evangelist, Shepherd, Martyr

Though there is no recounting of the story of the appearance of Jesus to Peter in the synoptic gospels, there can be no doubt that it happened. In fact, the account we just looked at from John 21 may represent Jesus's first appearance to any member of the Twelve. History, even salvation history, is often messy and full of unexpected twists and turns. Peter himself turns up with great regularity in the New Testament, especially in the first half of Acts as one of the two main leaders of the Jerusalem church, as an evangelist, and indeed as a pioneer, going to a Gentile named Cornelius's house and so paving the way for the Gentile mission of Paul. There is too much material on Peter to be able to do justice to the Christian life of the man after Easter, so we will focus here on some key vignettes. These passages will show us that Peter, who was in the inner circle of Jesus, made the transition into the inner circle of Christian leaders in the early church.

FROM JERUSALEM TO SAMARIA TO ANTIOCH AND BEYOND

By the time Luke arrived in the Holy Land in the late 50s with Paul, Peter was likely long gone. Accordingly, we must assume that Luke got his information about Peter's work in the Holy Land from an indirect source—presumably someone in Jerusalem, such as James, though he may have gleaned some material about Cornelius and Peter in Caesarea itself.[60] Let us consider what we do know about Peter's life in the Holy Land after Easter.

First of all, we know from Acts 1–12 that Peter was in Jerusalem, Judea, and Samaria for a considerable period of time—in fact, well into the 40s (and thus more than a decade after Jesus's death). We can date the end of this period with some precision because we hear in Acts 12 about King Herod's seizure and execution of James Zebedee, and then the seizure and escape of Peter. The Herod in question is Herod Agrippa I, and because we know that fact we can date this latter occurrence reasonably precisely: it transpired about A.D. 43.[61] Thereafter, Peter seems to have gone elsewhere, returning briefly perhaps a few times, including in the year 50 for the big council meeting in Jerusalem that is recorded in Acts 15. This comports with what we hear in Galatians 1:18–2:10, where we are told that Paul went up to Jerusalem three years after his conversion and spent two weeks with Peter. Interestingly, Paul always calls him by his Aramaic nickname, Cephas.

This first visit by Paul would have happened somewhere around A.D. 36–37, depending on whether Paul was converted in 33 or 34. He then makes a second visit up to Jerusalem in A.D. 48, referred to in Galatians 2:1–10; and in his account of that trip he speaks about Peter in a different way. While Peter is present to give the right hand of fellowship to Paul in Jerusalem, he is said to already be recognized as the missionary for Jesus to the Jews ("just as Peter had been to the Jews" is the precise phrase in verse 7, speaking of past activity). Then we find Peter in Antioch in A.D. 49, where he falls afoul of the Judaizers and Paul rebukes him for withdrawing from eating with Gentiles.[62] As noted above, we know Peter returned to Jerusalem for the council in A.D. 50 and strongly supported Paul's position regarding the Gentile mission, but thereafter Acts is silent about Peter.

We pick up his trail again in 1 Corinthians 1:12, 3:22, and 9:5, where he was clearly known to the Corinthian congregation when that letter was written (about A.D. 54–55). This familiarity suggests that he had perhaps been there. The link with Corinth may indicate that he was heading west. After this, however, the trail grows very cold. Paul writes his magisterial letter to the Romans in about A.D. 57 and does not mention Peter or send greetings to him in Rome. In view of all the Jewish Christians he does greet in Romans 16, it is unimaginable he would not have had a greeting for Peter as well, had he been there. But where could he have gone?

We've got some options: 1 Peter 1:1 refers to God's elect in Pontus, Galatia, Cappadocia, Asia, and Bithynia. These are regions in the middle and western part of what we call Turkey today. Some of these regions were also evangelized by Paul, but not all of them—in particular, not Pontus, Bithynia, or Cappadocia. This seems to suggest that Peter had been to these various and vast regions and evangelized there. This could have taken many years. But at the end of 1 Peter 5:13 we hear that Peter is in Babylon with two Pauline co-workers, Silas and Mark. This suggests that he has finally reached Rome, and we may date this stay to sometime in the early to mid 60s, before Nero's crackdown after the fire in A.D. 64 and before Peter's martyrdom as a result of that crackdown, as attested by Clement of Rome in the late 90s. We will say more about the close of Peter's life at the end of the chapter, but now that we have the chronological framework pieced together, we can examine some of the individual narratives in more detail.

PETER AT PENTECOST AND ENDURING PERSECUTION (ACTS 1–5)

Luke, in his presentation of Peter and Paul, pursues a strategy of parallel construction for these two central figures. For example, we have eight speeches by Peter in Acts and eight or nine by Paul. Let's extend this comparison with a brief chart that shows the distribution:

Peter	Paul
2:22–29	13:26–41
3:1–10	14:8–11
4:8	13:9
5:15	19:12
8:17	19:6
8:18–24	13:6–11
9:36–41	20:9–12
12:6–11	16:25–41[63]

What Luke is suggesting, both by the amount of the material devoted to these two figures and by the nature of the material, is that these were the two great spokesmen and chief evangelists for early Christianity—Peter more in the earlier part of the period covered, Paul in the latter part. Our concern in this particular section is with Luke's characterization of Peter as a leader, not with the exegetical particulars.

Peter is already a leading figure in Acts 1:20, when a decision has to be taken on replacing Judas among the Twelve. It is he who stands up and tells the 120 disciples it is necessary to find a replacement. The disciples then produce two candidates, and the one who is chosen is named Matthias. Peter is then already established as the spokesman for the group in this narrative in Acts 1, and this lays the groundwork for the more crucial story of Pentecost in Acts 2. It should be noted, however, that Mary, some brothers of Jesus, and various female disciples are present at the choosing of the new disciple, and apparently later at Pentecost as well.

Let's look at Peter's role as it is revealed in the paradigmatic speech that sets the agenda for the Christian mission and for the program of the book of Acts as well. That speech, found in Acts 2:14–36, reveals Peter to be a powerful, Spirit-filled prophet like those alluded to in Joel 2, which Peter quotes: "I will pour out my Spirit upon all people. Your sons and daughters will prophesy. Your old men will dream dreams. Your young men will see visions." The quotation of Joel is of no small importance, because the passage indicates that both men and women will be inspired by God to speak his word. I would suggest that the reason Peter picks this text is that he has seen it fulfilled in the upper room, where both men and women were present and empowered by the Holy Spirit, and he had already seen both women and men see and proclaim the risen Jesus. It appears that Luke wants us to think that women like Mary, Mary Magdalene, and Joanna were present and were filled by the Spirit at Pentecost as well.

This Acts 2 speech of Peter has been called something of a rhetorical masterpiece. It falls in two parts, with the promise in verses 17–18 (echoing Joel, as quoted above) preparing for the reception of the Spirit in verse 38 ("Repent, and be baptized …, and you will receive the gift of the Holy Spirit"); and the prophecy in verse 21 ("And anyone who calls on the name of the Lord will be saved") being reiterated and reinforced in the final exhortation in verse 40b. We are told that the Eleven are standing with Peter when he makes his speech, which highlights the fact that Peter is the representative and spokesman for the group—and more to the point, the interpreter of what has happened, fending off suggestions of impropriety and inebriation.

It is interesting that the call for the audience to repent, which note is also sounded in the next speech in Acts 3:19, sets the tone for the approach of the witness about Jesus to Jews throughout Acts, where the call for Jews to repent and the offer of forgiveness becomes characteristic of the missionary approach.[64] Even more striking is the appeal that the audience be baptized, which comports with the earlier appeal of John the Baptist and implies the scandalous notion that the audience needs to start over with God, lest they be judged. Peter is not being diplomatic here; he pulls no punches! Here, as in the rest of Acts, the mission is first to Jews but also to Gentiles, which makes clear that Luke is not operating with the notion of Gentiles replacing Jews amongst God's people. Jews are appealed to throughout the narrative, and some respond.

Peter, in his Acts 2 speech, makes it evident that an eschatological event has happened at the Pentecost festival, an event empowering both men and women to receive revelation from God and share it—even share it by means of miraculously speaking a human language the speaker doesn't know. This story is not about glossolalia, the gift of speaking in an angelic language, for the text indicates that the speakers were using various foreign languages. Until Peter interprets the meaning of the event, however, there is no repentance and there are no conversions. The lesson is that conversions are caused by persuasion aided by the Spirit, not merely by witnessing miracles or miraculous witnessing in foreign languages. At Pentecost, Peter doesn't only preach the Good News; he also informs the audience what to do next when they are ready to repent and believe.

One interesting feature of Peter's speech is his summary of the career of Jesus and his emphasis on the fact that Jesus's death was part of God's plan, even though this does not alleviate the need for those humans responsible for Jesus's death to repent and receive forgiveness. (This focus on God's hand in the death of Jesus is highlighted in 1 Peter as well.) He places even stronger emphasis on God's raising of Jesus from the dead and on Jesus's taking on the roles of Lord and messiah after the resurrection. These arguments, and his call to repentance, reveal Peter to be a masterful rhetorician and a decisive evangelist. Fulfilling the early promise of this rhetorical ability, Peter eventually leads many Jews from the Holy Land and from all over the Diaspora (meaning "dispersion"—thus the area outside the Holy Land settled by Jews) to Christ. This comports with Peter's job description in Galatians 2:7, where Paul speaks of Peter's work with "the circumcised."

In the very next chapter, Acts 3, Peter is depicted as not only a masterful evangelist but also a miracle worker, healing a crippled beggar by using the name of Jesus. Peter is paired with John (presumably John son of Zebedee) early in this account, but it is Peter alone who performs the miracle and Peter who speaks to the cripple, and the healing becomes another occasion for Peter to preach in the Temple precincts. What is most important about the speech that ensues is Peter's acknowledgment that the Jews who acted against Jesus acted in ignorance. Peter's mode of preaching in Acts 2 and 3 is to draw on and explicate Old Testament texts so as to interpret both the Christ event and the things currently happening in and through the lives of Jesus's followers. Clearly Peter is depicted by Luke as believing that he is living in the age of eschatological fulfillment.

The situation escalates in Acts 4 into a confrontation with Jewish authorities and the Sanhedrin; and this time, even though Peter is seized, far from denying Jesus, he gives bold testimony to Jesus in the council meeting; and the audience is said to recognize Peter's courage. In fact, the narrative concludes with a request by the authorities for Peter not to speak of or teach about Jesus again, but Peter flatly rejects the request and does not give in to their threats. He even says that they should judge for themselves whether it is right to obey God rather than human beings, or the converse. There would be no more denials of Christ and his message by Peter!

Acts 5 provides us with a very different sort of story about Peter, a story apparently involving a judgment oracle or punitive miracle inflicted on Ananias and Saphira. Peter is depicted here as a person who has spiritual discernment of facts not in evidence, particularly the fact that the church and God have been lied to by Ananias. This account in fact suggests that Ananias died of cardiac arrest caused by the shock of his deception being unmasked.

The concern about Peter and the other apostles' activities accelerates. When there is a second demand in Acts 5:27-28 for Peter and the others to stop teaching about Jesus, there is a second, equally adamant refusal by Peter. This time it results in a flogging, but Peter and the others leave the Sanhedrin rejoicing that they had the honor to suffer for Jesus, a theme that will crop up in 1 Peter as well. The mounting tide of concern and abuse being heaped on Peter and the apostles does not seem in any way to slow them down.[65] Indeed, Peter and his associates refuse to hide their light under a bushel, even going out to Samaria and evangelizing, and laying hands on Samaritans so that those foreigners might receive the Holy Spirit.

Peter is depicted in various of these narratives as both tending and feeding the sheep, fulfilling the mandate we heard about in John 21. He is painted as Peter the leader of the inner circle of the disciples, Peter the proclaimer, Peter the healer, and Peter the possessor of supernatural insight into human character and the motives of the heart. Let's see what the next two Peter narratives in Acts add to our understanding of this apostle.

THE CORNELIUS EPISODE (ACTS 10:1–11:18)

In the Lukan outline of things, Acts 10:1-11:18 must be seen as one more step along the way to a religion that is more universal in both geographical scope and social dimension. Here Luke recounts the all-important story of the shifting of a Gentile synagogue adherent into the Christian movement—and not incidentally, one with considerable social standing and status. This convert, Cornelius, had achieved upward mobility through a career in the army, and Luke is keen to tell his tale in full, perhaps especially because he wants to make clear to Theophilus, the high-status man to whom he's writing, that such persons have a place in the Christian movement. It is a measure of how important this story is for Luke that he repeats portions of it three and even four times between Acts 10 and 15, indicating that it is one of the main things precipitating the council recorded in Acts 15.

It is also no accident that Luke tells Cornelius's story right after recounting the conversion of Saul of Tarsus in Acts 9. In his mind these two stories are the ones most responsible for changing the approach to Gentiles in the early Christian movement. I will say more about Acts 9 and its parallels in Acts 22 and 26 in the chapters on Paul. Suffice it to say here that Paul's response to the vision he had and Peter's response to the vision *he* had precipitated a crisis for the Jerusalem church. What Luke wants to stress is that the move of the church in a Gentile direction comes directly from God above—hence the focus on the visions. This inclusiveness was always part of God's divine plan, according to Luke.[66]

I referred above to Peter's vision, but this story is in fact about a *double* vision—one that Peter has but also one that Cornelius has. The action of the story, including Peter's meeting with messengers sent by Cornelius to summon Peter, his journey to Cornelius's house, his dialogue with Cornelius, and the sermon that Peter preached to Cornelius and his household all are precipitated by divine intervention in the form of visions, and then are followed by divine intervention in the form of what has been called the Gentile Pentecost—the Spirit falling on Cornelius and his family and their subsequent baptism (10:44–48).

Since Luke does not in his two-volume work focus much on the issue of keeping kosher, or of the notions of clean and unclean more broadly, it is likely that Luke is relying on a historical source here about Peter. We can pretty much rule out the possibility that he made it up: it is hard to imagine Luke, who idolized and was a sometime companion of Paul, making up a story about *Peter* being the first missionary to the Gentiles! Besides, the story transpires in Caesarea Maritima, where Paul was under house arrest for two years. Luke had plenty of time to find out about Cornelius and Peter when he visited that city in the company of Paul in the late 50s. This material, then, comes from what we may call his Caesarean, or even his Petrine, source.[67]

Roman legions in the east were often composed of auxiliaries, and Cornelius was a centurion in such a force. He was likely named after the famous Roman general P. Cornelius Sulla, whose name was adopted out of gratitude by slaves whom the general freed in 82 B.C. Our Cornelius is probably a freedman descended from those slaves. He was part of a cohort called the "Italian," so we are apparently meant to think of him as a Roman freedman, and thus a Gentile proper—the very sort of person whose conversion story Luke would be keen to tell Theophilus.

It is not clear when this episode took place, either in an absolute sense or in relation to the conversion of Paul, who was converted only a few years after Jesus's death (and thus in the early 30s). This episode may well have transpired in the 30s also, perhaps in the year 39 or 40.[68] It is not clear whether we are to see Cornelius as still on active duty, or as retired and still living in Caesarea after Herod Agrippa I began ruling in the area. The grammar of Acts 10:1–7 suggests that he is still an active soldier.

We are told from the outset of the story that Cornelius is a devout God-fearer—which is to say, a devout Gentile synagogue adherent—giving generously to those in need and devoting himself to prayer. In other words, he performs the normal spiritual duties of a Jew. One of the things Cornelius is said to have been praying about is becoming a part of the Christian movement. In his vision Cornelius sees an angel who instructs him to send messengers to Peter, who is staying at the house of one Simon the tanner up the coast in Joppa.

At about this juncture Peter happens to go up on a roof to pray, but he becomes hungry while he is praying and falls into a state of ecstasy and, not surprisingly, has a vision of food! We are to imagine that he sees a tablecloth of some sort come down from heaven, and it is full of creatures—all kinds of four-footed animals and reptiles and birds, probably meant to indicate both land and sea creatures (which means both clean and unclean creatures).

Peter hears a command to get up, kill, and eat, and he emphatically refuses. Verse 14 has his response as, "By no means!" Perhaps Peter thought he was being tested by the vision. Some commentators have wondered why Peter would refuse all these animals, when surely some of them were not inherently unclean; but in fact if clean animals are lumped together with unclean ones, they become "common," as the story here says, and so are in effect unclean as well. There is a distinction in the story between the common and the unclean, raising the issue of contamination from the unclean to the clean animals. The divine response to these scruples in verse 15 is that Peter should not declare unclean what God has made clean. Peter comes across as a slow learner, for this interchange is said to transpire three times. (Should we see this as one more example of Peter denying the Lord three times?) There was a Jewish tradition that when the messiah came, all the animals in the world previously considered unclean would be clean,[69] but this vision is clearly about people as well as food.

Peter is not portrayed in an idealized way in this particular story, not only because of the aforementioned slowness but also because he is said to be puzzling about the vision when the messengers come, so absorbed that he has to be prompted by the Holy Spirit to take notice of the three men seeking him. He is in fact told by the Spirit to go down and speak to the men. Peter ends up inviting them into the house to spend the night, suggesting that Peter is beginning to catch the meaning of the vision, since truly scrupulous Jews would try to avoid all contact with Gentiles.[70] We are surely meant to see some irony here, because all the while Peter is protesting about food, and receiving Gentiles, he is staying in the home of a man whose trade, tanning animal hides, makes him and those who have contact with him unclean!

The next morning Peter arises and goes to Caesarea with the men, but he takes Christian witnesses with him—some "brothers." When he arrives, it becomes evident that Cornelius has made considerable preparations to receive Peter—assembling his family and his intimate friends, probably his retainers or clients. This was to be quite the occasion. Cornelius makes obeisance to Peter, who will have none of that, stressing that he is just a mortal, not to be treated as a divine man or magician.

By the time we get to verses 28–29 it becomes clear that finally Peter has puzzled out the meaning of his vision. He states that while Jews strongly frown upon fraternizing with Gentiles, God has now shown him that he should not treat Gentiles or anyone else as unclean.[71] Cornelius proceeds to explain why he has summoned Peter, telling the tale of his vision. What is striking is that God has told Cornelius, but not Peter, that Peter was to address Cornelius and his inner circle. We are apparently meant to hear an echo of Acts 1:13–14, where the believers awaited Pentecost. This story, then, would recount the equivalent groundbreaking event for Gentiles. By divine decree, no one is any longer to be treated as unclean (which of course has implications about eating patterns and unclean foods).

In verses 34–43 we have a summary of a sermon broken off by direct intervention of the Holy Spirit, who falls on the Gentiles present, including Cornelius. The sermon begins with the notion that God is no respecter of persons, especially when it comes to justice and fairness issues. This is a very different idea than the modern notion that religious or theological differences don't matter. It is precisely because the one true God treats all fairly that differing concepts of God make such a difference. One recognizes God's fairness to all when one recognizes the character and nature of the one and only God. Anyone who fears God and does what is right is acceptable to God, says Peter. *Acceptable* does not mean *saved*, however; it means being in an acceptable condition of repentance so that one may hear the message of salvation. God has sent the one Lord, Jesus, to make peace with both Israel and the Gentiles.[72]

Peter then gives a brief but comprehensive review of the earthly career of Jesus, the most comprehensive review in any of the Acts sermon summaries. Peter tells his audience that Jesus's death, like his ministry, is a fulfillment of scripture and thus part of the divine plan, and he stresses that he witnessed all these things and so is well qualified to be one of the Twelve and to proclaim this message at this time. The key to forgiveness for Cornelius and others, Peter says, is to believe the words of the earlier and the latter-day prophets about Jesus, which in this case includes the words of Peter himself, who is portrayed as a prophet here, breaking new ground under order of divine vision.

One of the regular features of conversion stories in Acts is that at some juncture God takes control and brings the new person into a right relationship by means of the Holy Spirit. Here in Acts 10 we have the fourth recorded outpouring of the Spirit. Peter compares this current event with the first of such outpourings, even though this event involves glossolalia rather than miraculous speaking in a foreign language.[73] Verse 44 is important: the Spirit fell on all who heard the Word of God, including Cornelius's relatives and friends. Thus not Cornelius alone, but he and his whole inner circle, become the test case of how Gentiles might enter the church.

Peter's companions are stunned that the Holy Spirit has fallen on a group of Gentiles, though they cannot deny the genuineness of what has happened. Peter responds with a rhetorical question, suggesting that nothing should prevent a person from receiving water baptism if he already has the Holy Spirit in his life. Notice that Peter orders his companions to baptize the new converts rather than doing it himself. He is depicted as being in charge here. And this account is as much about him as it is about Cornelius. One could say that it's about two sorts of conversions—the conversion of the imagination of Peter as to how God was now operating when it came to non-Jews, and of course the spiritual conversion of Cornelius and his inner circle.

Peter thereafter must deal with the fallout in Jerusalem—which is considerable, not least because the new Christians will not be required to be circumcised or keep the laws of clean or unclean. In Acts 11:1–18 Peter is criticized and then has to give a full accounting to the Jerusalem church as to what has happened. The conclusion of that meeting is that the audience agrees that God has granted to Gentiles the repentance that leads to life. What is not yet settled is whether there could be a systematic mission to Gentiles that does not include ritual restrictions on how they keep their new faith. It would be some years before that issue was to be debated.

The Cornelius episode could be treated as something of an anomaly, a divine exception, until Paul comes along pushing a mission to all Gentiles. Acts 12 tells us that well before that mission to the Gentiles, Peter fell afoul of Herod Agrippa, was jailed, miraculously escaped, and briefly visited the house of John Mark's mother, where the community was praying. Peter left instructions to tell James and the brothers he had escaped, and then the narrative simply says, "He left for another place" (12:17). We are not told where, and apart from the cameo appearance Peter makes at the council in Acts 15, we hear no more of him in Acts. He completely disappears from this chronicle. We must examine Peter's role at that council now.

PETER THE ADVOCATE IN THE COUNCIL (ACTS 15)

Peter, it must be said, was a person who could be pressured into things. We saw this with the story of his denials, and Galatians 2:1–10 offers witness that he succumbed to the pressure of the Judaizers in Antioch and drew back from table fellowship with Gentiles sometime in the late 40s— which is to say, well after his visionary experience about what is clean and unclean. This was not a matter of conviction for Peter, for Paul upbraided him for now living like a Gentile but hypocritically withdrawing from eating with Gentiles. Galatians 2:12 accuses Peter of being afraid of the circumcision party. But Peter was to have his chance to redeem himself on this matter at the council spoken of in Acts 15, which transpired after Paul wrote Galatians.[74]

Because of the crucial nature of the council that took place in the year 50, and because of Peter's important role in that council, we must now give more attention to the particulars of this text. Our concern here is not with Paul's or James's role in the debate, or even with the decree of James (which we will deal with in Part 5); our concern here is with Peter's speech and role in this momentous event. On this occasion Peter stands up to the circumcision party and sides with Paul.

The context of Peter's speech is important. According to Acts 15:5 the Pharisaic Jewish Christians had already stood up and thrown down the gauntlet, saying that "the Gentiles must be circumcised and be required to obey the Law of Moses." This demand had led to much discussion amongst the apostles and elders.[75] Only thereafter does Peter arise and offer his brief impassioned speech, set out in summary form in verses 7–12. One can immediately note that it is based on the Cornelius episode and alludes to that occasion, but it also appeals to what this audience will have already heard from him as recorded in Acts 11:4–18. It was Peter who answered the criticism of the circumcision party in 11:2–3, and it is Peter again who does so here. Peter suggests that considerable time had transpired since the Cornelius event. Indeed, it must have happened at least a decade earlier. Unfortunately, apart from Galatians 2:11–14, which places Peter in Antioch, we have no clear idea what Peter had been up to for at least the last seven or eight years before the council.[76]

The Cornelius episode is characterized, in the council account, as having happened "in the early days" of the church. Peter boldly says that in those days God had chosen him to be the first broker of the Good News to the Gentiles. We should not make too much of the contrast of this remark with Galatians 2:7–8, since of course Luke knows that Paul is the one who was called to be the light to the Gentiles on an ongoing basis, as suggested in Acts 9:15. Peter is simply claiming to have been chosen first to deliberately approach the Gentiles and break the ice, so to speak.

Peter stresses that the Cornelius event had happened due to the prodding of God by a vision, and that God had given that Gentile household the Spirit before they could keep the Law fully or be circumcised. Indeed, he gave them the Spirit before they were baptized in water. No ritual requirements, either Jewish or Christian, had to be met before God accepted them. Peter's conclusion is that therefore God accepted them without observance of the Law. Then Peter makes the emphatic point that those who want to require the Law of them are putting God to the test (and denying the validity of Peter's vision and his interactions with Cornelius).

Peter speaks of the burden of the yoke of the Law, something that may well echo what Jesus suggested by contrasting his own yoke as light compared to the Law.[77] It may be that Peter was impressed by Paul's earlier argument with him about freedom for the Gentiles when it came to the Law—in this case, food laws.[78] Peter concludes his impassioned appeal by stressing that it is by the grace of the Lord Jesus that both Jews and Gentiles are saved—sounding a good Pauline note. Peter clearly had lived out this credo prior to the pressure of the Judaizers; now he was reasserting it again vigorously, at the decisive turning point in early church history. There is no basis for the notion of a Judaizing Peter, but there is a basis for a portrait of Peter as subject to pressure, and as sometimes capitulating.

Peter's speech at the council is followed by a brief recounting by Paul and Barnabas of the wonders God is bringing about amongst the Gentiles, including miracles both physical and spiritual. The combination of Peter's speech and their witness prompts James to issue a decision on behalf of the group. Clearly enough, James is seen at this juncture as the head of the Jerusalem church, and it is he who concludes this matter. Peter has come back to Jerusalem, and his speech helps tilt the decision in the right direction; but he is no longer in charge there. We may well ask, then, What happened next to Peter?

PETER THE EVANGELIST AND LETTER WRITER (1 PET.)

In the opening section of this chapter I sketched out the Petrine chronology, and I have already mentioned the passing references to Peter in the Pauline corpus that suggest he went to Corinth. I have also noted the prescript to 1 Peter, which suggests he went to various places in Turkey that even Paul apparently never really evangelized, including Pontus, Bithynia, and Cappadocia. Presumably, in light of Galatians 2:7, he chose to go to places where there were considerable numbers of Jews. By the time he was writing 1 Peter in the 60s, however, he seems clearly to be safely ensconced in Rome, though we don't know when he arrived or how long he stayed. Acts does not mention Peter being there, and it takes us up to A.D. 60 or so. Paul's later letters written in the 60s (Colossians, Philippians, Ephesians, Philemon, and of course the even later Pastoral Epistles) likewise say nothing about Peter being in Rome, nor do any of the other New Testament documents apart from 1 Peter.

All we can safely say is that Peter must have shown up in Rome after a long period of evangelizing in Turkey and elsewhere, presumably after Paul was released from house arrest the first time in A.D. 62. In 1 Peter 5:13 we learn that Peter is there with Mark, whom Peter calls his son. I would suggest that this puts us somewhere around about A.D. 64–65. Peter has begun to share the gospel with Mark, and Mark has begun to take it down and compose a document he would finish somewhere around A.D. 68. The scapegoating of Christians in Rome has not yet happened, though the fire that Nero would attribute to Christians (and use to justify their persecution) may have already transpired. 1 Peter would prove to be Peter's last full letter. We must consider it closely, so far as it reveals something to us about Peter himself. Thereafter we will consider 2 Peter 1:12–21, which I take to be a Petrine fragment in a composite document, and John 21:18–19.

That Peter is both the stated author (1 Pet. 1:1) and the implied author of this document (1 Pet. 5:1: "a witness of the sufferings of Christ") is clear. The question then arises as to whether this is a pseudonymous document, later penned in Peter's name, or a genuine letter of Peter. I have dealt at length elsewhere with the problem of claiming Pauline or Petrine letters as pseudonymous documents. Such a claim implies deception, and indeed there is plenty of historical evidence that persons in the first century were concerned about the issue of literary fraud and intellectual property. Anonymous documents like Hebrews did not raise such questions, but pseudonymous ones definitely did.[79] In the early church this letter was universally judged to be authored by Peter, using Silas/Silvanus (who is named in 5:12) as a scribe, and I see no reason to dispute this view.[80] Peter is here exercising the authority Jesus gave him to feed and tend the sheep, and he is exercising it broadly as he speaks to Jewish Christians in a wide range of places in Turkey. In other words, this letter is an encyclical—a letter directed to a group of churches rather than to an individual person or congregation.

The first interesting feature to notice about this letter is that Peter has been influenced by the Pauline form of writing letters, as well as by some Pauline themes. This is not a surprise, of course, because of the contact between Peter and Paul, but Silas too was involved in various Pauline letters. Thus, for example, we have the Pauline greeting "grace and peace," the author starts by asserting he is an apostle (though later he refers to himself as an elder), we have the classic Pauline phrase for those who are Christians—"in Christ"—and we hear of suffering with Christ.[81] That Peter was indebted to Paul in his thinking and forms of expression is even more evident in 1 Peter than it was in Acts 15, which we considered earlier.[82] It reminds us that the inner circle of Jesus was rather small. We shouldn't be surprised, then, that there was cross-fertilization between Paul and Peter, or Paul and James, or Paul and the author of Hebrews—but it is interesting that it seems always to be Paul who is the influence on the others, rather than vice versa. The one great theological mind in the New Testament that seems not to have been much influenced by Paul is the Beloved Disciple, though John of Patmos seems to know the Pauline diction and epistolary style.

To judge from 1 Peter 4:12, Peter is either reflecting on or anticipating persecution, and in fact he speaks of a "fiery trial," to which we may add the reference in 1 Peter 1:7 to being "refined" by fire. Is this a coincidence, or is he mirroring the situation of the Roman fire of 64, and Nero's response of setting Christians alight in his gardens (according to the Roman historian Tacitus)? It is possible.[83] In any case, a good deal of this letter reveals a context of persecution, and so it is not a surprise that it reflects on the suffering of Christ, particularly as a fulfillment of Isaiah 53. Like the Master, so the disciples when it comes to suffering. It is also no shock in this sort of social context that Peter stresses submission to governing authorities.

In 1 Peter 2:4 Peter calls Jesus the "living stone." There is a certain appropriateness to this turn of phrase, since it was Jesus who first called Peter Cephas! Especially interesting is the interplay between Matthew 16:23, where Jesus speaks of Peter as a stumbling block to him, and 1 Peter 2:8, where Peter calls Jesus a stumbling block for others. In another turnabout, in John 21:15–17 Jesus designates Peter a shepherd to his flock, while here in 1 Peter 2:25 Peter assigns the role of head or chief shepherd to Jesus himself.[84] In 1 Peter 1:17 Peter highlights God's impartiality, a theme that he also speaks of in Acts 10.

In addition to these parallels between 1 Peter and other scriptural texts, there are signs that Peter took with him some of the lessons he learned from the historical Jesus. For example, in 1 Peter 3:9 he stresses not returning or repaying evil with evil or insult with insult in a way that is close to what Jesus says about nonretaliation in Matthew 5:38–44, and in 1 Peter 3:18–22 he highlights Christ's victory over the fallen angels or spirits on his way to heaven, reflecting exorcisms that Peter witnessed Jesus performing during the ministry.

I could say much more along these lines, but suffice it to say here that 1 Peter reflects the lessons of a lifetime that Peter learned both from Jesus and from partners in ministry, such as Paul.

THE PETRINE LEGACY (2 PET. 1:12–21)

2 Peter is in all likelihood not a document written by Peter. Rather, it is a composite document, as a careful comparison of Jude with 2 Peter 2 shows.[85] There is, however, a Petrine fragment in 2 Peter—namely, 2 Peter 1:12–21—as I have demonstrated at some length elsewhere.[86] This fragment has the same grammar, syntax, vocabulary, and style that we find in 1 Peter and is unlike the rest of 2 Peter. Therefore, the fragment deserves our attention as coming from Peter himself, even though the document was assembled at the end of the first century, when there was already a collection of Paul's letters circulating widely in the church—a collection that was viewed even then as scripture (2 Pet. 3:15–16).[87]

Peter is reflecting on the end of his life in this fragment, which may well be the last thing he wrote down before he was taken away and martyred.

In 2 Peter 1:14 he says that he knows he will soon put "this tent" aside, and so he is striving to make sure that his audience will remember the things he has taught them. He says in 2 Peter 1:16 that he was not following cleverly devised myths (a reference to Greco-Roman traditions, no doubt) when he spoke of the power and coming of the Lord Jesus, and he could say this with some authority because he had been there at the transfiguration as an eyewitness of Jesus's majesty. He refers to the fact that God confirmed the identity of Jesus directly, for the voice from heaven said, "This is my beloved Son; with him I am well pleased" (see Matt. 17:5). Those original experiences with Jesus—experiences that only the inner circle of the Twelve (namely, Peter, James, and John) were privy to—are being remembered here. Peter calls on that history to validate the truthfulness of the gospel that he preaches. He had the eyewitness experience of seeing Christ in glory and hearing God confirm Christ's identity. There could be no greater witness to the truth about Jesus than God, after all.

But Peter also refers, in that fragment, to the fact that the Lord had confirmed to him that he would soon die. He may well mean that the Lord had told him that what he had spoken of long before was now about to come to pass. Earlier, in John 21:18–19, Jesus had told Peter, "But when you are old you will stretch out your hands and someone else will dress you and lead you where you do not want to go." The Fourth Evangelist then adds that Jesus said this to let Peter know about the kind of death he would have—that is, not a death by natural causes.

Jesus here speaks as a sage using a traditional metaphor that contrasts the freedom of youth with the constrictions and restrictions of old age, but with a special reference to death. The reference to the stretching out of the hands is indeed a common metaphor for crucifixion.[88] While Clement of Rome, writing near the end of the first century, suggests that Peter met his end in Rome in the 60s,[89] much later hagiographic Christian tradition speaks more explicitly about Peter's crucifixion—specifically, crucifixion in an inverted position.[90] Yet Peter, as John 21 intimated, had lived a full and long life by the time he met his end, and no doubt he was pleased to have met it in the way Jesus did, and for the same cause. His 1 Peter is full of discussion of this approach to suffering, which he then had the honor of modeling, becoming a Christian martyr. He had run the good race, fought the good fight, and finished the course in Rome in a fashion like unto his Master, and at a time near to the time of Paul's demise. Clearly Peter was one of the giants of early Christianity, and really the only one, so far as we can tell, who made the transition from being in the inner circle of the Twelve before Jesus's death to being in the inner circle of leadership in the early church.

WHAT WE'VE LEARNED AND WHAT THAT KNOWLEDGE TELLS US ABOUT JESUS

Peter is a towering figure in the historical chronicles of the New Testament—that is, the gospels and Acts—but he is a more elusive presence in the homilies, letters, and apocalyptic writing of the New Testament. We may be thankful, then, for 1 Peter and the hints in 2 Peter and John 21, which reveal a bit more about Peter's life and ministry after the year 50. As noted earlier, though, there is nothing in any of this material to suggest that Peter was one of the founders of the church in Rome or the bishop there, though clearly he was an apostle and an elder in Rome near the end of his life. The later Gospel of Peter (a second-century document) provides us with no additional historical data about Peter, nor do the even later legends that call Peter the bishop of Rome or the first pope.

Peter is a larger-than-life figure anyway, and does not need the embellishments of later hagiographic traditions. Even our earliest witnesses attest loudly and clearly to his importance. Standing equally firmly in the life of the historical Jesus and in the early church from the beginning of the ministry of Jesus in Galilee until the gospel spread throughout the Roman Empire, Peter saw the church go from a Jewish sect to a world religion, from a Jewish-centered entity to a predominantly Gentile entity. He lived long enough to fight and make up with Paul, disagree and yet support his Jerusalem church colleagues, visit in Paul's churches, and start a few congregations of his own amongst the Jews in what we call Turkey. He fulfilled his calling as "apostle to the Jews" so faithfully that a whole stream of Christianity, Roman Catholicism, was to honor him for all he had started and accomplished. He is also the one figure from both the life of Jesus and the early church for whom we have a reasonably complete curriculum vitae, even though there are years in the 40s and 50s A.D. when we are not at all sure where he was and what he was doing.

But what do we learn about *Jesus* from Peter's post-Easter career? First, if we give even a cursory glance at 1 Peter, it becomes clear that Peter has learned well the theology of suffering and death that Jesus himself enunciated and that is indebted in both the case of Jesus's Passion predictions and of Peter's later reflections to Isaiah 53. It is clear enough that Jesus is seen as the suffering servant of Isaiah in 1 Peter, and this insight likely goes back to Jesus himself.

Second, Jesus saw himself as a shepherd of his people, and Peter was commissioned to take up a similar role toward his Jewish kin. This notion of servant and shepherd leadership found both in the Jesus and in the Petrine traditions reminds us that Jesus assumed some authority to speak and act in relationship to Israel. Remember that the sign on the cross called him King of the Jews (in particular). This reflects the claims of the historical Jesus to have been sent to the lost sheep of Israel, a phrase that is probably just a cipher for Israel itself. Peter continued this commission but focused particularly on Diaspora Jews, going beyond the scope of his Master's ministry but in the same direction. The implicit message of this ministry, whether exercised by Jesus or by Peter, was that Jesus believed Israel was lost and needed to be redeemed—indeed ransomed, as Mark 10:45 puts it. Peter's own ministry to the Jews emphasized the "Jesus for Jews" theme and the understanding that Jews too, not just Gentiles, needed redeeming. Though Peter may not have understood it before Golgotha, certainly afterward he understood why Jesus had predicted his own redemptive demise.

Notice as well that the authentic testimony in 2 Peter 1 to the transfiguration provides independent confirmation that something remarkable happened to Jesus on a mountain and that there was believed to be divine confirmation (even if it was a vision) that Jesus was the Son of God. In other words, this is not an idea the church dreamed up after Easter or Pentecost. Peter the eyewitness could testify to the fact both before and after the lifetime of Jesus.

But there is more. The book of Acts is replete with Peter's preaching about Jesus being a teacher, a miracle worker, a savior who died on a cross and rose again. Nothing that Peter talked about did he learn only *after* Easter; all of these things Peter saw or was taught about during the ministry of Jesus. If we ask where Peter's preaching at Pentecost and immediately thereafter came from, the answer is most likely to be, From his personal experience of what Jesus said and did during his lifetime. Peter had not paused to take courses in Christian theology or homiletics prior to Pentecost! Instead, his proclamation on these matters came from his own knowledge of what Jesus said and did. The Jesus that Peter knew was the historical Jesus; he did not suddenly morph into the Christ of faith due to the Easter experience. Nor did Peter and the earliest disciples have amnesia after Easter, forgetting what the historical Jesus had said and done. Just as there is some continuity between the historical Peter before and after Easter, so Peter vouchsafes that the same can be said about Jesus. It was "this same Jesus," the historical Jesus, that Peter was to proclaim as the risen Lord and that Peter was to emulate (even in his pattern of martyrdom).

Now we must consider another crucial figure in the inner circle of Jesus: Mary the mother of Jesus.

PART THREE

THE MOTHER OF JESUS

FIVE

As It Was in the Beginning

It cannot have been easy being the mother of Jesus. Scandal surrounded both the outset and the terminus of Jesus's life, and Mary was the only one who was there for both the bookend events, not to mention the many troubling and terrific events in between. One thing for sure: it was never boring being the mother of Jesus.

Beyond that, what do we really know about this woman? What can we say for sure? From the outset we must reconcile ourselves to there being gaps in our knowledge. For example, we know little or nothing about Mary's parents—certainly nothing from any first-century sources. Because from a historical point of view it is important to resist the tendency to fill in any gaps, I propose to limit the parameters here to what is arguably the earliest historical data we have. This comes from the canonical gospels. In my view, the only way to get to the bottom of things regarding Jesus's origins (via, in this chapter, Mary's origins) is through a careful reading of our earliest texts in their proper historical, literary, and sociopolitical contexts.

First of all, let's be clear about Jesus's mother's name: it's Miryam, based on the name of the famous sister of Moses, though we will use the conventional name, Mary, to avoid confusion. Mary was a devout Jewess who spent much if not all of her life in the Holy Land and focused her attentions on one or another of her children most of the time. But before we write Mary off as being just another person who was close to the historical Jesus, we need to remember that she is the only one of the inner circle of Jesus who came to be venerated—indeed, almost worshipped—as *Theotokos*, the "God-bearer," and whose life spawned a cottage industry's worth of expansions and legends about her character and her significance. Yes, Peter has gotten a fair amount of press, but the Gospel of Peter and other texts that highlight him or other members of the inner circle do not indicate the kind of direct devotion that we find in the case of Mary. In short, something called "Mariology" developed, but there has never been any

Peterology or Jamesology so far as we can tell. This later development of remarkable beliefs about Mary needs to be accounted for, since it differs to such a degree from what we find in the developing legends about other members of the inner circle of Jesus. Why was it that indeed it turned out as Luke predicted—that all nations, or at least many, would call her blessed?

MOTHER MARY IN LUKE'S GOSPEL

Luke, in his historical preface in Luke 1:1–4, tells us that he relied on eyewitnesses and the early proclaimers of the Word for his information. The author of Mark's gospel presumably falls into the latter category, but what should we make of the former category? If the information we have in Luke 1–2 reflects an authentic recounting of what happened at the beginning of the story of Jesus, it could ultimately have come only from Mary herself (or perhaps Joseph). So what should we make of these chapters? I have suggested elsewhere that Luke was privy to this material because he spent two years in the Holy Land in the late 50s while Paul was under house arrest in Caesarea Maritima, during which time Luke surely must have gone to Jerusalem and interviewed many persons, which may well have included Mary.[91]

Some scholars have suggested that Luke 1–2 is somehow different in character from the rest of Luke's gospel, that it's the gospel equivalent of primeval history or family legend. The problem with this assessment is that Luke, immediately before giving us this material, asserts that he got it from eyewitnesses, and the form of the prologue in Luke 1:1–4 strongly indicates that he intends to write as a Hellenistic historian, albeit a rhetorically adept one.[92] Figures like Thucydides and Polybius and Xenophon didn't write their histories solely on the basis of family legends and the like; they sought out historical sources, as Luke says he is doing. And certainly the fact that there are miracles and angels mentioned in Luke 1–2 does not distinguish this material from various portions of the rest of this gospel or from other Hellenistic historiography. Luke's account is a bit different from most Hellenistic historiography, of course, because *salvation* history is being written here; Luke is quite sure that God and his agents were involved in dramatic and dynamic ways. Nevertheless, Luke is also quite sure that his account falls into the category of history, and not simply myth or legend. So let's lay aside our modern skepticisms and stereotypes about the lack of critical judgment that ancients reflected in their worldviews, and see what a *prima facie* reading of this material tells us about Mary.

Starting at Luke 1:26 we hear the tale of an angel being sent to a tiny town called Nazareth in the hills of Galilee to make an announcement to a young virgin named Miryam, probably no more than twelve to fourteen years of age. Miryam, who is pledged to be married to a man in Nazareth named Joseph, has a close encounter with an angel, who greets her and tells her the Lord is with her. This deeply confuses her.

This element in the story is too improbable *not* to be true. No one, in that day, would have invented a story about a messiah coming from Nazareth. Nathaniel was speaking for many when he said, "Can anything good come from Nazareth?" (John 1:46). Cities had honor ratings in antiquity, and it was expected that famous people would come from notable and noteworthy places. Nazareth clearly did not qualify.

Mary is troubled by the rest of the angel's announcement—that she will become pregnant with the messiah who is to reign over the house of Jacob forever—because she is not yet married. She asks how this can be and is told that a miracle will happen in her body, and that while this is transpiring the Holy Spirit will overshadow her and protect her from harm. Her response to this is simple and direct, the words of an obedient and trusting follower of God's will: "I am the Lord's servant; may it be to me according to your word" (1:38). Luke portrays her as the paradigm of a disciple, coping well with even difficult and potentially life-threatening news.

This element in the story, that of the virginal conception, is also too improbable *not* to be true, even if the story has been told in a way that puts the best possible face on the situation. I say this for several good reasons:

1. Mary lived in a patriarchal honor-and-shame culture in which pregnancy out of wedlock was considered shameful and could lead to serious consequences. The least of these was the dissolving of one's betrothal contract; at the worst, one could even lose one's life. A writer who wanted to make a positive impression on his audience in that culture wouldn't make up a story about pregnancy out of wedlock for his heroine.

2. Isaiah 7:14, which is often cited as prophesying a miraculous virginal conception of the messiah, was not so understood in early Judaism. In Hebrew the text actually reads, "A young woman of marriageable age (*almah*) will conceive." The Hebrew text does not focus on the virginity of the woman, though it would have been assumed. But the verse would have been understood by Jews to mean that a woman *who was a virgin up until she was first impregnated by her husband*

would conceive and give birth to a royal offspring.[93] Early Jews were not anticipating a virginally conceived messiah and did not read Isaiah 7:14 to suggest such a thing. In short, it was an actual event in Mary's life that led to the interpretation of Isaiah 7:14 in that fashion, not the other way around.

3. No evangelistic religion in its right mind would make up a story likely to suggest to the skeptical outside world that its savior figure, Jesus, was illegitimate.[94]

4. The story of the virginal conception is not a good parallel with the Greek and Roman stories of gods mating with human beings, not least because there is no mating or divine rape in the Lukan or Matthean stories; rather, a miracle happens within Mary's womb! Nor does the gospel story very closely parallel other early Jewish stories of remarkable births. For one thing, the Christian story is about a miracle that happened at conception, not at birth.

In short, this story has scandal written all over it, from day one, and yet both Luke and the author of Matthew's gospel feel constrained to tell what happened in Mary's life, even though it creates difficulties for their narrative in general. If all they were concerned to do was refute rumors of Jesus's illegitimacy, there were easier ways to accomplish that end than making up a story about a virginal conception. They could have focused on Joseph's claiming Jesus to be his son, for example. What we have in both gospel accounts is more than a narrative about surprising beginnings; it is a narrative about *unprecedented* beginnings, for this story is frankly not like the stories of other ancient figures, such as Caesar, who were seen as prodigies from the outset. Virginal conceptions mess up claims to being a direct descendant from Romulus and Remus on one's father's side, or the like. Pedigree is all-important in establishing one's honor claims in an honor-and-shame culture.

So Mary, absent visible honor, had to live with shame in Nazareth, though initially she ran off to visit her cousin Elizabeth, and then later the census drove her to Bethlehem for the birth. She was probably mighty glad to get out of tiny Nazareth, where tongues were likely already wagging about her being pregnant before the wedding.

If we fast-forward for a moment to Mark 6:3 we hear Jesus referred to by a crowd as "Mary's son," which is more than a little surprising. In a patriarchal culture, even if one's father was dead, one was still identified by that father—for example, "Joseph's son." But not so in this earliest of gospels. Mark tells us that the crowd took umbrage, presumably in part because they thought they were being lectured to by a man with shady origins.[95]

This question of origins is no small matter, for ancient persons believed that one's origins often determined one's identity and potential, and that it was one's birth and death that most revealed one's character. Mary, as Jesus's mother, had to live with these sorts of issues from day one. Jesus was conceived in a way that would have seemed dubious to many, and he died in the most shameful way possible. In this context, the extended treatment of Mary in Luke 1–2, as she deals with her unique situation and son, becomes less surprising.

The beginning of Luke 2 makes evident that Luke is attempting to present his account as a historical monograph of sorts, tying the macro-history of the Roman Empire to the micro-history of the story of Jesus.[96] Of course, in Luke's view, the more important story is the story of Jesus. No little ink has been spilled on Luke 2:1–2, which is generally read to say that Quirinius was governor of the Syrian province (which included Judea at that point) when Jesus was born. Since Jesus was born somewhere between 1 and 4 B.C., not long before the death of Herod, and since we know that Quirinius took a famous census in about A.D. 6, various scholars have suggested that Luke made a chronological blunder.[97] This depends on a particular kind of reading of the grammar of Luke 2:2, however. It is equally feasible to translate the passage as "This registration happened first, [before] Quirinius was governor of Syria."

The reason for mentioning Quirinius is obvious enough: he took a famous (or infamous) census in A.D. 6 when he was governor of Syria, a census that helped precipitate a rebellion of some Jewish Zealots against Roman rule. (Head-counts for the purpose of composing tax lists were always contentious matters in the Roman provinces, and Judea would have been no different.) This census was an obvious historical landmark that many would be familiar with. Luke uses it to provide Theophilus with a general frame of reference. Luke is saying, in essence, "You remember the *cause célèbre* that happened when Quirinius took a census as governor of Syria. Well, there was in fact a less famous census before that one, the very first census of its kind, which precipitated a journey by Jesus's family to Bethlehem." Chronological precision was not required even in very good Hellenistic historiography, and so Luke is content to let Theophilus know that the census he has in mind transpired before A.D. 6.

While there is likely some rhetorical hyperbole in the reference to "all the [known] world being enrolled," it is true that Augustus did pursue a policy of taxation right across the imperial provinces of the empire; and because Judea was part of an imperial province, an enrollment there is perfectly feasible. We know that in the Syrian province women as well as men were subject to the poll tax, and we know that in the parallel case in the province of Egypt people did go to ancestral or main homes to be enrolled. Thus there is nothing improbable about Joseph and Mary going to Bethlehem together to be enrolled.[98]

As Luke 2:5 makes evident, Joseph and Mary were engaged and not yet married, but Mary was pregnant. Betrothal in early Judaism involved a contract that was as binding as modern marriage is today. Formal dissolution was required to undo such a commitment. Jewish women were usually between eleven and thirteen years old when betrothed; the men were generally a bit older.

Luke then goes on to talk about Jesus's birth and where it took place. We are not told in 2:6 that Mary was already in labor when they arrived in Bethlehem, as tradition sometimes has it; rather, she went into labor "while they were there." As for where "there" was, tradition has likewise distorted history. If Bethlehem was the town where Joseph and Mary's relatives lived, it is natural to expect that they would have first sought accommodations with their relatives; and in fact that is likely the case. The word *kataluma* in verse 7 should probably not be translated "inn," as is typically done. Bethlehem was such a small village on a minor road that it is not clear it would have had a wayside inn. Furthermore, when Luke wants to speak of an "inn" he uses the Greek word *pandocheion* (see, for example, Luke 10:34), not *kataluma*. Elsewhere, when Luke uses *kataluma* he means "guest room" (see Luke 22:11, where it refers to the guest room in a house where Jesus and the Twelve eat the Last Supper). Thus, Luke likely says nothing about the holy couple being cast out of an inn and Mary having to bear the child in a barn.

Strangely enough, it was St. Francis, with his love for animals, who was the first to set up a manger scene with animals in a barn setting. Historically, it is far more likely that Mary and Joseph had their child in the back portion of the ancestral home where the most valued animals were fed (and, in the winter, perhaps kept), because the guest room in the family home was already occupied. Jesus's beginnings were humble enough without mythologizing them into a story about being cast out by the world. Rather, Jesus was wrapped in strips of cloth and laid in a corn crib or manger in the family home. Nothing suggests that the birth itself was miraculous or unusual. The miracle is said to have happened at the *conception* of Jesus.

The episode about the shepherds in verses 8–20 (the angels bringing them the news of Jesus's birth, and the shepherds going to see the baby) takes up more space than the discussion of the birth itself. It has a certain plausibility to it since Bethlehem was one of the main areas near Jerusalem where sheep were raised for sacrifices in the Temple. Due to their profession, shepherds were viewed as unclean peasants by some early Jews, but Luke sees them as exemplars of the marginalized for whom the birth of a savior would be seen as Good News indeed.

Throughout the Bible angels are harbingers of divine activity and messengers of God. Here at first we have a single angel of the Lord. Presumably we are to think it is the same one who spoke to Zechariah in Luke 1:11. The text speaks of the glory of the Lord shining around the angel and the shepherds, a reference to the *Shekinah,* the bright and shining presence of God. This naturally frightens the shepherds, but they are told of good news of a great joy for "all the people." This may mean "all Israel," but it may also foreshadow a wider people including Gentiles, especially in light of the fact that we should read this gospel as the first part of a two-volume work. Furthermore, the angel refers to Jesus not merely as the Jewish messiah but also as a savior, a more inclusive concept. The shepherds are told that the "sign" or proof of the angel's words is the baby that they will find wrapped in strips of cloth and lying in a corn crib. The angel emphasizes the idea that this savior is "born to *you*"—in other words, especially for the least, the last, and the lost.

The savior language is notable on another account: it matches the rhetoric that the propaganda mill of the imperial cult used to refer to the Emperor Augustus, first when he was born and later when he "pacified" the entire region around the Mediterranean crescent. The infant of humble origins, Jesus, is being portrayed here as the *real* savior, compared to the Emperor Augustus, who is just a pretender or parody or counterfeit. The language of the imperial cult about Caesar being a god walking upon the earth in the flesh is countered here by the claim that this Jewish child is savior, messiah, and even Lord, and that his coming will bring peace on earth for "humans of good will/ pleasure," which presumably means those who receive or respond to the Good News positively.

The story goes on to suggest that a host of additional angels are celebrating the birth of Jesus by singing. Clearly they see this humble birth, far from detracting from the glory of God, in fact adding to God's glory. The shepherds take the announcing angel as being God's very mouthpiece, for they speak of that "which the Lord has made known to us." Thus it is that the shepherds travel in haste to Bethlehem, see the confirming sign, and then go forth as the first evangelists or proclaimers of the Good News, telling about the encounter with the angels and the confirmation of the angelic word upon visiting Jesus and the holy family.

It is, after all, the angelic word that helps the audience to correctly interpret the event, such that this child is seen as someone special—indeed, as someone divine and yet human. This is why in verses 18–19 "all" who hear the shepherds' proclamation marvel, and Mary stores or treasures up what she hears, trying to figure out its meaning.[99] Nothing comparable is said of Joseph, but this same thing is said of Mary again at 2:51. She is thus portrayed as teachable and on the way to being a true believer.[100] John Nolland's translation here captures the spirit of the text—"Mary stored up all these things, trying in her heart to penetrate their significance."[101] At the very least this means she was mystified by some of these events and did not quite grasp their significance, but was trying hard to do so. This could later be said to be the mark of a disciple in training.

In verse 21 Mary and Joseph are portrayed as good Jews who have Jesus circumcised on the eighth day. As for the naming of their son, they dutifully accept what the angel had said would be the name: Jesus (Yeshua, or as we would say, Joshua), meaning "God saves."

The next few verses have raised some questions over the years about the degree of Luke's knowledge of Jewish and biblical practices. It needs to be recognized, though, that Luke is incorporating three separate religious ceremonies that are recorded in the Old Testament: the purification of a woman forty days after childbirth, the presentation of the firstborn to God, and the dedication of the firstborn for service to God.[102] Luke has simply combined elements of each of these rituals here. Better said, he has compacted the story to suggest that Mary went through all the appropriate processes. Several aspects of this story are interesting.

The purification ritual involved both a burnt and a sin offering, and Luke's account informs us that Mary and Joseph followed the form of the ritual a poor person would follow—that is, offering two pigeons or turtledoves. This tells us something about the social situation of the holy family. They were observant of the Law, but they were not wealthy enough to afford a lamb at this point.

This makes the likelihood of their staying with relatives in Bethlehem even greater. In addition, a sin offering was involved. Thus this story must surely count against later Christian traditions about the absolute purity or sinlessness of Mary. Luke portrays her as a normal Jewish woman performing her ritual duties.

Luke also refers to "their sacrifice" (v. 24). Normally, it would be only Mary who needed to offer a sacrifice as part of her ritual purification. But since Mary and Joseph were not well off, it is quite believable that they could not afford a midwife and instead had Joseph and other family members help with the delivery of Jesus, and thus he himself would have been ritually unclean as a result.[103] Again, Luke does not paint an idealized portrait of Mary or Joseph. They are good Jews who are having difficulty coping with and understanding the extraordinary nature of their son and the things they are being told about him. Luke paints a very human, poignant, realistic picture of Mary and Joseph as parents—anxious, concerned, striving to be obedient and understanding. We should not be too hard on them, however, for as New Testament scholar Raymond Brown stresses:

> Luke's idea is that complete acceptance of the word of God, complete understanding of who Jesus is, and complete discipleship is not yet possible. This will come through the ministry of Jesus and particularly through the cross and resurrection. It is no accident that the final reaction of the parents of Jesus in the infancy narrative is very much like that of the disciples of Jesus after the third passion prediction: "They did not understand any of these things, and this word ... was hidden from them" (18.34). But Luke does not leave Mary on the negative note of misunderstanding. Rather in 2.51 he stresses her retention of what she has not yet understood and ... her continuing search to understand.[104]

Now we jump ahead to the story in Luke 2:41–52 that tells of Jesus in the Temple as a boy. The account begins with another strong stress on the piety of Joseph and Mary, telling us that the couple went to Jerusalem every year for the Passover festival. The year when Jesus was twelve, they stayed until the festival was completed, and then Mary and Joseph began the return journey to Galilee, not realizing that Jesus had stayed behind in Jerusalem. Before we accuse them of bad parenting, we need to bear in mind that huge crowds made the pilgrimage from Galilee to Jerusalem for Passover.[105] We must also bear in mind that Jesus was not a child any longer, and that ancient Jewish families operated by and large as extended families; so it is understandable that Mary and Joseph might have assumed for a day or so that Jesus was with the relatives. When after a day's journey they noticed him missing, they began looking for him among the relatives. When they did not find him, they returned to Jerusalem—but it was not until the third day that they found him in the Temple.

It is not a surprise that Luke portrays Mary and Joseph, after such a search, as at their wits' end. Verse 46 says that Jesus was found assuming the posture of a teacher—namely, sitting—and listening to other teachers and asking questions. Luke adds that all who heard him were stunned by his level of understanding and his probing observations. Jesus is thus portrayed as a sage in training, and even apparently outdoing his teachers. We are told that Mary and Joseph are flabbergasted by this scenario. Mary blurts out, "Child, why have you done this to us? See here, your father and I have been in agony looking for you." Here is the heart-cry of a distraught mother, but she is not dealing with a delinquent son. In an honor-and-shame culture, when a child was thought to be disobedient or rebellious, that behavior was seen as shaming the parents—hence the question here about why Jesus did this *to them*. Notice that Mary speaks of "your father." When Jesus answers, though, he speaks in terms of "my [heavenly] Father." This reflects the earlier presentation in Luke of the virginal conception. Mary should have anticipated this sort of answer.

Nevertheless, Jesus's response in verse 49 is not the expected one. He is surprised his parents had not anticipated that he would be in the Temple. Had they forgotten the remarkable things presaged about him by various persons, angelic and human, around the time Jesus was born? Jesus asks, "Did you not know it was necessary for me to be in the [house] of my Father?" The word "house" is missing from the Greek text, but it is a more likely insertion than "business." Here, for the first time in Luke's gospel, Jesus is portrayed as God's Son.[106]

Notice the reference to necessity. This is a common theme in Luke and Acts, and it always refers to *divine* necessity. Jesus is a young man who already has a sense of calling, and he is preparing for his life's mission or work. He must in the first instance be doing the things his heavenly Father planned for him to do. There is a strong stress on the sovereignty of God over all these salvation-historical events in Luke-Acts. But clearly Jesus's human family does not understand: they are nonplussed by his response. Verse 51 shows how the family crisis is resolved—namely, Jesus goes home with them to Nazareth and is said to be obedient to them. He must obey God first, but he will obey his parents and reflect the filial piety expected of Jewish children. Mary may not understand, but she will reflect and ruminate on these events.

Ancient historians and biographers did not spend much time on telling tales of their heroes' childhood or youth, in part because they were quite innocent of the notions of Freud and Jung about the importance of early childhood influences in shaping character. Most ancients believed you were born with a certain personality, and you were stuck with it. The personality would *manifest* itself over time, but not many people thought it would *develop* over time. This makes Luke's penultimate description in this account all the more striking: Jesus grew in wisdom and in stature. Jesus is portrayed as fully human in this story, a person who grows and develops, yet very remarkable. Luke then concludes that Jesus grew in favor with God and human beings. At this point in the story, then, Jesus has not yet stirred up opposition; all seems well.

Sometimes the silences in a story are as pregnant as what the story says, and this seems to be the case with Luke 2:41–52. Notice that at no juncture in the story do we hear about other children of Mary and Joseph, even though Jesus is now twelve. Theophilus would never have deduced they already had other children if he only had the canonical gospels to consult, and certainly would not have taken the story in Luke 8 about the brothers and sisters of Jesus to mean anything other than that they were actually brothers and sisters of Jesus—or, more properly speaking, half-brothers and sisters, since Joseph was not Jesus's father. The story in Luke 2:41–52 implies that Joseph is not in fact Jesus's father, but in a way that deflects possible scandal by stressing that he had divine origins, a heavenly Father.

When we think of all the hoopla that has developed around the celebration of Christmas, it seems miles apart from the simple story of a poor Jewish couple bringing their first child into the world under less than ideal conditions and circumstances. It is hard to miss the joy and excitement, and at the same time the anxiety and fear, that Luke portrays as the human emotions with which Mary and Joseph respond to the divine initiative. Luke goes out of his way to portray the humanness of these characters, but without in any way toning down the miraculous elements in the story. Luke, like most ancient (pre-Enlightenment) historians, readily combines the mundane with the sublime, the ordinary events with the supernatural ones. Herodotus, the father of Greek historical writing, provided a clear precedent for including divine characters and divine actions in the narrative. Luke follows this example, but in Luke's account God acts mainly through his surrogates, whether it be an angel or a human yet divine figure like Jesus. God is seldom portrayed as directly acting in these accounts.

But as for mother Mary, we have learned much from Luke 1–2. She is a good pious Jewess looking forward to being married, who is shocked when she learns she is about to be pregnant by highly irregular means. Yet Luke's portrayal suggests that she bounces back well: she and Joseph go on to have this child, and they follow the normal Jewish procedures in terms of ritual purification and taking their firstborn up to the festivals in Jerusalem.

Mary is portrayed as lacking understanding, but not lacking faith and trust. Not yet knowing all the truth about her son, she is pondering and processing things, and learning to accept surprise. There is nothing in this text about Mary being sinless—indeed, there is the suggestion that she thought she was like others in this regard. Nor do we find anything here suggesting her immaculate conception, another later Christian idea often read into a story that is innocent of it. In other words, Luke avoids anachronism and hagiography in his account, the marks of a good historian at work.

MATTHEW'S MARY

What can Matthew 1–2 add to this discussion of Mary? Not as much as we might like, unfortunately, but we can make several points. First, there is a most peculiar patriarchal genealogy full of begats in Matthew 1—which Mary ends up in, as the wife of Joseph. Talk about a genealogy taking a left turn at the end! But it's a necessary turn: Jesus can be worked into this genealogy of Joseph only if Mary is included in it. Thus we have a clear though indirect testimony to the virginal conception right from the start in Matthew's account: the genealogy and the passage that follows it seek to explore and explain that conception. There is a recognition of the difficulties caused by Jesus's "unusual" origins, so in a sense this material can be seen as an exercise in apologetics—showing how Jesus could be born only of Mary and yet still be the Son of David through Joseph. Modern genealogical sleight of hand has nothing on our author.

It was unusual to list women in a patrilineal genealogy *unless* the father was unknown, or there was a bifurcated line with two wives producing two sets of sons, or the women were famous figures or related to famous figures (as is the case in Matthew's genealogy). Matthew's genealogy mentions five remarkable women—Tamar, Rahab, Ruth, Bathsheba, and Mary. One plausible conjecture that takes these women as a group argues that these other women are mentioned because they, like Mary, had irregularities in their past but were nonetheless vehicles through whom God moved along his plan and brought royal figures to Israel.[107]

Mary, then, is to be seen in this genealogy as a vehicle of the divine plan; Joseph, as a righteous man; and Jesus, as indebted to both of them for who he is—naturally in the one case and legally in the other case. The

First Evangelist is setting things up here to portray Jesus as a sage, the Son of David, but one far more like Solomon than Solomon's father. In fact, it can be argued that this genealogy is meant to trace Jesus's link to Solomon and Isaac, for they are respectively a son of David and a son of Abraham, and this is what Jesus is said to be at the beginning of the genealogy in verse 1 of the book of Matthew. Early Judaism's concept of legal paternity is involved here as well: Jesus would be entitled to Joseph's genealogy if he was legally accepted and adopted by Joseph, which apparently he was.[108]

Matthew's account, like Luke's, also suggests scandal. Joseph resolves to put Mary away quietly. Talk about an unrealistic strategy in a small town like Nazareth! As noted earlier, betrothal in early Judaism was a formal contract. Thus any dissolution would have involved witnesses who might well talk afterward.

Here's how Matthew tells the tale. His main focus is on Jesus, whereas the Lukan story also addresses the family of and birth of John the Baptist. The explanation for this difference is quite simple: Luke is writing a historical monograph, not a biography of Jesus, and his focus is on what he deems to be the pertinent events in salvation history. The First Evangelist, however, is writing an ancient Jewish biography of Jesus. Matthew 1:18–25, which gives a brief account of Jesus's origins, should probably be seen as something of an apologetic tale, explaining how Jesus could be born of Mary and not of Joseph and yet still be in the Davidic line. Raymond Brown points out that Matthew 1 is about who and how (that is, the virginal conception), while Matthew 2 is about where and whence.[109]

With the mention of Mary in the genealogy, as well as other women, one might have expected a focus on Mary in what follows in Matthew 1:18–25, but in fact Matthew focuses almost entirely on Joseph. Like Jesus, he is given the title "son of David." In fact, it is through Joseph and the naming of his son that Jesus becomes a son of David. The portrayal of Joseph is important in several ways: he is a son of David caught between a rock and a hard place—specifically, between the Law (since he is a righteous, law-abiding Jew) and his love for Mary. It is not unlike the way Solomon, a literal son of David, is portrayed in 1 Kings as he faces decisions about important and in some cases life-and-death matters.

In other words, Joseph is portrayed as a wise man, doing the right thing repeatedly in response to heavenly dreams. This sets the stage for the portrayal of Jesus himself as a sage—indeed, as the embodiment of Wisdom, Emmanuel (or "God with us"). In the first two chapters of Matthew, Joseph—as the wise father obedient to heavenly directions—initiates action three times after being instructed by an angel in three dreams. The reception of the dreams and the guidance should not be taken to indicate that Joseph was otherwise dense—in other words, that if there had not been divine intervention, he would have done something stupid. To the contrary, Joseph is depicted as a good Jew following the Law, a man who is spiritually open enough to accept correction and direction when he misunderstands what God and the Law require of him. Again, he is a son of David (that is, one like Solomon) who provides something of a pattern for his own adopted son of David—Jesus.

Matthew 1:18 presents us with two key phrases in the Greek. The first of these is the term *genesis* in reference to Jesus's origins.[110] Here, as in Matthew 1:1, the issue is more than Jesus's birth, though that is included. As New Testament scholar Jack Kingsbury notes, "The term 'origin' is much broader in scope than 'birth.' 'Origin' has to do with relationships: one's relationship to mother, to father, to lineage, to forebears, and even to one's own people, or nation."[111] In fact, the double use of this language in verses 1 and 18 summons us to consider Jesus's relationship to God, especially when this language is used in conjunction with the Emmanuel (or Wisdom) theme that surfaces not only at the beginning of the story but in Matthew 28 as well. It is sometimes thought that Jesus is a son of David simply by virtue of Joseph's adopting him; however, our author sees Jesus as a son of David like unto Solomon—not merely because of adoptive and fictive kinship, but also because he is imbued with divine Wisdom by God, and thus is royal like Solomon because of what God has granted him.

The second Greek phrase of interest in 1:18, used to describe the relationship of Mary and Joseph at the time of Jesus's conception, is *prin e suneithein,* which is usually read as either "before they had marital union" or "before they married or cohabited."[112] If the former is the meaning, then the verse would imply that Mary and Joseph consummated their marriage after the birth of Jesus. If the latter was intended, it would simply be a statement about Mary's pregnancy before marriage. There is a third option, however—namely, that both marriage and its consummation are intended by this phrase. It is difficult to imagine a Jew (or a Jewish Christian like our author) separating these ideas regarding a couple committed to marriage. Thus it seems very likely that this phrase is meant to imply that marital union did transpire after marriage; and indeed, as the gospel continues, various passages suggest that Mary and Joseph had further children.[113]

The awkwardness of the phrase comes from Matthew's concern with explaining that God alone was responsible for Mary's conception and that

Jesus was the result of God's, not Joseph's, creative action. I. Broer has rightly said that Matthew is really concerned about Joseph's conduct only until the point that the birth and marriage happen, in order to show the fulfillment of scripture.[114] Mary then is depicted as having the greatest honor for a Jewess: she is the mother of the messiah and so through her not merely scripture but Israel's destiny is fulfilled.

Matthew 1:18 goes on to add that Mary was found to be with child by means of the Holy Spirit. This must actually mean that Joseph found her to be pregnant, though he did not know that it was by holy means. Matthew is reminding his audience here that the pregnancy was by action of God. Joseph's intention in the next verse to send Mary away is clearly precipitated by an assumption on Joseph's part that something unholy had happened. Joseph did not wish to subject Mary to the scandal of a public breaking-off of the betrothal, yet Joseph's allegiance to God's Word and will came first. What was he to do?

Joseph is then depicted as the model follower of God's will, for he gives up a Jewish father's greatest privilege (siring his firstborn son) in order to obey that will. Verse 20 suggests, however, that Joseph is afraid to take Mary as his wife once he knows that she's pregnant. This is an understandable fear, given that his whole family's reputation could be ruined by willing participation in scandal. The angel reassures Joseph that what Mary has conceived is from the Holy Spirit. While Mary will give birth to the child, the angel says, Joseph should assume the father's duty of naming him, and the name should be Jesus, as in Luke's account, "for he will save his people from their sins." Already at the naming, then, Matthew foreshadows the role that this particular son of David will play.

The text goes on to say that Joseph takes his wife, "but he was not knowing her until she gave birth to a son" (24b–25). This wording has caused no end of controversy, especially in Roman Catholic circles. The focus of verse 25 is on the fact of Mary's virginity before the time she gives birth to Jesus, but since the verb is in the imperfect tense it also focuses on the period during which Joseph abstains from intercourse with Mary—namely, prior to the birth of Jesus. The imperfect tense probably implies subsequent sexual relations between Joseph and Mary, because in that tense the verb implies a definite limited duration of abstinence (as opposed to the aorist tense, which indicates an action at a particular point in time, usually in the past).[115]

Mary's virginity after the birth of Jesus is likely ruled out by this verse.[116] The passage ends with the affirmation that Joseph was again obedient and gave the child the name the angel had told him to: Jesus.[117] It "remains an odd fact that although Jesus's name occurs some one hundred and fifty times in Matthew," observes H. Clarke, "none of the human characters use it in addressing him"[118] in this gospel. However, this is surprising only if one forgets that Jesus is not portrayed in this gospel as a mere mortal, one human amongst many. He is portrayed as the mind and Wisdom of God in the flesh: God with us.

Joseph fades from the scene in this gospel quite dramatically after Matthew 2, and in view of the popularity of this gospel, it is not surprising that there were various later apocryphal attempts to fill in the rest of his story. The Proto-Evangelium of James, from the second century, proved especially influential in painting a picture of Joseph as an older man who took Mary as his second wife and stepmother to the children he had by his first wife. There is no good basis for this speculation in Christian documents from the first century, however, including no basis in the canonical gospels themselves. It appears likely that Joseph died prematurely, probably before the beginning of Jesus's ministry, which explains his absence from the stories in Matthew 13 and elsewhere in this gospel. More we cannot say on the basis of good historical evidence.

WHAT WE'VE LEARNED AND WHAT THAT KNOWLEDGE TELLS US ABOUT JESUS

More is said about Mary in the birth narratives of Luke and Matthew than elsewhere in the gospels. She is the only figure other than Jesus for whom the gospels give us a representative chronicle of life.

What we discovered in the above exploration is that Mary's story is fraught with peril and potential scandal. God's divine intervention produces something unexpected, perhaps even initially unwanted, in Mary's life, and that development sends the story off in surprising directions. Indeed, there is one surprise after another, first in Nazareth, then in Bethlehem, and finally in Jerusalem. No wonder Mary is portrayed in Luke's gospel as pondering the significance of these matters and groping for understanding! She is on pilgrimage to holy cities, but also on pilgrimage toward understanding her role and that of her son in God's salvific plan.

Mary is also portrayed as a good and pious Jewish mother, concerned about her son and his future, and forewarned that heartache is coming her way because of her son and his life-trajectory. Nothing in Luke's or Matthew's stories suggests that Mary made a vow of virginity at the outset of her adult life or marriage—indeed, the hints in the text suggest that she went on to have other children, who then quite naturally are referred to as the brothers and sisters of Jesus later in the narrative.

The same texts that tell us about Mary also teach us about Jesus. We learn, from Luke and Matthew's birth accounts, about Jesus's relationship to God: Mary's son is Jesus ("God saves"), Emmanuel ("God with us"), and a wise son of David, the savior of the world.

If there was danger and potential scandal at the outset of Jesus's life, what did Mary encounter during his ministry? As we shall see in the next chapter—*more* danger and potential scandal.

SIX

What's a Mother to Do?

The maternal instinct dies hard. We have already seen this in the story of Jesus and Mary in the Temple, but we continue to see it in the first two stories we will consider in this chapter: the wedding feast of Cana story and the Beelzebul controversy story. As we will see, it was not just when Jesus was an infant or a child that Mary tried (with varying results) to exercise her maternal authority in their relationship. The authors we will consider here are not simply trying to portray Mary as a good, if somewhat overprotective mother. No, there is much more to be gleaned from these stories, including some surprising revelations about Mary's relationship with Jesus.

JESUS THE CATERER (JOHN 2:1–12)

We need to deal with some silliness first. Contrary to some current interpretations, the Cana wedding account is not about Mary being the mother of the bridegroom and Jesus getting married. Whatever else one might want to say about this story, clearly one doesn't talk about the bridegroom at a Jewish wedding being "invited" to the wedding, as John does in 2:2, and after a Jewish wedding the groom does not go home with his mother, as Jesus does in John 2:12! No, this is a story about Jesus being the emergency backup caterer at a wedding in a small town called Cana. What most interests us about this story is what it reveals about the relationship between Mary and Jesus.

We are told that the mother of Jesus is already present at the wedding feast; then Jesus and some of his disciples arrive, apparently separately. The story seems to take place when Jesus is in transition from leaving his family to beginning his ministry, though we cannot be sure about this. Because the story casts Mary in a somewhat negative light as a pushy mother, it is not likely to be a creation of later church piety. In terms of the narrative's role in the larger plot of the Fourth Gospel, stories involving

Jesus and Mary frame the ministry here, with the second account coming in John 19:25–27, which we will deal with shortly. Like all good Johannine stories, the wedding feast story operates on two levels: the historical level and the deeper theological or spiritual level. On the latter level it intends to suggest that Jesus began to replace the institutions of Judaism (in this case, Jewish purification water rites) with what he himself could offer (the new wine of the gospel). But our current interest is in the historical level of this study.

Some comments are in order about Jewish wedding parties of Mary's time. First, such parties could go on for days, and running out of wine must have been a rather frequent occurrence. There were certainly caterers for such weddings who knew this and could have made up for the short-fall quickly. In other words, Mary's request did not reflect an emergency situation, and certainly not one that Jesus needed to remedy. He could have responded, "A failure to plan on their part does not constitute an emergency on our part." In fact, that is in essence how Jesus did respond, as we shall see. The wine at such parties was certainly alcoholic, though it would have been regularly watered down after the first and best wine had been served undiluted.[119] The idea was to serve the best wine first, before the crowd was too inebriated to appreciate it.

Now let's look at the story in a bit more detail. According to verse 3, Mary goes to Jesus when the wine runs out and simply says, "They have no more wine," clearly implying, "Do something." Now this is interesting at several levels. It shows that Mary knows that Jesus can perform miracles, even though in the Johannine outline Jesus has yet to perform one. It also shows that Mary was not above trying to pressure her son into helping, to avoid having the families of the bride and bridegroom shamed at their own wedding party. In short, her intentions were surely good.

The attempt to assert maternal influence on Jesus produces a rather abrupt and surprising response, however. The Greek of the next verse can be translated literally, "What to me and to you, woman?" Scholars debating the nuances of this question have suggested a variety of possible interpretations: (1) "What is that to me and you?" with the implication that it is someone else's problem; (2) "What do you have to do with me?" but that seems too abrupt and goes beyond the strict grammar of the sentence; (3) "Why are you involving us in this matter?" a looser reading; or (4) "That is your business; do not involve me." What all of these readings make clear about this phrase is that it's off-putting. It's some sort of rebuke, even if a gentle one. When a phrase like this occurs elsewhere in the Greek Bible, it surely indicates an attempt to disengage from something or some request.[120]

Notice as well that Jesus calls his own mother "woman." Now while this is a respectful form of address, it is not the normal way one would address one's mother; indeed, it seems to be a form of disengagement from maternal authority. Mary seeks to assert her authority, but Jesus indicates that this is not appropriate, at least at this juncture. Though Jesus uses the respectful "woman" form of address with other women in other accounts (John 4:21; 20:13; Matt. 15:18; Luke 13:12), there are no known precedents in other sources for someone using such a term for one's own mother. Jesus addresses Mary this way only here and from the cross in John 19. (I will say more about that when we get to that story.)

But this is not all of Jesus's response. He adds, "My hour has not already come," or—if we take it as a question, which the syntax and grammar allow—"Has not my hour already come?" The latter seems unlikely in light of the initial response to the request and the fact that elsewhere in this gospel Jesus's "hour" refers to the climax of his ministry and what happens on the cross. That is likely what is meant here as well. The implication is that while Mary does not now have a claim on Jesus, in his "hour" she will have such a claim, and Jesus will do something for her personally—which turns out to be handing her over to the Beloved Disciple.

And yet, and yet … Jesus *does* respond to the situation. And his mother seems to expect that he will: she tells the servants present, "Do whatever he tells you." She does not press the issue with Jesus; she simply trusts that he will act in an appropriate way, and so he does, becoming the last-minute caterer who provides the best wine of all—indeed, provides gallons and gallons of Gallo, so to speak. Jesus clearly didn't have a problem with parties and celebrating. He was no killjoy.

Thus we can say about this story that Jesus responds in a way that distances him from Mary's maternal authority but does not fail to respond to the need of the moment. As I noted elsewhere, "Jesus' heavenly Father, not his earthly mother, must determine when his hour is to come and what he is to do until then."[121] Jesus is disengaging without being disingenuous, but Mary keeps trying to assert that maternal authority over him—especially in our next story, which will be seen as something of an attempt to rescue Jesus from a situation perceived to be dangerous.

New Testament scholar John Ashton, in his helpful study of the Cana wedding account, sums up its import nicely:

So the mother of Jesus occupies a mediating position, ranged in the first place with the hosts and guests, associating herself with their need, and eliciting, by her plea on their behalf, a sharp retort that contains a charge of misunderstanding; and in the second place with the servants, who are waiting to do Jesus' bidding. This mixture of incomprehension and compliance is surely part of the *meaning* of the story.... In the context of an appeal to Jewish readers and listeners to come forward and declare themselves for Christ, the significance of Jesus' mother ... is as a representative of those who do just that, *those for whom misunderstanding is not a permanent obstacle to discipleship.*[122]

Here in the Johannine depiction, Mary is portrayed as not yet a disciple (in fact, verse 12 distinguishes her and the brothers from the disciples) but perhaps on the way to becoming a disciple. But here again, as in Luke 2:41–52 (where the twelve-year-old Jesus is found studying and teaching in the Temple), Mary is brought up short by something Jesus says. Her attempt to assert maternal authority produces a stronger response here than in the Luke passage (perhaps because he is older now and has begun his ministry), though in both cases Jesus appears in the end to be an obedient son.

What can we discern about Mary's understanding of Jesus from this story? First, we notice that while Mary assumes she still has some authority over Jesus, Jesus does not make the same assumption. His response to her is abrupt and unusual, though not completely dismissive. But Mary knows that Jesus can do something—indeed, she seems to think he can do something miraculous. This suggests that Jesus has displayed his power already in some venue that Mary knows about. Interestingly, Anne Rice's new novel, *Christ the Lord: Out of Egypt,* explores this "hidden" period before the public ministry and comes to the same conclusion.[123] Jesus was a miracle worker from early on, and his family knew of his extraordinary abilities. The miraculous aspect of what Jesus did in Cana is not played up at that occasion, in the sense that no apologetic hay is made out of the miracle with the audience at the wedding. The end of the story suggests that only his disciples put faith in him as a result of this event.

This story about a relationship in flux shows that Jesus performed miracles early on: both his mother and his disciples already believe, at the time of this wedding, that he can perform a miracle. Miracles, then, don't show up only in public forums during Jesus's actual ministry; they characterize his life, according to what his mother knew of him.

HAVING THE DEVIL OF A TIME (MARK 3:21–35)

Mark, our earliest gospel, is both stark and dark. It presents a mysterious Jesus operating in an apocalyptic scenario and mode. For example, Jesus is depicted as doing regular battle with the powers of darkness. Jesus the exorcist is in fact on display from the very first miracle story in Mark, in the first chapter. While there is not a single exorcism story in the Gospel of John, exorcism is the first thing that Mark wants to tell us about Jesus when it comes to miracle-working, and it's a regular feature of the characterization of Jesus thereafter. While John's sign narratives begin in a party atmosphere, Mark's begin with tension you could cut with a knife—a healing on the Sabbath, and in the synagogue, and not just any kind of healing, but an exorcism.

We turn now to Mark 3:21–35, bearing in mind that Jesus is already in the middle of doing battle with demons before this story is told. This second exorcism account begins by presenting us with the unflattering picture of Jesus being misunderstood by his own family. The text says that the family, including Mary, went out to take Jesus home, because "they were saying" he was out of his mind. Although "they" could refer to either the family or the public here, at the very least the family thought he was not in control of the situation. Yet the verb here, which occurs again in 6:17 and 12:12, is a strong one, referring in those later texts to attempts to arrest Jesus. Here it must mean at least that the family members have come to restrain Jesus—in other words, it implies a forceful action. Interestingly, Mark's statement about the family was clearly too offensive for either Matthew or Luke, who both omit it.[124] This is one of the reasons we know with considerable certainty that we are dealing with a tradition of historical substance here.

On the basis of the honor challenges Jesus had been issuing to the authorities, it is understandable why his family might think he was courting disaster and had taken leave of his senses. "Since madness was often regarded as due to possession by a demon," notes New Testament scholar Marna Hooker, "it is arguable that their judgment on the situation was close to that of the scribes in the next verse," who assumed that Beelzebul was in control.[125] Seen from the perspective of honor-and-shame conventions, it is possible to understand the action of the family as an attempt to protect their own family honor, rather than protect Jesus in particular. They did not want him to disgrace the family.[126] As Jesus begins to speak in parables, he refers to a house divided against itself, a reference that could in fact be taken as an allusion to Jesus's own household.

This unflattering interpretation of Jesus's family's understanding of him seems confirmed in verses 31–35, where Jesus contrasts his physical family with the family of faith (that is, "whoever does the will of God").[127] This contrast between the two families would have no real force if Jesus's family did not share the crowd's opinion that Jesus had taken leave of his senses. Jesus's language leaves open the door for his physical family to join the family of faith, assuming they opt to do the will of God; but Mark does not suggest that the family, even later, walked through that door, nor does Mark 3 suggest that Jesus granted his physical family an audience on this occasion. In fact, Mark 6 continues the picture of misunderstanding and rejection, as we shall see, claiming that a prophet lacks honor even in his own home.[128]

As in the wedding at Cana story, misunderstanding is again a part of the relationship between Jesus and Mary. Apparently Jesus's exorcisms were frightening the family. Could Jesus really be in league with the devil? What would happen to the family if Jesus publicly shamed them? Mary and the siblings try crisis intervention, perhaps to protect Jesus, perhaps to protect the family name. Jesus's reaction is to present his vision for a new community, based on spiritual kinship rather than physical relationship. The upshot is that Jesus's natural family has no part in Jesus's movement or ministry, and family and friends have no special advantages in the Dominion that is coming.

This concept is radical in a traditional patriarchal culture where blood is thicker than water. Jesus's challenge to the traditional authority structures of Palestinian society is now complete: he has repudiated the "old fabric" (2:21) in order to make way for the new order. The fundamental unit of "resocialization" into the Dominion (or kingdom of God) will be the new family, the community of discipleship. This is not to say that Jesus sets out here to deliberately discredit or dishonor his physical family; rather, he places the honor of God above his family.[129]

This remarkable story seems entirely unconcerned about matters that later exercised the early church fathers, such as whether Mary remained a virgin after Jesus was born, and if so, whether the brothers and sisters Mark referred to were children of Joseph by a previous marriage or perhaps cousins.[130] Nonetheless, this remarkable story tells us a good deal about Mary. First, as mentioned earlier, it sounds a note of disharmony between Mary and Jesus. Second, it establishes that Mary and the rest of the family are not within the circle of Jesus's disciples. Third, it suggests that Mary is the ringleader of her little posse: she is mentioned first, separate from the brothers, at references in verses 31, 32, and 33. While we may surmise that her maternal drive to protect her son is part and parcel of her motivation, the story also suggests that she's worried that the rumors are true: Jesus is dancing with the devil—or, more charitably put, he is out of his mind to be dabbling in exorcisms.

Inasmuch as this story is followed a few chapters later in the Markan outline by Jesus's visit to his hometown synagogue, and that's the next time we hear about the family, we must assume that this earlier story prepares the way for the later assertion that Jesus is without honor in his own home. And on this note we turn to that story.

A PROPHET WITHOUT HONOR AT HOME (MARK 6:1–6)

Mark 6:1–6 presents us with a story bristling with animus and controversy. In this account, Jesus goes to his hometown with his disciples at some juncture—we don't know exactly when—well after the ministry has begun and Jesus is a known figure in Galilee. We must presume he has been invited to do so, because the text says that when the Sabbath rolls around, Jesus teaches in the synagogue and many are amazed or dumbfounded. The people who hear him ask questions such as, Where does Jesus get his ideas from, and what wisdom has been given him such that he can perform miracles? (Performing miracles was thought to be a learned art: one had to know the right formula, potion, or practice to effect a cure.) They also asked, Is this not the carpenter, Mary's son, and aren't his brothers and sisters here with us? When the crowd takes offense at him, Jesus responds with his famous saying about a prophet not being without honor except in his home region, amongst his kin, and within his own household. Even more interestingly, Mark's narrative says that Jesus cannot do many miracles there, apparently due to the people's lack of faith. We need to unpack various aspects of this intriguing tale.

The full family is apparently not present on this occasion in the synagogue (only his sisters are), but they are mentioned first by Jesus's listeners and then by Jesus himself. Mark 6:1–6 is connected with the passage we just looked at, in that both texts suggest that Jesus's physical relationship to his family proves to be a stumbling block for them, keeping them from seeing Jesus as he truly is. In both places, too, Jesus places his relatives and even his own household in a category other than that of believer or disciple.

The story begins by speaking again of Jesus leaving one place and entering another—in this case, entering "his own country." The term *patrida,* which means "fatherland," refers to the specific region where his family lived—that is, Nazareth and its environs. The disciples are described as following along behind Jesus. Nothing is said about what he did there until the Sabbath, when he begins to teach in the synagogue, presumably the only such meeting place in this small village.

The result of Jesus teaching in the synagogue is not accolades but astonishment; we are not told what he says, but we learn that the people are "knocked out" (the literal meaning of the Greek) by what Jesus says. They dispute neither that he has wisdom nor that he performs mighty works; they are just dumbfounded that such things come from a hometown boy like Jesus. More than just a matter of familiarity breeding contempt, their reaction comes from the ancient mentality that geographical and hereditary origins determine who a person is and what his or her capacities will be. They see Jesus as someone who is not merely exceeding expectations but is overreaching. This will in fact be the last time in Mark that we find Jesus in a synagogue, and it's the last mention of Jesus teaching, embroiled once again in a controversy in that locale which is supposed to be sacred space. The issue seems to be suspicion about Jesus's character. As Robert Gundry observes, "Uncertain origin implies uncertain character."[131]

A significant textual problem is revealed in some important manuscripts of this verse, which have the people refer to Jesus as "the son of the carpenter, the son of Mary," rather than the more widely supported reading, "the carpenter, the son of Mary" (with the former perhaps being a case of assimilation to Matthew 13:55). On the principle that the reading which best explains the other variants is likely to be original, the latter rendering calling Jesus a carpenter is to be preferred. If this gospel had as its primary audience Gentiles, a later change to "son of the carpenter" would not be surprising, because unlike in the Jewish world, in the Greco-Roman world (especially among the elite) such manual labor was seen as demeaning. Celsus, for example, in his polemic against Christianity, verbally sneered at the fact that this religion was founded by a carpenter (see *Contra Celsum* 6.34, 36). In addition, it is hardly likely that the phrase "the son of Mary" would have been added later to this text, yet some texts have simply "of the carpenter, the son."[132]

The phrase "son of Mary" may reveal one reason why Jesus's words, however wise, are not immediately received by the audience. How can the offspring of undistinguished or even dubious origins (was Joseph *really* the father?) interpret the Torah as he does? It is Mark alone who records that Jesus places his own family in the group with those who stumble over his apparently ordinary or questionable origins.[133] More importantly, it may very well be that the phrase "son of Mary" is itself intended to be a slur.[134] It may, on the other hand, simply indicate that Joseph is deceased, though as noted earlier it was a regular Jewish practice to continue to identify a child by the name of his deceased father.

Verse 5 stresses that such was the unbelief in his hometown that Jesus was unable to do any mighty work there except lay hands on a few sick persons and heal them. The focus, then, is not so much on Jesus's inability as on the people's lack of faith. Clearly Mark sees a connection between faith and healing, as the previous stories in the second half of Mark 5 show. We may perhaps put it this way: while faith in itself does not necessarily produce a miracle, lack of faith limits the reception of help readily available from Jesus.[135] The story ends in the next verse, as so often in Mark, with amazement or wonder—though here it is not the crowd but Jesus who is amazed. He is astounded at the unbelief he encounters among those who ought by rights to most appreciate him—his family and hometown folks.

The problem with hometown folks is that they know both too much and too little about a person who has spent some time away. What they know has to do with their memories of that person's growing-up years; they typically know little about what happened to him while away. Therefore, they continue to evaluate the person on the basis of their old information. The crowd's reaction to Jesus's preaching assumes that Jesus can't possibly know more than the other locals about the scriptures since he received the same sort of synagogue training they did. Jesus is also judged on the basis of his (possibly questionable) lineage. In a world where gender, geography, and generation are thought to determine one's identity, Jesus's audience is offended that Jesus seems to be claiming he knows more than they do, more than he ought to do on the basis of his family and heritage.

More surprising than the crowd's lack of faith is the fact that Jesus's family does not stand up for him—not even his mother! This suggests, as does the above-mentioned reading of "son of Mary" as a slur, that Mary was not held in very high esteem in this town. It also supports the earlier conclusion that Mary and the brothers and sisters were not within the circle of the disciples at this juncture. In addition, this story provides further rather strong evidence that Mary did go on to have other children after having Jesus. She lived out the role of a normal and good Jewish woman, but she lived with a cloud of suspicion over her head: with Joseph apparently dead, her eldest son did not permanently take over the work of the carpenter's shop; instead, James—the next eldest son—and the other brothers and sisters supported the family. (As noted above, Jesus is explicitly called "the carpenter" in this passage, and so he may have been for years. Remember that Jesus did not begin his ministry until he was about thirty.)

It cannot have been easy for Mary and the family to cope when Jesus, the eldest son, decided to "go walkabout" in Galilee with some hand-picked disciples, none of whom were family. This story and the Mark 3 account discussed earlier, in which he redefined the notion of family to include brothers and sisters of faith, perhaps reflect the fallout from that breaking away. In this context, then, it is not surprising that we hear nothing about the positive involvement of the family during the whole rest of Jesus's ministry. Indeed, John 7:3–5 suggests that there was the sort of sibling rivalry between Jesus and his brothers that existed between the Old Testament Joseph and his brothers in a much earlier period. Thus the next time we hear of Mary, she is at the cross—and at the cross *without* Jesus's brothers and sisters. To that final story we will turn in a moment, but first some concluding remarks about Mary in Mark's gospel.

There is absolutely no sign in these Markan stories that Mary is living out of any other paradigm than that of a normal first-century Jewish woman. She remains at home; she is not a traveling disciple of Jesus. She has multiple children, all of whom are still associated with her, and she is deeply worried about her eldest son, fearing that he may have lost his bearings.

There is likewise no attempt in these stories at hagiography. They bear all the earmarks of historical authenticity, including troubling and offensive elements such as the slur "son of Mary," which later hagiographers would leave out. Even Mary does not fully understand her son during his ministry, according to Mark's accounts, and her attempts to protect him and take him home are rebuffed. Instead, she is told indirectly that she and the rest of the family need to join the family of faith, the circle of the disciples. At this juncture in their lives they are outsiders looking in at the inner circle. Only at the crucifixion will Mary cross the line into the inner circle of disciples and the family of faith. To that story we must now turn.

THE SON OF MARY AT A DEAD END (JOHN 19:25–27)

Mary cannot have been pleased with her other sons' advice to Jesus, given as they were going up to the festival in Jerusalem. Their advice was, "You ought to leave here and go to Judea so that your disciples [some other group than these brothers] may see the miracles that you do. No one who wants to become a public figure acts in secret. Since you are doing these things, show yourself to the world" (John 7:4–5). This of course contrasts with what we saw in Mark 3 when Mary and the brothers try to convince Jesus to come home. Another interesting aspect of this suggestion is the implication that Jesus has Judean followers or disciples in addition to his Galilean ones. Here however we must consider the one story where Jesus and Mary interact in the Passion narrative, the exchange from the cross in John 19:25–27.

John 19:25–27, in some ways the climactic scene of the Johannine Passion narrative, is the second of the bookend stories about Jesus and Mary that frame the ministry:

> Standing near the cross of Jesus were his mother, and his mother's sister, Mary the wife of Clopas, and Mary Magdalene. When Jesus saw his mother and the disciple whom he loved standing beside her, he said to his mother, "Woman, here is your son." Then he said to the disciple, "Here is your mother." And from that hour the disciple took her into his own home.

Once again we see Jesus addressing Mary simply as "woman" (*gunai*) here. Rather than disengaging from her and her authority, as he does in John 2, he exercises his authority to integrate her into the family of faith, turning her over to the Beloved Disciple (who clearly is not a member of Jesus's physical family). I am convinced that this account has historical substance, not least because the Beloved Disciple, an eyewitness, is there to participate.[136]

In order to understand this story, which presents the resolution of the tension between the physical family of Jesus and his family of faith, we need to consider three things:

1. As noted earlier, Mark 3:31–35 makes perfectly clear that Jesus, during his ministry, considered his *followers* his primary family—the family of faith, or those who do the will of God.

2. John 7:5 ("For not even his brothers believed in him") and the verses leading up to it support the Markan stories we just considered in asserting that the brothers of Jesus were unbelievers during the ministry.

3. We know from Acts 1:14, where Mary is among the disciples in the upper room, that Mary at some juncture joined the inner circle of Jesus's followers. This act of adherence must surely have transpired

before that upper room event, and there is no good reason it could not have happened beginning at Golgotha.

Notice that John, from the outset, sets Mary alongside other women—most importantly, alongside the paradigmatic female disciple, Mary Magdalene. It is interesting that this is the only list of the women associated with Jesus that does not name Mary Magdalene first. In fact, this list puts Jesus's relatives first (Mary and her sister), and then names two female disciples (Mary the wife of Clopas and Mary Magdalene, unless Mary of Clopas is also a blood relative of Jesus's mother). There is no interchange at all between Jesus and these other women, only with Mary; and that is an interchange that Jesus initiates. We know that, historically speaking, close relatives of a crucifixion victim were sometimes allowed to stand near the cross, especially if they were women, and especially if the cross was guarded.[137] We also know that a dying man on a cross could legally make certain testaments or dispensations in regard to his property or family.

The words of Jesus are not responded to by Mary or the Beloved Disciple—not verbally at least, though the Beloved Disciple takes Mary to his home thereafter. The arrangement Jesus makes is interesting in two ways: the Beloved Disciple is entrusted into Mary's care as a son, but the reverse seems also to be true. This means that Jesus does not anticipate that Mary will cease to exercise the role of mother as she enters the family of faith, but now her role will involve *spiritual* motherhood. Mary learns that she is to be a mother as a disciple, not a mother and also a disciple. The two roles are fused, but not confused. Notice that she obeys the directive and goes with the Beloved Disciple after Jesus's death.

Jesus is in effect asking this disciple to take care of his mother, since henceforth he will be unable to do so. This was part of the responsibility of the eldest son if the husband was dead, and so we see an example of filial piety here, exercised by Jesus quite literally at the last minute. The situation is more strained than we can imagine, because when it comes to Jesus himself, no family member undertakes the required task of seeing that Jesus gets a decent burial. This was one of the main duties of a family to a deceased family member, and yet in the case of Jesus it is undertaken by people who aren't family. Even Mary is not involved apparently.

There is a plausible explanation for this historically. Crucifixion, as we saw earlier, was seen as the most shameful way an ancient person could die. Given the fact that the brothers did not believe in Jesus, and given the honor-and-shame culture in which they lived, it is understandable that they may have felt that Jesus did not deserve an honorable burial. Alternatively, they may have been too ashamed to hang around and watch Jesus die and then place him in the tomb.

For Mary, this event is clearly a turning point. Whether she saw it as a fulfillment of the prophecy given in Luke 2:35 we cannot be sure, but certainly the whole trajectory of Jesus's life has been one test of faith after another for her, ending in what appears to be a tragedy. Here finally she submits to Jesus's authority, no longer trying to manage the situation. Here she becomes a disciple, joining the Beloved Disciple's household. This signals a clear break with Nazareth and the past, especially given that it is not just any disciple whose home she becomes part of, but "the disciple whom Jesus loved"—that is, the paradigmatic disciple. Like the other disciples, she leaves family and home and kin to follow Jesus. Even as the other disciples are abandoning Jesus and scattering to their own families, Jesus's mother is united with the family of faith in the person of the Beloved Disciple.

Since so much has been made of this scene, especially in the later Roman Catholic tradition, it's worth summarizing what we can say historically:

1. If this event—Mary standing with the Beloved Disciple beneath the cross and receiving a dispensation from Jesus—happened, it is noteworthy that while the Beloved Disciple is called a disciple in this scene, Mary is just called "woman."

2. Nonetheless, the Beloved Disciple is now called Mary's son, just as Jesus had been.

3. We are led to believe that the Beloved Disciple's discipleship status and role as representative disciple antedate Mary's role as spiritual mother in the church.

4. Thus Mary is not depicted as the mother of the church here, but rather as a spiritual mother *in* the church and to the Beloved Disciple, so to speak.

5. Neither Jesus's mother nor the Beloved Disciple is addressed by personal name in this scene. This is because our gospel writer sees them as types or models. Standing beneath the cross, and becoming one because of what Jesus has done while on the cross, they foreshadow the church. We may perhaps also see a symbolic foreshadowing here of the equality of man and woman beneath the cross.[138]

In this scene, as John tells it, Mary typifies the traditional role of mother, but she learns how to exercise that role in a new spiritual way and in a new context. It can be no accident that once Jesus achieved this rapprochement between his physical and spiritual families—that is, once he accomplished all that God had set out for him to do—John has him say, "All is completed" (John 19:28). Nothing less than the reconciliation of man and woman at the foot of the cross was at stake.

MARY'S PENTECOSTAL EXPERIENCE (ACTS 1:14)

There is, sadly enough, little information on what happened to Mary after that fateful day in the year 30 when Jesus was crucified. We have only the bare hint in Acts 1:14 that she and Jesus's brothers and the "certain women" we saw in our earlier discussion of Joanna and Mary Magdalene were present in Jerusalem and in the upper room some fifty days after Easter: "All these [disciples] were constantly devoting themselves to prayer, together with certain women including Mary the mother of Jesus, as well as his brothers." But we can ask some probing questions about this Acts text and see if it won't give up some additional information about Mary.

The story of what happened at Pentecost can be summed up quickly. This weeklong Jewish festival commemorating the revelation of the Ten Commandments to Moses—a festival that each year brought Jewish visitors from distant lands to Jerusalem—became on the year in question the occasion when the Holy Spirit fell upon the disciples. Responding to that gift, they went forth into the Temple courts to tell the Good News about Jesus to all the visiting Jews. In the Christian church, the event is viewed as the occasion when the disciples received empowerment from on high so that they might boldly and effectively proclaim the story of Jesus.

Notice that Mary is called in this story "Mary the mother of Jesus"; her importance is seen in her relationship with Jesus. She and the brothers of Jesus—a reference I would take to mean James and Jude at least—are depicted here as devoting themselves to prayer. It is interesting that Luke has chosen to mention Mary, and associate her with a special work of the Holy Spirit, at the outset of both of his two volumes—Luke and Acts.[139] Clearly here she is seen as a Spirit-filled disciple, fully within the inner circle of Jesus. But what happened to her after that? This puts us in the realm of conjecture, but let's consider the possibility that we have a clue: that she continued to be in the care of or closely involved with the Beloved Disciple. This might mean that when the destruction of Jerusalem was imminent in the late 60s, she and the Beloved Disciple fled somewhere else. But where? Galilee? Syrian Antioch? Egypt? Or more further afield to Ephesus? Perhaps there is a further clue in the text we will consider now, Revelation 12:1–6.

THE WOMAN CLOTHED WITH THE SUN (REVELATION 12:1–6)

Apocalyptic prophecy is tricky material to interpret, especially when it has several possible referents and is deliberately meant to be multivalent. Still, Revelation 12:1–6 may tell us something about Mary and her fate. Certainly many Roman Catholic exegetes have thought this text was about Mary. Indeed, it is the basis of the Mary Queen of Heaven name of so many Catholic churches. Thus there is a clear tradition of seeing this text as having something to do with Mary—but what precisely, and will it yield up some historical information about Mary's fate after Pentecost?

The passage begins by telling us that the author saw a great sign or portent appearing in the *ourano*—"heaven" or "sky."[140] Either rendering is possible, but as the story unfolds, "heaven" seems the more likely translation. We hear of a woman clothed with the sun, with the moon under her feet and a crown with twelve stars. (Much conjecture has been offered as to whether this crown might represent the constellations or, more specifically, the twelve signs of the zodiac.) The destiny of the whole race lies in this woman, a conclusion that draws on the notion that stars control one's future or fate. But the story is about this woman's travail on earth, not her role in heaven. In other words, it has nothing to do with later Marian theology about Mary being an intercessor in heaven for believers.

The conjecture still favored by most Roman Catholic scholars is that this woman is Mary. Two factors are usually thought to count against this conclusion:

1. Later on in this chapter of Revelation, we hear about "the rest of her offspring" (*semeia*, here meaning "seed"; v. 17). If we take 12:1–6 to refer to Mary in particular, then this would be a reference to Jesus's other physical kin, Mary's other children. Such a reading would argue against Mary for Catholics, since most do not believe she had children other than Jesus. It is more likely to refer to believers, however—perhaps, in particular, persecuted believers, or those about to be persecuted.

2. There are parallels between this text and Isaiah 66:6–9 that strongly suggest that the woman is Mother Zion—or, as Paul would put it,

the new Jerusalem that is our mother (Gal. 4:26). In other words, the woman represents the community of God's people, a view that allows a certain continuity between the Old Testament and New Testament people of God. Jesus was born a Jew into the Jewish faith community; Gentiles are the community of God's other children. Jesus is in a sense viewed as a special child of God.

But this cannot be the end of the discussion, because in the Johannine tradition Mary is said to be the one who was to be spiritual mother to the Beloved Disciple. I would suggest, then, that this figure is both the literal mother of the male child Jesus, and also the female image of the people of God. Again, the text is multivalent!

As the passage continues, the woman is depicted as being in anguish, about to give birth. A second portent appears in the sky or in heaven: a red or fiery (or bloody) dragon with ten horns and seven crowns, waiting to devour her child. The horns, which draw on the apocalyptic imagery referring to nations in Daniel 7–8, suggest awesome strength, while the crowns may indicate an attempt to usurp all power. There is a deliberate contrast here: the dragon's crowns are called *diademata,* whereas Mother Zion's crown is called a *stephanos,* the laurel wreath for victors. It is possible that the twelve stars in her crown refer to the twelve tribes of Israel rather than to the zodiac, symbolizing the whole people of God.

Next we are told that the dragon's tail drags a third of the stars from the sky, casting them to earth. Stars were seen as gods by pagans and as angels by Jews—in this case perhaps fallen ones.[141] The action concludes with the birth of the child—a male who is to rule the nations. He is taken away to God, and the woman flees to the desert, to a place prepared for her by God.

What do these events mean? Certainly there does not appear to be anything here about a primordial fall of Satan and his angels from heaven. Rather, we have either (1) a depiction of what happened as a result of the triumphant death, resurrection, ascension, and assumption of power by the male child—in which case, the whole church age is seen as a time of being *in extremis;* or (2) a depiction of the events at the end of human history, the final tribulation before the end. Some would say that this is a false dilemma: John never pictured a long church age, and thus he could depict the final tribulation as potentially near at hand.[142]

Let's take a closer look at the child. He was a male destined to shepherd all the nations with an iron rod. Psalm 2 is clearly in the background here, coloring the imagery, which conveys the child's absolute power over the nations, and possibly even his power to judge. John is also drawing on traditions in regard to the birth of Apollo, which the Emperor Domitian appropriated to suggest that he was a divine being and the conqueror of evil. As M. G. Reddish stresses, "John's reuse of this ancient myth challenges the divine claims and arrogant presumptions of the imperial cult. Christ, not the emperor, is the real victor over the malevolent forces of chaos, darkness, and wickedness. John unmasks the Roman power for what it truly is—a tool of Satan, and a god worthy of worship."[143] It was not Roma, but Mother Zion who was the real mother of the divine Son of God.[144] But it was also Mary who was the real mother of Jesus.

The text says that the male child was seized and carried off to God and to his throne. Now there are various ways this might be understood. Some commentators think that Jesus's birth and death/resurrection/ascension are in view here. Others think that the only focus is the death and resurrection/ascension, for it is at this point that Jesus becomes Son of God in power, properly speaking. However, we are told explicitly that the woman bore a son; in fact, the only reference to sonship is connected with the birth.[145] I thus conclude that the birth and the death/resurrection/ascension are in view here, incorporating the whole earthly career of Jesus. The passive voice verb "was seized and carried off" implies that God did the seizing. This means John sees God's hand in Jesus's death. What the forces of darkness thought would mean the end of the male child, God used to give him a promotion and further power and authority even over the dark powers.

And what do we make of the woman fleeing into the desert? Since the woman represents the people of God, it is probable that we have an allusion to God's people fleeing into the desert in the Exodus. John indicates in his vision that the people of God will be "nourished" (by God), just as the ancient Israelites were. This text does not say the people of God are raptured into heaven or any celestial place; the image here is of protection on earth from the wrath of the dragon, something one would not need protection from in heaven.

But is there more to this than what we have just concluded? Could this not also allude to Mary herself fleeing into the wilderness, which from a Jewish point of view would be anywhere outside the Holy Land? Could this not also allude to the fact that Mary, the actual mother of the actual male child, is now seen as someone who in her person and in her life experience typifies the people of God in female form? There is a tradition from at least the second century that Mary and the Beloved Disciple fled to Asia and lived in Ephesus. It is possible that this text alludes to this tradition, which may or may not be true. Clearly, Revelation 12 was a text written to the church in Ephesus and others in Asia as well. It would be assumed that they would understand its meaning.

In conclusion, let me stress that we *cannot* deduce from this story that Mary plays some sort of role in heaven for the church. A portent in the sky is not the same thing as a powerful figure in heaven.

THE MOTHER OF THE SAVIOR (1 TIM. 2:13–15)

There may be one other slender and indirect reference to Mary in the New Testament that reflects a theological evaluation of her importance. We must turn to that text now before we sum up what we have learned about Mary in this chapter, and before we move on to the discussion of her spiritual son—the Beloved Disciple.

1 Timothy 2:1–15, a text fraught with peril, has been the subject of no end of debate.[146] Here I am interested only in the conclusion of this text: "For Adam was formed first, then Eve; and Adam was not deceived, but the woman was deceived and became a transgressor. Yet she will be saved through the childbearing, provided they continue in faith and love and holiness, with modesty" (vv. 13–15). This amounts to something of a midrash, or creative exposition, on portions of Genesis 2:7–3:12, which tells of the Garden of Eden and the tree of the knowledge of good and evil, the creation of Adam and Eve, and their interaction with the serpent. The phrasing in 1 Timothy can be seen as an after-the-fact illustrative paradigm (in this case, a negative one) that provides a further clinching warrant for the imperatives given earlier in the passage, including imperatives against women teaching without first listening and learning, and against usurping other's authority.

In order to understand the use of the story of Adam and Eve here, certain factors not directly mentioned in 1 Timothy are crucial. In the first place, according to Genesis 2:16–17 only Adam received the initial prohibition against eating from the tree of the knowledge of good and evil. Nothing whatsoever is said about God instructing Eve at this juncture; indeed, she had not even been created yet. One is left to assume that it was Adam who told Eve about the prohibition, and apparently he did not do a very clear job of it.

This leads to the next point in 1 Timothy—namely, that Adam was first in creation, but Eve was first in the Fall. In fact, the text says that while Adam was "not deceived" (*epatethe*), Eve was "truly deceived" (*exapatetheisa*). Indeed, so deceived is she said to be that she, to use a literal translation, "happened [or entered] into a state of transgression." This theme of Eve's deception is also found in 2 Corinthians 11:3, where Paul suggests that it could happen to any of the Corinthians, male or female. It is unlikely that Paul thought falling prey to deception was an inherent flaw in women to which men were not subject. Notice that Paul is quite ready to blame Adam for the fall in Romans 5:12–20. I suggest that the reason for the mention that Adam was formed first, before speaking of Eve, is to remind the audience of the context of the story in Genesis 2. That story is quite clear that Adam alone was formed and was present for the original instructions about what was prohibited. Eve was not there for proper divine instruction; hence she was more susceptible to deception. Nothing is said here about the woman being more susceptible *by nature* to deception.

The verb "truly deceived" seems to refer to what happens when someone is misled about something one has been taught, or when one is subject to being misled *because one has not been properly taught in the first place.* Notice that in the Genesis 3 story Eve tells the snake she is not even to touch the apple, something God never told Adam. But where did she get this idea? Surely we are to think that either it came from Adam or she made it up.

With that background, then, the question is, What's the connection between 1 Timothy's verses about Adam and Eve and verse 15? Here much depends on the translation. One could argue that the phrase should be rendered "but she will be kept safe through childbearing" rather than "she will be saved" (as we have it above), seeing here a promise of a reversal of the curse on Eve of pain and danger in childbearing if one is a good Christian woman. Unfortunately, the translation "be kept safe" instead of "be saved" is unlikely here. Our author uses an entirely different word elsewhere for the idea of being kept safe.

We find help in the definite article before the word "childbearing." It prompts us to ask which particular childbearing is meant, especially since the wording is in the singular ("she will be saved"). Surely the answer is Jesus, born of woman, born under the Law (as Galatians 4:4 puts it). In other words, the curse on woman incurred through Eve is reversed through Mary. Human fallenness came through a woman, and so did human salvation. This was the view of many of the church fathers about this verse, not least because they recognized that the pastoral epistles had elsewhere strongly insisted that salvation was by grace through faith, not by producing offspring while maintaining a highly moral lifestyle!

There is, however, a problem with a purely messianic reading of 1 Timothy 2:15—namely, that *gune* here in the singular ought to mean the same thing that it does in 2:11, where it is a generic term for woman. It seems unlikely that Paul is saying "Mary" in particular was saved through the childbearing of Jesus, a reading that puts the focus on her being the type and Eve the antetype. Rather, I would suggest that while the subject in 2:15 is surely women in general (which would *include* Jesus's mother), "the childbearing" is indeed a reference to a particular birth—that of Jesus. The point is that it was through woman the Fall came and through woman redemption came as well. In support of this I note first that the following verb "if *they* continue/remain ..." is in the third-person plural. This is supported by Paul's reference, earlier in 1 Timothy, to the fact that Jesus came to save *sinners* (1:15). Our own text has made emphatic that Eve was indeed the first and paradigmatic sinner. The passage in question concludes then with the affirmation that women, like men, must persevere in the faith.

Thus while there may not be a direct focus on or allusion to Mary in this text, there is certainly an indirect one, since she especially is the one involved in the salvific childbearing, and since here she stands with other women who stand to benefit from that salvific childbearing. Here, then, is a text that helped to spark the later discussion of Mary as *Theotokos*—the "God-bearer." Mary, as "woman" (like all other women), is said to be saved by "the childbearing" that reversed the curse. Whether intentional or not, this text was to prompt the later Christian reflection on Mary as the reverse of Eve, the one who helped bring salvation rather than sin into this world. This in turn also helped prompt the notion of Mary's sinlessness, in contrast to Eve's corruption as the primordial sinner.

WHAT WE'VE LEARNED AND WHAT THAT KNOWLEDGE TELLS US ABOUT JESUS

We may be tempted to say—what a long, strange trip Mary's pilgrimage to faith in her son and service to her Lord was. But we have highlighted some interesting points. Mary does not seem to have been a full-fledged disciple until at or after the death of Jesus. The fact that neither she nor his brothers or sisters were among his disciples before that must have been a cause of some frustration and sadness to Jesus—a sadness reflected in his prophets-in-their-hometown remark. But Mary at least never gave up on Jesus, though she kept trying to intervene in his life in ways that were not always helpful or appropriate. And Jesus remained a good son, taking care of his mother at the end even though she did not fully understand him and his ministry.

Mary is not depicted as the mother of the church in the New Testament, but she is depicted as a spiritual mother in the church, a symbol whose experience mirrors and illustrates that of the church and of all women. As such, she can be seen as a model of discipleship for women especially, perhaps in particular in regard to how they can exercise their maternal instincts in a spiritual way that benefits the church at large—that is, the family of faith—not just their own family.

We have seen plenty of evidence that Mary was a pious Jewish woman who had visions, went on pilgrimage, engaged in Jewish rituals, listened to prophets, and tried to protect her son, the Son of God, from potential harm. She was often found in the presence of her other children, particularly in and near her hometown of Nazareth. We find her in the upper room praying with others for the decision-making process of picking leaders, and we have no reason to doubt that the Holy Spirit fell on her, as it did on all the others at Pentecost. Finally, she was a full-fledged follower of Jesus and could be a spiritual mother to others.

It is conjectural, but there is a tradition that suggests Mary left the Holy Land and went to Asia with the Beloved Disciple. This may well be true, for we hear nothing about her in Acts after Acts 1:14, and Luke's chronicle does not take us up to the Jewish War in A.D. 66, when the Jews revolted against their Roman overlords in the Holy Land, or to the death of Paul and Peter at about that same time. We will never know for sure. But clearly more light can be shed on the inner circle of Jesus if we seek to plumb the depths of the figure called the Beloved Disciple. To this we must turn in a moment, but here is the place to say something about later Marian traditions.

The New Testament says nothing about Mary's parents, her immaculate conception, her perpetual virginity, her continuing role in heaven as a person to whom prayers can be directed, and the like. The real problem for several of these notions is not so much that they aren't mentioned in the New Testament, however; it is that what the New Testament *does* say about Mary does not suggest she took a vow of virginity, or that she shared the sinlessness of her son, or that she had a later special role in heaven. If thinking your son is mad and shouldn't be involved in exorcisms isn't a sin in the moral sense, it is at least an example of being severely out of tune with the truth about Jesus. The New Testament leaves the impression that Mary doesn't become a disciple of Jesus and really understand him until the end of his life. Furthermore, the New Testament, with its mention of brothers and sisters of Jesus who are always in the presence of Mary (when they certainly could have been called cousins or children of Joseph only, if that's what they were), suggests that Mary assumed the rather normal role of a Jewish mother—bearing and raising various children, Jesus being the eldest.

It is important to say, on the other hand, that the New Testament rightly makes much of Mary as the mother of Jesus, much of her faithfulness to respond to the angelic message; she is rightly seen as an image or symbol for the church, the body of true disciples of Jesus. This is important, especially since she presents us with an image of a female disciple. The ideas of Mary being a perpetual virgin and Joseph becoming an ascetic do not develop until the Proto-Evangelium of James, toward the end of the second century (and well after the ascetical movement had begun in Christianity). These ideas reflect a change in views of human sexuality that happened in Christianity once it ceased to be a subset or sect of Judaism—which is to say, once it became a predominantly Gentile entity. The more you view Mary in the light of life in early Judaism, the less likely it becomes that these later ideas reflect the historical situation of Mary's life. Rather, they reflect the developing piety of the second-century church, a piety that would continue to develop along that same trajectory, well into the Middle Ages.

What does all this discussion tell us about Jesus? For one thing, we learn that Jesus did not simply play the role of the traditional eldest son who takes over the family business once the father dies. Jesus, instead, sets out to preach and teach and heal throughout Galilee, and he receives a cold reception when he returns to his home synagogue. He even suggests that he was without honor within his own home. And his family found his exorcisms troubling, though Mary seems to have had no qualms about asking Jesus to perform a miracle in Cana. To what should we attribute this misunderstanding of Jesus, even on the part of Mary? Luke 2 suggests she was pondering what he would be like and what he would do but could not take it all in. The Simeon story in that chapter suggests that she was even warned that Jesus would become a catalyst for great historical change and that this would lead to a deep wounding of her self. But she could not have anticipated that her son would be crucified. It does not appear that anyone in early Judaism was looking for a crucified messiah, for they did not understand Isaiah 53 to be disussing the messiah. This was apparently something that Jesus first contemplated.

We also learn from John 19:25–27 that of course Jesus continued to care about his mother right to the end of his life, even if the relationship was strained. While the family of faith had become Jesus's primary family, he deeply desired his physical family to be part of that community, and so in the end it came to pass, partly through his own actions. Finally, Acts 1:14 reminds us in a pertinent way that something dramatic must have happened to Jesus beyond the horrors of crucifixion. Otherwise, we would not find his mother and brothers in the upper room awaiting the anointing from on high long after the crucifixion. What we know of the trials and tribulations of the mother of Jesus provides us with an indirect witness to the truth of the creed: "crucified under Pontius Pilate, dead, and buried, the third day he arose from the dead." Mary, too, came to see Jesus in light of the resurrection and, with her other children, truly became his disciple and one of the first "Christians" in Jerusalem.

But what of Mary's relationship with the Beloved Disciple? And who was he anyway? To this we must now turn.

PART FOUR

THE DISCIPLE WHOM JESUS LOVED

SEVEN

Unknown but Beloved

There are many Johns in the New Testament, the most prominent of whom are John the Baptist, John son of Zebedee (one of the Twelve), and John Mark, the author of the earliest gospel and the sometime companion of Paul and Barnabas. To this we may add John of Patmos, if he is someone different than John son of Zebedee. We may certainly conclude that John was a popular name among Jews in that era! But which John is the one associated with the Fourth Gospel? And if that John is the same as the Beloved Disciple, why doesn't the text of the Fourth Gospel indicate this directly? Furthermore, should we assume that the person who wrote the book of Revelation is the same as the person responsible for the Fourth Gospel? And what about the "old man" or "elder" who authored the Johannine letters? Is he any of the above Johns? It's hard to tell the players here without a program. Let's begin with a brief orienting summary and then move on to unpack the relevant data.

First, the only New Testament document that specifically mentions a John being involved with it is the book of Revelation. Revelation 1:1 refers to the servant John who received the revelation. Depicted as a prophet or seer, this John—John of Patmos—is never called an apostle or identified with John son of Zebedee. In fact, the majority of scholars who have studied Revelation have concluded with good reason that its language and style are so different from the other Johannine documents that it is unlikely that John of Patmos wrote those other texts.

Second, though this will come as a surprise to some, both the Fourth Gospel and the Johannine epistles are formally anonymous—that is, no author is named within their texts. The superscripts to these documents (by which I mean wording such as "The Gospel according to John," or "The Second Letter of John") were added after the fact, probably in the second century, based on ideas that some early Christians had about who may have written these documents. We must bear in mind, however, that these are later *guesses,* sometimes based on oral tradition, sometimes not.

Nothing in the documents themselves indicates that John son of Zebedee is the author. In fact, the Fourth Gospel suggests that it may have been penned by the Beloved Disciple, who is not mentioned until John 11 or perhaps John 13. The Johannine epistles give us only a slight clue to authorship, calling the author "the old man" or "the elder," but the majority of scholars are convinced that these letters are close enough in style and substance that they seem to go back to the same person who wrote the Fourth Gospel—the Beloved Disciple apparently.

There are a variety of good reasons to think that this author is not John son of Zebedee, not the least of which is that the Fourth Gospel leaves out all the special Zebedee stories we find in the synoptics involving events that John was a special eyewitness of (for example, the raising of Jairus's daughter, the transfiguration, and the request for special seats in the kingdom). Yet there is a strong stress in the Fourth Gospel on the author being an eyewitness of other events in the life of Jesus. The most reasonable conclusions are the following: (1) John of Patmos wrote Revelation but not the gospel or epistles of John; (2) the Fourth Gospel and the Johannine epistles were not written by John son of Zebedee either; (3) rather, those documents were penned by the Beloved Disciple, who is someone else—a Judean disciple of Jesus, as we shall see.

Now let's unpack these ideas a bit more. Bear in mind that we are dealing with a mystery wrapped in an enigma, to borrow an old phrase. We must look closely at this question of who the Beloved Disciple may be and which parts of the Johannine corpus he may have generated. The urgency of doing so should be clear: whatever else one can say, he was an intimate of Jesus and of Mary. We are clearly in the inner circle and the inner sanctum of Jesus when we are dealing with him.

I use the word "him" advisedly. Some have conjectured that the reason for the anonymity here is that the Beloved Disciple was a woman—specifically, Mary Magdalene. The problem with this conjecture is that it crashes on the hard rocks of the text of John 19:25–27, which names both Mary Magdalene and separately the Beloved Disciple, who is called Mary's "son," standing at the foot of the cross. In addition, we know that the Beloved Disciple was someone who hosted the meal recounted in John 13 and reclined with Jesus on a couch. In early Jewish society, which was a very stratified culture with specific male-female boundaries, a woman could not have reclined with Jesus. Indeed, women were not likely to be reclining at this meal at all, even separately; if traditional Jewish protocol was being followed, they were more likely to be serving.[147] Finally, most scholars think that the Johannine epistles were written by the same person who was identified as the source of the Fourth Gospel materials, who called himself an old man or male church elder (*ho presbuteros*). Clearly this person was not a woman.

An equally unfruitful conjecture is that the Beloved Disciple was an ideal figure of a disciple, not a real person. This theory also crashes on the hard rocks of John 19:25–27, which says that Jesus turned over his mother to this quite specific person; and again, Jesus reclined at table with this person. Furthermore, John 21 suggests that this person was fishing with Peter in Galilee on one occasion when Jesus appeared. No, this is not an ideal figure of a disciple; it is a real person whose community dubbed him the Beloved Disciple, though as noted above, at the time of the epistles he called himself simply an old man or elder. Who then could he be?

JOHN OF PATMOS AND THE JOHANNINE CIRCLE

It is important in a historical study like this to move from the more certain to the less certain, so we will begin with John of Patmos. As the vast majority of scholars recognize, Revelation is not a pseudonymous document. Its author identifies himself at the beginning of the work as someone named John. But which John? Later Christian tradition identified him as John son of Zebedee, but this notion developed at least a half century after Revelation was written (the earliest possible witnesses are Justin Martyr and Irenaeus from the mid and late second century, respectively— Justin, *Dial.* 81.4; Irenaeus, *Adv. Haer.* 4.20.11) and during an era when connecting sacred documents to apostolic witnesses was considered crucial, especially if such documents were to be given some sort of canonical status.[148] There was an urgency on the part of the orthodox to connect the Fourth Gospel to one of the Twelve or an eyewitness, especially because the Gnostics liked this Gospel too much.

How then does the author actually identify himself? At the outset John claims to be a visionary and a testifier and a servant. If that latter term was intended to carry the fuller resonance it sometimes does in the Old Testament prophetic corpus, in the Pauline writings, and elsewhere, he is claiming also to be a prophet. References in Revelation 10:11 and 22:9 make it apparent that this is the way the author chiefly views himself. In short, the author is John the seer, who offers up prophetic testimonies and proclamations.

The discussion of which John this might be has been necessarily complicated by the attempt to try to figure out the interrelationships among all the writings that came to be associated with the name John, only one of which—Revelation—explicitly names its author John. Linguistic study of these writings makes it quite unlikely that these five documents were all written by the same person. These differences were noticed as early as the middle of the third century by Dionysius of Alexandria, who was then quoted favorably by Eusebius. Various differences in diction, for example, rather strongly favor the conclusion that the person who produced the final form of Revelation did not also author the other Johannine documents, which among themselves *are* similar. Yet it is also true that there are terms like *Logos* that are applied to Christ only in the Fourth Gospel and in Revelation. In addition, there are passages that reveal similarities of diction and usage between those two works.[149]

The question, then, is how to explain the similarities as well as the differences between these works. While a person's style does evolve over time, a total change in style and usage is most unlikely. And that's the sort of change we're talking about. The gospel is written in rather plain and simple Koine (a common form of Greek), whereas Revelation uses a vocabulary that is complex and a syntax that is often prolix.[150] For example, one out of every eight words in Revelation is a word found nowhere else in the New Testament. Only some of this can be explained by the different subject matter in Revelation and the Fourth Gospel and Epistles.[151] On the whole, then, this internal evidence strongly favors the conclusion that the person who wrote Revelation did not also write the Fourth Gospel or the epistles. Nonetheless, John the seer apparently has some sort of relationship with those who wrote the rest of the Johannine corpus and/or with their communities.

In my view John the seer is a prophet from the Johannine community operating at a time when there was no apostolic presence left in that community. (See, for example, Revelation 22:14, which views apostles as a foundation of the church, apparently in the past.) Were this man John son of Zebedee, it would be passing strange that he does not identify himself as an apostle or as an original disciple of Jesus in the letter portion of Revelation, where credentials would have contributed to the rhetorical establishment of the author's authority in relationship to his audience. Nor does he identify himself as the old man/elder, as the author of the epistles does. In fact, there is nothing in Revelation that establishes John's *personal* authority. His vision has the authority of a revelation from Jesus for which John is the mouthpiece—which is to say, he reflects the derived authority of a prophet. This leads to two conclusions: John of Patmos is not likely John son of Zebedee; and it is even less likely that he is the Beloved Disciple or the old man/elder of the Johannine epistles.

THE OLD MAN AND THE BELOVED DISCIPLE

It seems unlikely that the Beloved Disciple is the same person as John son of Zebedee. I come to this conclusion because the Fourth Gospel has all sorts of unique traditions about what Jesus did in Jerusalem and its environs; and yet it has none of the special Zebedee Galilee traditions we find in the synoptic gospels, as noted earlier, nor does it have the synoptics' Galilean miracle tales (with the exception of the tandem feeding of the five thousand/walking on water).

Since the John to whom tradition attributed the Fourth Gospel and the Johannine letters was not specified, there was considerable controversy in the early church about whether John the elder was the same person as John son of Zebedee. Even as late as the time of Eusebius, it was debated whether 2 John and 3 John should be included within the canon because of their author's old man/elder designation,[152] whereas the Fourth Gospel and 1 John were not disputed in this way, it having been assumed they were penned by John the apostle, son of Zebedee. In fact, we can go well after the time of Eusebius and hear Bede in the eighth century still saying about 2 and 3 John, "Some think that this and the following letter are not of John the Apostle but of a certain John the Presbyter, whose tomb has been pointed out in Ephesus up to the present day. Indeed, Papias, a hearer of the Apostles and bishop in Hierapolis, frequently mentions him in his works. But now the general consensus of the church is that John the Apostle also wrote these letters."[153]

The problem with this entire debate is that it is hard to deny that the vocabulary and style of the three letters is similar enough to suggest a common author, and at the same time there is enough similarity between the gospel and especially 1 John to suggest a common author or source for these documents as well. Some have argued that the style of the Johannine epistles places these letters into the category of an assumed higher style chosen for some particular rhetorical aim or end, but in my view that is not the case. That there is rhetoric, and indeed rhetoric of some finesse, is clear. However, the letters should not be seen as examples of "speech in character," as if the writer were speaking in someone else's voice. In other words, the style appears to be genuine, not a matter of artifice, and so it tells us something about the author.

The "old man" speaks for himself quite clearly and directly. He sees himself as an authority figure who can address both local and more remote congregations in a definitive way. It is my view that these letters provide us with a glimpse of the author and his view of his audiences probably sometime in the 80s. The elder, or old man, is addressing congregations that are experiencing serious internal difficulties and that are familiar with many of the traditions later (perhaps in the early 90s) enshrined in the Fourth Gospel. At a still later date—in the middle 90s and during the reign of Domitian—John of Patmos was to address some of these same communities, drawing on the Johannine tradition in some respects, but making his own modifications.

Let's assume, then, that the same person wrote both the Fourth Gospel and the Johannine epistles, and that he's a different man than both John son of Zebedee and John of Patmos. Now the question becomes, Is the elder the Beloved Disciple?

To answer that question, we have to know more about the Beloved Disciple. Most scholars will say that he is first mentioned directly in John 13:23, where he's depicted as reclining next to Jesus at the meal mentioned earlier. This has also led to the conclusion that he must be one of the Twelve, since this is the Last Supper meal—or is it? We have here nothing like the so-called words of institution: "This is my body…. This is my blood." In fact, we are told in John 13:1 that this meal transpired before the beginning of the Passover festival—in other words, earlier in Holy Week. Prior to this meal, the last meal mentioned that Jesus took was at the house of Lazarus, Mary, and Martha in Bethany, just outside of Jerusalem. John 12:2b, which tells of that early meal, reads very much like John 13:23. There is another important connection between the meal at that household and the meal in John 13. The latter account refers to "the one whom Jesus loved." It is incorrect to say that this is the first time in this gospel that such a phrase has come up. We in fact find it on the lips of Mary and Martha in John 11:3: they importune Jesus, begging him to come because "the one whom you love is ill." Can this be mere coincidence? Since the author of these gospel traditions tends to do nothing by accident, and much that he writes is highly symbolic, I doubt it. If we link John 11:3 with John 12:2b and 13:23 in that order (which is how the texts would have been heard, since this gospel was used as an oral narrative to proclaim the Good News), it seems more than reasonable to conclude that our author indirectly tips his hand here: when he refers to "the Beloved Disciple," he means Lazarus, a Judean disciple.

This conclusion explains much about this disciple and this gospel. Lazarus had a close, indeed intimate, relationship with Jesus such that he was singled out as one whom Jesus especially loved, but he was not one of the Twelve. Rather, he was a Judean eyewitness of Jesus's ministry. This conclusion also explains why it is that this gospel is bereft of so many of the Galilean miracle accounts and various other Galilean tales. Instead we have Judean miracle tales about the man born blind, the man at the pool of Siloam, and of course the raising of Lazarus. And of course, if the Beloved Disciple is the one who took Mary into his own home, we know now how he learned of the Cana miracle tale: from Mary herself. But there is more.

This person had direct access to the house of Caiaphas the high priest, so that he could follow Jesus in after his arrest, as John tells us in 18:15.[154] Would a Galilean fisherman have had such access, or is it more probable that a Judean follower of Jesus—one who lived in the vicinity of Jerusalem—would? Surely in terms of historical probabilities the latter is more likely. Consider as well the fact that the synoptics are quite clear that while the Twelve had deserted Jesus and were not present at his crucifixion, the Beloved Disciple is clearly there near the cross. If those accounts are right, then the Beloved Disciple cannot be one of the Twelve. Or again consider the tradition suggested in John 21:22–23 that the Beloved Disciple would not die until Jesus returned. Surely such a tradition would be *more* likely to arise about a person who both had been raised from the dead by Jesus and had lived to a considerable old age. On the basis of cumulative evidence, I conclude that it is likely that the Beloved Disciple was a Judean eyewitness and disciple of the ministry of Jesus, who could testify to what Jesus said and did, particularly when he was in the vicinity of Jerusalem; and the most likely candidate to be this disciple is the one whom John 11:2 says Jesus especially loved—Lazarus.

CRY FOR THE BELOVED DISCIPLE (JOHN 11:1–44)

We are now in a position to review data from the Fourth Gospel and the Johannine epistles to see what more we can learn about this intimate of Jesus, beginning with John 11.[155] In the following chapter we will consider the Beloved Disciple's later ministry in Ephesus and its environs, but here we must focus on the gospel tales.

The story of the raising of Lazarus in John 11 is the climax of the so-called book of signs—that is, the first half of the Fourth Gospel, which records the seven sign miracles. This climax is no surprise at all if the person raised is the author of the traditions in this gospel. He would naturally include (indeed highlight) his own story in the narrative. In addition, this narrative deliberately foreshadows what will happen to Jesus, not only in the death and resurrection of Lazarus but also in the anointing of Jesus, which foreshadows his burial. We have met Lazarus's sisters elsewhere in the Lukan narrative, in Luke 10:38–42, and that earlier characterization matches up remarkably well with the portrayal here. We know, then, that this was a Judean family of Jesus's disciples with whom he had a special relationship.

The Lazarus account is the longest continuous narrative in this entire gospel, which makes sense if it is a firsthand report from the author and his family about what happened. It is also the most miraculous of the sign narratives. The story begins on an ominous note. Lazarus, the one whom Jesus loves, is very ill, so Mary and Martha send a messenger pleading for Jesus to race to Bethany. Their message to Jesus—"He whom you love is ill"—is as open-ended as Mary's announcement to Jesus that the folks in Cana have run out of wine (compare 11:3 and 2:3). Likewise, Martha's later statement that God will grant whatever Jesus wishes parallels Mary's instruction to the servants in Cana: "Do whatever he tells you" (compare 11:22 and 2:5). In both stories the hope is that Jesus will find a way to act despite the apparently hopeless nature of the situation. Just as the best wine was saved for last in John 2, so here the best miracle is saved for last. Just as Jesus brought new life to the wedding party celebrating the union of two lives, so here he brings new life quite literally and reunion to a family he has known and loved. But it is one of the major themes of this gospel that Jesus can act only when the Father gives him the go-ahead, not when a human being—whether his mother, a brother, or a disciple—importunes him. Thus, while it may appear that Jesus is unfeeling toward someone he is said to love, in actuality he is simply obeying the Father's directives.

The case of Mary, Martha, and Lazarus demonstrates that there were stay-at-home disciples of Jesus from the first; not all the disciples traveled with Jesus. But Jesus was in their home on more than one occasion, as Luke 10 and John 12 show. Nonetheless, Lazarus is introduced as a new character in the narrative in John 11:1–44, though the audience is expected to know who Mary is: "the one who anointed the Lord with perfume."[156] Almost immediately Lazarus is named as the one whom Jesus loved—the only male disciple in this entire gospel to be so singled out by name as one whom Jesus loved. This fact is so striking that we have to account for it.

This story is filled with pathos. Not only do Mary and Martha lose Lazarus, but they may also lose their right to the property they have been inhabiting. Males were normally the heirs of all property in that culture, in order to keep it in a particular kin group. The focus of the story, though, is on the faith response (or lack thereof) of Mary and Martha.[157] We are not told what illness Lazarus suffers from, but it proves to be fatal.[158]

Jesus, hearing that Lazarus is ill, makes the astonishing pronounce-ment that it is for God's glory. What he seems to mean is that God will use this occasion to reveal his life-giving and powerful nature. In any event, Jesus remains two more days where he is before announcing that he is going back to Judea. His disciples are dismayed, for they fear the Jewish officials there.[159] Thomas finally says, "Let us also go, that we may die with him." The portrait of Thomas here comports with what we find later in John 20. He is skeptical and lacks faith. His response to Jesus's announce-ment should not be seen as an indication of courage.

When Jesus finally arrives in Bethany (which is described as two miles from Jerusalem), Lazarus has already been in the tomb for four days. This is significant because some early Jews believed that the spirit of the deceased departed after three days, and at that juncture there was no hope of resuscitation.[160] We are then told that many Jews (again, likely a refer-ence to Jewish officials) had come to mourn with the family. This and the story in John 12 about anointing Jesus's feet with costly nard both suggest that we are dealing with a family of considerable social status, well known in Jerusalem, which comports with the Beloved Disciple knowing Caiaphas the high priest. Grieving would normally go on for about a week after someone of importance passed away. Thus this process is still in full swing on the fourth day after Lazarus has died, when Jesus arrives.

It is interesting that the two sisters have the same lament, almost word for word, for Jesus: "Lord, if you had been here my brother would not have died." Martha adds, "I know that he will rise again in the resurrection on the last day." This faith statement should not be taken to mean that Martha is expecting Jesus to raise Lazarus on the spot. Rather, she expects perhaps a promise that he will be raised with the righteous on the last day. This becomes clear when she objects to Jesus having the tomb opened, as there will be a foul odor of the decaying corpse. Early Jews did not have the embalming arts that Egyptians did. They simply used spices in the wind-ing sheet to retard the odor, especially during the mourning period. But here the tomb is already sealed up with a stone, meaning that no one is attending to or visiting the body at this juncture. The objections of the sis-ters reflect the fact that they do not yet understand that *Jesus is the resurrec-tion and the life.* Contact with Jesus produces miraculous results, even for a man four days dead.

The theme of Jesus's great love for this family is continued as Jesus weeps (apparently in part over the lack of faith of those around him). Nev-ertheless, whether the faith exhibited is weak or lacking in this case, Jesus will act; and he raises Lazarus. Not surprisingly, the response to Jesus's great miracle is mixed—some put their faith in Jesus, and some go to the officials, precipitating the council that leads to Jesus's arrest, trial, and execution. The raising of Lazarus is apparently the straw that breaks the camel's back for the officials.

This leads to a further point. Skipping ahead again to Caiaphas's house on the day of Jesus's arrest, if the man mentioned there with Peter is in fact Lazarus, we can understand why he is there. It is talk of his own resuscitation that has led to the arrest of Jesus, and perhaps he is seeking to head off disaster. He is known to the high priest, after all. Perhaps he has even heard rumors of a plan to try to kill him (that is, Lazarus) as well, as John reports in 12:10—the ultimate irony. But what sort of plan could it be to execute a man who had been raised from the dead, as if death could put a stop to what Jesus was doing?

Some have objected that Lazarus could not have been the man who went to the high priest; they claim that a former dead man would not have been allowed into Caiaphas's house, especially if it was leprosy (see Mark 14:1–3) that killed him. But that objection is unwarranted. A good Jew would rid himself of a state of ritual uncleanness by going through the *mikvah,* the ritual purification bath, offering a sacrifice, and asking a local priest to certify that he was "clean" and free of disease or unclean spirits. We may presume that Lazarus, being a good Jew, went through these steps; and since he lived near Jerusalem, we may assume that the priest in question had passed on this information to the high priest in Jerusalem.

BANQUETING WITH THE DEAD (JOHN 12:1–11)

The story of the meal in John 12 begins as though it's a separate tale ("Six days before the Passover Jesus arrived in Bethany, where Lazarus lived …"), and so it probably is. In all likelihood the placement of the Lazarus story is theological rather than chronological: it provides a fitting climax to the narration of the sign miracles and aptly foreshadows what will transpire with Jesus. This then means that the meal takes place some considerable time later than the raising. The meal is in fact said to be given in Jesus's honor, not as a celebration of Lazarus's raising. Still, the gospel writer pointedly remarks that Lazarus is reclining at table with Jesus, a comment that prepares us for the Beloved Disciple reclining with Jesus at what many assume to be the Last Supper in John 13:23. Now, it is important to note the protocol for such banquets, the pecking order that determines where the guests sit: the host normally reclines on the couch with or next to the chief guest. This strongly suggests that the Beloved Disciple is the host at the meal depicted in that later account, meaning that it takes place in his home—that is, in the home of a Judean disciple, not a Galilean one.

But back to John 12:1–11, which includes not only a shared meal but the anointing of Jesus by Mary. This story is more circumstantial than other anointing stories in the New Testament, and it names the woman who anointed Jesus—Mary of Bethany. The other stories include a Markan account that looks to be an abstraction from the original eyewitness tale (which we find here) and a Lukan account that relates a different sort of anointing at a different house by a different woman—a sinful one.[161]

The irony in this story is thick, for Jesus in effect interprets Mary's act as anointing him for burial as he sits next to the man he just raised from the dead! Mary here takes the role a servant would normally play. Anointing a person's feet was done for hygienic purposes, to keep the skin from cracking due to the heat, and it was an especially welcome gesture of hospitality. However, in our story, Mary has chosen not to use ordinary olive oil but rather nard, an expensive perfume, the ancient equivalent of Chanel No. 5.[162] It was something someone would normally use in small quantities only, and certainly not for anointing feet. Mary uses a whole pound—much more than she needs to use. So her gesture is meant to be seen as an extravagant act rather than a normal act of hospitality. It is a gesture of great love, and presumably gratitude for what Jesus did for Lazarus. When Judas Iscariot complains about the waste, Jesus deflects his criticism by making the novel suggestion that Mary is anointing Jesus in advance for his burial. This is the probable meaning of "Leave her alone; let her keep it," since the ointment itself has all been poured out.[163] This burial comment more closely links the story of Lazarus, sitting next to Jesus and recently out of the tomb, with Jesus, soon to enter a tomb.

For our purposes the importance of this narrative is twofold. First, it demonstrates the ongoing relationship of Jesus with this Bethany family, whose home he was in on more than one occasion. This is a family Jesus cared greatly about, an intimate part of his family of faith. Second, as noted earlier, this story establishes Lazarus as one who reclines with Jesus at meals, which prepares us for the Beloved Disciple reference in John 13. John 11 (the account of Lazarus's raising) prepared us for John 13 by naming Lazarus as one whom Jesus loved—the only male so named in this gospel. Now John 12 further prepares us by indicating that their relationship included sharing a couch in a dining setting. We then have the two clues we need for the story in that next chapter.

THE LONG FAREWELL (JOHN 13–21)

One of the objections, perhaps the major one, to seeing Lazarus as the Beloved Disciple is that John 13:23 does not mention him by name. This is not a very compelling objection for the very good reason that we know not only that the Beloved Disciple is the one whose memoirs are enshrined in this eyewitness gospel testimony but also that he was *not* responsible for the final compiling and editing of his memoirs. Other references make this abundantly clear. Notice, for example, how the Beloved Disciple is spoken of in the third person in John 19:35: "The man who saw this has given testimony, and his testimony is true." This would be a strange way for Lazarus to speak of himself. Or again in John 21:24 even more clearly: "This is the disciple who testifies to these things and wrote them down. We know his testimony is true." Who is the "we" here? Clearly it is someone or some ones distinguishable from the Beloved Disciple. The most reasonable conjecture is that "we" is the community of which this man was later a part and that it assembled his testimony after he died.

It is quite believable that that community, in love and reverence for their founder, called this man the Beloved Disciple; it is much more difficult to believe, with all that Jesus said about servanthood and humility, that there was a disciple who singled himself out with the title "the one whom Jesus loved [best or most]." In other words, phrases such as "the one whom Jesus loved" and "the other disciple" weren't *self*-references; they were ways that this community referred to their founder. Lazarus, on the other hand, identified himself simply as Lazarus. This gospel in various ways reflects both the original source, Lazarus—as well as redaction by a later hand (something we see, for example, in the advance reference to Mary's anointing in John 11:2). And perhaps we know who gathered Lazarus's memories and edited them—John of Patmos when he returned to Ephesus after Emperor Domitian died. This would explain why this gospel was labeled in the second century as written by an elderly John.

The good historian will do his best to account for all the data with an adequate theory. In my view, the theory that best incorporates the data suggests that Lazarus, the Judean disciple, is the source of this gospel material, some parts of which reflect his hand more directly than others, and that someone else edited and preserved the traditions he wrote down— perhaps John of Patmos. Bearing these things in mind, we can now look at the rest of the stories about the Beloved Disciple through the eyes of the community—as they saw him playing a crucial role during the last week of Jesus's life, at the cross, at the empty tomb, encountering the risen Jesus.

It was these things that equipped him to bear witness to Jesus, even though he was not one of the Twelve. (In this respect he was somewhat in the position of Paul, who likewise never claimed to be one of the Twelve.) Indeed, in due course, the Beloved Disciple was to call himself the old man/elder, as suggested earlier.

John 13:21–27 is a very interesting story, because it suggests that the Beloved Disciple is one of Jesus's confidants, one whom the others trust to ask Jesus the awkward question of who will betray him, and one to whom he directly entrusts the information that the betrayer is Judas. The portrayal of the Beloved Disciple in this account is tender. He is said to recline on Jesus—indeed, to recline on Jesus's bosom—and this surely recalls John 1:18, where Jesus himself is said to be in the bosom of his Father. This disciple is much like his master. G. R. Beasley-Murray observes, "The Evangelist introduces the Beloved Disciple as standing in analogous relationship to Jesus as Jesus to the Father with respect to the revelation he was sent to make known; behind this gospel is the testimony of the one who was 'close to the heart' of Jesus."[164]

If one envisions that the Beloved Disciple is introduced here to the audience, it is certainly not likely that he should be seen as synonymous with John son of Zebedee. The outsider hearing this tale would never have guessed that identification, whereas if he had already heard John 11–12, he might well guess it was Lazarus. This story suggests that the Beloved Disciple is from Judea, if he is the host of this meal, which is why he reclines with Jesus. Notice that nothing in John 13 suggests that this is a meal confined to the Twelve and Jesus. Indeed, the host of a Passover or earlier festival meal would normally be present with those who were feasting in his house. But which of the Twelve had a house in Jerusalem? Fishermen from Galilee are unlikely candidates.

We do not hear of this disciple again until John 18:15–16, where Peter and "another disciple" follow Jesus into Caiaphas's house. That he is the same person as the Beloved Disciple is made perfectly clear in John 20:2, where Mary Magdalene runs to Peter "and the other disciple, the one whom Jesus loved." What is interesting about the portrayal here and in John 20–21 is that the Beloved Disciple comes across as being more in the know than Peter, having more contacts and recognition in Jerusalem than Peter, being closer to Jesus than Peter, being less problematic than Peter, not denying Jesus like Peter, not needing to be restored like Peter, and knowing how to get to Jesus's tomb faster than Peter. Taken together, we may see this portrayal as an attempt by the later Johannine community to help legitimize itself, even though their founder was not one of the Twelve.

That he is nonetheless a disciple is implied in 18:17, where Peter is asked, "You are not *also* one of his disciples, are you?" Though Peter denies Jesus, the Beloved Disciple never does—indeed, among the men he is last at the cross and first at the empty tomb.

In our study of Mary, we already examined John 19:25–27 (which puts Mary and the Beloved Disciple near the cross) so we need not traverse that ground again, but here we can say that Jesus's decision to entrust his mother to the Beloved Disciple showed extraordinary trust in the man from Bethany. Jesus's trust speaks volumes about his friend. He was not only the one whom Jesus loved; he was the one whom Jesus trusted with his other loved ones.

John 19:34–35 brings us once more in contact with our man. This time he is depicted as one who saw the piercing of Jesus's side and watched the blood and water flow forth. This is interesting in light of the later reflections we find in 1 John 5:6–9, a passage we will take up in the next chapter. This scene is important because it bears witness to the true humanity of Jesus; he is no apparition on the cross, a theme heavily stressed in 1 John.[165] Here our man is depicted as reflecting on the mystery and meaning of the Passion of Jesus, and he affirms that his testimony about this event is truthful. In subsequent verses he notes that it was he who understood, perhaps later under the guidance of the Spirit, how scripture was being fulfilled in what was happening to Jesus on the cross.

Not only is the Beloved Disciple, unlike the Twelve and the brothers of Jesus, present when Jesus dies; he is also the one, along with Peter, to whom Mary Magdalene comes running to announce the empty tomb in John 20:2. Hearing the news, he outruns Peter to the tomb, though Peter enters the tomb first. Neither of these men sees the angelic presence that Mary will see, but the text tells us that the Beloved Disciple "saw and believed" (20:8). But believed what?

The next verse says quite explicitly that the disciples did not yet understand from the scriptures that Jesus must rise from the dead. Is the Beloved Disciple being depicted here as believing in the resurrection of Jesus on the basis of the evidence of the empty tomb rather than on the basis of scripture? Various scholars have thought so.[166] It is more likely, however, that what is meant is that the Beloved Disciple believed that Jesus's life had come to an orderly conclusion and that Jesus, perhaps like Elijah, was being taken up into the presence of God. Had Jesus not previously spoken of being taken up into the presence of the Father? Unlike Mary Magdalene, the Beloved Disciple does not suspect that the body has been stolen or moved somewhere. He simply goes home trusting all is well, as 20:10 suggests.[167]

We encounter this disciple one final time in John 21:7, in the account where Jesus appears to the disciples as they are unsuccessfully fishing (an account we looked at in our earlier discussion of Peter). The Beloved Disciple hears Jesus call to them from the shore and says to Peter, "It is the Lord!" He is not named in 21:1, which lists a number of fishermen by name and adds that "two other disciples" are present. The Zebedees are mentioned together not separately in that list, and no attempt is made to connect the reference to them in verse 1 to the reference in verse 7 to the Beloved Disciple. In fact, this is the only clear reference to the Zebedees in the whole gospel! This certainly suggests that the Gospel of John was *not* written by John son of Zebedee—especially since John 21 is a epilogue, likely added later to the bulk of the Johannine stories.

It is likely, then, that our author is one of the two unnamed disciples referred to in verse 1. Verse 7 depicts the Beloved Disciple as a person who recognizes the voice of Jesus, as every good disciple is said to do—only here he is the *only* one who does so (cf. John 10:4). The story thereafter focuses primarily on the restoration of Peter, though the Beloved Disciple comes up again in verses 20–23, a passage that we will consider later. It seems likely, given those later verses, that this chapter was added to this gospel material to clear up how it could be that the Beloved Disciple had died and yet Jesus had not yet returned. One can see how such a question would arise if *Lazarus* was the Beloved Disciple and Jesus had raised him from the dead. Surely (the thinking would be) he would not have died again before Jesus came back. I will say more about this at the conclusion of the next chapter.

WHAT WE'VE LEARNED AND WHAT THAT KNOWLEDGE TELLS US ABOUT JESUS

Jesus had various close disciples. Some were from Galilee, like the Twelve and Mary Magdalene; some were from Judea, like Lazarus and his two sisters. In this chapter, I have made the case for one of those close disciples being the man whom Jesus raised from the dead in Bethany—Lazarus. I have argued that the evidence of this gospel taken as a whole certainly does not point to the Beloved Disciple being a Galilean disciple, much less John of Zebedee, but rather a Judean disciple, most likely Lazarus.

We have examined a series of important texts in this gospel and considered detailed questions regarding the authorship of the various Johannine documents. All this evidence points in one particular direction: the Beloved Disciple was an important follower of Jesus, not to be equated with either John of Patmos or John son of Zebedee. This disciple in fact was so important that Jesus entrusted his own mother into the man's hands when Jesus died. As we shall see in the next chapter, he then took his gospel to Asia, where he founded the Johannine community, a community made up of a network of churches, largely comprised of Jewish Christians. Johannine Christianity, like Pauline Christianity, was to prove to be a major stream of the early Christian movement. Yet neither community was instigated or led by one of the Twelve! This is a point worth stressing. Much of the westward spread of the Christian faith was due to the work of believers who were not members of the Twelve!

We cannot know how close Jesus and Lazarus really were. We cannot know how often Jesus visited with Lazarus and his sisters. We cannot say how involved Lazarus was with the disciples in Galilee, if at all. Perhaps he got all of his information about the Galilean ministry from Mary and Peter and the others. Perhaps he learned much during his time in Galilee after Easter. What we *can* say is that this disciple was an eyewitness to the crucial climax of Jesus's ministry and its Easter sequel. The tradition is clear that Jesus raised this man from the dead, something that would surely change anybody's worldview and opinion of Jesus. It may well be this very fact that explains why the Fourth Gospel is such a distinctive testimony to Jesus, differing from the synoptics.

But what was the Beloved Disciple's legacy, other than testifying to what he heard and saw at the end of Jesus's life? We will examine this question in the next chapter.

EIGHT

The Legacy of the Beloved

Paul and Barnabas reached Galatia for the first time in about A.D. 48–49, and then again on their second missionary journey sometime in the early 50s. It appears that no efforts by other Christian missionaries had yet reached this area, but this was to change thereafter. If we take seriously the division of labor inaugurated already in the 40s when Paul visited Jerusalem for the second time after his conversion—a division that had Peter focusing on Jews, and Paul focusing on Gentiles (Gal. 2:1, 7)—we can see that the strategy of the early church was not to carve up the empire by geographical regions, but rather to have missionaries focus on different ethnic groups.

This division was not a hard and fast one, of course, since Paul would often preach in synagogues and find Gentile God-fearers there the most likely candidates for conversion, as both Acts and his letters demonstrate. Equally, figures like Peter and James wrote documents to Jewish Christians in areas that one might call Pauline (including Asia), if one were mistakenly thinking of evangelism as something done by region rather than by ethnic group. But such a geographical strategy and analysis would always be problematic, since Jews were spread all over the Diaspora.

James and others of the Jerusalem church were probably working with Peter on the evangelism of Jews. What about the Beloved Disciple? As it turns out, this seems to have been his bailiwick as well.

SEARCHING FOR THE JOHANNINE CHURCHES

There are many imponderables in the study of the Johannine literature, not the least of which is that it is not clear where the Christians are who are being addressed in 1, 2, and 3 John. Are these letters written to a largely Jewish Christian or Gentile Christian audience? Where are the recipients located?

Writing at the end of the second century, Irenaeus mentions a tradition about the Beloved Disciple residing in Ephesus and writing a gospel there (*Adv. Haer.* 3.1.1). He identifies him as John the disciple of the Lord, but he does not call him one of the Twelve. Clement of Alexandria, writing in the late second century, attests to an old tradition about a John who returned from exile on Patmos and lived in Ephesus into the reign of Trajan—which is to say, up to and perhaps beyond the very end of the first century (cited in Eusebius, *Hist. Eccl.* 3.23.6). But which John was that? The newly published Fragment of Polycarp 63r, also dating to the second century, refers to a John appointing Polycarp bishop of Smyrna. Irenaeus mentions that Polycarp had been instructed by apostles and had conversed with many who had seen Christ "but also was appointed bishop by apostles in Asia" (*Adv. Haer.* 3.3.4). Notice the reference to *apostles* (plural) in Asia. The apocryphal Acts of John 18, likewise written sometime in the second century, also speaks of the ministry of a John in Miletus, but again it is not clear which John.

Earlier than any of these traditions is the discussion about these matters by a scholar named Papias, someone who himself had spoken to "the elder John" and distinguished him from John the member of the Twelve (see Eusebius, *Hist. Eccles.* 3.39.3ff.). In fact, there is now an analysis of Papias Fragment 10:17 that is likely correct in saying that Papias affirmed that John son of Zebedee died early as a martyr, as did his brother James (see Acts 12:2).[168] This analysis certainly strongly favors the conclusion that the Beloved Disciple was not John son of Zebedee, and it also counts against the theory that John of Patmos was John son of Zebedee.

Perhaps it would be best to start with the observation that Acts 18 tells us already of a Jewish Christian missionary named Apollos who went to Ephesus, not as a part of the Pauline mission, but apparently on his own. It may be that the Jewish mission in Ephesus began in that fashion in the 50s, quite without the Jerusalem church sending anyone to that locale. In any case, it is clear that by the time John of Patmos was writing there were numerous churches in Asia, seven of which he was prepared to address and take responsibility for. These churches had clearly existed in places like Ephesus for a very long time indeed—long enough for them to develop both problems and promise over a generation or so. John of Patmos wrote to these churches probably in the early 90s,[169] using concepts and terms we find elsewhere in the Johannine literature. This suggests that the Fourth Gospel tradition about Jesus as the Logos, and other Johannine ideas we find in the epistles and gospel, had been circulating in these churches for some time and were familiar to John of Patmos's audience.

This in turn suggests that 1, 2, and 3 John were written perhaps in the 80s, and thus before either Revelation or the final form of the Gospel of John was made public. (As noted in the previous chapter, differences in Greek style argue for the gospel and epistles having been written by one person and Revelation by another.)

According to Eusebius (*Hist. Eccl.* 3.5.3) there was a prophetic oracle given in the Jerusalem church in A.D. 66–67 to flee from Jerusalem because it was about to be destroyed, and many Christians left and went across the Jordan to Pella. But it is surely likely that they also went elsewhere. Perhaps this was the juncture when the Beloved Disciple and others (perhaps even Mary) went to Ephesus. By then no longer a young man, the Beloved Disciple apparently was followed to (or found in) Ephesus by another Christian, a prophet, who became a member of his community—John of Patmos. We may hypothesize that because the Beloved Disciple had been an eyewitness of Jesus and his ministry, he became the central figure in the founding of churches made up largely of Jewish Christians in Ephesus and the surrounding area in Asia. We catch up with him in the Johannine epistles well after these churches were started, and in fact after they'd had to deal with schism. We turn to these letters at this juncture.

THE BELOVED DISCIPLE BECOMES AN OLD MAN

As we have seen, the second and third letters of John announce that they were written by a person who identifies himself as *ho presbuteros,* meaning "the old man" or "the elder." This label *could* even mean "the older man" (of two Johns?). However, it does not seem likely that we should take this term in a comparative sense (the older of two or more persons), since we find no such comparisons in these documents. Perhaps we should rule out "elder" as well. As Raymond Brown points out, this man seems to disavow the teaching office associated with local church elders at 1 John 2:27.[170] Furthermore, if he is the elder in a local congregation, why does he assume he has the authority to address congregations in a remote location some distance from his own? By the same token, if he is one of the Twelve, why does he never suggest this? As an "old man," then—and an eyewitness of something or someone crucial (Jesus as the Word?)—he speaks with authority.

We have a genre issue to consider here, for 1 John is not a letter at all, but rather a homily or rhetorical exhortation, whereas 2 and 3 John are, of all the letters in the New Testament, most like other ancient letters in length and scope. Either of those latter documents could have fit on one sheet of papyrus; 3 John is in fact the shortest document in the New Testament. There has to be some good reason that such brief letters were preserved and included within the canon. Only 3 John is in fact a personal or private letter to an individual, whereas 2 John is written to a congregation at some distance from our author. Likewise, only 3 John mentions names of persons our author is concerned about, evidence of its personal nature. Indeed, one could say 3 John is more personal than even the letters to Timothy and Titus, which, with the exception of 2 Timothy, are more pastoral letters from an apostle to his apostolic delegates.

THE BELOVED'S AUTHORITY AND WITNESS

It is necessary to probe into social and contextual issues to ferret out information about the Beloved Disciple, who by the time the Johannine epistles were written was indeed an old man. One of the most telling pieces of data is the overlap between John 14–17 and material in 1 John. The person who heard Jesus say the things cited in the gospel chapters is the same person who wrote the Johannine epistles: the Beloved Disciple. And he acted on his own authority, not claiming to be one of the Twelve and yet claiming to be an eyewitness.

We have some clues about the author of 1 John in the prologue itself (1 John 1:1–4), which begins, "We declare to you what was from the beginning, what we have heard, what we have seen with our eyes, what we have looked at and touched with our hands, concerning the word of life." In this passage, which has obvious connections with the prologue in the Gospel of John, who is "we"? In these introductory verses it appears to refer to eyewitnesses, though later in the homily it refers to the author and the audience.[171] (Actually, at the very end of the 1 John prologue, "our" joy probably likewise encompasses both the author and the audience.)[172] The "you" throughout these verses is clearly the audience in Ephesus, who are not eyewitnesses.[173] This way of putting things helps establish the authority of our author, and clearly enough it also involves the implicit claim that he himself is among the eyewitnesses who saw Jesus in the flesh. This in turn comports with the theory that the "old man" who wrote these shorter documents is none other than the Beloved Disciple, spoken of in the gospel as an eyewitness, and so *not* a second- or third-generation Christian. Supporting this conclusion is the fact that the phrase "seen with the eyes" appears some ninety-one times in the Greek Old Testament, and in all but one case it refers to directly witnessing something with one's own eyes. Furthermore, the verb "to contemplate/observe" with the eyes is used unambiguously in 1 John 4:12 to refer to physical sight, as here.[174]

There is a strong emphasis, then, from the beginning of this sermon in 1 John about the total impact that Christ, the "word of life," had on the Beloved Disciple and others while he was on earth.[175] Jesus was listened to and observed, the meaning of his words and works and person was contemplated, and close fellowship was had with him—in fact, he was even touched.[176] Alfred Plummer puts it this way: "A climax: seeing is more than hearing, and beholding (which requires time) is more than seeing (which may be momentary); while handling is more than all."[177]

The phrase "word of life" at the end of the passage quoted above certainly refers to eternal life, since that is a major theme in this sermon; but because Jesus embodied both eternal life and the word, "word of life" also describes his impact. He is preeminently the Word of Life beyond all ordinary speech or persons. But again the point here is about how he came across, how he impacted our author and others—how he was encountered and perceived and received.

Eternal life, here as elsewhere in the Johannine literature, does not refer merely to life everlasting, though that is meant as well, but also to a different quality of life, an unending spiritual life that has unlimited potential and is full of *joie de vivre*. It is a life that binds the believer forever to God and to other believers. As such, it already transcends time, for we have it already in time; but it will go on beyond the temporal existence we now experience. Jesus is not simply identical with this life, since it exists in his followers as well, but he clearly most fully embodies it and also bestows it. The person who has Jesus has life with a capital L, but also a lot more, including endless joy. Moody Smith puts the matter well: "Jesus is the bringer of eschatological life, the life that is final but without end, the life of God's new age."[178]

Life certainly is a major theme in 1 John, just as it is in the gospel (the noun "life" occurs some thirteen times in 1 John, the verb once), and about half of the references (six to be exact) in 1 John are more explicitly to eternal life. Clearly, then, our author reflected deeply on the meaning of his personal and eyewitness encounter with Christ, and he was determined to pass that along to his congregations.

In all three letters of John we find a pastor who is doing his best to mend divisions caused in large part by schismatics who left the community and by an authoritarian figure in one of the satellite churches. Given the conflict within his audience, it is probably no accident that the Beloved Disciple has adopted the ambiguous term "old man/elder" to assert his authority over the situation. Elders were those who had authority in the synagogue, something presumably much of his largely Jewish Christian audience knew well. But in a culture that honored seniority and years of experience, the voice of an old man was also assumed to carry wisdom and thereby authority. But as we have seen, the Beloved Disciple does not claim to be more than he was—an eyewitness of Jesus the Word, and an experienced Christian sharing his wisdom. He does not feel the need to use the term "apostle" as Paul does, perhaps because of his Jewish audience, nor does he seek to imply he was one of the Twelve, although that would surely have supplemented his authority. Rather, he is comfortable with who he is—a witness to the truth about Jesus.

At the end of the grand homily we call 1 John, the "old man" returns to a theme that he reflected long on—the human reality of Jesus and how his death as a human provided atonement for sins. About Jesus he says in 1 John 5:6–9: "This is the one who came by water and blood—Jesus Christ. He did not come by water only, but by water and blood. And it is the Spirit who testifies, because the Spirit is the truth. For there are three that testify: the Spirit, the water and the blood; and these three are in agreement. We accept human testimony, but God's testimony is greater because it is the testimony he has given about his Son."

Our author sees the death of Jesus as God's own testimony about the Son and his salvific significance. As I have shown in detail elsewhere, the reference to water here is not a reference to baptism, but rather a reference to physical birth, just as blood is a reference to physical death.[179] The stress in the Johannine epistles is on Jesus having come in the flesh—which is to say, on the incarnation and death of Jesus, which are seen as the means of salvation for humanity. The schismatics that these epistles attempt to counter are those who deny that the historical Jesus is the incarnation of the Son and also the Jewish messiah.

In 1 John 5:6–9 we hear an echo of what was said in John 19:34–35, where we had the same language of water, blood, and testimony—human testimony, that of the Beloved Disciple. These documents, the gospel and the epistles, are integrally connected, and they are connected because the eyewitness referred to in John 19 is also the author of the letters, and he is sharing his own human testimony in both the gospel and the epistles. Without cavil, he became one of the greatest theologians of the early church, and perhaps also one of its greatest and most beloved pastors, for it was likely the church that gave him the title the Beloved Disciple.

THE DEMISE OF THE BELOVED DISCIPLE

We cannot say precisely when, but it appears likely that somewhere in the early 90s the Beloved Disciple passed away in Ephesus. There is a Byzantine basilica of St. John, now in ruins, on the edge of Ephesus, which celebrates his life, all the while confusing him with John of Patmos. It is not clear which of those two men are buried there; it may be either one. But do we know anything else about the Beloved Disciple's death? Let us consider John 21:20–23 now.

It is Peter who raises the question about the fate of the Beloved Disciple in John 21:21. True to his customary *modus operandi,* Jesus answers with a rhetorical question: "If it is my will that he should remain until I come, what is that to you?" Now, this way of putting it is deliberately ambiguous. But when it is said of someone whom Jesus raised from the dead—namely, Lazarus—one can immediately see how speculation gets started. The form of the Greek conditional sentence that is Jesus's rhetorical question indicates only a possible, not a real condition.[180] The reply to Peter basically means that the matter is none of Peter's business. He must focus on what God has in mind for him, which ultimately proves to be martyrdom.

The Fourth Evangelist, the man who assembled the Beloved Disciple's memoirs after the old man had passed away, is eager to dispel the rumor that Jesus had promised that the Beloved Disciple would live until the parousia. Why? Because the Beloved Disciple had lived a very long life and then had died before Jesus returned, causing considerable dismay in the Johannine community. In other words, these verses are an exercise in damage control. The Fourth Evangelist goes on to explain that while the man had ceased breathing, his words of life and testimony continued to live on. And what a legacy he left his community—a wonderful gospel, one superb sermon, and two pastoral and personal letters.

WHAT WE'VE LEARNED AND WHAT THAT KNOWLEDGE TELLS US ABOUT JESUS

Early Christianity surely had few eyewitnesses of Jesus who lived into the last decade of the first century, but there *were* a few. This should remind us to beware of making facile assumptions about whether the Johannine gospel could be in touch with the real historical Jesus and be an eyewitness testimony to him. The answer is yes: it could be and is. The Johannine literature is the distinctive witness of someone who had a unique perspective on Jesus, someone deeply steeped in Jewish wisdom literature, who knew how to convey profound ideas in beguilingly simple Greek. He was someone for whom Jesus performed a profound miracle, and it changed his life and worldview forever. He knew personally what resurrection meant: he had experienced it. For him "I am the resurrection and the life" was more than a claim of Jesus; it was how he had encountered Jesus beyond and back from the grave. He had not merely seen Jesus, he had touched him; and he had not merely touched Jesus, he had been befriended by him; and he had not merely been befriended by Jesus, he had been loved by him, loved even to the point that Jesus raised this man from the dead and then died for him and others—for as Jesus had said, "Greater love has no one than he lay down his life for his friends" (John 15:13). Of course, the Beloved Disciple had also studied with Jesus and heard his words—as the echoes of 1 John 14–17 make so very clear.

And so it was by this means that a Judean eyewitness disciple who did not travel with Jesus became one of the crucial witnesses to the Christ event, and he continued to give testimony into the last decade of the first century, founding (with his helpers) numerous Jewish Christian churches in various cities in Asia. In the end we may be tempted to shout with him, if we have reflected long and hard on the substance of his gospel and letters, "We have seen his glory."

Despite all the problems, despite all the trials, despite all the defections, this man passed on the torch of eyewitness Christianity to another generation, as Polycarp and Papias and Ignatius and Irenaeus could attest. There is nothing in the Johannine epistles about whether indeed Mary was with the Beloved Disciple during these days in the 80s and into the 90s. Perhaps she had long since died. Perhaps in her honor the Beloved Disciple called one of his churches "the elect Lady," as some have speculated. We cannot know for sure. But we can say with considerable certainty that eyewitness Christianity survived until the very cusp of the second century, when its inner-circle testimony was passed on to another generation of Christians.

The connection between Jesus and the church of the second century in some cases involved a very short chain. Indeed, it was a chain with only one link in the case of the Johannine epistles and only two in the case of the Fourth Gospel, which required an editor to collect and put together the Beloved Disciple's testimony once he died. The importance of this immediacy can hardly be exaggerated. Early Christianity through to the end of the first century was in large measure the product of the hard work of the inner circle of Jesus, including both apostles and non-apostles, and it involved both largely Jewish and largely Gentile communities of Christians.

There was no rival form of Christianity of a Gnostic sort in the first century, nor of a sort that involved appreciating Jesus only as a great sage and not as Christ, the Son of God, the crucified savior. As the Beloved Disciple says emphatically in his letters and gospel, those who do not believe that Jesus is the Christ—that he came in the flesh, died on the cross, and rose from the dead—are not Christians.

This is the language of sectarian faith, of course—but then all of the inner circle of Jesus, and the communities those disciples helped to form, were constituted by sectarian believers. This becomes clear as we consider other members of the inner circle of Jesus and the way they helped shape early Christianity—especially Peter, who as we saw sought to create Jewish Christian communities that focused on the crucified and risen One who was messiah, savior, Son of God, Lord.

Finally, let's summarize what the material bequeathed to us by the Beloved Disciple tells us about Jesus. The first and perhaps most important conclusion we learn from examining this material closely is that there is no major gap between the historical Jesus and the Christ of later Christian faith. If indeed Jesus presented himself, at least in private to his disciples, in a fashion even close to what the "I am" sayings of the Gospel of John suggest—sayings not addressed in our discussion above, but including such pronouncements as "I am the good shepherd" (10:11) and "I am the resurrection and the life" (11:25)—then Jesus had a messianic understanding of himself as far more than an ordinary mortal. Indeed, if the Beloved Disciple's testimony really is "true," as John 21 claims, then we must assign Paul a considerably less exalted role than the suggestion that he invented a divine view of Jesus, or invented later Christian theology about Jesus.

Furthermore, and even more strikingly, the Beloved Disciple is not just a clear witness to what Jesus thought about himself and how he presented himself as a messianic figure; he is an equally clear witness—indeed, one with direct personal experience—that Jesus could in fact do miracles and even raise the dead. The exalted view of Jesus in the Fourth Gospel and the Johannine epistles reflects how an eyewitness was impacted by the words, deeds, life, and relationships of the historical Jesus himself. That eyewitness presented what he learned in his own distinctive fashion, of course, writing in his own style and with an eye to the wisdom of Jesus and to Jesus as the incarnation of divine wisdom. And of course it may have taken some time for the Beloved Disciple to reach the conclusions he did about Jesus. We don't know how long these ideas gestated in his mind.

But what we can say is that the high Christology, the view of Jesus as both human and divine, is found in this eyewitness testimony just as it is found in the chronologically earliest New Testament documents—the letters of Paul. Furthermore, the Beloved Disciple, like Paul, believed that Jesus's death and resurrection are the fulcrum of the Jesus story, the events that changed (indeed shattered) history. These were not ideas invented late in the first century by second- or third-generation Christians. Rather, these were the ideas and events that generated and shaped the thought-world of the Christian movement in the first place.

According to the Old Testament, the testimony of two witnesses validates the truth of anything. We have seen in the Beloved Disciple a powerful witness to a powerful and messianic Jesus. When we tell Paul's tale, we will find a similarly exalted view of Jesus. The question is, Will we believe these earliest witnesses to Jesus, or will we exchange their testimony for the later musings of Gnostics, Marcionites, and others who turned Jesus into a talking head, an idea man without a story, whose incarnation, death, and resurrection were not crucial to unveiling his identity and his mission in life? We must decide whether to believe the testimony of the earliest witnesses (some of them *eye*witnesses), who spoke of an exalted, divine Christ, or the conclusions of later writers. We must decide which group is more likely to have known what Jesus was really like. The answer of this study is of course that the members of Jesus's inner circle were likely to have known him first and known him best. But did this include Jesus's own brothers?

PART FIVE

THE BROTHERS OF THE LORD

NINE

O Brother, Where Art Thou?

The true name of James is Jacob, named after his grandfather and the patriarch of a much earlier era in Jewish history. Though there are several Jameses mentioned in the New Testament, it is possible to sort out which is which by careful examination of the way each James is identified and the person with whom each James is associated. The James we are concerned with is always associated with Mary and with the other siblings of Jesus in the gospels. He is identified as James the brother of the Lord by Paul, and Jude is identified as his brother in Jude verse 1. He is identified as a servant of Jesus in James 1:1.

To tell the story of James/Jacob, we must begin before he ever became a disciple, in fact long before he became a disciple. He was not a follower of Jesus during his ministry, as John 7:3–5 makes very clear. But we can certainly say some things about his life as it led up to his becoming a follower of Jesus after the death and resurrection of his brother. What sort of life and upbringing would someone like James have had as a Jew in Galilee in the first century?[181]

How do we know that James's family was devoutly Jewish? There is first of all the clue that the names of the children in the family are names of famous patriarchs (James and Joseph) or of Maccabean war heroes (Judas and Simon, Mark 6:3). It is clear they were proud of their Jewish heritage, and in particular the heritage they had as a free people following God's will. Second, we have the evidence of the family of James making repeated trips up to Jerusalem for the Jewish festivals (cf. Luke 2:22 and 2:41–52 to John 7:5). Third, there is the evidence that Jesus's family attended synagogue services (Mark 6:1–3 and parallel). Fourth, the story in Luke 4:16–30 indicates that Jesus could read the Hebrew scroll, which suggests he had training in the home or in the synagogue to do so, since Aramaic and not Hebrew was the family's spoken language. Fifth, independently of one another, both Matthew 1–2 and Luke 1–2 depict Joseph and Mary as devout Jewish individuals who have religious visions, dreams, and even encounters with angels. There is clearly a decided attempt to depict them as holy persons. Equally importantly, Luke 2:41–52 tells us they trained their children in their faith, for it is surely not accidental that we are told that Jesus was taken up to the Temple when he was at the proper age to become a "son of the commandments" (bar-mitzvah), and there is a strong emphasis on Jesus's own ability to convey his faith and its teachings. Notice once more that there are no references in this important story of James, Jude, or any other siblings of Jesus.

According to Mark 6:3 Jesus himself was a carpenter, a worker of wood, and according to Matthew 13:55 so was his father. This suggests that Joseph passed on the family trade to his sons, and so we may quite properly envision James as being trained in this trade as well. What would being a woodworker have entailed? For one thing, it was viewed by early Jews as a clean or ritually unobjectionable trade, unlike for example tanning of hides, which meant one touched animal carcasses and became ritually unclean. It is possible that Jesus's family was involved in the building of some of the structures in Sepphoris, a city on the rise during the reign of Herod Antipas. There is both archaeological and literary evidence of the manufacturing of furniture in this vicinity.[182] Carpenters would not have been at the bottom of the social structure of society, for tenant farmers and day laborers were certainly poorer, as were shepherds and agricultural workers, so neither Jesus nor any of his brothers should be called a peasant. Furthermore, if there was a good deal of building going on in nearby Sepphoris, even a woodworker who simply specialized in furniture might expect to make a living that could support the family. Despite protestations to the contrary, an artisan was by no means a peasant, and in an area like Nazareth next to Sepphoris it is unlikely that any enterprising artisan lived on peasant's wages or according to a peasant lifestyle. We need to stop generating romantic notions about agrarian peasants and then trying to place Jesus into that socioeconomic slot.

We know that different Galilean villages specialized in different trades, and that the wheat of Sepphoris was famous.[183] It is thus possible that some of Jesus's family was involved in agricultural pursuits. Certainly both the parables of Jesus and some of the wisdom teaching found in the book of James strongly indicate that these men were familiar with agricultural trades. Besides politics, religious life, and work, the fourth major factor in daily life in Galilee in this era was of course the family.

Family however in Jesus's day was in various respects different from what it is today. For one thing, almost all marriages in early Judaism were arranged marriages. At their essence they were property transactions meant to secure the future of one family through an alliance with another. The heavily patriarchal structure of the society made it such that basically marriages were arranged by the two male heads of their families. There was no dating or romance or courtship in the modern sense, but there was a formal betrothal, as was the case with Mary and Joseph, which had a legal status. For it to be dissolved required some sort of formal action. In Jewish culture, unlike in the Greco-Roman world, all extramarital sexual activity was seen as immoral or sinful, especially in the case of women. It is interesting that not only did the Jewish tradition more strongly emphasize limiting one's sexual activity to the confines of marriage, but it also more strongly stressed honoring one's parents.

One of the more interesting facts that is recorded in 1 Corinthians 9:5 is that the brothers of Jesus were married, as was Peter, as were the rest of the apostles, but Paul himself was not married at the time he wrote this letter (though he may well have been a widower or even divorced).[184] Now if Paul could have referred to a married Jesus at this juncture he surely would have done so, and equally clearly he could have known about this since he had had time to talk with Peter and James and John and others who would certainly have known about Jesus's marital status (see Gal. 1–2).[185] What this means of importance for our study is that James and Jude and the other brothers of Jesus lived more normal Jewish lives than Jesus did, and we can say with some assurance that in James's case at least, this meant not only being married but eschewing itinerancy.

Family could also include extended family, and it is interesting that in his famous saying about prophets being not without honor Jesus mentions an increasingly narrow circle in which that seemed to be true in his home town, among his relatives, and within his own home (Mark 6:4). Jesus apparently had relatives in Nazareth, but notice that he distinguishes them from those within his own home. This probably suggests Jesus did not have an extended family situation involving other married siblings or slaves within his own household at that juncture. This means of course that James did not either at this juncture, which suggests that James and the other siblings are clearly younger than Jesus, since we know from 1 Corinthians 9:5 that they later went on to get married. Paul's point in 1 Corinthians 9:5 would have been moot if in fact his rhetorical question "Do I not have the right to travel with a Christian wife like Peter and the Lord's brothers do?" was not grounded in reality.

JAMES IN THE CONTEXT OF JESUS'S MINISTRY

But what would happen to a family where the eldest son, who was the chief or primary heir, decided not to continue in the family business and support the family, but instead embark on a career as an itinerant teacher and preacher? This is an important point, and it is seldom contemplated what the ministry of Jesus might have done to the social structure of Jesus's family, especially if, as may be the case, Joseph died before or during the time of Jesus's ministry. What responsibilities would someone like James have had? In the absence of Joseph or Jesus, James becomes the de facto head of the family, along with his mother. He would be responsible for supporting the family through their woodworking trade.

Let's consider another point as well. How might James have viewed Jesus prior to his death and resurrection? If the opinions expressed in John 7:3–5 at all represent James's view, then it appears he would have seen Jesus as something of a self-seeking person who should go up to Jerusalem to prove himself or demonstrate his messianic potential. As we have already noted, the situation seems to be somewhat similar to the sibling rivalry situation we find in the story of Joseph the patriarch and his brothers in Genesis 37. Notice in John 7:3–5 that Jesus does not go with his brothers up to Jerusalem, but does then turn around and go to the festival without them. This sort of distancing from the family activity can be also seen in the Cana story in John 2.

Considerations such as these have led scholars to quite properly ask a pertinent question: If there was distance between Jesus and his family, and particularly between Jesus and his siblings during his ministry, how is it that we find James among the leaders of the Jerusalem church apparently from the outset of things (see Acts 1:14)? F. F. Bruce rightly says, "It might have been expected that the disgrace of his execution would confirm in their minds the misgivings which they had felt about him all along."[186] An adequate historical answer needs to be given to this question, and we will turn to the matter in due course.

If we needed further proof that Jesus was somewhat estranged from his siblings, we need look no further than what happened at Jesus's death, when by all accounts he was not buried by his family or his inner circle of disciples, even though his mother may have been present at his death (John 19:25–27). I suspect the issue of shame is primary here. If Jesus was perceived to have shamed the family during his ministry, the fact that he died in the most shameful means possible in the ancient world would quite possibly have been the final straw severing the ties of Jesus from his siblings, unless something dramatic happened to rectify the matter afterward. Notice too, that according to all the gospels, Jesus was not buried in a family plot, but in the tomb of Joseph of Arimathea. This suggests there was no family plot in Jerusalem, which is no surprise since the family was only visiting Jerusalem during festival times, while still residing in Nazareth.

This raises some interesting issues in regard to the James ossuary, the burial box of James, and his burial in Jerusalem. Presumably James's burial after his martyrdom in 62 would have been an isolated not a family burial, a burial by the Jewish Christians in Jerusalem. Perhaps in the end, James too, like Jesus, had come to see the family of faith as his primary family. Notice as well that in all the accounts of Jesus's entombment, he is not buried in the ground, but laid out in a tomb.[187] This is important, for it suggests that the practice of reburial in an ossuary was going to happen to Jesus once the flesh was no longer on the bones, though the process never got that far. There was then a potential precedent within the family for James being laid out in a tomb and then his bones being transferred to an ossuary.

As for the ongoing controversy about the James ossuary, only a few things need to be said at this juncture: (1) the Israeli Antiquities Authority's attempt to claim that the inscription is a modern forgery has not been substantiated in the subsequent discussion of the matter;[188] (2) those who originally authenticated this inscription continue to stand by its authenticity, including Andre Lemaire, who was the first to recognize its genuineness; (3) all are agreed the ossuary is a genuine first-century Jewish burial box; and (4) further study of the inscription is required once the ossuary is made available again after the current legal squabbles.

At this point we must stress what the linguistic evidence actually suggests about James indeed being Jesus's brother, rather than say a cousin or a half-brother. This issue is important because Eusebius, the church historian, says that James became the first bishop of Jerusalem in part *because* he was the brother of Jesus. There is another explanation that could be added, namely that he became a church leader because he also saw the risen Jesus, as the early list of appearances in 1 Corinthians 15:5–8 suggests.[189]

James and Jesus's other siblings are always called his brothers and sisters in the gospels. There was indeed a word for cousin in Greek, *anepsios*, and it is never used of James or the other siblings of Jesus. It is interesting how the second-century Christian writer Hegesippus distinguishes between those who were cousins of Jesus (*anepsioi*), and James and Jude, who are called brothers of Jesus.[190] The two terms clearly do not mean the same thing in Greek. But James and Jude were brothers who did not own up to their kinship with Jesus when he died and was buried in Jerusalem in another family's tomb, despite the Jewish views about filial piety and being sure your family members get honorable burial. Nothing from the pre-Easter life of James explains how he became an important leader in the early Jesus movement. Mere kinship to Jesus cannot explain it, or otherwise we would have expected to hear about how various of his brothers and sisters played important roles in the early church. This is not what the historical evidence suggests. We now have, in addition, the evidence of the James ossuary to support the contention that James was a brother of Jesus (through Mary), and at the same time that James was the son of Joseph. This information alone rules out the cousin theory, if the inscription is genuine on this ossuary.[191]

JAMES AND THE RESURRECTION OF HIS BROTHER

According to Acts 1:14, both Mary and the brothers of Jesus (which surely must include James and Jude, but where were the sisters?) were present in the upper room praying at Pentecost when the Holy Spirit fell upon the followers of Jesus.[192] How had it happened that James was present on this occasion when in fact he had not been a follower of Jesus during Jesus's earthly ministry? The answer to this question is found in 1 Corinthians 15:5–8, which provides us with the earliest list of those who saw the risen Jesus.[193] The listing of those to whom Jesus appeared seems to be in chronological order, for Paul uses the Greek words for "then" and "afterward" more than once, and concludes the list with himself using the qualifier "last of all." It is a probable suggestion that Paul is quoting an old witness list from Jerusalem, just as the traditions mentioned in verses 1–4 are said by Paul to have been passed down to him from others as sacred tradition.[194]

Paul first mentions an appearance to Cephas, and then an appearance to the Twelve (which actually were the Eleven at that juncture), then an appearance to more than five hundred believers at once, most of whom are said to be still alive in the early 50s, then there is mention of an appearance to James, then to all the apostles, and then finally to Paul. There are many interesting features to this list, not the least of which is the only named persons in the list are Cephas and James and of course Paul.

This list should be compared to what Paul says in 1 Corinthians 9:5 where he mentions the Lord's brothers, Cephas, and the other apostles. If

James son of Zebedee, one of the original Twelve disciples of Jesus, was meant by Paul when he says James, there would be no reason to single him out from the other members of the Twelve. No, in this case Paul is talking about three appearances to individuals (Peter, James, and Paul), and also appearances to groups of people. The Gospel traditions are such that the appearance to James is not mentioned, but then the individual appearance to Peter is not recounted either, as we have already noted, but only mentioned in passing in Luke 24:34.

If this list is in chronological order, then it is possible to suggest that the appearance to James came later, possibly in Galilee, but if James was in Jerusalem for Passover, more likely it happened in Jerusalem. It is also noteworthy that James is distinguished from both the Twelve and the apostles, when it comes to appearances. Since James the brother of Jesus is the only James Paul mentions elsewhere in his letters, the reference here is surely to the person Paul calls a pillar of the Jerusalem church in Galatians 1. In other words, it appears that James, like Paul, was a convert to the Jesus movement because at some juncture he saw the risen Jesus, for nothing prior to Easter accounts for his having become such a follower of Jesus, much less a leader of Jesus's followers.

At this juncture we must reveal a startling fact. It appears that none of the persons we are studying in this volume would have even been disciples of Jesus after the crucifixion if he had not appeared to them! We can say this with assurance about the brothers of Jesus, about Paul, and about Peter who had to be restored and about the Beloved Disciple. The Beloved Disciple and Mary simply went to the Beloved Disciple's home after the crucifixion (John 19:27). There is no reason to think that they would have continued to be Jesus's disciples and have shown up in the upper room at Pentecost had they not seen the risen Lord, or in Mary's case at least received the witness that he had risen from those who did see him and renounced their previous cowardly lack of faith, or denials, or desertion. John 21 makes clear that the Beloved Disciple, though not one of the Twelve, did see the risen Lord. The only persons we do not have direct evidence for are Mary and Jude, but surely their presence in the upper room in Acts 1:14 attests that they too were there because of the resurrection, either having seen Jesus when he appeared to "more than five hundred at once" (1 Cor. 15:6) or having been told directly by those who had seen him.

Here we are able to reach a major conclusion of this study. None of these major figures who constituted the inner circle of Jesus would have become or remained followers of Jesus after the crucifixion if there was no resurrection and no resurrection appearances of Jesus. The church, in the persons of its earliest major leaders, was constituted by the event of the resurrection, coupled with the Pentecost event! The stories of these figures, especially their post-Easter stories, are the validation of this fact. There would be no church without the risen and appearing Jesus.

JAMES THE JUST

Though James had not believed in Jesus before Easter, he developed quite a reputation for Christian piety after Easter.[195] There is a late embellishment to the statement in 1 Corinthians 15:7 about Jesus's appearance to James found in the apocryphal Gospel according to the Hebrews.[196] It states that James took an oath to eat no bread until he saw the risen Jesus. When Jesus did finally appear to him, "he [Jesus] took bread, gave thanks, and broke it, and then gave it to James the Just, saying to him, 'My brother, eat your bread, because the Son of Man has risen from those who sleep.'" This story is legendary, but it preserves several historical kernels about James that need to be considered. The trick is to figure out what is grounded in history and what reflects later Christian interests in extreme forms of asceticism.[197]

First, both within the Christian tradition and in the writings of the Jewish historian Josephus, James is presented as someone with a reputation for ascetical piety and righteous character. This is why he came to be known as James the Just. Among the various things that this reputation means is that James took very seriously the importance of being faithful to both the Law and various Jewish traditions not specifically recorded in the Law. This tradition in fact comports with what we learn of James from Galatians 1–2 and from a text like Acts 15, as we shall see.[198] James was concerned with maintaining continuity with early Judaism in various ways, one of which entailed the continued keeping of the Law. While in the end James turns out to be something of a mediating figure between the Pharisaic[199] Jewish Christians to his right and Paul and those interested in a Law-free Gospel to his left, nevertheless James is not one who embraces an approach that basically allows concerns about inclusion of Gentiles in the church to dictate how Jewish Christians ought to live.

The second feature of the legendary account is the emphasis on James's ascetical piety. Indeed one could read this story as suggesting that James followed time-honored ascetical practices, such as fasting, in order to be able to see the risen Jesus. The decree in Acts 15 reflects a concern about food, and in particular where Gentiles should not eat, namely in the presence of idols in pagan temples. Yet one should not push the ascetical reading of James too far, for 1 Corinthians 9:5 indicates that James, unlike Jesus, was married.[200] But sexual asceticism is one thing, dietary asceticism another. Yet it is right to emphasize that James was Torah-true and believed in righteous deeds as an important part of being a follower of Jesus. This is the truth behind the famous utterance of James found in James 2 insisting "faith without works is dead!"

The third feature of the story that bears mention is the reference to Jesus as the Son of Man. Paul never calls Jesus the Son of Man, and indeed outside the Gospels and one reference in Acts, this is a title applied to Jesus nowhere else in the New Testament except in allusions to Daniel 7 in the book of Revelation. It seems very clear that because the title Son of Man would not have connoted to the Gentile world that Jesus was a human but also divine figure, as Daniel 7 suggests, this title was soon abandoned in the Gentile mission despite the fact that it is the most common form of self-identification found on Jesus's lips in the gospels. This suggests something important. Jewish Christianity, which continued well beyond the New Testament period, continued to maintain continuity not only with its Jewish heritage, but also with the heritage Jesus passed on to his followers, including the way that he spoke of himself as Son of Man.

JAMES THE LEADER OF THE FIRST CHURCH

Precisely because all the earliest followers of Jesus were Jews, including of course the members of Jesus's own family, it needs to be kept squarely in view that these people did not view themselves as founding a new religion. When we talk about James as the leader or head of the earliest church, we are not talking about James intentionally setting up a separate religious entity. As the Old Testament quote in Acts 15:15–18 suggests, James views the matter as a case of Old Testament promises to Jews being fulfilled, and of Gentiles joining a Jewish messianic movement centered on Jesus, not Jews joining some new religion. In other words, James and the earliest Jewish Christians need to be viewed as promoting a sectarian form of early Judaism, not unlike the Qumran sect did.[201] Craig A. Evans puts the matter helpfully as we try to locate James and his church in the context of early Judaism:

> In sum, we could say that if we drew three circles to represent the Judaisms of Qumran, the Rabbis, and James, the circles would overlap. But the centers of these circles, centers which represent the essence of the respective Judaisms, would not. We would have three

overlapping circles, but three distinct, separate centers. The Judaism of Qumran is focused on the renewal of the covenant, with great emphasis on cultic reform. The Judaism of the Rabbis is focused on studying and obeying the Torah, the key to life in this world and in the world to come. The Judaism of James is focused on faith and piety centered on Messiah Jesus.[202]

This is a very important point, and it is further confirmed by the use of Aramaic on the inscription on the ossuary of James, which reminds us that even in the 60s the Jewish character of this form of the Jesus movement was still very much to the fore. If we are used to thinking of the Jesus movement as a largely Gentile affair dominated by Gentile concerns and customs by the 60s, which is to say, by the time that Paul is concluding his missionary efforts, then we need to remember that this was not true of the character or basic constituency of the mother church in Jerusalem. There was more than one strain of early Christianity, and the discovery of the ossuary reminds us of this in a powerful way.

What of the evidence about James as the first leader of the post-Easter Jesus movement? There is first of all the indirect evidence in Acts, not merely of the presence of the brothers of Jesus at Pentecost in the upper room in Acts 1:14, but also of a text like Acts 12:17. It is clear from the context that the James mentioned here is James the brother of Jesus, for Luke had already mentioned in Acts 12:2 that James son of Zebedee had been executed by Herod Agrippa.[203] Notice how Peter says that the message should be taken to James and the brothers.[204] The urgency of James's knowing is highlighted. This suggests he already had an important leadership position at that time, which must be in the 40s.

J. Painter has suggested that Acts 12 should be read as a flashback indicating how James the brother of Jesus came to leadership in the Jerusalem church, namely because Peter had to go elsewhere and the other James had been executed.[205] There is probably some truth in this assessment, but it is doubtful his leadership happened simply by default. It needs to be remembered that the father of church history, Eusebius[206] recognizes no Petrine leadership of the Jerusalem church. Indeed he quotes Clement of Alexandria as saying that Peter, James, and John after the ascension of Jesus chose Jesus's brother James as the first bishop of Jerusalem (*Hist. Eccl.* 2.1.3). Allowing for the use of the later Christian terminology "bishop," this tradition could well be grounded in fact. Eusebius has his own view, which is that when Stephen was martyred James became the leader (2.1.2). We need to consider an important text in Galatians at this juncture.

It is generally recognized that Galatians is one of Paul's earlier letters. In my judgment it may well be his very first letter, written in about 49 before the major Jerusalem council mentioned in Acts 15.[207] In any case, it is a genuine Pauline letter that recognizes at an early date the great importance of James, as well as Peter and John. Galatians 1:18–19 chronicles Paul's first postconversion visit to Jerusalem, where he visits with Peter for a fortnight, and he says he saw none of the other apostles except James the brother of Jesus. We can date this meeting rather precisely. Paul says this visit transpired three years after his Damascus road experience. This would certainly place the event in the 30s, perhaps as early as 37.[208] This text then suggests that within only a few years of Jesus's death (which likely took place in 30), James was already a recognized leader in Jerusalem of the Jesus movement. Notice too that in this very earliest reference to James in the New Testament at Galatians 1:19 he is distinguished from the other James by being called "the Lord's brother."[209] It appears that the one label that was constantly applied to this James, early, middle, and late in his life, is that he was the brother of Jesus. It is thus not at all surprising that this is part of how he is identified on his ossuary as well.

Galatians 2 goes on to mention James again in connection with Paul's second visit to Jerusalem, which transpired about A.D. 48. This was the famine relief visit mentioned briefly in Acts 11:30, but it was also an occasion on which Paul had a private meeting about his gospel and missionary work with the "pillars"—James, Peter, and John. It must be remembered that Paul is being polemical in Galatians 2, and somewhat defensive about his gospel, and so when he calls these men reputed to be leaders (v. 2), or reputed to be pillars (v. 9), it is not because there was any doubt about their leadership, but rather it reflects Paul's concerns about his own status and whether his mission to Gentiles would be recognized as legitimate. It also reflects the fact that early Jews placed importance on people's honor ratings, as in fact was common throughout the Greco-Roman world. Notice that in 2:9 James is listed first among the "pillars." What are we to make of this terminology?

The Greek term *stuloi* suggests that these three men are seen as the main supporting columns in the eschatological temple or tent currently under construction by God through the gospel.[210] The term frequently occurs in the Greek Old Testament (LXX) in reference to the support of the tabernacle, and later the Temple columns (1 Kings 7:15–22; 2 Chron. 3:15–17). In fact these columns in the Temple were even named Jachin and Boaz (cf. 2 Kings 23:3 to 2 Chron. 34:31). This notion of the earliest leaders being the supporting columns of the eschatological people of God is probably supported by Revelation 3:12 and 1 Clement 5:2 as well.[211] There was a great deal of speculation about the destruction and rebuilding of the Temple and the people of God in early Judaism,[212] and Jesus himself had some things to say about this matter (Mark 14:58; cf. John 2:19; Acts 6:14) as did Paul (1 Cor. 3:16–17; 2 Cor. 6:16). It is not surprising, then, that there was a theology among the earliest Jewish followers of Jesus that suggested God was rebuilding his people and that James was one of the pillars in that reconstruction. It is then all the more significant that James himself will speak about the rebuilding of God's people, under the metaphor of the re-erecting of David's tent in Acts 15:16–17. James views the eschatological order of things as follows: (1) rebuild the Jewish tent; (2) then Gentiles will come into it.[213]

There is another important feature of Galatians 2:9. Paul mentions being given the right hand of fellowship, and he had also mentioned a fear of running in vain unless the pillars approved his mission and gospel. This makes perfectly clear the degree of importance and authority that James and the Jerusalem leaders had not only in Paul's eyes, but also in fact. The phrase "to give the right hand" describes the gracious gesture of a person in a superior position.[214] This tells us that already in the 30s James is a major leader of the Jesus movement. But there is more to be mined from this text.

Paul goes on to relate an incident in Antioch in connection with Peter that transpired in the mid–40s. Here we learn that there is a problem in regard to Jewish and Gentile believers eating together there. Paul also tells us that some men who came from James in Jerusalem were sent to check the situation out. Notice that Peter, according to Galatians 2:12, withdraws from fellowship meals with Gentiles when these men from James come. This in itself suggests that James is the recognized head of the Jerusalem church, such that even Peter defers to his judgment. Notice that it does not say men came from the Jerusalem church, but men came from James himself.

What I would suggest we see in the three references to James in Galatians 1–2 is the gradual ascendancy of James over the Jerusalem church. Peter is mentioned first in the earliest reference in Galatians 1:18, but thereafter James is mentioned first and seems to be in control of things. This impression is confirmed in Acts 15 at the famous council meeting. There Peter and Paul both confer, but James is the one who concludes the matter. I will say more about this crucial meeting shortly.

Let's be clear about what Acts and Paul, and not just later Christian tradition, suggest about James as a leader in the Jerusalem church. First, Acts does not use the term "bishop" to refer to him. The leaders in Jerusalem are called elders at Acts 11:30, in continuity with the Jewish tradition, and in 15:2 they are called apostles and elders. 1 Corinthians 9:5 speaks of the other apostles and the Lord's brothers, but there the Lord's brothers and the apostles are distinguished. And as we have seen, Galatians suggests that James is a pillar, indeed apparently the chief pillar of the Jerusalem Christian community, which was viewed as the eschatological reconstituting of God's people.

One of the things that is never suggested about James is that he was an itinerant apostle. He never seems to travel. Rather he is always in Jerusalem, people come to see him, and he sends out emissaries and messages to other churches. Perhaps this is why he is not usually called an apostle in Christian tradition, for the term *apostolos* refers to one sent out, to an agent or a missionary. Nor for that matter is James later called pope. He is however certainly listed in the earliest lists of bishops of Jerusalem in both Eusebius (*Hist. Eccl.* 4.5.3–4; 5.12.1–2) and Epiphanius (*Pan.* 66.21–22).[215]

It may be important as well that no honorific title is applied to James on his ossuary. The inscription simply reads "James son of Joseph, brother of Jesus." Such titles were not uncommon in grave inscriptions in the first century, but there is none on James's ossuary. It may be that he wanted it that way. If we can judge from James 1:1, this man preferred to be called a servant of God and of Jesus. There is no evidence that he himself insisted on some exalted title. What Paul says in Galatians 2 is that he is reputed to be a pillar, which implies someone else's way of giving James an honor rating. Nevertheless, both Galatians and Acts make very apparent how very important James was. If an independent-minded missionary apostle like Paul felt he needed James's support for his work to not be in vain, and if Luke portrays him in Acts 15 as the one who resolved the major crisis prompted by the Antioch incident, James was clearly a central figure in early Christianity.

This bears emphasizing precisely because of the "big three"—Peter, James, and Paul—it is almost always James who gets neglected in the discussion. This is understandable in view of the fact that some 35 percent of the New Testament is written by Paul, and his Gentile mission set the trajectory of the majority of the church in an increasingly Gentile direction as the first century progressed. It is also understandable because Peter is the one figure who was a major disciple of Jesus both before and after Easter, and there are two letters attributed to him in the New Testament. Furthermore, he took on enormous significance later for the church in Rome and in the Roman Catholic tradition. James has labored long in the shadow of these two towering figures. Yet it is James to whom both Peter and Paul answer and defer, according to Galatians 1–2 and Acts 15. This fact must not be underestimated when calculating James's significance for the early Jesus movement.

THE ANTIOCH INCIDENT REVISITED

I have already spoken of the fact that Galatians 2 records an incident in Antioch that transpired around A.D. 48 which involved tensions between James, Peter, and Paul, and more broadly between Jewish and Gentile Christians in the important city of Antioch. After Jerusalem, Antioch was the most important city, with the possible exception of Damascus, in the early days of establishing a following for Jesus among Jews and also Gentiles. According to Luke, it is the city where Jesus's followers were first called *Christianoi,* which literally means "those who belong or adhere to Christ" and is the origin of the term "Christian" (Acts 11:26). A significant number of Gentiles came to Christ in that city, and it raised the issues of table fellowship and also the more serious matter of whether Gentiles would be required to conform fully to the Mosaic Law in order to be able to be followers of Jesus, including whether they were to be circumcised.

There can be no doubt that a good number of Jerusalem Jewish followers of Jesus believed that Gentiles must become Jews in order to be followers of Jesus, indeed in order to be saved. Was this James's view as well? Some scholars have thought so and have imagined a major split between James and Paul on this issue. The evidence, however, does not really support this conclusion, as we shall see. For now the following needs to be pointed out.

First, the mention in Galatians 2 of men going from James to Antioch and causing a split in the community, at least temporarily, such that even Peter and Barnabas stopped accepting Gentile hospitality, should be coordinated with what Luke says in Acts 15:1: "Certain individuals came down from Judea to Antioch and were teaching believers, 'Unless you are circumcised, according to the custom taught by Moses, you can not be saved.'" This brought Paul and Barnabas into sharp dispute and debate with them. Luke goes on to say at Acts 15:5 that some of the believers who belonged to the sect of the Pharisees stood up in the Jerusalem meeting and made the same demand. It is natural to see the former group who went to Antioch as part of the Pharisaic Christians in Jerusalem. This might well help explain why there was an explosion on Paul's part about this matter in Galatians 2. After all, Paul had left behind being a Pharisee in Jerusalem when he gave his allegiance to Jesus, and it was his view that the Mosaic Law should not be imposed on Gentile converts. In his view it was neither necessary nor sufficient for their salvation. From Paul's point of view, some in Jerusalem were not understanding the radical implications of a gospel that proclaimed salvation by grace through faith in Jesus as a means of entering the community of God's people. These Pharisaic Jewish Christians Paul accused of trying to "Judaize" his converts, not just in Antioch, but also in Galatia. Indeed this very matter is what prompted him to write his letter to the neophyte Galatian Christians.

The crucial question became, How then shall we live as Jews and Gentiles in Christ? Would there be separate communities for each kind of Christian, which only occasionally and in limited ways met together? But how then would that fulfill the prophecies about the reconstruction of God's people, including the incorporation of Gentiles into that people? There was no issue more crucial to the Jesus movement in the middle of the first century, and standing right at the heart of the matter with Peter and Paul was James, and it was he who would resolve the matter, as we shall see in the next chapter. But here we should sum up the matters discussed in this chapter.

WHAT WE LEARNED AND WHAT THAT KNOWLEDGE TELLS US ABOUT JESUS

In this chapter we have seen that James was a crucial early leader of the Jesus movement, known for his Jewish piety and faithfulness to the Torah. Indeed, he gained a reputation early on for being something of an ascetic. This aspect of his faith should not be exaggerated since, unlike his brother Jesus, he was married. His asceticism may have been shaped by his following of Old Testament teachings about Naziritic vows, which did not require celibacy but did involve abstinence from some foods and normal practices, such as allowing one's hair to grow (see Numbers 6). Notice that in Acts 21:24 Paul is asked by James and the leaders in Jerusalem to undertake a Naziritic vow. Hegesippus and perhaps the Gospel of the Hebrews, which we spoke of at the beginning of this chapter, seem to confirm that James was a Nazirite or took on Naziritic vows from time to time.[216] This might explain why James got a reputation for spending time in the Temple, for Nazirites were to remain present in the vicinity of the Temple (Num. 6:18–20). This theory could also explain why James stayed in Jerusalem and is never said to travel.[217]

James is depicted in Galatians as a pillar of the new eschatological temple known as the people of God, and it is clear enough that at least by the time of the events recorded in Acts 12 he is clearly the leader of the Jerusalem church, as becomes especially clear in Acts 15 and Galatians 2. Others may confer, but James will conclude. Others may evangelize or act as an apostle or missionary, but James will authorize. It is James who will write the encyclical letter to the Gentile Christians according to Acts 15, and it is James who will write the encyclical letter to Jewish Christians that is found in the letter in the canon called James. James stands at the center of things: missions and messengers go out from him and come back and report to him. Even in the late 50s. Paul is still gathering money to take to James and the saints of the Jerusalem church in hopes of cementing the union of Jew and Gentile, and Jewish mother church and largely Gentile diaspora churches in Christ (see Romans 15). But what kind of leader was James? Was he a partisan for a hardline Jewish Christianity that was to make it difficult for Gentiles to follow Jesus? Or was he more of a mediating figure? We will address this question in our next chapter.

But most importantly, we have arrived at the juncture that a crucial fact has come to light. *None of these major figures who constituted the inner circle of Jesus, including Jesus's own brothers, would have become or remained followers of Jesus after the crucifixion if there had been no resurrection and no resurrection appearances of Jesus. The church, in the persons of its earliest major leaders, was constituted by the event of the resurrection, coupled with the Pentecost event. The stories of these figures, especially their post-Easter stories, validates this fact. There would be no church without the risen and appearing Jesus.*

There is more to be said as well. Those who would like to see Jesus as some kind of radical who was more like a Cynic philosopher than a Jewish sage have to explain why Jesus's brother turned out so differently than he did. How could James believe that he was faithfully following the example and teaching of his brother if his piety and practice and teaching were so radically different from Jesus's own piety and practice and teaching? How could James have thought that Jewish Christians should be practicing Jews if Jesus had taught that the whole Law was abolished? At the same time one can ask, How could James have been willing to agree that Gentile converts did not need to keep the Law in toto, if in fact Jesus had insisted that all converts to the Jesus movement had to become Jews? James is a witness to the fact that Jesus must have been in some respects a traditional Jew and in some respects not. We can only assume as well that someone like Peter would only accept James as head of the Jerusalem church if he was convinced that James's approach and teaching were essentially in accord with and in the spirit of Jesus's life and teachings. Peter was in a position to know about these things in detail, and both Acts and Galatians attest to Peter's acceptance of James in the chief leadership role, even though he was a Johnny-come-lately to the Jesus movement. This is extraordinary and surely could not have been accepted by Peter if James was really so radically different in focus, teaching, and tenor from Jesus. In short, a non-Jewish Jesus doesn't work any better than a non-Jewish James. If the roles of Mary Magdalene and Joanna attest to the more innovative and distinctive side of Jesus's ministry, James attests to the more traditional side of it. If we combine these portraits we see Jesus presenting himself as a thoroughly Jewish, though creative messianic figure who claims certain kinds of authority within the context of Israel that the Jewish religious leadership and even the client rulers found threatening but that others found helpful, healing, even eschatological. But what about the teaching of James? Could it have mirrored Jesus's teachings in some way? We will pursue this in the next chapter.

TEN

James the Mediator and His Letters to Gentiles and Jews

Nearly all scholars are in agreement that Acts 15 provides us with the Lukan perspective on one of the most important of all early church events, the so-called Jerusalem council.[218] Unlike the meeting Paul refers to in Galatians 2, which was private, this was the most public and potentially volatile of all early church meetings. Had Paul been describing the same meeting in Galatians 2 as we find in Acts 15, there can be no doubt he would have cited the Jerusalem decree to his Galatian converts, for it did not require of them circumcision. The silence of Galatians in regard to a non-requirement of circumcision of Gentiles by the Jerusalem church is deafening. Galatians was surely written before any such definitive meeting.

At the midpoint of the first century, in about 49 or 50, James was to preside over the first major turning point in early Christian history. Doubtless there would not have been a council at all if there had not been considerable success in the Gentile mission, indeed so much success that it threatened to overwhelm the original Jewish Christian flavor of the Jesus movement and turn it into something else altogether. According to Luke, Paul's first missionary journey (mentioned in Acts 13–14) coupled with the crisis in Antioch (mentioned in Acts 12) had made it necessary to address the issue of whether Gentiles could be accepted as followers of Jesus without becoming Jews (or at least proselytes or God-fearers).

But there was another important factor here. It was also earlier in A.D. 49 that the Emperor Claudius had expelled Jews and Jewish Christians from Rome due to a row over Christ.[219] On any showing A.D. 49 was a tumultuous year, and one can well imagine that Jewish Christians in Jerusalem, especially the Pharisaic ones, were feeling very much on edge and possibly worried about a reaction throughout the empire as the Jesus movement emerged from the synagogue and took on a life of its own.

What would happen if it became the generally received opinion in the empire that the Jesus movement was not just another form of early Judaism which was respected as an ancient religion, but rather a new "superstition" not protected by Roman tolerance for ancient and indigenous religions of various peoples such as the Jews?[220]

Nerves were undoubtedly on edge when Paul and Barnabas went to Jerusalem for this meeting. The Jerusalem church might quite rightly feel that Jews would be unapproachable if they thought that Jesus's followers were not expecting their converts to remain faithful to the Mosaic Law in some way. But how to adjudicate this matter without compromising the heart of the gospel preached to Gentiles and Jews, namely salvation by grace through faith in Jesus? Who constituted the people of God, and on what basis? What place did Gentiles have within the people of God? An interrelated series of issues was at stake.

A careful analysis of Acts 15 will show the following: (1) Peter seems to enter the discussion basically from the Pauline view of the matter; (2) Paul and Barnabas simply recount the miraculous signs and wonders God did among the Gentiles when they were on their missionary tour (15:12); (3) the Pharisaic Christian position does not prevail, because James does not agree to circumcision of Gentiles; (4) but at the same time James does not simply echo Peter's speech either. James is a mediator, and he takes a mediating position on these volatile issues. We must examine first James's brief homily (15:13–18), James's judgment (v. 19–21), the letter from the apostles and elders to Gentile believers in Antioch and elsewhere, and then his letter written to his fellow Jewish Christians in the Diaspora.

THE SERMON OF JAMES (ACTS 15:13–18)

The first thing to notice about James's sermon is that he picks up where Peter left off. He seems to be providing scriptural support for Peter's argument that the Gentiles should not be required to keep the entire Mosaic Law.[221] First James says, "Brothers, listen to me. Peter has told you about the time God first visited the Gentiles to take a people for himself. And this conversion of Gentiles agrees with what the prophets predicted." James then cites some form of Amos 9:11–12. In fact, it appears that James is combining Amos 9:11–12 and Zechariah 2:11 in his Scripture citation. The latter text says, "Many nations will be joined with the Lord in that day and will become my people. I will live among you and you will know that the Lord Almighty has sent me to you." Amos 9:11 says, "In that day I will restore David's fallen tent."

The point of the quote is to show that God would rebuild David's fallen tent and that in doing so Gentiles would be included in the people of God. James seems to be an early advocate of restoration-of-Israel theology. The Lord returns to rebuild Israel's tent *so that* all other peoples may seek the Lord. James's point is that no one should be surprised at the influx of Gentiles in the present eschatological time since it was prophesied long ago. It would appear that this homily is meant to prepare the audience for hearing a judgment that supports including Gentiles in the Jesus movement, and without requiring that they become Jews and keep the entire Mosaic Law. What then was the nature of the compromise James was to offer the divided Christian body on that day?

THE DECREE OF JAMES

We find the decree in essence in three places in Acts: Acts 15:20, 15:29, and 21:25. Unfortunately there are also three different forms of the decree found in the various manuscripts of Acts. The version that is likely the earliest, providing an explanation for the later modifications, is the version that includes the following items: (1) *eidolothuton,* which means food sacrificed to and eaten in the presence of idols; (2) blood; (3) things strangled; and (4) *porneia.* If Gentiles avoid these items, then fellowship with Jewish Christians is possible. But what is the import of these items for Gentiles, and what is James really asking? Is James actually imposing on Gentiles the food laws found in Leviticus 17–18 or perhaps the Noachic restrictions found in Genesis 9:3–4? This is often how the decree has been interpreted in the past, but there are real problems with this view. For one thing, Genesis 9:3–4 is about abstaining from meat with blood in it, and nothing is said about "idol meat" or associations with pagan worship. Furthermore, the restrictions in Genesis 9 were regarded in early Judaism as being for Gentiles living in Israel, not Gentiles living in the Diaspora. Notice nothing is said about sexual immorality in this Genesis text either. What then of Leviticus 17–18? Is James appealing to this text and applying it to Gentiles? Again these are rules for Gentiles living within Israel, not for the Gentiles being addressed in the letter that the Jerusalem church sends out. In neither the LXX of Leviticus 17–18 nor in Genesis 9 does the key term *eidolothuton* occur. Furthermore, Leviticus 17:10–14 prohibits the eating of blood, but nothing more. Nor is the text about food partaken of in the context of an act of idolatry. Nor is anything said in Leviticus about things strangled. Nor is the term *porneia* used in Leviticus 18, which describes sexual aberrations that occur between people too closely related by blood. Are these Levitical restrictions really what James wanted to impose on Gentiles? It seems very unlikely, especially since there is another, and much more viable, explanation of the decree.

Let's suppose that the decree is as much about venue as it is about eating and being sexually immoral. Let's suppose that we should have asked, Where would Gentiles regularly encounter and be tempted by these four items? What would be the most basic requirements, even going back to the Ten Commandments, that God requires of people? Obviously the Ten Commandments suggest that a person must give up idolatry and immorality to properly worship the God of the Bible. Suppose this is what James is requiring in the decree by saying, "Stay away from pagan temples, where there is idol worship involving idol meat and blood and things strangled, and sexual immorality."

The proof that this is what James is requiring here is that the term *eidolothuton* is in fact a technical term meaning meat sacrificed and eaten in the presence of an idol.[222] It is not a term for meat simply found in a Gentile meat market somewhere. Furthermore, the term *porneia* comes from the word *porne* (from which we get "pornography") and has as its root meaning prostitution, and in this case temple prostitution.

To sum up, then, James is requiring that Gentiles forsake their pagan past, with its idolatry and immorality, and give up attending the worship and banquets found in pagan temples. He is not imposing food laws per se on Gentiles. If Gentiles would consistently do what James requests, it would be a witness to Jews in the Roman Empire that the heart of the Ten Commandments was being honored by them. We know from a text like 1 Corinthians 8–10, which discusses the very matter of attending idol feasts, that Gentile Christians had a real temptation to continue following that social practice, even after their conversion, and we know that Paul warned that it was scandalizing Jewish Christians, as well as Jews in Corinth. In my view, Paul is seen to be implementing the decree in 1 Corinthians 8–10.

The implications of this interpretation of the decree are important for our understanding of James. James, then, is not imposing a modicum of food laws from the Old Testament on Gentiles. He is urging a hard and fast break with their pagan past, especially with pagan worship and dining practices in temples. In this regard, James and Paul are by no means far apart.[223]

Where James and Paul seem to have differed is on whether Jewish Christians, not Gentiles, should be required to continue to be observant of the Mosaic Law. Paul's answer was no, it could be a blessed option, but not required (see 1 Cor. 9). James's answer seems to have been yes, it was required that Jewish Christians continue to be observant, not least because of the hope of winning more Jews to the following of Jesus. The divide would come then over what Jewish Christians would be expected to do, to have fellowship with the ever-increasing majority of Gentile Christians. Some Jewish Christians would be prepared to become temporarily unclean through dining with Gentiles, and then go through ritual purification. Others would not be prepared to do so, and thus a stream of strongly Jewish Christianity would go its own way, having very little contact or fellowship with Gentile Christians. In fact I would suggest that the New Testament bears witness that this is exactly what happened. We have various documents addressed almost exclusively to Jewish Christians in various places, both early documents like the homily of James, documents from the 60s like Hebrews, and later documents like the Johannine epistles or the Gospel of Matthew. What then of the letter of James to Gentiles in the Diaspora?

THE LETTER OF JAMES AND THE CHURCH TO GENTILES

The irenic tone of the letter found in Acts 15:23–29 is immediately apparent. The letter mentions that the Jerusalem church recognizes that some went out from them and upset the Gentiles, doing so without authorization. This is why they sent two representatives of the Jerusalem church, Judas and Silas, with Paul and Barnabas to convey or interpret the sense of the letter and the decree it contains. Notice too that there is a concern about burdening the Gentiles (15:28), an issue raised by Peter in his speech (15:10). Beyond the few items listed in the decree, nothing was to be added. Judas and Silas are described as prophets and thus in tune with what the Spirit would lead them to say about the decree.

Something else to notice about the letter and this gesture is that Paul and Barnabas are not entrusted with the letter's delivery or interpretation per se. The letter is placed in the hands of the representatives of the Jerusalem church. This avoids the potential problem that Paul and Barnabas might have been accused of slanting the decree in a direction the Jerusalem church would not necessarily endorse. This shrewd maneuver removes that potential problem. Overall, the picture of James is of a leader who, while not merely a compromiser, was able to be flexible enough not to stifle the Gentile mission. If the test of good leadership is that the leader does not take the way out which is easiest for his own immediate situation, but rather does what he thinks best for all concerned, then James does that as well. This will become especially apparent in the next narrative that refers to James, namely the story of James's final meeting with Paul, recorded in Acts 21.

JAMES, THE COLLECTION, AND PAUL'S ARREST

Paul was on any showing a very controversial figure, and his statement in 1 Corinthians 9:20-21 that he could become the Jew to the Jew and the Gentile to the Gentile, because he was no longer under the Mosaic Law but rather under the Law of Christ, was bound to raise many eyebrows in Jerusalem and elsewhere. We will talk more directly about Paul in the last section of this book, but here we must deal with his interaction with James. In Acts 21 we do find an example of this sort of pragmatic approach to Jewish customs, when Paul is asked by James to demonstrate that he respects the Law by submitting to a vow of sorts. This ironically proves to be Paul's undoing, for while he is in the Temple precincts he is recognized and labeled as one who teaches Gentiles to break the Mosaic Law. We must consider this narrative in more detail and see what it reveals to us about James himself, and James in his relationship with Paul.

The story is told by Luke, who is probably present with Paul on this occasion. Paul has arrived in Jerusalem after making "the collection," a gift from the Gentile churches to the Jerusalem church for famine relief in about A.D. 58 (Rom. 15:25-27—"But before I come to Rome I must go down to Jerusalem to take a gift to the Christians there. For you see the believers in Greece have eagerly taken up an offering for the Christians in Jerusalem who are going through some hard times").[224] Luke says that he and Paul were well received by the Jerusalem church, and this presumably meant the collection was received as well, though it would not ultimately have the effect Paul desired of binding the Gentile churches to the mother church in Jerusalem.[225] Notice that we are told that on day two of their visit, they went to have an audience with James (21:18), and all the elders were present as well. Paul gives a status report on his Gentile mission, which led to God being praised by the Jerusalem leaders.

There is then a request, or perhaps request is not a strong enough term, made of Paul. Because there are thousands of Jews who have believed in Jesus but who are also zealous for the Law, who have heard the report that Paul teaches Gentiles to turn away from Moses, Paul must join four men in their rites of purification, and he must pay their expenses (v. 24—possibly out of the collection funds?). The intent of this act is to show that Paul lives in obedience to the Law. This request is not said to come specifically from James, but at the least he agrees with it. But were they asking Paul to violate his principles? Was this an example of making a good show of things, when the reality was really otherwise? Would Paul have seen this as an opportunity to show he could be the Jew to the Jew? Perhaps Paul would have viewed this in such a light, but of course the most it could demonstrate is that he was sometimes observant of the Law and was happy to do so on those occasions.

The importance of this story for our understanding of James is this. It shows that James was himself very much concerned that the witness (to observant Jews and to those who were already converts and were still observant Jews) not be undone, especially by Paul failing to keep the Law while visiting Jerusalem. Since paying for others' purification rituals was not obligatory but optional under the Law, it would show Paul was an extremely pious Jew. The plan, however, backfired, and Paul, after having been taken prisoner by the guards of the Temple precincts in Jerusalem, spent the next two years under house arrest in Caesarea Maritima, where the proconsul lived.

Should we take seriously the suggestion that there were many observant Jews among the early Jewish Christians in Jerusalem? Yes I think we must, and it must be noted that they apparently were quite content with having James as their leader, which speaks volumes about James. He too was an observant Jew, and he believed other Jewish Christians should be as well. This can only mean that he would have had some differences of opinion with Paul about this matter, since Paul saw such observance of the Law as optional once he became a follower of Jesus. But would James undertake to critique Paul, or the frequent misunderstandings of Paul (as in Acts 21:21), in print? Some scholars think this is what we find in the canonical document called James. We must examine this letter to Jewish Christians at this juncture.

DID JAMES WRITE JAMES?

Scholars are divided on whether James the brother of Jesus could have written the letter that bears his name, but it is fair to say that most scholars think that either James wrote this letter (perhaps with the aid of a scribe who knew Greek well), or at the least it contains his source material even though a later editor arranged and polished the material.[226] The Greek of the letter of James is quite good Koine Greek and even has considerable rhetorical polish, which has led some to think the letter could not be by James in its present form.[227] This sort of reasoning, however, is questionable. Consider, for example, the case of Paul. His letters reflect considerable rhetorical sophistication, a skill he probably derived from spending time learning rhetoric in a school in Jerusalem! Whether James also received such training or not, there were plenty of scribes in Jerusalem who had received it, and James himself could have had a letter composed to Greek-speaking Jews or Jewish Christians in the Diaspora.[228]

There are several clues that suggest that this letter does indeed ultimately derive from James. First, there is the self-effacing way the author identifies himself as a servant of Jesus. The degree to which this letter echoes the teaching of Jesus supports this identification as one who is a servant of the master teacher, Jesus. A later Christian writer would be likely to have called James the brother of Jesus, or James the Just of Jerusalem, or the like. The identification in James 1:1 is simple and believable. Second, it is assumed that the audience will know which James the author is speaking of. There was only one James that is ever referred to in the New Testament without further qualification, and that is James the brother of Jesus.

Notice, for example, the respect shown to James and the authority he is assumed to have in Jude verse 1, which reads, "Jude, a servant of Jesus Christ and brother of James." As Richard J. Bauckham has shown at length, the brief letter of Jude was indeed probably by another of Jesus's brothers,[229] and it is significant then that both these brothers identify themselves as servants of Jesus. Notice also how Jude identifies himself in relationship to James as well, whereas James does not reciprocate this practice in his letter.[230] This too suggests that the James in question does not have to establish his authority or further identify himself for his audience, and it also suggests that James is the elder and more famous brother of the two. The conclusion is likely that we do indeed hear the authentic voice of James in the letter that bears his name, even if he had a scribe help him compose the letter or if there was some light editing of the letter after the fact by another Jewish Christian.

THE AUDIENCE OF THE LETTER OF JAMES

The letter of James is addressed to "the Twelve Tribes in the Diaspora."[231] This phrase is a natural way to refer to Jews outside Israel, but it is not a natural way to refer to the church. But in fact it needs to be remembered that the earliest Jewish followers of Jesus, including James, did not see themselves as starting a new religion. It is clear enough from the content of James that this homily, for it really is more of a homily than a letter, is addressed to those Jews who are followers of Jesus outside the Holy Land, but the author does not use any specifically Christian terms to identify the audience, such as "those in Christ" or the term *Christianoi* from which we get the term "Christian."[232] This appears to be because "early Jewish Christians thought of themselves, not as a specific sect distinguished from other Jews, but as the nucleus of the Messianic renewal of the people of Israel, which was underway and would come to include all Israel.... What James addresses in practice to those Jews who already confess the Messiah Jesus, he addresses in principle to all Israel."[233] This form of addressing the audience, however, tells us something else.

This letter was written from Israel, not from somewhere in the Diaspora, and there was certainly no place in Israel more appropriate for such a circular letter to go forth from than from Jerusalem and from the original Jewish Christian community. In my judgment, it appears likely that this letter was written probably ten years prior to James's death or a bit later (so from about A.D. 52 on), after the Jerusalem council, and after the impact of Paul and his gospel had become rather widespread and well known in the Diaspora. If this is correct, then there is an important connection between the letter of James and the letter to the Gentiles that resulted from the council cited in Acts 15. James, after he chose to write to Gentile Christians in the Diaspora, then chose to write to Jewish Christians in the Diaspora, explaining to them as well how they ought to live. Part of the function of this homily called "James" was to help the audience to not be misled or confused by some reports about or versions of Paul's message as well as to confirm them in their commitment to various Jewish ways of viewing life and religious practice. The circular letter of James turns out to be a remarkable window into the mind of James and the way he thought about his fellow Jewish Christians.

JAMES AND THE JESUS TRADITION

The letter of James has many special features, one of which is that it uses many words (sixty to be precise) that are not found anywhere else in the New Testament. James clearly has his own style and vocabulary. And yet he also reflects a profound indebtedness to the teachings of Jesus and other forms of early Jewish wisdom literature. The material we find in James reflects the long and rich heritage of Jewish wisdom literature, which includes proverbs, aphorisms, riddles, parables, and various sorts of sage advice about topics having to do with the everyday life of a religious Jew. Such topics would include what one does with one's money, prayer, how to handle an illness, curbing one's tongue, and the like. We find this sort of more generic advice in Proverbs, Ecclesiastes, Wisdom of Solomon, Sirach, and elsewhere. But most importantly James is indebted to his brother's wisdom teaching found in the Sermon on the Mount. A careful comparison of portions of especially the Matthean form of the Sermon on the Mount and James is very interesting.[234] Consider the following list:

James 1:2	Matt. 5:11–12/Luke 6:22–23
James 1:4	Matt. 5:48
James 1:5	Matt. 7:7
James 1:17	Matt. 7:11
James 1:22	Matt. 7:24/Luke 6:46–47
James 1:23	Matt. 7:26/Luke 6:49
James 2:5	Matt. 5:3, 5/Luke 6:20
James 2:10	Matt. 5:18–19 (cf. Luke 3:9)
James 2:11	Matt. 5:21–22
James 2:13	Matt. 5:7/Luke 6:36
James 3:12	Matt. 7:16–18/Luke 6:43–44
James 3:18	Matt. 5:9
James 4:2–3	Matt. 7:7–8
James 4:4	Matt. 6:24/Luke 16:13
James 4:8	Matt. 5:8
James 4:9	Matt. 5:4/Luke 6:25
James 4:11	Matt. 7:1–2/Luke 6:37–38
James 5:2–3	Matt. 6:19–21/Luke 12:33
James 5:6	Matt. 7:1/Luke 6:37
James 5:10	Matt. 5:11–12/Luke 6:23
James 5:12	Matt. 5:34–37[235]

What this list shows is that James clearly knows a collection of Jesus's sayings in some form. These parallels by themselves rule out the theory that we should see the book of James as a sort of nonmessianic and non-Christian Jewish tract that has been slightly Christianized at some point.[236] No, the letter of James is deeply indebted to the Jesus tradition. Furthermore, the brief wisdom narratives found in James 1:23–24, 2:2, and 2:15–17 also reflect a specific indebtedness to the Jesus tradition, for this form of wisdom material was not characteristic of Jewish wisdom literature before Jesus. What is most striking about James's use of the Jesus tradition is that he rarely quotes it, nor does he attribute it to Jesus. Rather he weaves various ideas, themes, and phrases from the Jesus tradition into his own argument. Sometimes the parallels are obvious and striking, for instance in the saying about perfection in James 1:4 ("You may be mature and complete/perfect") and Matthew 5:48 ("Be perfect ... as your heavenly Father is perfect"), and the saying on peacemaking in James 3:17–18 and Matthew 5:9 (the only two references to peacemakers in the New Testament). On the basis of the parallels between James and the Matthean form of these sayings of Jesus, P. J. Hartin has concluded, rightly I think, that it would appear that the more Jewish form of Jesus's sayings found in Matthew are in general likely to be closer to the original form in which Jesus uttered such sayings, as opposed to the more Hellenized and even Gentilized form of the sayings found in Luke.[237]

THE CONVENTIONAL AND COUNTER-ORDER WISDOM OF JAMES

James is interested in conveying conventional wisdom of a practical sort, but he also offers some counter-order wisdom as well. Let's consider some samples of this material. At the very outset of his exhortation James makes clear that wisdom from above is what must be sought to deal with life's trials and temptations (James 1:2–6). The hearer[238] is not exhorted to learn the teachings of Jesus or the Law, but rather to pray for wisdom from above. James seems to operate with the same theology as Jesus of the importance of fresh revelation to guide God's people through dark times. This approach is much like what we find in the Wisdom of Solomon 7:7–8: "Therefore I prayed and understanding was given to me; I called on God, and the spirit of wisdom came to me."[239] Unlike some of the sages from much earlier in Israel's history (for example, some of those who contributed to Proverbs), James does not exhort his audience to observe life or nature to gain wisdom. It is rather something one gains from God directly or receives from one's teacher.

A second feature of James's wisdom is that it is wisdom from and for the marginalized and oppressed minority. For example, what James says about riches and the rich in James 2:6 and 5:1–5 ("Your gold and silver have corroded") sounds a good deal like what Jesus says in Matthew 6:19 ("Do not store up for yourself treasures on earth"). Here again James stands with Jesus and against the older Jewish wisdom, which stressed that riches were a blessing from God. In the view of both James and Jesus, the men from Nazareth, riches were a temptation and a snare to vulnerable human beings.

There is a danger in taking the letter of James as reflecting his mind on all the subjects he thought important for Christians to reflect on. James here is focusing on inculcating a specific sort of community ethic and ethos, and so his comments are inwardly directed (James 4:11; 5:9). He says things like "Let not many of you become teachers" (James 3:1). He does not say, "Go make disciples of all nations," but this is in part because of his audience and the purposes he has in writing this document. It seems clear from Galatians 2:8–9 that James was all for sharing the Good News with both Jews and Gentiles, for that text says that James extended the right hand of fellowship to Paul and Barnabas and agreed they should go evangelize the Gentiles.

What sort of ethical concerns does James focus on? Here are a few of his emphases: (1) caring for widows and orphans in the community; (2) keeping oneself unstained by the world; (3) fulfilling the royal Law according to scripture; (4) bridling one's tongue and passions; (5) persevering in faith through trials and suffering; (6) confessing sins to one another in the community; (7) praying for the sick and suffering; and (8) retrieving the erring community member.

Again and again there are echoes of earlier Jewish wisdom literature, particularly that from the so-called intertestamental period (Wisdom of Solomon and Sirach).[240] For example, compare James 1:27–2:9 to Sirach 35:15–16, which reads: "For the Lord is the judge, and with him there is no partiality. He will not show partiality to the poor, but he will listen to the one who is wronged. He will not ignore the supplication of the orphan or the widow when she pours out her complaint." Or again the same stress on carefully controlled speech is expressed in Sirach 23:7–15 and 27:4–5 as we find in James 3:1–12, especially when it comes to avoiding cursing and abusive speech. What can be said about this material is that, much like the exhortations found in 1, 2, and 3 John,[241] the function of this material is to help prevent a certain kind of Christian community from losing its sense of identity, by setting up carefully controlled boundaries affecting speech, behavior, and relationships. This comports quite well with what we have seen in Galatians 2, where men came from James complaining about Jewish Christians eating with Gentile Christians, and so being a bad witness to other Jews, as well as becoming ritually unclean themselves. It also comports with what we find in Acts 21, where efforts are made to get Paul to present himself as an observant Jew in the Temple, so the evangelism of Jews would not be harmed by the Pauline evangelism of Gentiles. We have once more turned to the discussion of James and Paul, and two topics raised in James deserve some discussion accordingly: (1) what James says about the royal Law and (2) what James says about faith and works.

JAMES AND PAUL REVISITED

Perhaps the most important thing that can be said about James's comments about the royal or perfect Law (James 1:25) is that James is not simply referring to the Mosaic Law, but the Mosaic Law is certainly included in what he is referring to. James stands in the tradition of Jesus ben Sira and other earlier Jewish sages (such as some of those who produced some of the Qumran documents) who drew both from the Law and also from other Jewish wisdom material for their teaching. They believed that all wisdom came from God and that not all of it was found in the repository known as the Mosaic Law.[242]

James was not, however, a Pharisee. There is no evidence in the New Testament anywhere that James took the position of the radical Pharisaic Jewish Christians who demanded that Gentiles be circumcised and keep the food and Sabbath laws.[243] Make demands on Gentiles James did, and clearly he also believed that Jewish Christians should remain observant Jews. This in part is what the letter of James is about. But notice nowhere in the letter of James is there any discussion about food laws, strict Sabbath keeping, or circumcision, or any other of the usual boundary marker issues that Paul had to deal with when he was confronted by Judaizers. This is probably in part because such matters were not up for debate amongst Jewish Christians, most of whom had been circumcised as infants and had long since been keeping the Sabbath and various food laws. The attempt to pit James against Paul, which found encouragement from Martin Luther when he called the Epistle of James a "right strawy epistle," is wrong, not because there are not differences of approach to the new faith community by James and Paul, but because James was more of a mediating figure between the Judaizers and Paul than is usually realized, and Paul was not a person who had an allergic reaction to the notion that faith without the fruit of faith in good works was a barren faith indeed.[244] Indeed, Paul was prepared to talk about the Law of Christ (cf. Gal. 6 to 1 Cor. 9). Paul was not anti-Law, any more than James was a legalist.

What James here says in his letter about obedience to God's word and charity and the like are not things Paul would have objected to. As it turns out, since for James the royal or perfect Law of God includes (1) various Mosaic provisions such as the Ten Commandments, (2) the wisdom teachings of Jesus, and (3) other early Jewish and perhaps even non-Jewish wisdom material, this hardly differs from Paul's approach to the Law of Christ. Galatians 6:1–2 makes evident that the Law of Christ includes the teachings of Jesus, and if we look elsewhere in the Pauline ethical material (see Rom. 12:9–15:6; 1 Cor. 9:19–23), it also includes various teachings from the Mosaic Law and other early Jewish material as well. Where James and Paul differ in these matters can be seen in 1 Corinthians 9:20–23. Paul believes that even for a Jew such as himself, observing the Mosaic Law is a blessed option, but not an obligation. James did not agree.

At the heart of the matter is a true difference of emphasis. James wants to emphasize the continuity of the Jesus movement with early Judaism's approach to the Law and what constitutes the people of God. Paul, on the other hand, wants to emphasize the new eschatological situation[245] that Christ's death and resurrection has precipitated, such that there has already begun a new creation, a new covenant, a new way of constituting the people of God. In Paul's view the Mosaic covenant, while glorious, has become a glorious anachronism (see Gal. 3:19–4:31). Christ, and faith in Christ, should be that which circumscribes the boundaries of the community of Jesus, not the Mosaic Law and its covenant obligations. It would appear that the anxiety expressed in Acts 21:21 was in a sense a prophetic word. In James's view, if Paul's approach to the Jesus movement prevailed, then it was likely that only a tiny minority of Jews would want to be involved in it, and the "church" would become a predominantly Gentile entity. This was James's concern, and so he set out to preserve a form of Jewish Christianity in which there was less discontinuity with early Judaism than in the Pauline form of Christianity. This brings us to the famous discussion about faith and works in James 2:14–24.

It appears clear from this text that James is concerned to correct a misunderstanding of the Pauline Gospel. This misunderstanding suggested that Paul was saying that one is "justified" by faith alone and that righteous deeds or obedience to God's commands once one believes is not required for salvation. There are in fact several misunderstandings here. First, note that James is addressing those who are already Jewish *Christians* (notice the reference to Christian brothers and sisters in James 2:15). James is not talking about how one becomes a believer in Jesus; he is talking about the behavior of those who already are believers in Jesus. James in 2:22 says that faith is made complete by deeds. He does not say deeds are a prerequisite to God accepting a person. Second, in James 2:24 James is speaking about final justification, or final right-standing with God at the last judgment. He is not referring to how one initially obtains right-standing with God in this life. His perspective here does not differ from that of Paul, especially the later Paul we find in Philippians or Ephesians or the pastoral epistles.

Yet at the same time, it is very clear that James uses in James 2 the Abraham story in a much more traditional early Jewish way to inculcate good deeds flowing out of faith, deeds like Abraham performed in offering Isaac, and so he makes a very different use of the Abraham story than Paul does in Galatians 3:6–9 and Romans 4:1–15.[246] Paul uses the Abraham story to show how a person gains right-standing with God by God reckoning or crediting a person's faith as righteousness.

The caricature that all early Judaism was grounded in legalism and works righteousness without any emphasis on grace and God's mercy taking precedence in the way God deals with people is simply false. The caricature that James embodies such a "works righteousness" approach in James 2 is equally false. Good works are simply the natural and indeed expected outflow of saving faith for a believing person. You will know the tree by the fruit it bears.

So we see two very different ways of using the Abraham story in Paul's letters and the letter of James. James uses the story to correct a misunderstanding of Paul's gospel which suggested that obedience to God's Law was optional once one was saved by faith. Paul uses the same story from Genesis 12 about Abraham to correct the notion of the Judaizers that in order for Gentiles to have right-standing with God at all they must be circumcised and keep the Mosaic Law. They are arguing against different misunderstandings of the implications of the crucial Abraham story in Genesis 12. It is a historical mistake to pit James against Paul in some radical way, as if Paul's message as he proclaimed it to Gentiles was being corrected by James. James is asking and answering the question, How then shall believers, in this case Jewish Christians, live, as illustrated by the Abraham story? Paul is asking and answering—How then shall believers, in his case mainly Gentile believers, be saved, as illustrated by the Abraham story? The focus of each writer is different.

R. J. Bauckham has this to say on the matter: "That there are very considerable differences between James and Paul is not in doubt. But they should not be exaggerated at the expense of the notable similarities … in an historical reconstruction that has an eye only for diversity in early Christianity. … In a canonical conversation … between James and Paul there would be much nodding of heads and smiling agreement as well as some knitting of brows and some exclamations of surprise."[247] It is quite true that the letter of James does not reflect the central Pauline message about salvation being grounded in the death and resurrection of Jesus, but then the letter of James should be compared to the more ethical sections of Paul's letters, such as we find in Romans 12–15, not the more theological sections, and James after all is addressing those who are already Christians. Bauckham keenly observes that the faith James is complaining about is mere intellectual assent that does not affect behavior whereas the works Paul is complaining about are the attempts to achieve right-standing with God by human effort.

He adds:

> The kind of faith which James envisages as existing "alone" without works, is mere intellectual assent to truths about God (2.19). Paul who never speaks of faith in that sense, would certainly agree that no one is justified by that kind of faith alone.... But the faith which, like Abraham's, is completed by works must be the kind of faith about which James is explicit in James 1.6–7: that wholehearted trust in God to which "double-mindedness" is opposed. About the nature of Abraham's paradigm faith Paul and James are agreed. No one who does "works" in the context of that kind of faith can be relying on them for acceptance by God. Such works constitute "the obedience of faith" (Rom. 1.5; 16.26). When Paul says that justification is not by works he does not have in mind at all these works done in faith. When James says that justification is by works he does not have in mind at all the works of self-reliance which compromise faith.[248]

The discovery of the ossuary of James has given us an opportunity to re-examine much of what has been thought about James in the past, but it also gives us an opportunity to correct caricatures of both James and Paul and their differences. The differences should neither be minimized nor exaggerated. If it is sometimes true that history is written by the "winners," at least fresh historical evidence gives us an opportunity to correct false impressions about a form of early Christianity that came forth from James and the Jerusalem church, even though eventually it was to largely die out by the Middle Ages.

All too often the book of James has been viewed as nothing more than a rehashing of conventional Jewish wisdom. I must confess that I have sometimes thought this was mostly true.

Bauckham, however, has made clear that there is another side or dimension to the wisdom of James. For one thing, James does ethics in an eschatological context much as Jesus does. He does ethics in the shadow of the eschaton, with one eye on the horizon for the coming Judge who is also the Redeemer. James 5:3, 7 speaks of the last days and the coming of the Lord. It is this coming that provides a sanction or added seriousness to all of James's ethical teaching. For another thing, like the teaching of Jesus, the teaching of James involves the same intensification of demand and sometimes some of the new teaching and new emphases of Jesus. This should not surprise us since there are so many allusions to the teaching of Jesus in this letter, as we have already seen in this chapter.

For example, James concentrates on the theme of wholeness or perfection in this letter, a theme he derives from the material in the Sermon on the Mount. This theme is enunciated by stressing whole-hearted loyalty to God, fulfilling the whole royal Law, doing that which comports with what one believes and speaks, and behaving in ways that bring wholeness and peace to the community. The opposite of this is saying one thing and doing another, or being double-minded. James follows his more famous brother in suggesting that God demands more under the new covenant than was demanded under the old one, because more grace and revelation have been given.

James follows Jesus in prohibiting oaths.[249] Why? Because an oath suggests that some things which one says are more clearly or absolutely true than others. In James's view, every remark should have the same truthfulness that oaths require. Speech is regarded as an indicator or barometer of one's moral character, which is one reason James has so much concern for the ethics of speaking truthfully (cf. 1:19, 26; 3:1–12; 4:11–12; 5:9, 12). Indeed he stresses the matter even more than his brother Jesus.

Perhaps the clearest indicator that James does sometimes emphasize themes of a counter-order wisdom, a wisdom that undermines rather than undergirds the traditional structure of his society, is found in what he says about not giving special treatment to those of higher status or who are wealthy. This is condemned as partiality and furthermore is an implicit dishonoring of the poor. In fact God is one who produces reversal of fortunes and reversal of status, for God is no respecter of persons and does not endorse human attempts at a hierarchy of being or society that suggests that the rich are better and deserve better treatment than the poor, or that men should have a higher place in society than women, or that one race or ethnic group is inherently superior to another.

Notice how James constructs community, just as Paul and other Christians do, not by using the language that creates hierarchy (that is, by calling those he addresses "son" or "daughter"), but rather by addressing the audience as spiritual brothers or sisters. Honor or shame is determined by speech and conduct, not by social considerations such as gender, wealth, power, and the like. Wisdom is derived from revelation, rather than a reasoning about nature or human nature or by passing along what might be called commonsense advice in the form of aphorism or maxims and the like. James does not want his audience to fit easily into a fallen world. Rather he wants them to build a countercultural community that reflects its own values.[250] This comports quite readily with the decree and the letter James sent to the Gentiles, according to Acts 15, in which he asked the Gentiles not to conform to the dominant religious values of their world by attending feasts in pagan temples and participating in all that went on in that locale. In a similar fashion in his letter to Diaspora Jewish Christians, James expects his audience to live by the new revelatory wisdom that comes down from above, and through Jesus, rather than simply returning to an old source like the material we find in Proverbs.

James was indeed a sage, but he was by no means simply reiterating material from Proverbs or the Wisdom of Solomon or following Jesus ben Sira's teaching. He had been too shaped by the wisdom of his own brother when it came to issues of truth-telling, impartiality, peace-making, nonretaliation, perfection, and generosity both human and divine, to do so. In fact, I would suggest that James's mediatory role and practice in the church was profoundly shaped by his convictions in these matters, convictions he derived from the teaching of Jesus. These convictions are reflected in the decree and letter to the Gentiles just as they are reflected in his letter to Jewish Christians in the Diaspora. Both these documents strive for concord and harmony in the Diaspora between Gentiles and Jews who follow Jesus, without compromising core ethical and theological convictions of the new movement. In this James simply sought to be what he calls himself in James 1:1—"a servant of God and of the Lord Jesus Christ."

WHAT WE'VE LEARNED AND WHAT THAT KNOWLEDGE TELLS US ABOUT JESUS

Sometimes those who are able to work out delicate compromises between persons or groups with differing opinions are viewed as not principled enough, as going in whichever direction the wind is currently blowing. This would be an unfair criticism of James. He was a Torah-true Jew who at the same time was committed to Jesus as the Jewish messiah and to the Good News about Jesus. He was the first great leader of the church who felt strongly about both the inclusion of Gentiles in this religious movement and the inclusion of Jews who would remain observant of the Mosaic Law. But how was this to be accomplished?

If James insisted, as did some hard-line Pharisaic Jewish Christians, that Gentiles must be circumcised, even as adults, and keep all of the requirements of the Law, this would undoubtedly stifle the possibility of including many Gentiles in the church. On the other hand, if some compromise position was not crafted, both Jews and conservative Jewish converts would be scandalized and might reject or abandon the Jesus movement. James chose to focus on the heart of the Law, indeed the heart of the Ten Commandments, which demand abstaining from idolatry and immorality. James did not impose food laws from Leviticus or Genesis on Gentiles living in the Diaspora. Instead he says in essence what Paul urges in texts like 1 Thessalonians 1:9 ("You turned from idols to serve the living God") or 1 Corinthians 8–10. He says that Gentiles must stop going to pagan temples and engaging in the practices believed to be common in those venues—worshipping false gods, eating meat with blood in it in the presence of an idol as part of an act of worship, and engaging in sexual immorality at the idol feasts. In other words, he wants the Gentiles to make a clean break with the pagan religious practices of their past (which in some cases Gentiles seem to have continued even after becoming Christians—see 1 Cor. 8–10).

This was the minimum requirement James felt must be met by Gentiles if there was hope for Jewish and Gentile followers of Jesus to be able to associate with one another, worship with one another, even have table fellowship with one another. Perhaps he also thought that when Jews and Gentiles dined together the Gentiles would be sensitive enough not to scandalize the Jewish believers by imposing their own beliefs about non-kosher food and drink on the group fellowship (see Romans 14).

In all of this, James was remarkably similar to Paul in his approach to such matters. He differed from Paul, however, in the fact that he felt Jewish Christians needed to continue to observe the Mosaic Law. Had James's own views actually prevailed in the Diaspora with Jewish Christians, both in their approach to their own practice and in their view and relationship with Gentiles, it is possible that more than a modicum of Jews might have continued to join the Jesus movement. As it was, Paul's views about the Mosaic Law and the fact that observance of it was optional prevailed, and the church became increasingly a Gentile enterprise. But perhaps, in the end, James himself did not want the Diaspora Jewish Christians to focus on boundary-marking rituals like circumcision, Sabbath observance, and food laws. Perhaps he saw something else as the heart of Jewish Christian piety. What might it be?

The letter of James has been not merely neglected but misunderstood. It has been not merely overlooked, it has been overburdened by the assumption that there is some anti-Pauline rhetoric in this document, as though Paul would be opposed to good works or obeying God's Word.

But this is unfair both to James and to Paul. The legacy of Luther needs to be left behind when it comes to evaluating these two figures in early Christianity and their writings.

We have seen in this letter James's concern for a faithful living out of the essential teachings of the faith. It is not important whether James himself wrote this letter or dictated it to a scribe. What is important is the sum and substance of the letter, which calls Diaspora Jewish Christians to believe and behave in a way that is in accord with the wisdom of Jesus, a revelatory wisdom that came down and comes down from above. This wisdom does in various ways echo earlier Jewish wisdom, but it is filtered through the lens of the distinctive emphases and ideas of the wisdom of Jesus the sage. James does not merely pass on tradition, even the Jesus tradition. He reforms and refashions it to meet the needs of those he addresses while remaining faithful to the core values that underlie and undergird such teaching. James shows his creativity not only in the way he handles the Jesus tradition but also in the way he responds to the misunderstanding of Paul's teaching. We noted how he could creatively use the story of Abraham and even the very same texts as Paul uses, for instance Genesis 12 and 15, to make very different points indeed (cf. James 2 to Rom. 4 and Gal. 3). James is no mere passer-along of tradition. He is a creative reshaper and applier of tradition.

Unlike Jesus, James had a long ministry in the Holy Land, and in particular in Jerusalem. He had an extended opportunity to shape a Jesus-centered community that was growing. The impact and legacy are evident in the accounts of his martyrdom and death, which show that even non-Christian Jews had great respect for James's spiritual and moral integrity, even if they differed with some of his theology. To these accounts of the death of James and to his legacy we will turn in a moment, but first we need to say something about what we learn about Jesus from all of this reflection on James.

The first thing to be said is that if we compare James's writings with Paul's, both of them from time to time draw on the sayings of Jesus and apply them, but both of them do so with a certain amount of freedom to paraphrase the source material. They are not slavish repeaters of the Jesus material, whether the audience is predominantly Jewish or predominantly Gentiles. The second thing to say is that we should not minimize their indebtedness to this body of Jesus's teaching. The themes of nonviolence, peace-making, tongue-curbing, avoidance of oaths, love and compassion for the marginalized, and the importance of good works even though one has been saved by the grace of God are evident in both these sources. The

Jesus that appears from behind these themes is a Jesus who was certainly not a Zealot or revolutionary in the traditional sense of the term. He was a peaceable king who blessed peacemakers, and both James and Paul tried to follow that mandate and shore up the rents in the seamless garment of Christ called the church whenever dissension and real difference threatened to tear it to shreds. The Jesus that also appears from behind the curtain of his sayings in James is a Jesus who sounds more like Matthew's representation in Matthew 5–7 than the Lukan form of the same material in Luke 6 and elsewhere. In other words, scholars of the sayings material shared only by Matthew and Luke are wrong to give preference again and again to the Lukan form of Jesus's sayings rather than the Matthean form. Luke has Hellenized the tradition for a Gentile audience, as James's use of a tradition that matches up with the Matthean form of the tradition shows.

This brings us to a further interesting point about the historical Jesus. The Gospel of Matthew in narrative form, and James in its opening salutation and closing remarks about the coming Lord, make clear that Jesus is not only a sage and a purveyor of wisdom, he is Wisdom come down from above, the revelation of God, even the incarnation of Wisdom. This raises an interesting question about James 3:17: "But the wisdom that comes down from above is first of all pure, then peace-loving, considerate, submissive, full of mercy and good fruit, impartial and sincere." What is interesting to me is that this is not only a fair summary of a good deal of what Jesus taught, it is also an accurate character description of the man. Notice as well that James 3:18 is where we find the quotation of the peacemakers saying of Jesus, which activity is said to raise a harvest of righteousness. The kind of righteousness James and Paul were interested in was the same kind Jesus was interested in—that which flowed from grace and love and peace. In other words, the nonviolent Jesus, the Jesus who turned the other cheek and laid down his life for what he believed, very clearly peers out from behind the curtain of James's use of his brother's teaching. The eschatological reign of God, which this Jesus believed he was bringing in, involved just such transforming qualities.

Jesus's kingdom language, like that of James, was not primarily a critique of mere human kings and kingdom, or human domination systems, and there is certainly no evidence either in the teaching of James or in his continued relationship with the Temple that he had concluded that Jesus was unalterably opposed to the Temple as if it were inherently evil. Jesus simply believed that all kingdoms and indeed all temples, including the one in Jerusalem, would finally be sifted by the refiner's fire of God's judgment. Jesus did not set out to wage war on the Roman Empire and its minions either literally or in his wisdom speech. Of this we find nothing in the teaching of James. Jesus had come to set the earth on fire by the positive, powerful, transforming redemptive grace of God, not by waging a campaign, even indirectly, of opposition to earthly reigns and realms. To him they paled into insignificance as earthly things that came and went, for God's own direct rule in the lives of human beings was breaking into the present as the Wisdom from above broke into people's lives and they were changed.

This of course was radical and threatening enough to get Jesus killed, despite the fact that Jesus made evident his kingdom was "not of this world." Indeed not. It was something that still had to be prayed for daily—"Thy kingdom come, thy will be done on earth as it is in heaven." This kingdom was something that came down from above and was in the hands of God, not in the plans of human beings, even though Jesus's followers were urged to implement its implications. The power, however, the transforming grace, came from God, always and everywhere, coming down from above. This Jesus believed and taught, and so he taught his disciples to pray, to storm the ramparts of heaven with entreaties, and so did his faithful brother James. In short, the Jesus of modern liberation theology was not the Jesus of history, nor the Lord his brother James knew and served. The real Jesus was not into empire smashing or empire building; he was into proclaiming and bringing the dynamic saving reign of God from above into human lives, one life at a time—a very different matter. Turning the world upside down was more a matter of praying for transformative power to act rather than playing politics of whatever sort. This is why James in the end submitted to martyrdom without violence, as his brother had done before him. He knew there was a higher power who would take care of such oppressors and right the wrongs in due course. He went the way pacifists go when they are also activists. To this martyrdom we now turn.

ELEVEN

James's Demise and Jude's Rise

The decade of the 60s was a volatile and indeed violent one for residents of Judea under the rule of one bad procurator after another. Jewish blood began to boil long before it began to be spilled in large quantities. In order to set the demise of James in its proper perspective, we need to consider first the context in which he was martyred. The picture is a dark and foreboding one, as Jerusalem spiraled down in a death dance into conflagration and destruction.

THE DEMISE OF A JEWISH WORLD

Roman rulers during the empire seem to have regarded Judea as a minor and yet troublesome province. It was hardly seen as a plum appointment for ambitious patrician Roman soldiers and politicians wishing to climb the ladder of success. It is fair to say that Rome generally tended to send very much less than their best potential procurators to govern this region in the 50s and 60s. We must back up a bit and consider first the last procurator who ruled for any extended time in Judea. His name was Felix and served under Claudius and then Nero as procurator of Judea from A.D. 52 until either 58 or 59. It might have been thought that he would govern in a clement manner since he was married to a Jewish princess named Druscilla in A.D. 54, but since observant Jews saw this as a violation of Jewish marital customs, it seems not to have helped much. Felix also had the problem of dealing with the fact that north of him in the Holy Land was Herod Agrippa II, who kept being given more and more land by Nero.

It is then not a surprise that Felix was somewhat paranoid, and Josephus's account of his reign reads like tales from the reign of the Marquis de Sade—a true reign of terror. Felix was always executing one zealot or another and seems to have made it his personal mission to root out Jewish messianic troublemakers such as Eleazar the revolutionary. This only produced more violence among the Jews, leading to the rise of the so-called *sicarii* or "dagger-men," who went around executing Jews who were collaborating with Rome, such as Jonathan the high priest. It was also during Felix's reign that the messianic pretender called the Egyptian rallied a group of Jewish followers and promised to bring down the walls of Jerusalem with a shout from the Mount of Olives. Felix sent out troops against this group, and the Egyptian escaped, which explains how Felix may have thought that Paul, when he was taken prisoner in the Temple precincts in Jerusalem, might have been this Egyptian.

The important thing to notice about all of this is that the Jewish Temple hierarchy was very concerned about maintaining the Temple and their roles in it, and once messianic figures or Jewish revolutionaries started executing Temple priests, they would certainly be opposed to any sort of messianic movements, including the Jesus movement, that might arouse the suspicions of Rome and might lead to their own loss of political power. No doubt, they kept a watchful eye on James and his fellow Jewish Christians in Jerusalem, seeing them as potential troublemakers who would endanger their fragile collaborative arrangement with the procurator.

Suffice it to say that in the time period of A.D. 52 to 68 or so, there must have been increasing pressure on the church in Jerusalem to appear truly Jewish and truly loyal to the Temple and its hierarchy. This is in part what must have been driving a request like we find in Acts 21:21–24 where Paul is asked to take part in a purification ceremony in the Temple with other Jewish Christians, and indeed to pay for the cost of these others doing so. It is fair to say that when Paul marched into Jerusalem with Gentiles and the "collection" in A.D. 58, he could hardly have picked a much worse or more xenophobic time to come in the 50s. Jews, Jewish Christians, and especially Pharisaic Jewish Christians would have become more concerned about the direction of the Jesus movement, not less, at the time when this event transpired. This is the backdrop not only to what happened in regard to Paul in A.D. 58–60 while he was under house arrest, but also what was to happen to James in A.D. 62.

The next procurator, Festus, arrived in A.D. 60 with Judea on the verge of falling into pure chaos. Bandits and zealots plagued the land; bad blood existed between Herod Agrippa II and the Temple hierarchy. Festus was a capable man, and he was able to prevent all-out war from breaking out, but Judea was nonetheless a seething cauldron waiting to bubble over. Festus could not have known he was facing a very divided Jewish leadership when he went to deal with them in regard to the matter of Paul, and in any case he was off the scene rather quickly, for he died in office, preventing a natural transition to the next procurator (Albinus). There was an interregnum, a gap between the rule of one procurator and the next, and so the high priest Ananus decided to seize the moment to strike at the heart of the Jewish Christian community. Josephus provides a remarkably frank and direct report of what transpired in A.D. 62 that is critical of the Jewish Temple hierarchy.

THE REPORT OF JOSEPHUS ON JAMES'S MARTYRDOM

It will be well at this juncture to allow Josephus to speak for himself in a rather full way, not least because he provides us with the only early account of James's martyrdom, for the New Testament is silent on the matter.

> The younger Ananus, who as we have said, had been appointed to the high priesthood, was rash in his temper and unusually daring. He followed the school of the Sadducees, who are indeed more savage than any of the other Jews, as I have already explained, when they sit in judgment. Possessed of such a character, Ananus thought that he had a favorable opportunity because Festus was dead and Albinus was still on the way. And so he convened the judges of the Sanhedrin and brought before them a man named James, the brother of Jesus, who was called the Christ, and certain others. He accused them of having transgressed the Law and delivered them up to be stoned. Those of the inhabitants of the city who were considered to be the most fair-minded and who were strict in observance of the Law were offended at this. They therefore secretly sent to King Agrippa urging him, for Ananus had not even been correct in his first step [of convening the Sanhedrin without Albinus's permission], to order him to desist from any further such actions. Certain of them even went to meet Albinus who was on his way from Alexandria, and informed him that Ananus had no authority to convene the Sanhedrin without his consent. Convinced by these words, Albinus angrily wrote to Ananus threatening to take vengeance upon him. King Agrippa, because of Ananus' action, deposed him from the high priesthood which he held for three months.[251]

This account has struck the vast majority of scholars as frank and unlikely to reflect later Christian padding or editing.[252] Josephus, it is true, is a tendentious writer, and it is fair to say that here his concern is not with James per se, whom he mentions only in passing, but with chronicling how the Jewish and Roman leadership acted. But it is often what one says in passing, which is less likely to reflect the ax one is grinding, that is most historically revealing.[253] This being so, we need to consider it carefully.

First of all, James is called by Josephus the brother of Jesus, just as is the case in the New Testament and also on the ossuary. The term used here is *adelphos*, not the Greek word for cousin, and this independent testimony to the relationship of James to Jesus is both early and important. Josephus is prepared to call Jesus the so-called (*legoumenou*) Christ, but is not prepared to call James the so-called brother of Jesus.[254] It is important then to say that it was not just early Christian writers who called James the brother of Jesus. At least one early Jewish writer did so as well.

Second, the attestation that James was a Torah-true, faithfully observant Jew is stressed. Indeed it is apparently the basis of the complaint of injustice to Albinus, and it seems clear that Josephus definitely agrees an injustice was done to James. It was the strict Jews who complained about the injustice done to James, presumably because they recognized him to be a good and faithful Jew, perhaps in spite of his messianic beliefs about his brother. Indeed the action against James was seen to be such an injustice that it led to Ananus being deposed.

Stoning was indeed a possible punishment for lawbreaking in the form of blasphemy, false teaching, or being a troubler and seducer of the Jewish faithful, and this is the punishment Josephus says James underwent.[255] This is indeed more believable in this volatile and very Jewish setting than the later Christian accounts that have him pushed from the pinnacle of the Temple and then struck thereafter as well.[256] In short, James, like his brother, suffered a travesty of justice at the hands of an unscrupulous high priest who was critiqued not only by Josephus, but also by other fair-minded Law-observant Jews of Jerusalem. There is nothing in this account that reflects later anti-Semitic or pro-Christian sentiments, and it deserves to be given its proper weight.

This account makes it clear that James had respect not only within his own Jewish Christian constituency but also among other Jews in Jerusalem, including very strict ones. This could hardly have been the case if James himself had not been a pious and observant Jew himself. It is then all the more remarkable that James was able to take a middle way between Judaizing Pharisaic Christians on the one hand and the Pauline line on the other, in order to try and forge a workable model of Christian community that could include both Gentiles without circumcision and Jewish Christians, even strictly observant ones. James was not only James the Just, faithful to the Law. He was James the Mediator, whose broader perspective on the true essence of the Law and of faith and grace shines through.

THE BURIAL OF JAMES

As we now can say with some assurance with the discovery of the James ossuary, James was buried in Jerusalem and buried in a thoroughly Jewish manner, appropriate and indeed distinctive to the period of Jewish history between the rule of Herod the Great and the fall of the Temple in A.D. 70. Notice that James was not carried back to Nazareth and buried there. No, his fellow Jewish Christians in Jerusalem were his primary family and community at the time he died, and they in all likelihood provided for his burial.

It involved a two-stage process in which the body was laid out and allowed to decay. Early Jews did not practice mummification, unlike Egyptians. Once the flesh had disappeared from the bones, then the bones would be taken and carefully put in an ossuary, which did not entail laying the skeleton out to its full length, but in fact taking apart the skeleton so it would fit within a rather narrow and often short container.[257] Early Jews who believed in resurrection had no difficulty believing God could reassemble the person and put new flesh on the bones and new breath in the body, especially in light of passages like Ezekiel 37:1–14. Respect for the dead and a belief in the resurrection of the righteous did not require burying them in a condition that mimicked what they looked like in this life.[258]

In fact it is plausible that Jews used the form of reburial involving ossuaries precisely because they believed in an afterlife, and the most prominent belief on that matter was the belief in a bodily resurrection. Is it an accident that the growth in this practice in Judaism parallels the rise of Pharisaism, the Pharisees being the most ardent advocates of bodily resurrection amongst early Jews? I think not, and early Jewish Christians very much followed in the footsteps of the Pharisees in regard to this matter. Their savior had been raised from the dead. They looked forward to a like destiny.

The ossuary itself is interesting in various respects. First of all, we do know that it was found in an area near or in the old city of David where there were Jewish tombs. In other words, James was not likely buried in a graveyard specifically for Christians. He was buried with his fellow Jews, and not likely in a family plot either. If James had been buried in a family cave where there were other ossuaries already in place, it is likely that, as with the case of Caiaphas's ossuary, the inscription would have been placed on the end of the box so his ossuary could be distinguished from other such ossuaries, which would have been placed lengthwise in the cave. Instead we have an inscription on the side of the bone box, and not one hastily scrawled on it for mere identification purposes. To the contrary, James's ossuary has what can only be called an honorific inscription, and an odd one at that, for it mentions not only the name of his father but also of his brother.[259] The Jewish Christians who buried James wanted to honor him in burial, and we may suspect that they expected some would come and visit the burial spot and see the inscription written on the side of the box. The association with his brother is indeed the most honorific part of the inscription, and it is what not only sets off the inscription from other grave inscriptions in early Judaism,[260] it also is the singular means by which this James could be clearly identified by those who visited the tomb. This James had been known by Jews and Jewish Christians alike as "the brother of Jesus," the most notable and in some minds notorious first-century Jew by that name. James's glory was in part a reflected glory, and he himself was perfectly comfortable with being known as a servant of Jesus. He was not one who sought honorific titles for himself, unlike various rulers and religious figures of his day. James was buried properly according to Jewish custom, and it is only by a providential accident that his ossuary has now been found. It of course needs further testing, especially in view of the discrediting of the Israeli Antiquities Authority report, but this must await the resolution of the trial of Oded Golan. I see nothing, however, at this juncture to cause me to change my earlier conclusion that the James ossuary is what it purports to be—the burial box of James.

THE IMMEDIATE AFTERMATH

What happened after James died? According to church tradition, he was replaced not by Jude or another brother of Jesus but by a relative of Jesus named Symeon, son of Clopas, as head of the Jerusalem church.[261] Symeon is actually called a cousin of the Lord whom all deemed appropriate to be the next bishop. This indicates that the connection with Jesus's family continued to be important to the Jerusalem church.[262] It is Eusebius who also tells us that at the outset of the Jewish War, Jewish Christians in Jerusalem were warned by a prophecy to flee, and they did so to Pella. This would mean that Jewish Christians would not have remained in Jerusalem for many more years after James's death. Somewhere in the mid-60s, or at least by 67–68, they would have fled due to the deteriorating situation in Jerusalem (food shortages and in-fighting between Jews, among other things). One reason to trust this tradition is that Pella is an odd choice of destination if one is making up a story about a location for early Christians to seek out. Damascus and Antioch would more likely have been chosen since they have clear and early connections with accounts in Acts about a Christian presence.

While it is not true to say that early Jewish Christianity died out because of the fall of Jerusalem and its Temple, it is true to say that it lost its central focus, for it was a Law-observant form of Christianity, and this included worship in the Temple. Thus in quick succession, first losing James, then losing a crucial part of the social context and religious focus in which it had been born and grew, this form of the Jesus movement experienced a drastic turn of events. But did Jewish Christianity return to Jerusalem after the Jewish War and before the Bar Kokhba Revolt in the early second century? Apparently some Jewish Christians did return, for Eusebius tells us that Symeon was not martyred until the time of the Emperor Trajan (in the early second century).

James had successfully established one form of the Jesus movement in Jerusalem, and it clung to its identity and location even despite severe trauma and difficulties involving not one but two Jewish wars (including the Bar Kokhba Revolt).[263] But it was definitely a weakened form of Christianity, and it was also dispersed, indeed to judge by the letters of James, Peter, and Hebrews it was dispersed all over the empire, including even in Galilee.

The death and burial of James is not recorded in the New Testament. This is in part because the only history book in the New Testament, the Acts of the Apostles, only takes us up to A.D. 60, and James died after that point in time. We must then rely on Josephus's account and to a lesser extent the later Christian accounts of the event. What we have seen so far in this chapter is that it is perfectly believable in the volatile and often violent situation which existed in Jerusalem in the 60s that James could have been martyred by Sadducean Jewish Temple officials. After all, the same priestly family seems to have been involved in some way, though indirectly, in the demise of James's brother Jesus.

The account of Josephus is a credible account, especially because the matter is simply used by Josephus as an illustration of the abuse of power by a high priest. Josephus only refers to James in passing, and there is no reason to doubt he is correct in saying that James's martyrdom was seen as an abuse of power and an injustice by some fair-minded Jews who protested to the incoming procurator. What Josephus's account does not tell us is how and where James was buried. We must turn to the early Christian accounts and the evidence from the finding of the ossuary for clues on this matter. What Josephus's account does suggest is that James was an observant Jew, and other such Jews took umbrage when he was unfairly executed.

Since stoning was a punishment reserved for certain particular crimes, it appears likely that James was accused of being either a blasphemer or a false teacher leading astray the faithful. In a detailed study Bauckham concludes: "Our attempt to explain Josephus' account of the death of James has therefore left us with two plausible possibilities: that he was executed as a blasphemer or as a *maddiah* [one who leads astray the faithful] (of course it is possible that he was convicted of both crimes). Both possibilities have the advantage of coherence with the policies of the Temple authorities towards Jesus and the Jerusalem church at an earlier stage in its history."[264] This is assuming that the action of the high priest was not merely one of pure maliciousness. Though Josephus portrays the priest in question as impetuous, this is simply his stock way of referring to young authority figures whom he thinks poorly of. It is more likely, since Josephus says the Sanhedrin was assembled, that a judicial verdict was passed on James, just as there was probably one passed on Jesus.

It is telling that this blow to the early Jewish Christian community did not immediately cause it to flee. Rather they must have stayed in the city long enough to allow the flesh to desiccate and to practice reburial on the bones of James. This means that the reburial likely would have transpired in A.D. 63 or 64.[265] This also means that the now-famous ossuary inscription would have been written on the eve of the real outbreak of the Jewish War. Jewish Christians were not abandoning their city at this juncture. Rather, they were carefully and quietly honoring their dead leader and continuing the community in the tradition he had taught them, which involved the practicing of Jewish customs and the speaking of the language only Semites used in the region—Aramaic.[266] Some final reflections on James are in order.

At the epicenter of early Jewish Christianity stands James—fixed like a rock in Jerusalem, no traveling evangelist he. If the measure of a man is seen in those he influenced, then James is clearly a giant. The intertextual echoes in 1 John and 1 Peter suggest that the two other major figures responsible for early Jewish Christians in the Greco-Roman world, Peter and the Beloved Disciple, were deeply indebted to the teaching and orientation of James toward these fledgling communities being birthed from Jerusalem to Rome. It is James whom we find steering the ship of Jewish Christianity in the remarkable homily called "the Letter of James." And what do we learn of the man from this remarkable polemical salvo?

We learn at least the following things. James did not have a problem assuming authority over those he had not personally converted or discipled. His sense of authority in relationship to the Jewish Christians in the Diaspora is clear in "James" the document, yet it is also clear since this homily is an act of persuasion, a piece of deliberative rhetoric meant to change the audience's mind and behavior, meant to help them renounce "friendship with the world" and do a better job of embracing "friendship with God." At the heart of the homily is the attempt to remove the inequities that existed in these congregations between rich and poor, haves and have-nots. But equally clearly, James believes that that sort of social program requires a higher vision, the embracing of a more heavenly counter-cultural wisdom, to be enacted even in part. He will dispense some of this wisdom in this homily and hope it becomes implanted in the hearts of at least many in the audience. He pleads for a living faith that works, that does good deeds of piety and charity. He insists on impartiality and generosity of spirit toward all, even the lowest of the low. Like Jesus he insists on the ethic of the Sermon on the Mount, not as an ideal, but as something that by grace becomes the Magna Carta of freedom and possibilities for a truly Christian community. Like Paul he believes salvation is by grace through faith, but that this does not settle the matter of how Christians should behave thereafter. Faith that is not perfected in godly works is no living faith at all, and for both James and Paul, in differing ways, Abraham is the benchmark of both faith and obedience.

James is wary of the cult of personality, prefers to call himself only the servant of Jesus, and warns strongly against too many desiring to become teachers in the community. Few could have matched his knowledge of the scriptures, the teaching of Jesus, and early Jewish wisdom literature (for example, Sirach, Wisdom of Solomon) in any case, and even fewer had his aptitude for and skill with rhetoric. He was the orator par excellence. It is a shame he has been viewed as a mere appeaser or compromiser in early Christianity, or even worse someone who opposed the bold missionary work of Paul with the Gentiles and his message of salvation by grace through faith. James was neither of these persons, but he was a skillful diplomat, as Acts 15 shows, working out a necessary compromise. And to judge from both Acts and James the homily, he was no hard-line Judaizer either, though he probably believed all Jewish Christians should continue to keep the Mosaic covenant, especially in the Jerusalem community, though he says nary a word in his homily about circumcision, Sabbath-keeping, or food laws. Were these really not the subject of some discussion in Jewish Christian churches in the Diaspora? It is hard to tell, but neither

1 John nor 1 Peter suggests they were either, and Paul's fulminations in Galatians and elsewhere pertain almost entirely to Gentile Christians and others who are part of his congregations. There is so much more we could say about James, but one more remark must suffice. He is the one person who held together the teachings of Jesus and early Judaism and the Jewish Christian churches with one hand, and at the same time extended the right hand of fellowship to Paul and his mission of salvation by faith. For this he deserves our eternal praise and admiration.

But we must now turn to another of Jesus's brothers of which we know a bit: Jude. We have already seen a piece of evidence that reflects the fact that he did not become the head of the Jerusalem church after James. What is his story, and what should we make of his letter and contribution to early Christianity?

A JUDAS WHO DID NOT BETRAY JESUS

The brother of Jesus we know as Jude was in fact named Judas. He is mentioned quite clearly as Jesus's brother in Mark 6:3 and Matthew 13:55—third in Mark's listing of brothers and fourth in Matthew's. His position in these listings may mean that he was not the next brother in line after James to be the head of Jesus's family (these things being determined by age), which may in turn explain why he did not succeed James as head of the Jerusalem church. Jude is also referred to by name in Eusebius's *Historia Ecclesiastica*, following the account of Hegesippus from the third century.

The fact that Jude's letter begins with the identification "brother of James" establishes the connection with the holy family beyond reasonable doubt. The fact that Jude also calls himself a servant of Jesus, as does James in James 1:1, does not count against his blood kinship with Jesus as some have argued; it simply reflects his humility and his use of a common title adopted by Christian leaders in that era to establish authority in a church setting. As Bauckham stresses, the connection of this Judas and this document to the holy family is secure because "the only man in the whole early church who could be called simply James [as in Jude's claim to be *brother of James*] without risk of ambiguity was James the Lord's brother."[267]

Bearing in mind that we have no evidence that James was itinerant—indeed, as we have seen, he sent and received messengers rather than traveling himself—Paul's reference in 1 Corinthians 9:5 to brothers of the Lord being accompanied by believing wives suggests that Jesus's brother Jude was an itinerant Jewish Christian missionary who was married and traveled with his wife. Since Paul does not suggest that Jude was a missionary to Gentiles like himself, and since Jude's letter likely addresses a Jewish Christian audience, it is very likely that, like Peter, he was a missionary to Jews. Jude refers to others (but not himself) as "apostles" in verse 17, thereby distinguishing himself from those followers of Jesus who were evangelizing non-Jews.

As for what we know of Jude from noncanonical sources, Julius Africanus tells us in the late second century that the family of Jesus spread the gospel throughout Israel starting from Nazareth and its vicinity. This likely confirms that apart from James, the family of Jesus was based in Galilee after Easter, which is perhaps another reason Jude did not succeed James as leader of the Jerusalem church.

Now let's see what information we can garner about Jude the brother of Jesus from a closer look at his brief letter.

HEY JUDE, DON'T MAKE IT BAD: A LETTER COMBATING FALSE TEACHERS

There has been considerable debate over the authorship and authenticity of the letter of Jude, and accordingly debate over its proper dating as well. Those like Bauckham and William Brosend, who are inclined to see this letter as genuine, date the letter early, perhaps as early as the early 50s. The one thing thought to count against this sort of dating is the aforementioned verse 17, with its reminder about the "predictions of the apostles of our Lord." Those inclined to see this letter as a pseudepigraph—a letter written by someone else who adopted the name and authority of Jude—see that verse as a clue that the document was written in the postapostolic era. There are several problems with this conclusion.

For one thing, it might just as well reflect the fact that while Jude sees himself as a servant of the Lord Jesus, he does not see himself as an apostle, perhaps because Jesus did not appear to him personally. (Seeing the risen Lord was an essential criterion for being an apostle of Jesus Christ, as opposed to being an apostle/agent/missionary commissioned by a church.) While 1 Corinthians 9:5 shows that Paul knows that the brothers of Jesus are Christians by the time he writes this letter, he does not call them apostles there, and he mentions only an appearance to James amongst the brothers at 1 Corinthians 15:7. Remember that John 7:3–5 makes clear that the brothers did not believe in Jesus during his ministry, while Acts 1:14 tells us only that the brothers came to the Pentecost meeting in the upper room convinced of Jesus's resurrection. Second, as Brosend points out, there is nothing in the construction of verse 17 that suggests that the apostles made these predictions in the *distant* past. To the contrary, this letter is full of the eschatological fervor and anticipation of the return of Christ that characterized the apostolic era in general.[268]

Another thing that supports an early dating of the letter of Jude is the fact that it has to have been written prior to 2 Peter: the vast majority of scholars now recognize that 2 Peter 2:1–18 and 3:1–3 are dependent on Jude verses 4–13 and 16–18.[269] That means this document must have circulated in Jewish Christian circles in the first century prior to the writing of 2 Peter near the end of that century.

As for the authorship of Jude, some people have quibbled about the Greek of this letter being too good for a Galilean carpenter, but as Bauckham argues, this complaint does not have much merit. For one thing, this letter reflects that the author knows the Aramaic edition of the book of 1 Enoch and of the Testament of Moses; furthermore, his use of the Old Testament does not suggest he is following the *Greek* Old Testament in general. Here is someone who apparently knows Hebrew, Aramaic, and some Greek. His skill in Greek should not be exaggerated, however. He has a good Greek vocabulary, but his skills with grammar and syntax are not honed. One could say he has an oral skill with Greek, as his rhetoric is powerful at points, but his written Greek is far from textbook Greek.[270] The view that best explains the evidence we have, both as to authorship and as to dating, is that the letter of Jude was written by a brother of Jesus, probably sometime in the 50s.

So what can this brief, twenty-five verse letter tell us about the author? It seems to be, like the letters of James, an encyclical, though it may have been written to a particular congregation. Very polemical, it focuses its wrath on false teachers who have infiltrated the letter's audience and are misleading and beguiling others into false belief and bad behavior. While Jude is a good rhetorician and can occasionally sound like his brother James in his use of sapiential speech and colorful metaphors (referring, for example, to shepherds who feed only themselves, clouds without rain, autumn trees without fruit, wandering stars for whom blackest darkness has been reserved), he more often sounds like an offerer of prophetic woe oracles, not unlike what we find on the lips of Jesus in Matthew 23. In many ways this letter reads like the epistles of John in their polemics against schismatics and false teaching. The function of Jude's harsh language is to get the audience to disassociate from false teachers, and in particular to recognize that they shouldn't be let into the church meetings, where they are "blemishes at your love feasts" and are given an opportunity to share their erroneous teachings and ways in an intimate setting.

Jude warns of both coming judgment, like that on Sodom, and coming eschatological salvation to enforce his ethical teaching here. However, he does not want to discourage mere doubters with his rhetoric; rather, they are to be encouraged.

Especially interesting is Jude's use of extracanonical documents. He uses material from the Testament of Moses that speaks about the struggle between the archangel Michael and the devil over the body of Moses, apparently choosing that text because the false teachers Jude is condemning slander celestial beings; and he appeals to 1 Enoch to reinforce his message about the coming of the Lord for judgment. Jude 4–19 can be said to be a skilled midrash on various Old Testament texts. The writer's midrashic technique resembles that found in the Qumran commentaries, and he shares the Qumran community's perspective not only that the Old Testament is replete with prophecies about the end-times, but that the author and audience are living in the age of the fulfillment of those prophecies.[271] This document, then, reflects the charged atmosphere of what can be called apocalyptic Jewish Christianity. It is therefore appropriate that this document was placed next to the book of Revelation in the canon.

Jude is Trinitarian in his thinking, speaking of praying in the Spirit, keeping oneself in God's love, and waiting for the mercy of the Lord Jesus to bring the gift of eternal life (clearly seen as in the future). Nor is he shy about stressing a high Christology, speaking about Jesus being the believer's only sovereign and Lord. His great worry is that the audience may fall away or defect to a false teaching, and so his famous concluding doxology promises that if they will rely on God, he can keep them from falling away. Jude is a fiery preacher of salvation and judgment who does not feel a need to pull his punches, but rather fights fire with fire to, by all means, rescue some. It could be that he intended this document as an honor-and-shame discourse—in other words, one meant to shame the audience into avoiding or even expelling the false teachers, and thereby honoring Christ and God and thus avoiding the dangers of apostasy.[272] The use of the purity language helps reinforce the rhetorical aims of the discourse.

There is much we can learn about Jude from what he says in this discourse. His letter is far more Christological than that of James to the Jewish Christians, and it is far more apocalyptic and eschatological than James's. Jude is more of a prophet and preacher and spirit-inspired exegete of ancient texts, while James is more of a sage. We can assume that Jude was seen by at least some in the early church as a paradigm of good teaching and preaching, for his work gets recycled in 2 Peter. Only Paul's work seems to be as obviously influential in other New Testament documents as Jude is on 2 Peter. This may be as much because of who wrote this short document as because of what is said. Jude is clearly no mere clone or copy-cat of either of his older brothers; rather, he carves out his own niche and serves the cause of Christ in his own way, with a strong sense of eschatological urgency. His work deserves far more attention than it usually gets, and it speaks volumes about the prophetic, eschatological, and highly Jewish character of the discourse in the Jewish Christian communities in and around the Holy Land. Jude deserves to be seen as a strong voice within the inner circle of Jesus.

But there are also a few things to be learned from what Jude does *not* say. Despite all his use of purity language, he does not argue about kosher food laws, or Sabbath-keeping, or circumcision, but rather about general ethical, spiritual, eschatological, and Christological concerns. This says a lot about where his focus was. One cannot characterize him as amongst the Judaizers or Pharisaic Jewish Christians we hear about in Galatians 2 or Acts 15, despite his use of esoteric Jewish materials and midrashic exegesis. In fact, no Judaizers or Pharisaic Christians are ever heard from directly in the New Testament, only indirectly. This makes clear that in the end that rigidly Pharisaic branch of early Jewish Christianity was not seen to represent even the Jewish Christians, as characterized by James and Jude; the inner circle of earliest Christianity did not include such hard-line figures any more than it included Gnostics or libertines. The differences between James, Jude, Peter, Paul, Mary, the Beloved Disciple, Joanna, and Mary Magdalene, while real, should not be exaggerated.

Clearly this letter of Jude, with its polemical tone, makes evident that even in the earliest period of church history there were a variety of Christian views and teachings that were seen as beyond the pale ethically, spiritually, theologically, and Christologically by the inner circle. All of the inner circle who wrote documents make this clear, some (for example, Jude, Paul, and the Beloved Disciple) offering more polemics than others against false teachers. There were boundaries to the Christian community, and they regularly were enforced and reinforced by the inner circle. Interestingly, the boundaries were insisted on even by those who could be called charismatics. Jude, for example, urges praying in the Spirit, and Paul stresses prophesying even when writing to a pneumatic church situation in Corinth; but this charismatic focus was not seen in any way as a cause to be less demanding at the ethical or Christological level of discourse. The equating of charismatic and libertine or charismatic and theologically broad-minded is a false one if we are talking about the inner circle of earliest Christianity.

WHAT WE'VE LEARNED AND WHAT THAT KNOWLEDGE TELLS US ABOUT JESUS

In the 60s the early Christian movement was to lose three of the inner circle—Peter, Paul, and James—leaving something of a leadership vacuum in both Jerusalem and Rome. In addition to this upheaval, Jerusalem itself was to receive a stunning blow in A.D. 70 with the destruction of the Temple, a blow from which it would not truly recover for the rest of the New Testament era. The center of the Christian movement would of necessity have to be located elsewhere. That era in Jerusalem was a volatile vortex into which early Jews and early Jewish Christians were both dragged, changing both forms of Judaism irrevocably.

It is telling that neither early Judaism nor early Christianity tried to go back to a Temple-centered religion focused on a theology of holy space and holy land, at least not after the brutal suppression of the Jewish Bar Kokhba Revolt in the early second century. It is a strange truth that the Jesus movement and the Pharisaic movement, both of which survived the two Jewish revolts, became supercessionist in character—that is, believing that the former form of their religion should be left behind for something better—a Word-centered religion in the case of Judaism, and a Jesus- and Word-centered religion in the case of Christianity.

History, it has been said, is most often written by the winners, but sometimes winning or losing is just a matter of location, of being in the right or wrong place at a certain time. This was certainly true of the more Torah-true form of Christianity that James nurtured in Jerusalem. While this form of Christianity was by no means snuffed out by the destruction of Jerusalem, it was forced out into backwaters like Pella and even Galilee. In my view we bear witness to something of the aftermath and residue of the Jerusalem crisis in the Gospel of Matthew, a gospel likely written in the 70s or 80s for Jewish Christians in Galilee (or, less likely, in Syrian Antioch). That gospel, like documents such as the Didache, reflect the tenacious attempt to preserve a more Jewish form of discipleship to Jesus—a form that was to continue on into the early Middle Ages, until anti-Semitism in the church forced it underground and largely exterminated it.

But it is perfectly clear that during the New Testament era both the more Jamesian and the more Pauline forms of early Christianity were alive and well. Both forms—the form which thought Jewish Christians ought to be Torah-true, and the form which thought adherence to the Torah was optional—were alive and well. The mediating figures, as we have seen in Acts 15, were Peter and James, who were closer to Paul and endorsed his ministry in a way the hard-line Judaizers did not. James was worried about a garbled Paul, or a Paul misinterpreted, just as Jude was worried about teachers who seemed libertine and the Beloved Disciple was concerned about the denial of incarnational Christology by the schismatics.

None of the inner circle would have argued with the view that faith without works is dead, and none of them would have been happy with an inadequately low Christology. Jesus was the risen Lord for all of them, and the sovereign mediator between God and humankind; they viewed the human race as lost without Christ. All of them manifested one or another form of what can be called early Jewish Christianity—even Paul, as we shall see in the next chapter.

But let us remember that there was already a strong sense of Christological orthodoxy and ethical orthopraxy in these communities. We have seen plenty of evidence that there were both Christological and ethical boundaries to the communities of Jesus which led to polemics against false teachers of various sorts, ranging from Judaizers to libertines to those with too low a Christology. These boundaries were defined and refined and further clarified in the period when the New Testament documents were written— that is, between A.D. 49 and the end of the century. What we have no hint of in the New Testament is polemics against later aberrations like Gnosticism or Marcionism; nor does any New Testament document—or, for that matter, any other first-century Christian document, such as the Didache or 1 Clement—suggest that there was a Gnostic or Marcionite stream of Christian tradition already extant in the first century. Likewise, we do not have any hard evidence of a purely low Christological stream of Christianity in that era, if by *evidence* we mean whole communities of this orientation. False teachers do not a stream of Christianity make.

All of the inner circle of Jesus were Jews advocating what they took to be a Christological reformulation of Jewish monotheism with the premise that the Old Testament was God's good revelation for God's people, including his Christian ones—something the author of the Gospel of Thomas and later Gnostic documents obviously struggled with. Jesus was confessed, worshipped, and proclaimed as the risen Lord in all of the communities addressed in the New Testament era that we know of. This is why false teachers were immediately singled out and castigated in those communities, and this is why they left.

It is simply historically false to suggest that the intellectual boundaries of Christianity were not defined until well after the New Testament era. The evidence that they already existed in the New Testament era is compelling. However, as offshoots and aberrations from the earlier and more apostolic faith arose in the second through fourth centuries, the church was forced to more clearly define Christological orthodoxy and ortho-praxy. Then indeed the boundaries were more rigidly and firmly put in place. But this is not because before the fourth century what existed was a "free-range" Christianity that would have considered Gnosticism (or, for that matter, an inadequate Christology or polytheism or libertinism) a legitimate variant on a Christian theme. It is because the specific problems raised by such later deviations had not yet formed, or had not yet *fully* formed, in the New Testament era.

Let's conclude this chapter by asking what we learn about Jesus by look-ing through Jude's eyes. The message of Jude suggests that he knew of his brother's strong apocalyptic rhetoric and compelling eschatological mes-sage. A non-eschatological Jesus doesn't work any better than a non-Jewish one! The nascent Trinitarian language in Jude makes perfectly clear that Jude did not see such language as incongruous with either the message of Jesus or Jesus the man himself. Indeed Jude, like the other members of the inner circle of Jesus, believed firmly that he lived in the eschatological age of false teachers and false teaching, a time when proto-orthodoxy was at a premium and needed to be maintained. He also believed fervently that Jesus would return, bringing in his hands eternal life. This is something a Jew could believe only of a divine figure. In this light, it is noteworthy that Jude talks about figures like Enoch but does not equate Jesus with them. Rather, he calls the latter the Lord Jesus Christ and tells us that the earliest apostles were apostles of the Lord Jesus Christ. This concept of Jesus did not arise in the late first century; it arose in the earliest circle of Jesus's fol-lowers in response to encountering the risen Jesus and in response to what they remembered of his claims and his teachings. For them, the historical Jesus and the risen Jesus who was the risen Lord were one and the same per-son, a man they worshipped, prayed to, and served—even in the case of Jesus's own brothers, who had known him since childhood!

This speaks volumes about the historical Jesus, however uncomfort-able it may make those who like the notion that high Christological views of Jesus were royal robes only later placed on this man. A late take on high Christology is historically false. As I once heard the great German New Testament scholar Martin Hengel say, the earliest Christologies were some of the highest ones, seeing Jesus as both human and divine. This is because those who knew him best and earliest knew that this was a fair representa-tion of how he presented himself, what he taught and did, and what the implications of his resurrection were. Such ideas characterized Jude's the-ology just as much as they characterized Paul's. Thus Paul cannot be seen as the inventor of such ideas about Jesus, as we shall now see.

PART SIX

PAUL:
JEWISH APOSTLE TO THE GENTILES

TWELVE

Paul the Change Agent

Paul was always going to be the odd man out when it came to Jesus's inner circle. First, he did not know the historical Jesus during his earthly career, though it is possible he heard Jesus speak in Jerusalem once or twice. Second, he did not become a disciple until a couple years after the death of Jesus, and well after Pentecost. How could he claim to have seen the risen Lord, who ascended after forty days of appearances? Third, he had violently opposed the Jesus movement before his conversion; it is no exaggeration that the church in Judea was afraid of Paul and afraid to believe he had been converted after the now-famous Damascus road episode. Besides all that, he was an out-of-towner—a Diaspora Jew, unlike all of the rest of the inner circle. Yes, he was always likely to be suspected of some sort of aberration, whether theological, ethical, or ecclesiological.

Something else that makes Paul the odd man out as far as we are concerned today is the sheer quantity of firsthand evidence we have about him from his own letters—more firsthand evidence than we have about any of the other members of the inner circle of Jesus, and indeed more than we have about Jesus himself! Our problem in these two chapters is how to boil down that considerable amount of information. What it will show us is that though Paul was set off from the others, we should consider him one of the inner circle, not least because he is the one who took the apostolic faith and what he had learned from the pillar apostles to more people than anyone else we know of; and no one disputes that he did indeed have direction from contact and conversation with Peter and James on various occasions.

It is not surprising, though, that even in the modern era Paul has been accused by some of being the first great corrupter of the teachings of Jesus, and by others of being the one who turned Christianity into a non-Jewish (or at least mainly Gentile) enterprise. Outsiders who are innovators have suffered this kind of polemic throughout human history. In the next chapters we need to look closely at the man who was, humanly speaking, most responsible for opening the doors wide so Gentiles could stand on equal footing with Jews in early Christianity, without having to become converts to early Judaism.

We have already seen too much evidence in studying the other seven members of the inner circle to think that Paul invented high Christology or the messianic community of Jews and Gentiles united in Christ. He was the *last* of all the apostles, not the first. Even Peter preceded him in reaching out to Gentiles. But Paul is responsible for kicking the mission to Gentiles into high gear and defining what that mission could and ought to look like. He is responsible for making numerous Jewish Christians as well as God-fearers rethink whether it was necessary for them to be Torah-true in the sense of keeping the Mosaic covenant. He was the change agent who helped steer the ship of Christianity in an increasingly more Gentile-friendly direction, especially as the Good News headed into the western part of the empire (for example, into Galatia, Asia, Macedonia, Greece, and Italy).

As we shall see, the real issue between Paul and some of the other members of the inner circle was not whether salvation was by grace through faith in the crucified and risen Jesus. Everyone in the inner circle agreed on that. It was not whether ethical imperatives were required by Jesus of the believer. On that too there was agreement. The issue was the more specific one of *how* Jewish and Gentile Christians should live (particularly how they should relate to the Mosaic Law), and how they should relate to each other if they followed different patterns or forms of obedience to God. And—oh yes, not incidentally, was it really necessary for *even* Jewish Christians to keep the Mosaic Law?

THE MULTIFACETED MAN FROM TARSUS

It is quite impossible in the space of only two chapters to do justice to as complex a person as Paul. We must be content to focus on certain key features of his personality, life, and ministry. Few of these factors are more important than his Jewishness, so we will start there.[273] The truth is that Paul viewed himself as a true, if Christologically and eschatologically oriented, Jew from the start to the finish of his life, though various of his contemporaries and detractors would not have agreed.

Perhaps the one thing all modern commentators agree on about Paul is that he was a Jew. What sort of Jew he was is another question, of course—one that has been heavily debated not only among Christians but also among Jews.[274] During this century, the pendulum has swung back and forth between viewing Paul as a Hellenized Diaspora Jew and viewing Paul as a rather traditional Palestinian Pharisaic Jew. There are, of course, opinions ranging between these extremes. Part of the issue under debate here is how much change actually occurred in Paul's life when he became a follower of Jesus. Was he simply a messianic Jew—that is, a Jew who believed his messiah had come? Or was he a Jewish Christian, with more emphasis placed on the discontinuity than on the continuity with the past? Wherever one comes down on these issues, surely the proper place to begin this discussion is with Paul's own remarks about his personal Jewish heritage.

It goes without saying that Paul's personal heritage cannot simply be ignored or dismissed as a key to understanding his identity. Here is a person who, long after his conversion, still reckons time by the dates of the major Jewish festivals and when pressed is quite ready and able to offer a mock boast about his honor rating as a Jew.[275] What is most significant about a passage like 2 Corinthians 11:22 (which reads "Are they Hebrews? So am I. Are they Israelites? So am I. Are they descendants of Abraham? So am I. Are they Christ's servants? I am more so!") is that Paul does not say "so *was* I" about being a Hebrew, an Israelite, and a descendent of Abraham, but rather "so *am* I." In short, he still claims his Jewish heritage. Yet at the same time, it is clear that he is able to sit lightly with significant aspects of his Jewish heritage, so that while he can identify with non-Christian Jews, he can also identify with Gentiles and thus apparently sees himself as neither *merely* one or the other.[276] Paul's Jewishness, then, is but one partial, but nonetheless key, clue to understanding who Paul was. It follows from this that we must give his autobiographical remarks careful scrutiny.

First, it cannot be stressed enough that the Paul we know from the letters talks about his Jewish heritage mainly when provoked. Consider the following:

- In Galatians 1:13–14, where Paul refers to himself in his earlier life as a zealous persecutor of Christians and one who advanced much further in Judaism than others of his age and ilk, he is writing in a polemical context.

- In 2 Corinthians 11:22, the passage quoted above in which Paul claims his Hebrew/Israelite heritage, Paul is responding to an honor challenge.

- In Philippians 3:4–6 ("circumcised on the eighth day, a Hebrew of Hebrews, of the tribe of Benjamin, a Pharisee who was blameless when it came to righteous obedience of the Law"), Paul is commenting in order to forestall potential honor comparisons by other Jewish Christians (the circumcision party) who probably made much of their Jewish pedigree.

The contentious rhetorical situation affects the way the material is discussed in the first two cases and may affect the third example as well. We will look at each of these texts in some detail at this juncture.

It is my view that Galatians is a polemical argument meant to prevent Paul's overwhelmingly Gentile converts in Galatia from having themselves circumcised and taking up obedience to the Mosaic Law. One of Paul's tactics in this letter is to get his audience to follow positive examples and avoid negative ones.[277] Among the negative examples to be avoided is Paul's pre-Christian behavior summarized in Galatians 1:13–14. Perhaps the most important reason to begin our discussion with this polemical text is that it appears to be a part of the earliest extant letter we have from Paul's hand.[278]

Of supreme importance in analyzing this text is recognizing the contrast between earlier life and present life, formerly and now, which involves a contrast between Judaism and the "assembly of God."[279] This text is the only example of the use of the term *Ioudaismos*, "Judaism," in the New Testament. We do find it in the Jewish literature of this period,[280] however, and in each case the term as used by Jews focuses not on the geographical reference or potential of the term (which, were this the focus, might lead to the translation "Judeanism") but rather the religious and social component. Paul is indicating that he had earlier been part of one particular social community pursuing a particular way of life and belief, and as part of that had been persecuting a splinter group that he saw as an aberration from Judaism. Now, however, he is in the community and following the way of life of those he once persecuted. Here Judaism is being contrasted with living a life in accord with the gospel, within the new "assembly of God," as Paul calls it.

Of course, Paul continues to view himself *ethnically* as a Jew. Thus he can speak of his kinsmen or kinswomen according to the flesh as "my people,"[281] but his point is very clearly that he has made a break with that community. His identity is no longer chiefly formed by that ethnicity. I would also argue, without going into a long discourse at this point about Paul's view of the Law, that he no longer sees himself as obliged to observe the Mosaic Law, for the time has come when God's people should go beyond being under the supervision of the pedagogue known as the Mosaic Law and should now become part of the new covenant community established through the person and work of Christ and following the Law of Christ.[282]

In short, Paul's approach to these matters is a sectarian one. In this he differs from various Jewish Christians in Jerusalem who are some of his dialogue partners mentioned in Galatians 1–2. In Paul's view, Jew and Gentile united in Christ are the assembly of God; Christians are not merely *in continuity with* the assembly of God. This new creation, this new assembly, is distinguishable from the Judaism of which Paul was formerly a part. In other words, Paul is the one who initiates the change in perception that leads to Christianity being a religious community separate from Judaism. Typical early Jews certainly would not have agreed that the Mosaic covenant had had its day and was becoming obsolete. Another Pauline co-laborer, the author of Hebrews, was to run with this ball even further down the field, stressing the discontinuity between the new covenant and the Mosaic one. It is interesting that in each case there is an insistence of theological and ethical continuity with the Old Testament *people* of God, but covenantal discontinuity such that those who are truly in the same line and on the same trajectory with the Old Testament saints are those who follow Jesus.[283]

The heritage of Israel is by no means being renounced by the Jesus movement, in Paul's view. Rather, it is being claimed and fulfilled by Jews and Gentiles united in Christ. The promises of God to Abraham are *fulfilled* in Christ. The continuity between the Christian assembly of God and the Old Testament people of God is thus theological, not ecclesiological. Both faith groups claim the same sacred scriptures. In fact, in Romans 9–11 Paul goes so far as to say that non-Christian Jews have been temporarily broken off from the people of God, with the hope that they may be grafted back in on the basis of grace and faith in Jesus Christ. This approach must not be called anti-Semitism, not least because Paul was a Jew and he believed that God had not cast off his first chosen people forever; but it is not inappropriate to call it a radical critique of Judaism.[284] It is understandable and was inevitable that the Pharisaic Jewish Christians in Jerusalem, as well as non-Christian Jews, would more often than not see this view as supercessionist in character, rather than as the logical fulfillment of what the Old Testament promised and prophesied.

Paul says that Christians know well about his former way of life in Judaism, clearly implying that he does not feel it necessary to follow that way of life any longer. It is understandable in these circumstances why a Jewish scholar like Alan Segal would conclude that Paul, whom he accepts was genuinely converted to following Christ, had thereby committed apostasy from Judaism. He also concludes that the two-ways model of salvation (that is, Gentiles saved through faith in Christ, Jews through the Torah) proposed by K. Stendahl, L. Gaston, J. Gager, and others as an interpretation of Paul's thought is not warranted by the Pauline evidence itself.[285] Paul's critique of Judaism, Segal believes, was more thoroughgoing than that.

Notice that Paul also is quite willing to admit that he had advanced further than most of his peers in Judaism. He uses the term *anastrophen* to describe his former way of life. This term certainly refers more to orthopraxy than it does to orthodoxy, but then early Judaism was much more of a way of living religiously than it was a set of doctrines to be believed. Nonetheless, there were certain fundamental convictions about God and the Law and about Jews that undergirded such a way of life.

Paul in Galatians 1:13b stresses that he persecuted to a very great degree the assembly of God, though at the time of the persecutions he would not have recognized his target as the assembly of God. He clearly must have believed that the Jewish Christians he persecuted were beyond the pale, apostate Jews who were heading in the opposite direction—that is, away from Paul, who was advancing in Judaism. The key factor linking both Paul's advancement and his persecution was zeal—in particular, zeal for the Law and Jewish traditions. Note that it is only after the fact, after his conversion, that Paul indicates he was ashamed of persecuting Christians.[286] There is no hint that he had an uneasy conscience while he undertook such actions. In fact, while he was persecuting he likely saw this activity as clear evidence of his positive zeal for the true faith and way of life. The Greek in Galatians 1:13 which we translate "persecution" refers to more than just vigorous dialogue or debate. There is little reason to doubt that Paul engaged in physical attacks on early Christians, perhaps much like those he endured himself later.[287] It is possible that Paul before his conversion was a part of the extreme faction of Pharisaism that tried to follow the examples of Elijah, or Phineas, or the Maccabees.[288] He may well have been willing to own a motto later attributed to Barry Goldwater— "Extremism in pursuit of virtue is no vice."

I would agree that Paul's zeal is a key clue to understanding the man both before and after his conversion.[289] We must not allow our modern distaste for violence propagated in the name of God or religion to put us off from analyzing this factor closely. Paul came to Christian faith in the middle of a career as a persecutor who believed that there was a fundamental contradiction between being a Torah-true Jew and being a Jewish follower of the crucified Jew Jesus. For Paul the Law and belief in salvation through faith in the crucified Jesus were seen as two opposing and contradictory means of defining the boundaries of the people of God. This conviction he held both before and after his conversion: he simply changed sides on the issue. "The incompatibility of Christ and Torah [as the factor defining the nature, limits, and shape of a religious community] was the constant element in the syllogism that on the one side of the conversion led to the persecution of the church, and on the other resulted in fierce resistance to the Judaizers."[290]

Paul refers to his Pharisaic Jewish heritage as something he at least largely gave up when he became a Christian—or, to put it as he does in Philippians, he reckoned it in the loss column in order that he might gain Christ. This is not because he saw this Pharisaic heritage as a bad thing; rather, he saw it as something no longer relevant, something obsolete now that Christ had come. Apart from Paul's stringent adherence to and zeal for the Law (perhaps especially for its distinctive practices), his belief in resurrection, his commitment to advancing in a Pharisaic lifestyle, and his commitment to and belief in the Hebrew scriptures and their prophetic character, it is not at all clear what more we can deduce about his Pharisaic background, because we know so little about pre-A.D 70 Pharisaism from other sources.[291]

Nevertheless, the evidence is strong that the Pharisees were centered or based in Jerusalem, not in the Diaspora. In view, then, of Philippians 3:5— the second of the passages cited above in which Paul discusses his Jewish heritage—we must assume that Paul's formative Jewish years were spent in the Holy Land, and in fact mainly in Jerusalem.[292] This conclusion is based on what Paul himself says, but it becomes virtually certain when we add Luke's remarks found in Acts 22:3, 23:6, and 26:5, which speak of Paul having been born in Tarsus but raised in Jerusalem (especially if it is true that Paul's father was also a Pharisee). This means that we must not make too much out of the connection with Tarsus. Judaism in general was Hellenized in Paul's day, even in Israel. Paul could well have gotten the rudiments of a good Greco-Roman as well as Jewish education right in Jerusalem.

Paul remained a zealous person after his conversion, but his zeal was transmuted into a vigorous commitment to spread the gospel message and to follow the nonviolent suffering example of Christ rather than following the example of earlier Jewish Zealots.[293] I have little doubt that most moderns, even most modern Western Christians, would have been taken aback by Paul. We would have seen him, both before and probably also after his conversion, as a fanatic. We would also likely have seen him as too driven and too single-minded—a person without a life apart from his ministerial work. Yet it is clear enough that Paul was no anomaly. He stood in a long and proud tradition of zealous Jews, and he was by no means the only Christian who carried that zeal over from his Jewish to his Christian life.

Now for the third heritage passage cited above. As we saw, Paul states in 2 Corinthians 11:22, "Are they Hebrews? So am I. Are they Israelites? So am I. Are they Abraham's descendants [seed]? So am I." Here we have, in ever-narrowing degrees of specificity, a description of particular kinds of Jews. "Hebrew" refers to the language and perhaps also the essential ethnic identity of the person in question; "Israelite" has to do with one's spiritual or religious allegiance; "Seed of Abraham" refers to one's ancestry and genealogical heritage. It is important to note that this description suggests that Paul's primary source of Jewish identity was gained *while he was in Israel*. He would not claim he was a Hebrew of Hebrews if in fact he had grown up in the Diaspora and did not know the sacred language. Of course, it is not impossible that his parents were not very Hellenized Jews who lived in Tarsus and taught him the sacred language there; but all other things being equal, it is more likely that Paul is suggesting that he, apparently like the "bogus" apostles he contrasts himself with in 2 Corinthians 11, grew up in the sacred central context of Judaism—in Israel. Those bogus apostles could not gain any rhetorical advantage over him by claiming they were true Palestinian Jews while he was just a Hellenized Diaspora Jew, because that wasn't true.

Something needs to be said about Paul's boasting here. He lived in a culture where the trotting out of one's pedigree or tooting of one's own horn was deemed not only acceptable but advisable. Now to be sure, Paul is boasting somewhat tongue in cheek. In fact, he says that he is playing the fool (2 Cor. 11:21). He is boasting in order to shame his opponents and to put his converts back in their place and in rightful relationship with Paul. In fact, Paul is following the proper ancient conventions for what was called inoffensive self-praise—but doing so to mock the false, pompous, exaggerated eloquence and rhetorical self-praise of his opponents.

Paul is an ancient person not above using contemporary conventions in regard to boasting in order to persuade his converts to do or be something. Yet he uses those conventions in surprising ways, to deflate and defuse the pompous examples and remarks of his opponents while presenting himself as a figure that inspires deep feelings of pathos. In all of this Paul is being a traditional Jew, but he is also participating in the larger Greco-Roman conventions of his age and using them to his advantage.

While Paul accepts that boasting is appropriate, he clearly believes that one ought in the main to boast in the work of Christ in one's life, in one's assembly, and in one's world, as we shall now see. In Philippians 3:3–10 Paul says directly that one ought to boast in Christ; in 1 Corinthians 1:31, quoting Jeremiah 9:23, he says that one should boast in the Lord. Galatians 6:14 suggests that a Christian should boast only in something which the world would see as shameful—the cross of Christ. This passage is full of intentional irony, as was 2 Corinthians 11:22, involving deliberate inoffensive boasting meant to shame the opposition. In the Philippians passage Paul first boasts of his Jewish pedigree and then turns around and says he now counts it as refuse or dung, not because it is not a good heritage, but because of its value in comparison to the surpassing worth of having and knowing Christ. Furthermore, here Paul goes beyond what we saw in 2 Corinthians 11:22. There Paul simply said, "So am I," but here he says "I more so," outdoing his potential rivals.

This is a typical honor-challenge kind of approach, where one tries to put oneself a cut above one's rival. If Paul's opponents could boast of circumcision, he could claim he was circumcised on the day required by the Old Testament. He was a Jew among Jews by birth and a Hebrew among Hebrews, speaking the native tongue (see Acts 6:11). Furthermore, as a Benjaminite he was named after the most illustrious member of that tribe—King Saul. The tribe of Benjamin was noted as the one that remained faithful to Judah. Furthermore, in terms of the sort of righteousness one could have from obedience to the Law, Paul says he was blameless or faultless. This is not to be confused with some sort of claim to being perfect. It means Paul could not have been charged with any violations of the Mosaic Law or have been accused of wrongdoing by a Jew.

Of course, Paul is saying all of this from the perspective of his Pharisaic past. This is how he would have evaluated himself *while a Pharisee:* he saw himself as devout and faithful and upright. In other words, we have no basis at all to think that Paul was plagued by guilt feelings or self-doubt while a Jew and that this was what drove him to consider Christ and finally convert. This all-too-prevalent, all-too-modern psychological approach to Paul fails to reckon with the clear statements Paul makes in Philippians 3, where he states that his conversion involved a revelation and a miracle. There is no evidence of tortured spiritual turmoil that led to this conversion. As Fred Craddock sees it, "We do not have in this text a portrait of a man at war with himself, crucified between the sky of God's expectation and the earth of his own paltry performance. Paul is not in this scene a poor soul standing with a grade of ninety-nine before a God who counts one hundred as the lowest passing grade."[294] We ought not to read Paul as an early example of the introspective conscience of the West.[295]

What we may say thus far about these three autobiographical texts is the following:

1. Paul is happy to still claim to be a Jew after his conversion.

2. He does not renounce this Jewish heritage as something wicked or worthless when he becomes a Christian.

3. Indeed, he seems somewhat proud of his performance as a Pharisaic Jew in keeping the Law, with the exception of his persecution of Christians, for which he did later come to have regret and remorse.[296]

4. Yet it is clear enough that something has eclipsed or surpassed the influence and importance of that heritage in regard to his present life, lifestyle, and self-evaluation. This new something has in fact so surpassed that heritage that Paul is prepared to regard the latter as worthless in comparison to the supreme value of knowing Christ and obtaining salvation through him.

All this helps us to understand our next text: 1 Corinthians 9:19–23. Paul is portraying himself in that passage ("To the Jew I act like a Jew, as one under the Law.... To the Gentile I become as a Gentile who does not have the Law") as a person who accommodates his style of living, eating, and dressing—*not* his theological or ethical principles—in order by various means to win both Jews and Gentiles to Christ.[297] Yet of course this would be the very rub for either a Jew or a true Judaizer, since Judaism involved at its very heart a way of living, eating, and dressing religiously.

It is important that we be struck by the oddity of hearing a Jew like Paul say he could become a Jew to the Jew, apparently without any sense of incongruity or reneging on his conviction that Christians are not under any obligation to place themselves under the Mosaic Law. Here is the clearest evidence we have that Paul feels no compulsion to be Jewish in the sense that he did before his conversion. He takes up Jewish orthopraxy as an evangelistic strategy, not out of habit or as a concession to those who think such things essential. Paul is quite clear that his orthopraxy should not be interpreted to mean that he himself is still under the Mosaic Law. Keeping the Mosaic Law, in his view, is a matter of *adiaphora*—that is, something that doesn't ultimately matter in the larger salvific scheme of things, since the new creation has already arrived. Again, the evidence is such that Alan Segal's conclusion about Paul is fully warranted from a Jewish point of view: Paul would have indeed been seen as a bad Jew, if keeping the Mosaic Law was seen as essential to being a true Jew. But perhaps there is another way to view Paul's Jewishness.

Perhaps we may say that Paul was an apocalyptic and messianic Jew, a Jew who truly believed that the new creation had come because the messiah had come, and that new occasions taught new duties. This new creation had eclipsed the need for not any and all sorts of law or ethical principles but for the specific form of God's Law intended to guard and to guide God's people until the messiah came. Paul is perfectly happy to command obedience to instructions of the Lord's or of his own, but he would prefer to persuade. He is perfectly happy to speak about the new Law of Christ meant for the new covenant situation that incorporates the heart or essence of the obsolete Mosaic Law, albeit transfigured and transmitted through the example and teaching of Christ. Like a good Pharisee, Paul still believes in a day of reckoning, a future final judgment and final vindication after a final resurrection of at least those who are in Christ. He still believes in the importance of good works and of working out one's salvation with fear and trembling. He still believes that the Good News about the promises and salvation of God is for the Jew first but also for the Gentile. He still celebrates a meal that he is happy to refer to as involving Passover or a Passover lamb.

Yet Christ has transformed all of this for Paul. Christ is the one who will bring in the day of judgment and provide the vindication. He will be the one sitting on the judgment seat, as Paul tells us in 2 Corinthians 5:10. The future resurrection will not happen until Christ returns. Likewise, the Lord's Supper focuses on Christ as Passover, not on the Sinai events of the Exodus. It is important to stress, as 1 Corinthians 11:23 makes clear, that this new interpretation of the sacred meal is not something Paul dreamed up. It is a tradition he learned from others—probably from the pillar apostles, who in turn got it from reflecting on what Jesus said and did at the Last Supper. In other words, Paul is just drawing out the radical and eschatological implications of the reinterpretation of Jewish ideas and institutions by Jesus. He simply sees more clearly the implications, including the implication of a new community, than did other members of the inner circle of Jesus.

The Law that Paul urges is founded on Christ as the norm and the norm-giver, Christ as the example and the lesson and the instructor. If this is Judaism, it is certainly not like the Judaism Paul says he left behind.

Obviously the ultimate litmus test of the type and degree of Paul's Jewishness is his views on the Law. I have treated this matter thoroughly elsewhere, but here I must summarize the major evidence we have and the conclusions we can draw on the basis of that evidence.[298]

PAUL AND THE MOSAIC LAW

Paul sees the Mosaic Law as part of scripture and thus as God's Word. Indeed, so closely are the two concepts identified for Paul that he can use the term *nomos* simply to mean scripture in general rather than the Law in particular.[299] He is even quite happy to cite portions of the so-called ritual Law to make a point for his Christian converts that he thinks God wants them to understand.[300] There is no evidence, then, that Paul makes a distinction between the moral and the ritual Law as being a viable source of truth to speak to Christians. He uses it all. The more important concern is to explain why and how he uses that broadly construed Law as he does.

Certain central convictions lie behind Paul's understanding and use of the Hebrew scriptures, including the Law:

1. His readers are those upon whom the end of the ages has come, meaning the time of the fulfillment of all scripture is at hand.

2. His hearers are then God's eschatological people, for whom the promises of God are yea and amen in Christ.

3. Having received Christ, believers have in him the key to understanding God's plan and Word.[301]

4. One must read the Old Testament in light of where God's people now are in the progression of salvation history—namely, they are no longer living under the Mosaic covenant, nor are bound to observe the Mosaic Law; rather, they are living in Christ and according to his Law.

Obviously, if one doesn't subscribe to Paul's Christology, one is not going to agree with Paul's Christological and eschatological and even ecclesiological understanding of the Law. Paul's views on the Law are complex, and they are bound up with his views on God, salvation, anthropology, and human relations, to mention but a few topics.

The failure to recognize the narrative character of Paul's thought and the role the Law plays in it, as well as the failure to understand the implications of covenant theology and what Paul means when he speaks of a new covenant and a new creation, is a serious one. Paul asserts repeatedly in Galatians, and by a variety of means and metaphors (see especially Galatians 4), that the Law had an important but *temporary* role to play in the old covenant, providing stipulations, strictures, promises, and curses in the ongoing story of God's people. If we are asked why Paul takes this view of the Law, we are pushed back to two facts. First, before and after conversion he saw faithfulness to the Law as being at loggerheads with belief in a crucified messiah, especially one who authorized a Law-free mission to Gentiles. Second, his own conversion came about as a matter of pure grace. As a result of this conversion, his view of Christ changed, and this necessitated a paradigm shift in his thinking about the Law and its role in the life of God's people. He now saw the Mosaic Law, while a good thing, as playing a covenantal role *only until the maturity of God's people*—that is, only until they came of age and no longer needed to be confined by a guardian or pedagogue. Just as a child, when he comes of age, is no longer obliged to obey his guardian, so God's people are now no longer under the constrictions and constraints of the Mosaic Law.

What is the problem, in Paul's view, if the Mosaic Law is used as the necessary *means or pattern for living*? Unfortunately, under that condition, the Law's effect (though not its original purpose) is to imprison those who are under it in a form of slavery, as if they were being watched by a guardian.[302] Indeed, it is to submit oneself not merely to a fading glory but to a ministry that leads to condemnation and death rather than to justification and life.[303] Furthermore, since God intended for the Law to be a temporary expedient until he sent his Son, to go back and submit to the Mosaic covenant now is not only anachronistic, it is tantamount to denying the efficacy and benefits of Christ's work on the cross, including the sending of the Spirit.

It is also the case that, in Paul's view, the Law is incapable of giving what Christ and the Spirit can give. The Law is not a bad thing, but it cannot empower someone to do good. Paul is opposed to the *mandatory* observance of the Law for either Jewish or Gentile Christians, as we have seen.[304] Paul knows that if Jewish Christians choose to be consistently Torah-true, the Christian community will be divided between clean and unclean, between sinner and holy one, between first- and second-class citizens. This is at odds with why Christ came in the first place. If fellowship is defined by the Mosaic Law, then it requires Law observance by all parties to have such fellowship. There is in Paul's mind, then, a conviction that Christ came not to renew existing Jewish or Gentile religion but to get beyond both and form "a more perfect union" between all peoples, classes, and genders. This is what Paul calls a new creation.[305]

There is a difference in Paul's mind between being under the Law covenant and listening to any and all parts of the Hebrew scriptures as God's Word. Paul's covenantal theology allows him to affirm that the Law tells the truth about human nature and human need, and about God, and about the need for the interrelationship between God and humankind. Paul does *not*, however, believe that God has made only one covenant or contractual agreement with humankind throughout all of human history, in various administrations or renewed forms. Galatians 4:24 and Romans 9:4 make this quite clear, for there Paul speaks of covenants *plural*.

In the ancient Near East, when a potentate drew up a new covenant (a new contractual arrangement with some subordinate kingdom or individual party, say), it was normal practice to reuse certain statutes that were in previous agreements or covenants. The subordinate party then would keep these stipulations *not* because they were once in the old and now defunct treaty or covenant, but because they were now in the new one. Furthermore, stipulations and codicils of the old treaty that *weren't* carried over were no longer binding.

Thus while Paul is quite capable of saying that Christians are obligated to *fulfill* (or allow to be fulfilled) various of the commandments we find in the Old Testament, this is not because they are under the Mosaic Law. Rather, it is because they are *also* now found in the Law of Christ, the new Law by which Christians must live. After all, Paul says that the whole of the (Mosaic) Law and its essential requirements are summed up in a single commandment—love neighbor as self—which Christians are still to fulfill.[306] While clearly Paul is talking here about the old Mosaic Law, he is saying that the essence of that old Law is summed up in this new covenant arrangement and should be taken to heart and obeyed *for that reason*. Frank Thielman puts this another way: the essential requirements of the Mosaic Law are fulfilled in the life of Christians "not because they continue to be obligated to it but because, by the power of the Spirit in their lives, their conduct coincidentally displays the behavior the Mosaic Law prescribes.... Paul is claiming that believers have no need of the Mosaic Law because by their Spirit-inspired conduct they already fulfill its requirements."[307]

This is part of the truth, but there is also the matter of consciously following the pattern or norm of Christ, which involves both his life and teaching; and it is this latter that Paul calls the Law of Christ. The Christian, then, has not only a subjective power, namely the indwelling Holy Spirit, conforming him to God's ways and the likeness of Christ in the person and presence of the Spirit in his life, he or she also has an objective model and standard to which conformity is expected—namely, the example and teaching of Christ called the Law of Christ. The new covenant is not without new objective imperatives. Paul is no antinomian, throwing out the Law altogether; and he is not attacking legalism, even in Galatians. Paul's answer to the question, "How then should Christians live?" is not "Submit to and keep the Mosaic Law" or even "Adopt Christ's interpretation of the Law and then follow it" (as if the Law of Christ were the Mosaic Law intensified or in a new guise), but rather "Follow and be refashioned by the Law of Christ while walking in the Spirit."[308]

I would suggest that a careful evaluation of Paul's view of the Law shows that Paul is a sectarian person. He takes his heritage with him into his new religious community—indeed, he says it belongs particularly or especially to that new community, and he transforms that heritage into a different key because his experience and understanding of Christ now call and provide the lyrics for all the tunes.[309] Previously he looked at all of life through the lens of the Law, but now he sees it all through the eyes of Christ.[310] And from this vantage point Paul can only say, as he does so powerfully in 2 Corinthians 3, that the old glory, the old covenant, the old ministry, the old law has had its day, and that the new and surpassing glory has already arrived and must be embraced.[311] Thus in the end it is perhaps better to call Paul a Jewish Christian than a messianic Jew. It is the discontinuity rather than the continuity between the adjective and the noun that best explains why he was as he was. James, by contrast, was a messianic Jew: he still insisted on a covenantal continuity with those who kept the Mosaic covenant.

PAUL AS A ROMAN CITIZEN

At first blush, it might seem an exercise in futility to try to talk about Paul as a Roman citizen, since Paul nowhere in his letters mentions that he has this status. Nevertheless, there are a variety of good reasons to think that he had such citizenship. The book of Acts states and implies at various points that Paul was a Roman citizen: Luke has Paul himself announce his citizenship in Acts 16:37, which extricates Paul from a sticky situation; again Paul makes known his citizenship in Acts 22:25–28, where we learn that he was *born* a Roman citizen; we're told in Acts 25:10–12 that Paul appeals to the emperor, going over the head of the local procurator in Judea, an act that only a Roman citizen could have managed successfully to do; finally, Paul is given lenient or even favorable treatment in Acts

28:16, strongly suggesting that he is a person of considerable status and is being treated with the respect and courtesy normally reserved for Roman citizens. Furthermore, a later church tradition that holds that Paul was executed by the Roman authorities not by crucifixion but by beheading, which was the normal procedure when executing a Roman citizen, also supports the theory of citizenship.

The references to Paul in Acts are relevant only if Luke is correctly characterizing Paul, of course. Some would argue that he isn't: there has been a considerable protest that the Paul of Acts is not in fact the Paul of the letters. To resolve that issue, let's look first at Paul's writings. What can we discern about the social status of Paul from his undisputed letters that might either confirm or cast doubt on the judgment of Luke that Paul was a Roman citizen?

It is clear from the undisputed Pauline letters (Romans, 1 and 2 Corinthians, Galatians, Philippians) that we are dealing with a person of considerable education and knowledge, and not just of Jewish matters. These letters suggest that Paul has some knowledge of Greek philosophy (particularly popular Stoicism), and he has a considerable grasp of Greco-Roman rhetoric. Furthermore, in Paul's attitudes about manual labor and patronage we see a higher-status individual deliberately stepping down the social ladder in order to identify with his converts and to be all things to all persons in order to win some.[312] Paul in general does not insist on his rights, but this in turn shows that he presupposes that he has such rights. There is in fact nothing in the Lukan portrait of Paul as a man of virtue and consequence, a rhetor and a person of social status, that does not comport with the hints we find in Paul's undisputed letters.

If we consider the matter of Paul's Roman citizenship in terms of general historical probabilities, it can be said that there were examples of Jews from before the middle of the first century who were Roman citizens. (After that time, Roman citizenship for Jews seems to have been more common.) Also, it was perfectly possible for a person to hold more than one citizenship at a time, so we cannot rule out Paul's Roman citizenship based on the mistaken idea that he could not also concurrently have been a citizen of Tarsus.[313] Finally, we may envision a situation in which Paul's family provided a great service to the Romans, perhaps by making tents for the Roman army (Antony's?), and as a result were granted citizenship.

One may rightly ask, however, why it is that, according to Acts and on the *prima facie* evidence of the Pauline letters, Paul seems so reticent to claim his Roman citizenship, at least until backed into a corner. Of course, no one disputes the notion that Paul's Jewishness was a more primary factor in determining his identity than was his Roman citizenship. As a Jew in a Greco-Roman world, even a high-status Jew, Paul would have experienced considerable status inconsistency, and he may well have downplayed or even had ambivalent feelings about his Roman citizenship. In addition, Paul would have wanted the claims of the gospel to stand on their own merits. He would not have wanted his own high status to encourage conversion in someone who sought to follow a teacher of high social status. No offense but the gospel itself, no inducement but its compelling persuasive message.[314]

After all, as Paul says clearly enough in Philippians 3:20, the Christian's real *politeuma* is in heaven. Whether this term means "citizenship" or "commonwealth" or "constituting authority," the point must be taken that Paul had loyalties that transcended whatever earthly status he might have had by birth or by social status and privilege. Paul did not recognize the emperor and his decrees as the ultimate authority in his life; rather, Jesus Christ was his Lord. Furthermore, there is clear evidence that Paul believed that the institutions or "forms" of this world were passing away in light of the eschatological situation already inaugurated in Christ. If we factor in all of these considerations, it is understandable that Paul might have chosen to use his Roman citizenship only in an opportunistic way—particularly in order to advance the gospel or, in the case of the drama played out in Acts 22–28, to get him to the locale where he wanted to go next to spread the Word.

Finally, he may have been reluctant to claim Roman citizenship because of the problem of being able to prove it if called upon to do so. Citizens would have had a small wooden diptych containing their certificate of citizenship, but such an item was too precious and too easily lost for most to be willing to carry it on their person when traveling far from home. Furthermore, if the authenticity of the certificate was disputed, the original witnesses who signed it had to be produced. This, of course, an itinerant missionary like Paul could not do.

Given all these factors, we must conclude that it is indeed likely that Paul was a Roman citizen, but it is clear that this fact did not dominate his life or sense of identity. It was one of the resources he would draw on *in extremis,* perhaps, or in order to advance the gospel, but it was not something that Paul wanted to boast about or flaunt. Anything but mock boasting was reserved for the touting of Christ and his cross.

If, as is likely, Paul was a Roman citizen, he would have had a three-part name, composed of the given name (*praenomen*), the name of the founding member of his gens or tribe (*nomen*), and the particular family name (*cognomen*)—for example, Gaius Julius Caesar. Now when a foreigner or slave gained citizenship, he would retain his own name as the last name or *cognomen,* but he would add the *praenomen* and *nomen* of the Roman who obtained citizenship for this person. It is noteworthy that neither in Acts nor in Paul's letters do we find recorded Paul's threefold Roman name. (For that matter, neither do we find any significant evidence of Paul's skill with Latin, though this was apparently not required of Roman citizens in his day.)

The name Paulos is the Greek equivalent of the Latin Paullus. The latter is attested as a *praenomen* rarely and as a *cognomen* quite frequently (for example, the proconsul Sergius Paullus introduced in Acts 13:8). This makes it altogether likely that Paulos was in fact Paul's *cognomen,* his family name. However, the way the name is introduced for the first time at Acts 13:8–9 ("who is also called ...") may suggest that it was a nickname, meaning the small one. It is in any case significant that Paul's change of names in Acts (that is, from Saul to Paul) comes not at the point of Saul's Damascus road encounter but rather when he begins to do missionary work in the Greco-Roman world—specifically, when he begins to approach a man named Sergius Paullus! This may suggest an initial missionary strategy, at least in the broad sense of assuming a Greek name. There was, however, a very good reason for Paul not to go around the Greco-Roman world calling himself Saulos. This latter was the word in Greek used to describe someone who walked in a lascivious manner like a prostitute![315]

We may conclude this all too brief discussion by saying that Paul's Roman citizenship would have provided him with certain advantages that would have assisted his work as a traveling evangelist. Besides having Roman justice on his side, he also would have had an instant *entrée* to any city in the empire, particularly a Roman colony city. As a person of considerable social status, he would have commanded respect, especially whenever he announced his citizenship. He would have had ready access to Roman roads, of course, and could have traveled with parties of other Roman citizens or even with Roman soldiers on a mission if need be. His positive interaction with the Praetorian guard while under house arrest, as described in Philippians 1:13, was no doubt a result at least in part of the officers' reluctance to ignore or despise a Roman citizen.

We must remember, however, that though Paul's Roman citizenship is an important factor in understanding his life and identity, especially his travels to and experiences in Rome, it is a less crucial factor than either Paul's Jewishness or his Christian faith.

WHAT WE'VE LEARNED AND WHAT THAT KNOWLEDGE TELLS US ABOUT JESUS

It is impossible to sum up, in the short space we have here, the enormous amount of complex information that Paul gives us in his various letters and that Luke doles out in Acts about his hero Paul. What this chapter and the next attempt to do, as earlier chapters have attempted with our other subjects in this study, is paint a portrait of the person who became part of the inner circle of Jesus. His career is well known to most, of course, from his dramatic conversion, to his various controversies and missionary journeys seeking chiefly to share Christ with Gentiles, to his attempts to win acceptability for the Gentile mission with the Jerusalem church, to his rhetorically powerful missives written to his converts and others, and finally to his martyrdom in Rome. His Christian life pilgrimage transpired over the course of about thirty-odd years, from the early 30s to the mid-60s. But a mere chronological rehearsal of the facts hardly scratches the surface of the man, so I have sought to go deeper and probe what made him tick. I will take this a step further in the next chapter, when I talk more fully about Paul as a Christian.

In summary here, however, I would like to stress several things. Paul, perhaps more than any other early Christian that we know of, and certainly more than anyone else we have examined in this study, thought systematically through the implications of the Christ event and what it meant for both Jews and Gentiles, considering particularly what changes it required of members of both groups if they were to be adherents of Christ. We cannot blame other early Christians for not seeing things as clearly as Paul did, or for resisting various of his conclusions, but we have to admit that history has proved him right. As Paul saw things, a gospel offered on equal terms to Jews and Gentiles required changes of them both, especially if they were going to have fellowship or *koinonia* in Christ, and share together in a world mission. Paul does not say, "If anyone (Jew or Gentile) is in Christ, he or she is a new creature" idly or lightly. He believes that people must really have a shift of values to become a Christian, changing not merely their thinking or their moral behavior, but in fact their very way of living. This is not an easy demand, of course, and it is not surprising that many Christians misunderstood it, ignored it, protested it, or even resisted it. They still do.

Yet Paul felt irrevocably called to be a change agent, even if the pillar apostles were not always sure that he was on the right track in presenting his Law of Christ ideas, or that he was right to so relentlessly pursue and persuade people in regard to his vision of the gospel and the changes it required of a person. Very few could really take the measure of his belief that one's new identity in Christ made obsolete all pecking orders and societal privileges based on ethnic extraction (neither Jew nor Greek), social status (neither slave nor free), or gender (no male and female—see Gal. 3:28). Paul had had a radical conversion, and he remained in various ways a radical to the end. Prophetic figures such as he was are almost always marginalized if not simply repudiated; they are hardly ever embraced.

Paul did not look for the rest of the early church leaders to embrace him, however; rather, he immersed himself in a profound love affair with his converts and with his task not only of evangelizing the lost but of discipling those he found, until they indeed had heard and heeded the call to be imitators of Christ. His love for and pastoral relationship with his co-workers in the Pauline mission is obvious and moving to read about. By dint of his conversion by vision of the risen Christ and by virtue of his work, he was certainly part of the inner circle of Jesus even if he wasn't always well received by the inner circle of the mother church in Jerusalem.

Few people have been more profoundly converted or changed than this man. It is thus not surprising that few people, if any, have had more success as a change agent of others than Paul. But what did it mean for and to Paul to be a Christian? In our penultimate chapter in this study we must examine that question at some length.

First, though, there are a few things that need to be said about what Paul can tell us about Jesus. Clearly Paul's knowledge of the Jesus of ministry is secondhand. He is careful to say in 1 Corinthians 11, when he tells the story of the Last Supper, that he is handing on what was handed down to him. He does the same thing again at the beginning of 1 Corinthians 15, when talking about the earliest interpretation of the death, burial, resurrection, and appearances of the risen Jesus. When he draws on the Jesus tradition—for example, in 1 Corinthians 7, where he offers, "The Lord says no divorce"—he makes clear that he got this data from someone like Peter or James or someone else in the Jerusalem church. Though Paul is only a secondhand witness to the pre-Easter Jesus, he is paradoxically the only witness we have such a volume of firsthand information about.

The real importance of Paul, however, lies not so much in what his writings tell us about Jesus of Nazareth during his earthly ministry, but in what he understood the meaning and implications of the entire Christ event to be. It appears that he understood Jesus's eschatological significance and the radical implications of his teaching, life, death, and resurrection more clearly than any of the other members of the inner circle of Jesus, or at least he understood these things *sooner* than the rest of them did. That Peter came to defend the Pauline gospel at the great council of A.D. 50, and to adopt and adapt some of it in his letter to Jewish Christians (1 Peter), is compelling testimony to Paul's importance; but it also shows that it was Paul who had first thought through these things to their logical outcome. The pillar apostles, including James and Peter and John, all agreed with the substance of Paul's preaching about Jesus and about grace for Jews and Gentiles and about the death and resurrection of the messiah; it's just that the ecclesiological implications sometimes escaped them in the heat of controversy.

I don't think, then, that we can talk about Pauline Christology or Pauline eschatology as if he had somehow *invented* these ideas. Although Paul was their most able and clear exponent, and in some cases their first exponent, other early Christians were equally prepared to talk about such things as the preexistence of the Son of God, and to call Christ God. The Beloved Disciple, who had been an eyewitness to at least the Judean parts of Jesus's ministry (particularly its conclusion), and who ended up evangelizing the very same region as Paul (Asia Minor), would certainly have agreed with Paul that a high Christology was the only Christology that adequately conveys the full significance of the Christ event and gives it an accurate and adequate interpretation. The author of Hebrews would have said a hearty amen as well (as Hebrews 1–8 especially shows).

We must recognize, then, that Paul's Jesus was not the creation or singular interpretation of Paul. He was also recognizably the Jesus that other early Christians talked about. The focus of the Beloved Disciple and the author of Hebrews was understandably on events in the life of Jesus—but it was on those events that had weight regarding salvation and eschatology: that he came in the flesh, that he died on the cross, that he rose from the dead, and that (as the author of Hebrews was to add) he ascended into heaven and intercedes for believers there. In other words, this remarkable interpretation of the significance of Jesus and his career—found already in our earliest New Testament documents, in Paul's letters, in the 60s in the homily of Hebrews, and thereafter in the writings of the Beloved Disciple—was proffered by eyewitnesses of Jesus (such as the Beloved Disciple), those who knew the eyewitnesses (such as Paul and Luke), and those who knew Paul (the author of Hebrews, for example). There is an obvious chain of witnesses to this high Christological and eschatological evaluation of Jesus: it does not show up for the first time at the end of the first century in the prologue of the Gospel of John, much less in the second century—no, it starts with those who knew Jesus.

What else do we learn about Jesus through Paul? Well, we can rule out a couple of things. Nowhere in the inner circle of Jesus, as Paul depicts it, do we find representatives of the Q community—that is, the imaginary community thought to have compiled the Q sayings—or anyone else whose presence would suggest that Jesus the sage was the only Jesus one needed to know about, or that the death and resurrection of Jesus weren't central to the Christian faith. Nor do we find in Paul's letters (or anywhere else in the New Testament, for that matter) any polemics against those who were touting Jesus as merely a teacher, pundit, or sage. There are polemics against those who deny "Jesus come in the flesh" in the Johannine letters, there are polemics against Judaizers, and there are polemics against cleverly devised myths, but entirely missing are polemics against hoarders of Jesus's sayings or proclaimers of Jesus the talking head. Why? Because there was no Q community in the early Jesus movement; and even if there was a Q document—a collection of Jesus's sayings—there is no historical evidence at all to suggest that it represented the entire Christology or eschatology of those who compiled and cherished that collection.

Likewise, we find in Paul no support for the ideas presented in the Gospel of Thomas. In my judgment, that gospel shows what happens when the teachings of Jesus are abstracted from their Jewish context and given a Hellenistic and perhaps even Gnostic spin in the second century. The Gospel of Thomas shows what happens when you fail to interpret the sayings of Jesus in the context of the story of Jesus's life, death, and resurrection. This document does not bear witness to either "the historical Jesus" in any direct way (with the possible exception of a saying or two), nor does it bear witness to his earliest disciples' or inner circle's beliefs and ideas. The general rule must be—the less Jewish and eschatological the material is, the less likely it represents either Jesus or his earliest disciples' views. The more Gnostic the document, the less it reflects the historical Jesus and his earliest interpreters.

I say all this here because it is all too easy to single out Paul and suggest that he is an aberration who betrayed the stream of tradition begun by Jesus and continued by the purported Q community and later the Thomas community. The problem with this whole argument is that the Q community has no face and no known witnesses and probably no historical reality; it is a scholarly construct. In fact, the stream of tradition goes from Jesus to people like Peter and James and the Beloved Disciple and the female disciples, all of whom we know existed and followed Jesus, and thence to Paul and to Pauline co-workers like the author of Hebrews. Thus Paul is not the starter of the Jesus tradition or even of high Christological reflection about Jesus, though he is one of the most able exponents amongst the earliest witnesses. In our next chapter we will consider further what Paul the Christian believed about such important matters.

THIRTEEN

Paul: In Christ and in Crisis

The discussion of Paul as a Christian has all too often focused exclusively on his conversion or call, without due consideration of the rest of his Christian life.[316] Yet when we meet Paul in his letters, even in his earliest letters, he has already been a Christian for at least fifteen years. Paul's letters do not reflect the musings of a neophyte Christian, but rather the author speaks to us as a mature Christian—a seasoned veteran, so to speak—throughout his letters. This means that even when we are reading remarks about Paul's conversion, we have the benefit of Paul's hindsight. Our discussion must begin, then, with the issue of Paul's conversion, but we must realize from the outset that Paul's remarks are deliberately selective, highly rhetorical, and lacking in immediacy. Time and reflection have no doubt affected Paul's perspective.

PAUL'S CONVERSION: SET APART AND CALLED THROUGH GRACE (GAL. 1:15–16)

Our first text of importance is Galatians 1:15-16. In this key passage, Paul refers to God's having set him apart before he was born, called him through grace, and revealed Jesus to him in order that he could preach the gospel to the Gentiles. This text is part of Paul's *narratio,* the narrative of those aspects of his conversion that have direct relevance to his discussions with the Galatians. This is certainly not Paul's personal testimony in anything like a full form; rather, it is a highly selective and carefully couched presentation on a subject that the Galatians have already heard something about.

The function of these autobiographical remarks is to substantiate a particular claim, not so much about Paul and his Christian origins but about the nature and origins of his gospel and secondarily about his apostleship to preach it. There is another dimension to these remarks, however. Paul is presenting himself as a paradigm of the gospel he preaches to the Galatian Gentiles. As G. Lyons observes, "The formulation of Paul's autobiographical remarks in terms of 'formerly-now' and '[hu]man-God' serves the paradigmatic function of contrasting Paul's conversion from Judaism to Christianity with the Galatians' inverted conversion, which is really nothing other than a desertion of 'the one who called [them] in the grace of Christ' (1:6) and a surrender of Christian freedom for the slavery of law."[317]

Paul offers us two specific denials a few verses earlier: he did not receive his gospel from human beings; nor was he taught it. On the contrary, he says, it came through a "revelation of Jesus Christ." The issue here is the source and nature of his gospel and the means and timing of its reception—namely, at the beginning of his Christian life. There is debate as to whether we should take the last clause ("revelation of Jesus Christ") to refer to a revelation of which Christ is the content or a revelation that comes from or through Christ. Clearly enough, in view of the rest of Galatians 1, Paul is not denying that he ever received any information about Jesus from human beings. Still, Galatians 1:16, where Paul says that God revealed his Son in him, suggests that Paul is speaking of a revelation that came from or through his encounter with Christ on the Damascus road. The most reasonable suggestion is that this revelation entailed an indication not just of who Jesus was but also of what the message was that God wanted Paul to convey—the Law-free gospel about redemption through faith in the crucified Christ proclaimed to the Gentiles. Paul admits that this sort of message is not the kind of thing human beings could come up with on their own. It has been revealed to Paul through the making known of the hidden—that is, through *apokalupsis,* or a "revelation." The term refers to the making known of a hidden secret about God's plan for human redemption.

Paul describes his experience in prophetic terms. In particular, in his statement that God set him apart before he was born, we should hear an echo of Jeremiah 1:5—"Before I formed you in the womb I knew you, and before you were born I consecrated you; I appointed you a prophet *to the nations.*" Isaiah 49:1–6 may also be alluded to here: "The Lord called me before I was born" (v. 1). Paul goes on to say that, having been set apart, he was called by grace. In other words, God has had his hand on Paul since even before the time of his birth and all along has had in mind for him to be God's spokesman to the Gentile nations. Paul's current occupation and vocation as apostle to the Gentiles is not a result of careful career planning on his part, then; indeed, it was against the flow of his pre-Christian behavior, especially his persecuting activities. We can see where Paul is going with these remarks: his focus is not on the personal salvific consequences of his encounter with Christ, but rather on that encounter as the basis of his ministry and message. The description is task-centered, not focused on the effects on Paul as a person apart from such activities.

Paul has framed this discussion in a careful manner to fend off criticism that he is guilty of chameleon-like behavior.[318] He does not wish to be seen as opportunistic or fickle. Ancients did not much believe in the idea of change or development in a person's personality, or at least they did not see such change—for instance, a conversion—as a good thing. It was rather the mark of a deviant and unreliable person who was not being true to type. Thus Paul takes pains to present this change in a rhetorically effective manner, making clear that it came about through an action from God.[319]

But it will not do to see the Damascus road event as simply a prophetic call. Verse 16, as we saw, speaks of a revelation of the Son either *to* or *in* Paul—probably the latter, in light of Galatians 2:20 and 4:6. The coupling of the word "revelation" with the phrase "in me" suggests that Paul had an apocalyptic vision of the risen and glorified Christ that changed the character and course of his life and indeed his very identity. It cannot be stressed too strongly that Paul is not talking about his "having made a decision for Christ" or his having voluntarily changed the course of his life. To the contrary, Paul is talking about God's having made a decision about Paul being his witness to the Gentiles from before the time he was born!

We must compare what Paul says here to 1 Corinthians 9:1, where he speaks of having seen the risen Lord. Paul in all likelihood would have rejected modern distinctions between objective and subjective if asked about the nature of this revelation. It was objective in the sense that it was from God and was not a result of his fantasizing or dreaming or wishing. At the same time, it was subjective in that the revelation came to, and indeed even in, Paul. It was deeply personal and transforming. The purpose of the revelation was to enable Paul to preach Christ among the nations. Thus there was a call that came *with* the conversion, not later. The verb "preach" is in the present tense, but the verbs "set apart" and "called" are in the aorist, or past, tense.

What do we know about conversions from one religion to another in antiquity? First, of course, the word "conversion" is not restricted to shifts between early Christianity and early Judaism.[320] In fact, most of the conversionist groups or sects in the first century involved Eastern religions— including, for example, the cult of Isis—in addition to Judaism or Christianity. It must be stressed that the ideological distance Paul traveled

from one form of early Judaism to an offshoot of Judaism was considerably less than, say, when a person would convert from the worship of Yahweh to the worship of Baal, or from the worship of the traditional Roman
gods to the worship of Isis. In view of the general belief in Paul's world
about people having a static or unchanging character, it is not surprising
that there might have been skepticism about Paul's conversion even
among Judean Christians.[321]

We know something about conversion and initiation by a pagan person into the Judaism of Paul's day—the sort of conversion with which Paul
would have been most familiar. Conversion to Judaism was almost always
a gradual process, at the end of which was the rite of passage—namely, circumcision and full conformity to the Law.[322] The very existence of God-
fearers—Gentile synagogue adherents who were in a sort of limnal state,
neither pure pagan nor full convert—supports this conclusion.[323] Of a different order is Josephus's description of his being initiated into various
different parties or sects within Judaism (*Life* 7–12). Initiation and conversion were not one and the same. In the case of the God-fearer, conversion
led to initiation. In the case of Josephus, we can hardly speak of conversion at all. In the case of Paul, Acts 9 strongly indicates that conversion
preceded initiation into the community through baptism and acceptance
on the part of Ananias and the Christians in Damascus.

We must not dismiss the evidence that Jews knew about and even in
some cases, however rarely, sought converts to their faith. Matthew 23:15
bears witness to this phenomenon, as does Josephus's discussion of the
royal house of Adiabene (*Ant.* 20.2.3–4) and perhaps some of the Qumran
data. My point is that Saul of Tarsus would have known what a conversion was, and what it meant for his life. It meant he would be viewed as at
best a renegade and at worst an apostate crossing the boundaries of Judaism and heading in the wrong direction—indeed, texts such as 2 Corinthians 11:24 ("Five times I received the thirty lashes from the Jews") suggest
that this is how he was viewed by his Jewish peers in the Diaspora synagogues.

There was a strong social dimension to conversion, especially in antiquity. It was not a purely private matter between an individual and the
deity. Rather, it was conversion to a deity *and into a community*.[324] However
intense Paul's experience on the Damascus road was, it eventually led him
to join the group he calls "the assembly of God." As Galatians 1:13–16
shows, he saw this assembly as a distinguishable entity from Judaism. Paul
found himself part of a new family whose members he called brothers and
sisters. Yet if indeed Paul went almost immediately off into Arabia on mis-

sionary work, and then was never really integrated into the Jerusalem church afterward, it is easy to see why he would have been viewed as a maverick or a deviant by many Jerusalem Christians—that is, as one not properly integrated into a proper Christian community. This is one of the startling things about Paul: he was seen as strange or even beyond the pale not merely by his fellow Jews but also by various of his fellow Jewish Christians! He was a sectarian person whose sense of identity as a Christian came in large measure from his own conversion experience and his own outreach work and the communities and co-workers those efforts generated, *not* from some preexistent community he became a longtime member of.

If we were to do a careful sociological analysis of what happened to Saul on the Damascus road, we would have to conclude that he underwent a thorough resocialization. His symbolic universe was not just altered, it was turned upside down. Those formerly thought to be insiders were out, and those thought to be out were found to be in the people of God! It tells us something crucial about Paul's new worldview that he can see the Jewish rite of passage as not fundamental for marking out those who were truly in the assembly of God. Notice too that Paul focuses clearly on the spiritual experience that changed human lives, and he was willing to sit lightly with the Christian initiation rite.[325] Conversion, not initiation, was the truly crucial thing in his mind.

It has become common in some quarters to argue that what happened to Paul on the Damascus road was a prophetic call, not a conversion from Judaism to something else.[326] I would suggest that this is right in what it affirms but wrong in what it tries to deny. Even with all the diversity in early Judaism, not Qumranites nor Samaritans nor Sadducees nor Pharisees were prepared to say what Paul in fact says—that the Mosaic covenant, though glorious, has been eclipsed.[327] Nor were any of these groups prepared to say that full converts to their party would not have to be circumcised and keep the Law. It is quite impossible to believe that Paul, the former zealous Pharisee, could have ever said, "Neither circumcision nor uncircumcision matters" (Gal. 6:15), had there not been a radical change in his worldview and symbolic universe. This change is quite properly called a conversion.

In all likelihood the reason some scholars overlook this fact is because they do not find the traditional language about repentance or forgiveness or being saved in our text. This overlooks the rhetorical function of this material, which is to explain the divine origin of Paul's gospel. Paul says nothing here about being saved or forgiven or repenting *not* because he does not believe such a thing has happened to him, just as it did to his Gentile converts (whom he is trying to get to follow his example), but because his remarks are meant to have another rhetorical effect. Paul is also presenting himself as a paradigm of how God's miraculous grace works and leads to a life of proclamation of the message of grace and living by that grace.

It would appear to be largely true, then, that many key elements of Paul's gospel, including the idea of salvation offered freely apart from observance of the Mosaic Law, go back to his own conversion experience and the revelation he received on that occasion.[328] Paul's gospel of grace was bound up with his own experience of grace and grounded in the content of God's revelation of his Son in Paul. After this revelation but clearly before he wrote Galatians or even visited the Galatians, he worked out the implications of this Good News for his beliefs about God, messiah, Law, salvation, and the identity of God's people.

PAUL'S LIFE IN THE SPIRIT

As noted earlier, some discussions of Paul as a Christian begin and end with a discussion of his conversion.[329] This is unfortunate, as there is much more that can and should be said. I would like to speak briefly about several key aspects of Paul's Christian life that reflect who he was:

- Paul's life in the Spirit and spiritual gifts

- Paul's future hope, for himself and for others, as part of his eschatology

- Paul's overarching concern for love and concord in the community of God

Apart from the seminal work of G. D. Fee, surprisingly few detailed works have been produced in the last two decades in English that meaningfully discuss Paul's own life in the Spirit.[330] This is in part because Paul himself seems reticent to talk about such things, not least because he is not, like many a modern Western individual, bent on revealing his innermost thoughts. Ancients in fact went out of their way not to discuss "unique" experiences that distinguished them from the crowd. Such discussions were seen as antisocial to the collectivist mindset.

Paul's Life in the Spirit (2 Cor. 12:1–10; 1 Cor. 14)

It is not surprising, then, that when Paul actually does boast about his own experiences (spiritual and otherwise), the boasting is clearly ironic or tongue in cheek. For example, let's consider 2 Corinthians 12:1–10. This text is set in a context in which Paul has just boasted about his weaknesses and his trials and tribulations (2 Cor. 11), mocking the customary boasting about one's great deeds. Paul moves on, in the first verses of the passage in question, to speak of his visions and revelations (though when he gets to specifics he does so in the third person—"I know a person in Christ who … was caught up into Paradise and heard things that are not to be told"—following the rules of inoffensive self-praise). While Paul is really claiming to have had this sort of experience once in a while, which makes him in various respects like John of Patmos, he is writing to a highly charismatic audience that would be eager to hear about such experiences. Paul knows the emotional impact of such claims on them, and so while he raises their expectations, in the end, as the passage progresses, he just teases and shames them.[331]

Paul then says that he had a vision that was a source of revelation to him (in other words, he not only saw but also heard and learned), but he coyly adds that he is not permitted to convey the contents of this revelation! It is possible that his opponents, "false apostles" who were bewitching the Corinthians, were claiming such experiences as well, and that he was mainly trying to deflate their boasting.

Paul tells us that this experience happened some fourteen years prior to the writing of this letter (in other words, during the years 40 to 44), which probably places it during Paul's "hidden" years in Syria and Cilicia.[332] Now it is possible that, precisely because Paul was not a modern individualist, the Corinthians would have been shocked to hear Paul recount this story, just as they may have been shocked to hear what Paul says about tongues and prophecy in 1 Corinthians 14. Some commentators have suggested that since Paul mentions an experience of fourteen years prior rather than something more current, such experiences must have been especially rare for him. On the other hand, Paul may mention this one because to him it was especially notable and outstanding. In favor of this last suggestion is the observation that the plural in 2 Corinthians 12:1—"I will go on to visions and revelations of the Lord"—suggests that initially Paul thought about relating more than one such vision or revelation.[333]

In the course of his discussion of this event, Paul says twice that he does not know whether he was in or out of the body when he was "caught up."

The language suggests an overpowering experience that overtook Paul. It was not something Paul deliberately worked his way into through spiritual exercises or ascetical practices. Paul says also that he got as far as the third heaven, which he calls Paradise, a term from the Genesis story about Eden.[334] Paul is probably not suggesting that there are any levels above the third heaven, for to say that he didn't ascend into the highest heaven is to weaken his mock boast. Paul's point is that he got all the way to the third heaven and that this was no planned trip. Perhaps, unlike the Corinthians, he was not seeking such adventures in the Spirit.

Paul then says he heard unutterable words, but he clarifies this by explaining that he is not permitted (by God? by the Spirit?) to repeat what he heard (v. 4). The Corinthians might well understand this in terms of their knowledge of mystery religions, which often had secrets that were revealed only to special initiates. The point of mentioning the utterance without disclosing the message is to make clear that God thought Paul was a special person. In short, the Corinthians had badly underestimated him. Yet Paul also does not want them to *over*estimate him just because he's had an "excess" of revelations (v. 6).[335] This impression that Paul was a visionary is clearly confirmed in Acts, and there are various texts in which Paul himself indicates that he both knows and teaches mysteries and has special revelatory knowledge.[336]

In our 2 Corinthians 12:1–10 text, Paul goes on to say that God gave him a "stake" (a sharp wooden object) or "thorn" in the flesh, lest he too give way to the wrong sort of boasting—a deflation device, in other words. This stake or thorn, likely a physical condition, had the effect of bringing Paul right down to earth. Despite Paul's repeated prayer, God chose not to remove this stake from Paul's flesh. While we don't know for sure what afflicted Paul, what we may have here is a visionary with a vision problem![337] It's clear from 2 Corinthians 10:10 that Paul's condition involved something obvious to an outsider, something that led to an evaluation that he was weak or sickly. Furthermore, as 2 Corinthians 12:12 goes on to say, when Paul was with the Corinthians, miracles happened. Apparently they didn't happen to him, though: he may well have been a healer who himself was not entirely well! Yet it is clear from 2 Corinthians 11:21–24 that Paul did not let this condition or other misfortunes slow him down. The point in any case is that Paul's weaknesses show that the power and the revelation came from God and not from the apostle. Indeed, God's power comes to full expression or completion precisely through and in the midst of human weakness. Paul says in 2 Corinthians 12:9 that this divine power made its home in him.

This likely draws on the image of the *Shekinah* glory descending on the Temple and its Holy of Holies.

It is quite possible that Paul here has patterned his description on the experience of Christ.[338] Christ faced a cross, Paul a stake or thorn. Christ prayed three times for the suffering to pass, and so did Paul. Jesus prayed that God's will not his be done, while Paul received an assurance that God's grace would be sufficient so he could endure this stake. Both the cross and the stake had to be faced and actually endured. Since Jesus was a suffering messiah, it is no wonder his agent was a suffering apostle. Increasingly, Paul's autobiography sounds like a version of a "series of unfortunate incidents."

The next point to make about Paul's life in the Spirit is that he did indeed perform miracles, though once again he does not boast of such things but mentions them only in passing. For example, we can mention the reference to miracles in 2 Corinthians 12:12—"signs and wonders and mighty works," which in this case surely refers to miracles of healing of various sorts. We may also point to Romans 15:18–19, which closely associates the performance of powerful works with the power of the Spirit working through Paul. This impression of Paul as a miracle worker is simply confirmed by various texts in Acts.[339]

We now come to the reference in 1 Corinthians 14 to the fact that Paul both prophesied and spoke in tongues. The former is simply implied, but the latter is specifically stated. Indeed, in an attempt to deflate the overly charismatic and chaotic Corinthians, Paul says, "I thank God I speak in tongues more than all of you" (14:18)—not, mind you, more than *any* of the Corinthians, but more than *all* of them! Nevertheless, it is quite clear that Paul affirms the gifts of prophecy and of tongues (glossolalia), both in his own life and in the lives of other Christians.[340]

Tongues passages such as 1 Corinthians 14:2 (which notes that glossolalia speakers speak only to God) and 14:14 (which refers to glossolalia as prayer of the spirit but not of the mind) strongly suggest that Paul sees glossolalia as an angelic prayer language (see 1 Cor. 13:1), something prompted by the Spirit in the believer and uttered to God. In Galatians 4:6 Paul says it is the Spirit who cries "Abba, Father." This is of course an intelligible utterance or prayer. In Romans 8:26, on the other hand, Paul says that the Spirit "groans" for us. Here, it seems, Paul is referring to glossolalia, where the Spirit helps the believer at a loss for words and intercedes through the believer with "inarticulate groanings or speech."[341]

This kind of utterance does have meaning, though it is not immediately intelligible to the human speaker. God knows the mind of the Spirit, however, and knows what the Spirit is saying through the believer. The Spirit intercedes for the saints according to God's will. In other words, while the human person may not know exactly how to conform his or her prayer to God's will, the Spirit indeed does, and will do so for the believer so that he or she may pray effectively.[342] For our purposes, what is important about this material is that Paul is speaking from experience here, including his own. The first-person plurals ("when *we* cry ... with *our* spirit ... the Spirit helps *us* ... for *we* do not know how to pray ...") must be taken quite seriously here.

Paul was not only a spirited man, as any reading of his more polemical letters will attest, but also a man of the Spirit. It is important that we not downplay this factor, and it is equally important that we not anachronistically contrast it with the notion of Paul being a profound and rational thinker. We are talking about a person who manifests both life in the Spirit and life of the mind, and in fact we see a marriage of the two. No doubt Paul might have said that the only people really in their right minds are those who are filled with and inspired by the Spirit to think God's thoughts after God has revealed those thoughts.

When we assess this data as a whole, it becomes clear that despite Paul's reticence to talk directly about such matters when he himself was the focus of the discussion, he was in fact much more like his Corinthian converts than many modern commentators would like to think. Paul was not being facetious in 1 Corinthians 1:4–7 when he thanked God for the Corinthians' spiritual gifts. Paul was indeed a man of the Spirit, a "charismatic" individual in more than just the secular sense of that term. His Christian life was punctuated and enriched with notable spiritual and ecstatic experiences.

Paul's Eschatology (Phil. 2:12–13; Phil. 3:10–13)

This is not to say that Paul was not also familiar with the notion of progressive sanctification in the Christian life, nor is it to say that Paul saw himself as already spiritually complete or totally perfect in this lifetime. In this regard the book of Philippians has several texts that are helpful.

We turn first to Philippians 2:12–13, which reads in part, "Work out your salvation with fear and trembling, for it is God who is the one working in your midst, and the willing and the doing are according to his pleasure." The first point of note about this text is that "your" is in the plural. This is an exhortation for Christians to *collectively* work out the salvation they share with fear and trembling. Paul is not exhorting each individual to pursue his or her own private salvation in this matter. This is especially unlikely in that earlier in Philippians 2 Paul talks about being self-forgetful and not regarding one's own interests.[343] Paul speaks of working out the shared eschatological gift of salvation within and by the community of faith *as a community*. It's not a human accomplishment, however: not only salvation comes from God, but also the energy and the will to do this working out of salvation. God's ongoing work in the body of Christ, which also includes individual Christians as part of that body, is indeed a part of progressive sanctification.

Lest we think that Paul is speaking only about his converts in this matter, we must examine Philippians 3:10–13, where Paul speaks of "knowing Christ and the power of his resurrection and the sharing in common of his sufferings, sharing the very likeness of his death, if somehow I might obtain to the resurrection from the dead. Not that I have already obtained or am already complete [or perfect], but I press on." We see here that salvation for Paul has several tenses. He speaks of having been saved, being saved, and going on to be saved.[344] In his own life, Paul makes clear that he does not yet fully know Christ, nor has he fully experienced the power of his resurrection. In the passage above, resurrection is not a present spiritual experience but a future condition, a being raised from the dead. It is only at that latter juncture that Paul expects to be complete or perfect as a Christian person. He has not yet obtained the goal of perfection, which amounts to full Christ-likeness in the resurrection body as in the spirit. Progressive sanctification and dynamic spiritual experiences can take us only so far in this life. We must still deal with the fact that outwardly we are wasting away while inwardly we are being renewed day by day (2 Cor. 4:16–17). However "charismatic" we may be, we must still live by and move on faith and look forward to the day of resurrection, when completion finally comes.

For Paul, life apart from a body is not seen as a full human life. Thus salvation is not seen as complete without the resurrection of the body.[345] This means that we must take seriously Paul's qualifying wording in Philippians 3:11, which reads, "… if somehow I might reach/obtain the resurrection from the dead." Paul's own view, then, is that even those who have preached Christ could in the end be disqualified if they do not remain in Christ and obey him to the end.[346] Even apostles must live by faith and are not eternally secure until they are securely in eternity or have obtained the resurrection. Until such time, one must work out one's salvation with fear and trembling.

Paul's ethical enjoinders have purpose and meaning not least because there is an eschatological tension in the life of the believer between already being saved and not yet being saved to the uttermost. One not only *may* but *must* work out one's salvation in conjunction with the body of Christ with awe and respect for what is happening and must happen in Christ's body. Grace-induced, grace-empowered obedience on the part of the Christian does indeed have something to do with the final outcome. Paul calls his converts to, and models for them, the role of athletic spiritual discipline and moral effort as one presses forward toward the goal of final salvation, of fully knowing Christ, of obtaining the resurrection from the dead. Even with all of the straining, of course, resurrection still comes as a gift from God, not something achieved by the believer, though there is a sense in which Paul can speak of a heavenly prize for faithfulness to the end.[347] The discussion of spiritual gifts and experiences and process in the life of the apostle and Christians in general is incomplete unless one also speaks about the fruit of the Spirit. The Spirit not merely gives experiences or gifts but also shapes character.

Paul's Concern for Concord in the Body of Christ (Gal. 5:22–26)

It is a striking fact that many of the undisputed Pauline letters in the end prove to be exhortations to concord and unity within the body of Christ. We see this sort of deliberative argument in 1 Corinthians, in Philippians, and even in Galatians. As a part of this overall strategy to produce harmony between Paul and his converts and within the congregations, the apostle is attempting to model and commend the fruit of the Spirit.

Galatians 5:22–26 is part of a larger discussion in which verses 22–23 ("but the fruit of the Spirit is love, joy, peace, patience, kindness, goodness, faithfulness, gentleness, and self-control") stand in direct contrast to what has just been said about the deeds of the flesh—deeds prompted by sinful inclinations and leanings. Many of the main virtues that Paul lists as fruit are not included in ancient virtue lists, and some of them, such as humility, would not have been seen as virtues by most ancient pagans.[348] Those ancient lists of traits or habits that were seen as desirable for contributing members of Greco-Roman society look in many ways different from Paul's list. Only some Jewish lists also comment on love, for example, as Paul does.[349] To be more specific, the first six virtues Paul lists are found elsewhere in the New Testament, mainly in the Pauline letters,[350] while the last three are what might be called characteristic Greek virtues. It is quite tempting, in fact, to see Paul's sketch of fruit (as has sometimes been suggested for a part of 1 Corinthians 13), as a sketch of Christ's own character and characteristic teaching on the subject.[351] What a list like this actually shows is that Paul, while drawing on the best of the pagan virtues, is largely trying to create a distinctive Christian ethos for the community of his converts. What then does Paul say about the fruit?

First, he speaks of fruit *singular,* not fruit *plural.* This suggests the unity and unifying nature of virtuous qualities, as opposed to the division and discord that the works of the flesh produce. The singular also suggests that *all* these qualities should be manifest in any Christian's life, including that of the apostle. The term "fruit" also suggests that we are not talking about natural virtues or personal attainments but rather about character traits wrought in the life of the believer by the work of the Spirit. To be sure, the believer must work out these qualities in his or her social interactions, but the Spirit is the source of the qualities originally.

Love is of course the signature Christian quality to which Paul refers here, as in 1 Corinthians 13. In Romans 5:5 ("because the love of God is poured out into our hearts through the Holy Spirit") he makes abundantly clear that he is not talking about natural human feelings, but rather about love poured into the hearts of believers by the Spirit. The noun *agape,* which Paul uses for this sort of love, is not really found in classical Greek writings, nor for that matter in Josephus, yet it dominates the New Testament discussion of personal relationships. Paul sees love as the means and the goal affecting all else: he talks about faith working through love, about serving each other through love, and about loving neighbor as self (Gal. 5:6–14). The similarity between Galatians 5:13–14 ("The whole Law is summed up in a single commandment, 'You shall love your neighbor as yourself'") and Galatians 6:2 ("Bear one another's burdens, and in this way you will fulfill the Law of Christ") should not be overlooked. The Law of Christ has to do with that which Christ taught and modeled—namely, love and self-sacrificial acts. There is no law against the fruit of the Spirit; indeed, it reflects the higher law of Christ.

It is quite impossible to read Paul's letters and not be impressed with the way he modeled the various forms of spiritual fruit, especially love. The evidence of loving service for the gospel and for his converts at great personal cost is writ large in these documents.[352] Paul set the example of Christlike loving service and then bid his converts, "Imitate me, as I Christ."[353] To our own culture, the appeal "Imitate me" will seem hubristic, but it would be a mistake to read Paul this way.[354] In the first place, one of the major pedagogical tools of ancient teachers was to use modeling, especially for beginning or immature learners. Quintilian, the great Roman teacher of rhetoric, stressed the importance of modeling and indicated how he used it successfully.[355] This tool requires a society where there is considerable respect for authority, for one's elders, for those in the know. In the second place, Paul appeals for imitation only to the extent and in the way that he models Christ, the great paradigm. Were Paul an individualist, this appeal could be seen as hubris. However, Paul sees himself as one who is in Christ, as one who is but a servant or messenger of Christ, as one who is embedded in the body of Christ, as one who is what he is by the grace of God (which is to say, because of what someone else has done to and for and in him).

When Paul speaks of imitating Christ, he makes clear that his own pattern for identity and sense of identity come from another—namely, Christ. Paul is modeling himself on the narrative pattern of Christ's whole career of self-sacrificial giving, as the so-called Christ hymn in Philippians 2:5–11 shows. There he calls his converts to have the "same mind" as Christ, but it is clear that he has already heeded that exhortation in his own life.[356] He is not interested in manifesting his own distinctive mind or imposing it on others. He wishes to embody and model the mind of Christ. This focus on Christ refutes the accusation, sometimes made, that Paul has a messiah complex: to the contrary, he clearly sees a distinction between himself and the One he seeks to imitate.[357]

What does imitation of Christ mean for Paul? At times it means being conformed to the pattern of Christ's death in the events of his life while trying to serve Christ. At other times it means consciously trying to act and live humbly, deliberately stepping down the ladder of social status so that he might relate to and help all, even slaves. Imitation of Christ, then, is for Paul both something that happens in his life and a choice, both a being conformed to Christ's image and a choosing to conform to it. Imitation involves both the indicative and the imperative of the Christian life, and imitation does not fully become image until the believer is made fully Christlike at the resurrection.

WHAT WE'VE LEARNED AND WHAT THAT KNOWLEDGE TELLS US ABOUT JESUS

The trinity of Paul's identity involves his Jewishness, his Roman citizenship, and his Christianity. In other words, a variety of influences went into making Paul who he was. He had a foot in more than one sector of the ancient world both by choice and by accident of birth, and thus he cannot be understood on the basis of any one of these three crucial factors. Some combination of them is required to make sense of the apostle to the Gentiles—and even then there is much that goes unexplained, not least because Paul's letters are not like the *Confessions* of St. Augustine. They only occasionally include biographical remarks, and those remarks are never there for their own sake. In part this is because Paul, like most ancient persons, did not go around talking about his unique inner self. Rather, he spoke of who he was in relationship to the Jewish and Christian communities of which he had been or was a part, and he spoke of *whose* he was as a follower and servant and imitator of Jesus Christ.

It would appear that, of Paul's trinity of factors, the least influential was his Roman citizenship and identity. The matter is barely hinted at in his extant letters. Certainly more important is Paul's Jewish background, much of which he carried with him, though in transformed and transfigured shape, into his Christian life. Yet when Paul himself compares his illustrious Jewish past with his Christian present, he is quite clear that he places all of his former life in the loss column in comparison with the surpassing value of knowing Christ and being in Christ.

The balance of the evidence suggests that Paul was a sectarian person. He had broken away from the community that mothered him and was now helping to found a new community that, though related in various ways to its forebear Judaism, was distinct. He derived his self-understanding from that new community and from its foundation, Jesus. His identity and life work were given him by another—God in Christ; in fact, God had an identity and a calling in mind for him before he was born.

We should then not be surprised, as some commentators are, that we "do not learn anything [in his letters] about his origin from Tarsus and his family, his twofold Roman and Tarsian citizenship, his Jewish (and his official tripartite Roman) name, the great significance of Antioch, and indeed of Syria and Cilicia generally over many years, . . . his biography, his mission in the interior of Asia Minor, the foundation and fate of the community of Rome, and the reasons for the acute danger to his life."[358] This is not because Paul was shy or because he just wanted to leave the past behind; it is largely because he was an ancient, not a modern, person. There is an irony in our lack of personal information about Paul, because few people have ever had a closer link between theology and biography, between belief and life, between experience and exhortation than Paul did. Paul not only taught about Christ; he lived a cruciform life. Paul not merely talked about the Spirit; he was a man of the Spirit.

If Rudolf Bultmann was right that Paul's essential exhortation to his converts was "Become what you already are," it is fair to say that Paul was busy hearing and heeding this same exhortation.[359] He was prepared to both live in and walk by the Spirit. He was prepared to both imitate and model Christ. We have no evidence from his letters that he ever had what we would call an identity crisis. No, he was very sure of who he was and ought to be in Christ.

We can no longer treat Paul as a late Western individual. In fact, Paul was not an "individual" in the modern sense at all. He believed, and it was largely true, that his identity was established by *whose* he was, not *who* he was; by who he was related to, not how he stood out from the crowd. In this he reflected the collectivist mentality of first-century culture. Yet he was viewed by those who opposed his ministry as not merely a sectarian person, but as a deviant person, an outcast, an "abortion" of an apostle, as he calls himself in 1 Corinthians 15:8.

As a sectarian person, Paul helped lead a group of people, including some Jews and many Gentiles, to define themselves as the people of God and take over for themselves the terminology and concepts that previously had been applied almost exclusively to non-Christian Jews. This social agenda, plus Paul's strident, zealous mode of pursuing this agenda, produced strong and even at times violent reactions to him and his ministry. Apparently one either loved or hated him. Controverted and controversial, he would have won no popularity contests. He was no advocate of the status quo in a world that expended considerable energy on maintaining it.

Yet when Paul set about his mission to change the world, his choice of weapon was rhetoric, the ancient art of persuasion, first in his oral proclamations and then in his letters, which served as surrogates for his presence in the communities he had started. The leaven of the gospel was, apart from the initial acts of evangelism, inserted into the lump of society indirectly, by working for social change within the communities he had founded. The discourse we find from Paul in his letters is community-based and community-directed. Like most of the prophets of the Old Testament, he directed words of praise and censure, of prediction and confirmation, to those who were already a part of God's people.

Paul was no ordinary wordsmith, no backwoods preacher, despite his rhetoric about proclaiming to the Corinthians nothing but Christ and him crucified. Paul partook fully of the rhetorically saturated oral culture and used the great love of rhetoric to his advantage in numerous ways, yet without compromising the integrity of his gospel. It is a measure of his success as a rhetor that he was able to sell socially disconcerting notions about servanthood, self-sacrifice, equality of personhood, love of enemies, grace rather than reciprocity, and a crucified Lord using the formal conventions of his day. Indeed, nothing short of grace itself could have convinced the Greco-Roman world about these sorts of values. To moderns, Paul's boasting seems a bit off-putting, but to ancients accustomed to boasting, the only striking thing would have been what he chose to boast about—a crucified savior, power in weakness, reversal of roles between the haves and have-nots, and the like.

It would be wrong to underestimate the social level of Paul. His education was considerable, his Roman citizenship important, and his deliberate agenda of stepping down the social ladder impressive. He was a clear parable of grace to the less fortunate of society. We must not be misled by his choice to occasionally make or mend tents. While Paul was not among the tiny minority of the Greco-Roman aristocracy, he was among the relatively elite echelon of society that came just below the patricians—and not just because of his education. What a paradox he was: a Roman citizen with considerable status, but also a Jew who continued to affirm various aspects of his Jewish heritage (which made him part of a minority that was despised by many Greeks and Romans) and a follower of Christ (which made him part of an even smaller and less well known—and perhaps less well liked—minority).

Yes, a paradox to be sure. On the one hand Paul was a prophet, which gave him considerable status in the Greco-Roman world, but on the other hand he chose to work with his hands, which would not have endeared him to the elite. On the one hand Paul advocated submitting to the governing authorities, but on the other hand he set about to deconstruct many of the major social values of Greco-Roman culture that the authorities spent no little time and money to support. On the one hand Paul seemed to support the patriarchal status quo, with its harsher aspects mitigated by love, but on the other hand he tried to give women more options by advocating singleness, give slaves more hope and sense of self-worth by advocating their personhood in Christ, give children a chance to avoid abuse, and finally rein in the power and authority of the head of the family by tying him to following the model of servanthood and love of Christ. It is not surprising in these circumstances that people today have a hard time deciding which anachronistic pigeonhole—chauvinist or feminist—to place Paul in. But this square peg will fit in neither of those modern round holes.

While recent discussions of Paul's thought-world and his theology have made some progress in looking at Paul as part of his old-world context, we've seen precious little progress in the debate about Paul's view of the Law. The key to understanding Paul's view is where he places the Law in the timetable of the story of God's people in relationship to where he sees God's people now, as a result of Christ's coming. That word "story" is crucial: the search for the heart of Paul's theology has to recognize that in an oral culture dominated by defining narratives, we need to be looking for the climax to a story, not the center of a body of thought. There *is* no static body of thought in Paul's theology. Rather it is the result of his thinking and theologizing into the various situations of his converts. It is not those situations that dictate what Paul says, of course; they are only the occasions for this or that particular articulation of his gospel and narrative thought-world. What we have in Paul's letters is theologizing on the basis of a symbolic universe and the stories within that universe—particularly the story of Christ, which is the gospel. To speak of Paul's theology is to speak of a modern creation, a modern putting together of the pieces of Paul's theologizing. To a certain extent this process is artificial, and it certainly involves various debatable interpretive judgments. Yet it is reasonable to conclude that the task is necessary if we are to have a full-orbed picture of Paul.

Paul's ethics are likewise grounded in his theologizing and his narrative thought-world. Again the story of Christ plays a crucial role, providing the paradigm for Christian living. Paul the exegete draws on the substance of Old Testament stories and commandments to address his converts, but he reconfigures these stories in light of Christ and in light of the eschatological situation he sees Christians living in, caught between already and not yet, between flesh and Spirit. The Paul who emerges from our explorations appears to have been remarkably flexible in an inflexible world. It is very odd language for an early Jew to speak of being a Jew to the Jew and a Gentile to the Gentile in his manner of living in order by all means to win some. This is not to say that Paul does not have fixed and unalterable commitments to the gospel and its theological and ethical ramifications, but it is to say that the way Paul theologizes and thinks ethically out of these commitments is remarkably adaptable to his audience's situation. His message is at one and the same time both coherent (with his thought-world) and contingent in its expression and application. The old distinction between eternal principles and culturally relative practices is in some ways still helpful, but only if one recognizes that the middle term between these two is the theologizing and ethicizing that Paul does in order to relate the former to the latter. In all this one must keep steadily in mind that Paul was a pastor, not an armchair theorist. He did not intend for his letters to become fodder for systematicians or fertile fields for doctoral theses; and yet both things have happened, and not without profit.

The definitive biography of the man is yet to be written and may never be written. But were the apostle to have written one himself, I am sure he would have stressed the cruciform and Christocentric pattern of his life.

He stood in the shadow of the Galilean and not infrequently reflected the character of the one he served. No higher compliment can be paid to a Christian than to say he lived out of and strove to emulate the story of Christ. It is no wonder so many have loved this passionate and paradoxical man and have striven to imitate him. We become what we admire.

I suspect that the historical Paul, were he to visit us today, would still be a social outcast and deviant, still be seen as a fanatic, even in many conservative religious circles. Prophetic figures tend to be heroes only long after they are dead, when their actual ground-shaking presence and power are no longer directly felt. Yet it is true to say that if Paul had not been the person he was, the Christian movement might not have become the Gentile-dominated entity it has been for almost the whole of the last two thousand years. There might never have been a Lutheran reformation or a Wesleyan revival or a Geneva awakening. If the measure of the stature of a person is the degree of impact that he and his life's work have on subsequent generations, then the historical Paul is clearly the most important figure in Christian history and the history of the West—after Jesus, of course. It thus behooves us to continue to search for ever clearer portraits of the man.

It is ironic that the last of the inner circle to become a follower of Jesus was the one who was to have the largest impact on the shape of the Christianity that came after him. It also ironic that this last one was in fact to provide the chronologically earliest and most ample contributions to the New Testament. Is this large contribution due to the fact that Paul and his co-workers won the day when it came to defining what the faith would be like? Yes, there is some truth to this view. Rome was the center of the empire, and Paul went there; and we see his large impact already in 1 Clement, and then in the letters of Ignatius, and then in many other writings.

The members of the inner circle that stayed at home or near home in the eastern end of the Roman Empire were not likely to have, and in fact did not have, the largest impact on the future character of Christian faith. One wonders what Jesus would have thought about all of this. Perhaps he would have said to Paul, "Well done, good and faithful servant," or perhaps he would have reminded his Jerusalem brothers and sisters about the Old Testament promise that many would come from the east *and the west* and sit down at table with Father Abraham at the messianic banquet. But surely if they were to come, somebody would have to go out and give them an engraved and grace-filled invitation. That person was Paul in the first century. Perhaps the last really do become first.

More than any other single figure, Paul was the change agent who steered a Jewish sect in the direction of becoming a world religion. There was no time for looking back in longing, for the eschatological age had already dawned, time was a-wasting, and Jesus had promised to return. New occasions (especially eschatological occasions) call for new duties, new mission strategies, and new flexibilities, but also for consolidating the gains already obtained.

Whether we look to the early letters of Paul or the late letters of the Beloved Disciple, all along the way we see boundary lines being drawn and firmed up—Christological, ethical, and practical community boundary lines. Paul and the rest of the inner circle believed in joining hands so that the circle would be unbroken in generations to come. Though that circle was inclusive, it was also exclusive: had there been Gnostic or Marcionite Christians in the first century, they would have been treated like the false teachers described in 2 Corinthians, the pastoral epistles, Jude, the Johannine epistles, and Matthew's gospel. And in due course those false teachers would have found themselves on the outside looking in.

The establishment of boundaries is not a cause for regret. A Jewish eschatological Christ-centered religion that was open to Jew and Gentile alike, to the well-educated and the illiterate alike, to men and women alike, to the young and the old alike, could not afford to be without some clear ideological boundaries, some clear sense of what they were and were not—especially since their identity was *not* to be defined by geography, gender, generation, social class, age, or wealth of possessions or knowledge. It was not to be defined by the things that usually determined what religion one was a part of in that world. There were, after all, not that many highly evangelistic, successfully conversionistic religions in antiquity. If with the apostle to the Gentiles one is going to say, "If anyone is in Christ, he or she is a whole new creation," one had best be prepared to say clearly what that does and does not entail.

And what it did not entail at the end of the day was simply being a part or sect of extant Judaism, nor did it involve becoming a part of the general pagan religious world that worshipped many gods and recognized emperors as gods who walked upon the earth. Instead—in some ways reluctantly, in some ways eagerly, in some ways intentionally, in some ways quite by accident—a new Christ-centered religion became fully formed in the first century by devout monotheistic Christians not waiting for later church councils to tell them what they did or ought to believe and embrace.

Later attempts to reinvent the Christian wheel in the second through fourth centuries were seen for what they were—Johnny-come-lately efforts that did not stand in continuity with the original form of the faith and could not trace their lineage back to the inner circle of Jesus, though they would desperately try to do so through vehicles like the Gospel of Thomas and the Gospel of Mary.

These later offshoots, then, should not be seen as "lost Christianities" that we should rediscover, if by rediscover one means endorse or embrace as a legitimate form of early Christianity. We certainly need to know about them, however, in order to know what early Christianity was *not* like. These aberrations should be seen exactly the way the church fathers and mothers of the second through fourth centuries saw them—as "heresies," the promulgation of "other" ideas not in continuity with the eyewitness and apostolic faith given in the first century. After all, those later Christians who lived in the second through fourth centuries and interacted with the living advocates of mutations of the Christian faith knew far better than we do today the real character of those offshoots and whether they comported with the Jesus movement and its earliest source documents. In our final chapter we will pursue these matters further.

Here it is sufficient to stress that Paul, the change agent, was right when he said already in his earliest letter, Galatians, that there is no other gospel than the one originally proclaimed by the inner circle of Jesus. There seems not to have been any major Christological dispute among members of that circle. We don't see Paul facing off with Peter about Jesus: they dispute, yes—but about table manners and table fellowship! We don't see James butting heads with Paul about Jesus or even about grace or the need for obedience; they differ on whether Jewish Christians should be required to keep the Mosaic Law. The differences within the inner circle are primarily ecclesiological and praxis-centered; they're not about Christology, *which is the defining element that made Christianity distinct from early Judaism and paganism.*

Why this basic concord on matters Christological within the inner circle? Surely it is because they all had seen the risen Lord, had all worshiped him together, had written hymns and prayers and confessions about him, and had taken that central message down the roads of the empire to share the Good News with others. It was the resurrection of Jesus that made the Galilean the risen Lord; and it was the appearances of that same Jesus that made his followers the founders of a new community of faith, the authors of most of its original source documents, and the evangelists of its great message.

To look through the eyes of Paul at the historical Jesus is an interesting exercise. What we learn about the man Paul is prepared to call the Son of David on the one hand (Rom. 1:3–4) and the Son of God (or even God) on the other hand (Rom. 9:5; Phil. 2:5–11) is remarkable. But I would stress again that we have no evidence that Paul was ever taken to task by his fellow members of the inner circle *for his Christological reflections*. That issue is not what he argues with Peter or James or the others about. This is remarkable for what it tells us about both the inner circle itself and what those fellow Jesus-followers thought about Paul's views in light of what they actually knew about the historical Jesus. As we saw in our earlier discussion of Joanna/Junia, Paul says that she was in Christ before him, shared jail time with him, and was notable amongst the apostles. Perhaps he learned much about Jesus from his time with her. But we have no hint that she ever corrected, contradicted, or disputed Paul's presentation of Jesus the Christ. If the leadership of earliest Christianity was really as diverse as some modern scholars have suggested, these sorts of silences make no sense at all.

The final important clue about Jesus that we glean through the study of Paul comes through Paul's imitation of Christ. Just as Paul was not an individualist in the modern sense, neither was Jesus. Ancient persons were not preoccupied with their own inner psyche or sense of identity, which helps explain why Jesus was not more forthcoming about how he viewed himself. But we see Jesus through Paul. When Paul speaks of imitating Jesus, he is referring to a reasonably clear line of demarcation in regard to the behavior traits of Jesus—something both he and his converts knew about. Jesus the man of the Spirit, the visionary, the miracle worker, the man of peace, the purveyor of wisdom, the prophet, the eschatological teacher—all these roles find an analogue in the behavior of Paul. You do indeed become the person whom you admire. In our last chapter I will say more about all this, and we will see if that inner circle actually joined hands in the end.

PART SEVEN

WILL THE CIRCLE BE UNBROKEN?

The Character and Characters of Earliest Christianity

It has been said that necessity is the mother of invention. It might be better to say that *experience* is the mother of invention. It was the experience of seeing the risen Lord that created the inner circle of Jesus, and the coming of the Spirit that birthed the church. In other words, naturalistic historical explanations alone will never adequately explain the crucial events that led to the rise of the inner-circle leaders within the Christian movement and the rise of the movement itself.

One member of the inner circle of the fledgling church, Peter, was already a follower of the historical Jesus before Easter, but this really didn't much help him since he abandoned his Master in Jesus's greatest hour of need. He pretty much had to start over after Easter. Another member of the inner circle, the Beloved Disciple, was a part-time pre-Easter follower, joining up whenever Jesus was in the vicinity of Jerusalem, but he wasn't one of the original inner circle of the Twelve or one of the core three. He was a Judean disciple—indeed, perhaps he was Lazarus, as this study has suggested. But even he was quite literally out to sea until he saw the risen Lord in Galilee. He also had to start over after Easter, though without the painful rite of restoration that Peter underwent.

Jesus's own mother tried to understand him and protect him, and she stood by him even in his greatest hour of humiliation, but she only really began to be his follower at the foot of the cross. It's a great shame we have little or no historical evidence about the role she played after Pentecost (unless Revelation 12 provides a small clue, as discussed in Chapter 6).

Joanna and Mary Magdalene were faithful to the bitter end; they didn't head off to Emmaus after the crucifixion. However, when they went to the tomb, even these faithful ones were expecting only to pay their last respects. They didn't expect to find the tomb empty, and they certainly didn't expect to have a close encounter of the first kind with the supernatural. They too only became full-fledged followers of Jesus when they were transformed and galvanized by the risen One. It is the greatest of pities that they left us no personal written record of what they did thereafter, though, as we have seen, Acts 1:14 suggests that they continued in the church in Jerusalem. In the case of Joanna, we are very fortunate indeed, if she was in fact Junia, to catch up with her twenty-five or more years later in Rome and hear about her courageous apostolic labors. Andronicus and Junia likely played larger roles than we understand at this juncture. We would love to know more about them, but the evidence is lacking. To be sure, they were not jailed for loitering! Maybe they were some of the first apostles in Rome.

In regard to the brothers of Jesus and that man born out of due season, Paul, there is no shard or shred of a hint that they began their pilgrimage as disciples of Jesus before they saw the risen Lord (or perhaps, in Jude's case, heard of it from eyewitnesses such as James). It is that experience of the risen Christ that in the end bound them all together and made them the inner circle of Jesus—only a miracle, nothing short of a miracle, could have so galvanized this diverse group of early Jews, who then went out and turned the world upside down. But of course they did not do it alone. They had many co-workers, and in a few cases they even shared some co-workers: Paul and Peter, for example, both worked with Silas and Mark.

Lost in the usual discussions of the rise of early Christianity is the fact that the Twelve—that is, Peter and Andrew (brothers), James and John sons of Zebedee (brothers), Matthew/Levi and James son of Alphaeus (possibly brothers), Philip, Bartholomew, Thomas, Thaddeus, Simon the Zealot, and Judas Iscariot—do not seem to have played a major role, as a collective entity. In fact, only Peter from among the Twelve seems to have figured largely in the rise of this movement. We do not hear again about various members of the Twelve in any of our earliest and best historical sources. There are some credible later traditions that some of them became traveling missionaries, such as the tradition that Thomas headed off toward India in obedience to the Great Commission, but the trail goes cold after that. Being an eyewitness was obviously more crucial, then, than being one of the Twelve.

Consider too the literary output of the early church. Of the gospels and the book of Acts, only Matthew's likely owes something to one of the Twelve, though Peter may stand behind Mark's gospel; and of the epistles, only 1 Peter appears to go back to one of the Twelve. This is further confirmation that it was not the Twelve, but rather the wider group of the apostles—the eyewitnesses of the risen Jesus—who became the early leadership structure and spearheaded the spread of the Good News. The Twelve in any case had been set up by Jesus as a paradigm of Israel, and primarily to take the Good News to Jews whether in Israel or elsewhere, with a promise of an eschatological role of being the judges of the twelve tribes of Israel at the end. We have no evidence that this mission had vast success. Only in the case of Peter do we see evidence, in his document 1 Peter, that some good things were accomplished in the Diaspora.

And yes, some people who were neither eyewitnesses nor members of the Twelve played major roles—figures like Priscilla, Aquila, Apollos, Titus, and Timothy (along with a few who may or may not have been eyewitnesses, such as Silas). After the year 50, in the writing phase of the New Testament era, figures such as Luke and the prophet John of Patmos play important roles.

And yes, it was James and Jude the brothers of Jesus who played an important role in keeping Jerusalem-centered, Torah-true Christianity alive, and James also helped birth what was to become the largely Gentile church heading west. Philip seems to have been an important figure, to judge from Acts 8—and once again he was not one of the Twelve, nor do we know if he saw the risen Lord. We suspect that he, like another non-Twelve member, Stephen, may have contributed more than we know to the mission in the Holy Land. The devastating events in the year 70 in and around Jerusalem helped make sure that the Pauline forms of early Christianity, and other forms birthed in the Diaspora (such as Johannine Christianity), were to prevail over this Torah-true form in the Holy Land, in spite of the sporadic persecutions of Nero and Domitian and later emperors.

The Torah-true form of Jewish Christianity that James represented continued to exist into the early Middle Ages, but it was not the stream that was to become the broadest and most inclusive. It is worth stressing, however, that this stream did *not* differ from Pauline Christianity in any significant way in its Christology or soteriology (salvation theology) so far as we can tell. It differed in its ortho*praxy* rather than its ortho*doxy*. And we know nothing whatsoever of a form of Christianity in the Holy Land that did not have Christ's death and resurrection as a central focus. Possible early collections of sayings of Jesus do not tell us anything about the contours or full belief system of a whole Christian community.

It becomes clear on closer inspection that Christianity spread in various ways and places and often without the help of apostles or the Twelve. Christianity was already in Rome before Peter or Paul ever got there, so we must beware of overdoing the "great person" approach to the spread of Christianity. There is, for example, no historical evidence that Peter was ever anything other than the apostle to the Jews. Even from Rome he was simply writing to his Jewish converts in Turkey. The evidence that he was the head of a mostly Gentile church in Rome is mostly lacking, though some have argued that the mention of Silas and Mark in 1 Peter points in that direction.

We might wish that there was clear evidence of Peter and Paul working hand in hand in Rome, or of the Beloved Disciple and Paul working together in Asia, but that evidence is lacking. The men and women of the inner circle whom we have examined in this book do not seem to have done much actual work together, though surely they strove to support each other in prayer, and Paul sought the blessing of the Jerusalem church and worked hard to bind his congregations to that church by the raising of the collection for famine relief in the city of Zion.

It is pointless to talk about "lost Christianities" if we are talking about the apostolic age, because there were no forms of Christianity like later Gnosticism already extant in the first century. Indeed, as far as we know there were no forms of earliest Christianity that did not worship Jesus as crucified and risen Lord, as has been aptly and thoroughly demonstrated of late by Larry Hurtado.[360] All of the later variants such as Gnosticism, which were deemed heresies in their own time as well as afterward, were offshoots and aberrations of the second- through fourth-century Christian churches. There is not a shred of solid historical evidence that such movements and sectarian split-offs existed in the apostolic age.

One cannot imagine a James or a Jude or a Peter or a Paul or a Beloved Disciple, with all of their polemics against sectarians and false teachers of various sorts, sitting down at table fellowship with the folks who wrote the various Gnostic gospels and tracts. Folks like Paul could hardly stomach having table fellowship with Judaizers, and Jude warns against love feasts with those he deems immoral.

Earliest Christianity, if we go back to the font, had narrow banks, but the streams flowing through them were deep, not broad and muddy. Better said, there was a central river that fed several clear streams that branched out in various directions in the first half of the first century. Whether we are comfortable with it or not, the earliest Christian leaders were remarkably similar in their beliefs about the divinity of Jesus, the way to salvation, and basic ethics. Beliefs about food laws, circumcision, and Sabbath-keeping were a different matter—a matter about which early Christians could and did agree to disagree. What this in practice meant is that Christianity would not remain simply a sect of Judaism, especially when the Torah-true stream of the faith failed to dominate the landscape of the empire.

As we have seen in this study, a very resilient form of Christianity, in the form of the Johannine community, was probably started by someone who was neither one of the Twelve nor an associate of Paul, though he was certainly an eyewitness of the risen Jesus and of his pre-Easter ministry. History is messy, even church history: the waters from the various important streams of early Christianity that flowed out of the central river sometimes intermingled. However, the streams tended to stay mostly within their own boundaries, heading in their own respective directions; and this trend continued into the postapostolic era.[361] The Pauline stream tended to go in its own direction, and the more Jewish Christian streams in their own directions, even when those streams all meandered widely through the empire.

A good case study of whether we can really talk about parallel but mostly independent streams of early Christianity can be done on the Pauline and Johannine communities in Asia, the former having apparently been basically a Gentile community, and the latter largely a Jewish community. What happened in Asia after most of the eyewitnesses and the inner circle had passed away? Did the Pauline and Johannine churches merge? Consider these words from the summary offered in the Mohr-Siebeck catalog of Paul Trebilco's recent *magnum opus* on Christianity in Ephesus:

> In this book, Paul Trebilco seeks to discuss all the evidence for the life of the early Christians in Ephesus from Paul to Ignatius, seen in the context of our knowledge of the city as a whole. Drawing on Paul's letters and the Acts of the Apostles, the author discusses the beginnings of the life of the early Christians in Ephesus, both before the Pauline mission and during that mission. He then shows that in the period from around 80–100 CE there were a number of different groups in Ephesus who regarded themselves as Christians: the Pauline group addressed by the Pastorals, the Johannine group spoken of in 1–3 John, the opponents of the Pastor, the Johannine secessionists, and the Nicolaitans. Some key features of the life of each of these groups are discussed, as the evidence allows; this testifies to the diversity of early Christianity in Ephesus.
>
> It is also argued that the Pauline group and the Johannine group in Ephesus were distinct and separate communities, although they maintained non-hostile contact. This is done by examining a number of different themes relating to these two groups: their attitude to the wider world, their material possessions and the use to which they were put, their leadership structure and understanding of the locus of

authority, the position of women, and their use of self-designations. Through discussing these themes, Paul Trebilco also describes a number of features of the distinctive identity of the Pauline and Johannine groups. He also argues that John the Seer in Revelation was seeking to address all Christians in the city and that Ignatius in his letter to Ephesus addresses all Christians in the city. Finally the information that Ignatius gives us about Christians in Ephesus in his time is discussed.

I quite agree with Trebilco's presuppositions that the Johannine letters were likely written by one person, as were the pastoral epistles (or at least they came from one person, though someone else may have been involved in the actual composition), and I concur with the following portions of his thesis as explicated in his book as well:

- The Pauline and Johannine groups in Ephesus were distinct and separate communities. This is shown by the hints about the structures of these communities and the very different sorts of rhetoric used to address them in the pastorals and the Johannine epistles. This conclusion lends itself to the suggestion that the Johannine communities were populated predominantly by Jewish Christians.

- The necessarily small size and character of so-called house churches—small groups of Christians who met in homes, sometimes because persecution prevented large public gatherings—"fostered the maintenance of difference, and the practicalities of house churches had an impact on the emergence and maintenance of diversity within the Christian communities of a large city."[362]

- The peaceful coexistence theory works far better to explain the data than the takeover theory (that is, earlier Pauline communities coopted by later Johannine ones), or even the merger theory. Trebilco helpfully adds, "It is noteworthy that neither group would have regarded the other in the same way as they saw their 'opponents'. Neither group would have failed the particular 'litmus tests' that the other group has used with regard to their 'opponents' and which their respective opponents had failed."[363] This is exactly right, and it means that for both these communities, while some diversity was allowed in faith and practice, there were also boundaries the crossing of which led to crises that required rhetorical responses of various sorts.

- The Johannine communities and their leader, the "old man" or Beloved Disciple, were more exclusivist and community-oriented, concerned about firming up boundaries with the world, whereas the Pauline followers maintained some boundary with pagans but were prepared (to judge from their leadership, Paul and Timothy) to translate "significant theological ideas into more acculturated forms."[364] This does not surprise us if we are right that the Pauline communities are largely Gentile and still quite concerned about reaching out to Gentiles, while the Johannine communities are much more Jewish Christian and operating in a more insular and inwardly looking mode.

We can conclude, then, that the Pauline and Johannine churches were basically separate communities in and around Ephesus, communities that may have had some contact and some knowledge of each other but did not exchange influence in either direction—not even influence from the founding figures of each of these communities. This is not a surprise, since as Galatians 2:7–8 indicates, there was an intentional division of labor from the beginning, with Paul targeting largely Gentile audiences and Peter and others targeting Jews. It appears that it was only in the second century that these communities in Asia began to be truly consolidated under one authority structure, a consolidation that may already have begun to happen when John of Patmos wrote Revelation 2–3 in the 90s (since he seems to have been addressing communities addressed both by 1 and 2 Timothy and by 1–3 John) and seems to have been still going on when Ignatius wrote his letters in the early second century.[365] There is still much fertile research that needs to be done on the social networks in early Christianity during the last three decades of the New Testament era, but that is a task for another time and another author.

What we see both in the apostolic and the early postapostolic age is a surprising lack of central organization. This is one reason why we have, on the one hand, documents like the Didache, warning people about prophets arriving from elsewhere and assuming authority in a local congregation; and we have, on the other hand, the efforts of figures like Ignatius in the early second century to create a central and hierarchical structure in the form of the monarchial episcopate. These phenomena indicate that neither the inner circle nor the apostles had left in place a structure that bound the various parts of the church together. The structure of deacons and elders and overseers that developed tended to be very local or regional, but certainly not empire-wide; and the mother church in Jerusalem never had a chance to establish such a structure due to the devastations of A.D. 70. Rather, that Jerusalem-based form of Christianity stayed in the eastern part of the empire and charted its own course.

Thus, when we get beyond the period of the inner circle, different forms of orthodox early Christianity, divided along ethnic lines by and large due to the shape of the original division of labor of the early church's evangelism, continued to grow and flourish and sometimes interact in important and positive ways. There was no centrally controlled monolithic development of the first-century church empire-wide. But if there was not ecclesiological unity, there was something else remarkable, something that kept these Jewish and Gentile streams within their proper bounds— the collection and dissemination of the original eyewitness source documents, which indeed go back to the inner circle, as shown in Chart 1.

CHART 1: THE INNER CIRCLE

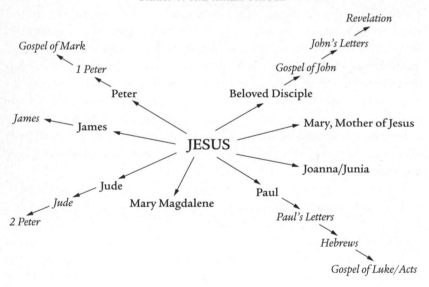

Some things to note:

- All twenty-seven of the New Testament documents can be traced back to the inner circle or those connected to the inner circle (with the possible exception of Matthew's gospel).

- No women were responsible for these documents.

- The New Testament documents were equally directed to Jews (the Gospel of Matthew, the Gospel of John, James, Jude, Hebrews, 1 Peter, John's letters, and Revelation) and to Gentiles (the Gospel of Mark, Luke, Acts, Paul's letters, and possibly 2 Peter, though the latter may have been more broadly directed).

When we realize that almost all the New Testament documents can be traced back directly or indirectly to the inner circle of Jesus, we gain some clarity as to why the movement had coherence and Christians were readily identifiable as Christians throughout the empire. I have told elsewhere the remarkable story of the production and copying of the New Testament documents, which cannot be repeated here.[366] Here it must suffice to say that this must have been something of a cottage industry that involved especially the collection of Paul's letters and the four gospels for copying and dissemination. This would have been before the end of the first century in the case of Paul's letters (see 2 Pet. 3:15–16), and somewhat later in the case of the four gospels, which seem to have circulated together in codex form by the year 125. The postapostolic era was not left without eyewitness testimony or new sacred traditions; and fortunately, a few of the original eyewitnesses lived almost to the close of the first century, further helping the transition. But there is another factor that bound early Christianity together and prevents us from accepting an evolution-of-ideas model when analyzing its ideology. I am talking about the Christology of the New Testament—that is, the things believed about Jesus by his followers. See Chart 2 for a breakdown of that Christology by source.

CHART 2: HIGH CHRISTOLOGY IN THE FIRST-CENTURY CHURCH

All the documents in the New Testament agree on the messianic status of Jesus. None of them consider him merely an ordinary human being, though his humanity is nowhere in doubt. The question, then, is how Jesus's more-than-ordinary mortal status is viewed in these documents. The chart below, broken into documents written specifically for Jewish Christians (on the left) and for Gentile Christians (on the right), indicates the Christological focus of each source and the approximate date of composition. (Note that the purpose of a document dictates the content. For example, the focus of the sermon we call the book of James is hortatory, not theological; nevertheless, it has some Christology.)

DOCUMENTS FOR JEWISH CHRISTIANS

Matthew: High Christology of Jesus as Wisdom, Emmanuel; written in the 70s–80s for those in Galilee or Antioch

John: High Christology of Jesus as preexistent Logos and Theos; written in the 90s for those in Asia

Hebrews: High Christology of Jesus as Wisdom, God's divine, preexistent Son; written probably in the 60s for those in Rome

1 Peter: Lord Jesus Christ, with the spirit of Christ dwelling in Old Testament prophets; written in the 60s for those in Asia, Pontus, Cappadocia, Galatia, Bithynia

Johannine Epistles: High Christology of Jesus as incarnate One; written in the 80s

James: Submerged Christology, but Jesus called Lord Jesus Christ (like title of divine emperor); written in the 50s; encyclical sermon for Jewish Christians outside Israel

Jude: Jesus called Master, Lord, Christ, with threefold "Lord Jesus Christ"; written in the 40s–50s; audience uncertain—possibly all Jewish Christians or even all Christians

Revelation: Jesus called by divine names and a host of others; written in the 90s for the largely Jewish Johannine community in Asia

DOCUMENTS FOR GENTILE CHRISTIANS

Mark: Jesus as Christ, Son of Man, Son of God; written in the late 60s for a largely Gentile Christian audience in Rome

Luke-Acts: Jesus as Christ, Lord, savior; written for Gentile patron Theophilus in the 70s–80s; location unknown (possibly Rome)

Pauline corpus: High Christology of various sorts (including Theos Christology); written from 49 to 65

2 Peter: High Christology, Lord, savior, Christ; written at the end of the first century, possibly for a general audience

CONCLUSIONS

As the above presentation shows, high Christology is found not only in documents largely for Gentiles, or only in Pauline-influenced documents, or only in documents from toward the end of the first century. Indeed, high Christology goes back to the Aramaic-speaking Christians in Jerusalem, who prayed not only to Abba, but prayed Marana tha, "Come, O Lord," to the exalted Jesus (see 1 Cor. 16). That group likely generated and sang some of the Christological hymns embedded in various New Testament documents (for example, Phil. 2:5–11; Col. 1:15–20) and made some of the confessions found embedded in various New Testament documents (see, for example, Rom. 1:3-4). High Christology ultimately goes back to Jesus's presentation of himself as God's Wisdom come in the flesh, and as the human but also divine Son of Man of Daniel 7. In other words, there is no easy evolutionary spiral from low to high Christology, from early to late Christology, from more Jewish to more Gentile Christology, or from Christology more for Jews to Christology more for Gentiles.[368]

Just as the majority of New Testament documents can be traced back to the inner circle of Jesus either directly or indirectly, so also can the high and often divine Christology found in documents for both Jewish and Gentile Christians be traced back to the inner circle of Jesus. It is not primarily a product of later non-eyewitnesses or third-generation, second-century Christians.

What is most telling about this chart is that we find both human and divine predications of Jesus in both Gentile and Jewish streams of early Christianity, and we find them both early and late in the first century. There was no evolutionary spiral from low to high Christology in the first century, not even when it came to calling Jesus "God" or "divine Lord." Indeed, some of the highest Christology is found in some of the earliest documents—Paul's letters, for example, and from there back to the Aramaic-speaking sources in Jerusalem whence he got some of his ideas. The central ideology of early Christianity about Christ was well in place by the end of the first century, then; it did not first coalesce only after the ecumenical councils of the fourth and fifth centuries, as some have suggested. Despite a profusion of Christological images and a plethora of titles in our varying first-century sources, those sources reveal that the inner circle and their co-workers were in general agreement in the first century that Jesus must be worshipped as divine, as well as understood and proclaimed as a messianic human being.

So in the end if we ask the question, "Will the circle be unbroken?" and refer it to the original inner circle of Jesus, the answer must be the escha- tological one that the song itself offers: "by and by, Lord, in the sky." Per- haps Jesus's answer would have been, "The circle will be reunified into a whole when the Son of Man returns and, at the resurrection, the Twelve are reconstituted and given roles in relationship to Israel." In the interim, those of us who are still part of this remarkable movement and cherish the original inner circle of Jesus must live as the church expectant, not the church triumphant, and be thankful for those early believers' remarkable lives and witness to the risen One.

But what about that risen One—the Jesus remembered by all of these members of the inner circle? What was he like, and did these disciples "reinvent" him in their imaginations after Easter? We have seen that the inner circle had more than enough living contact with the historical Jesus to remember who Jesus was, what his teaching was like, and what claims (implicit or explicit) he made of a messianic nature. After all, the inner cir- cle was constituted partly by members of Jesus's family, and partly by some of his earliest disciples (Peter, Joanna, Mary Magdalene), and partly by nonitinerant disciples who were eyewitnesses (for example, the Beloved Disciple). Given those relationships, there is good reason to think that these early disciples transmitted their ideas about Jesus to those whose lives they touched.

Paul is an excellent example. He speaks of consulting with the pillar apostles Peter, James, and John, and he chooses to use the rather technical language Jews used for the careful transmission of sacred tradition. So even Paul, who did not know the pre-Easter Jesus, was passing on what he had received of the story and teachings of Jesus. Even Paul was not recre- ating Jesus according to the measure of his dreams or desires. Had he done so, he would surely have been corrected by Peter or James, whose opinions he respected and whose approbation he sought. Paul can be accused of turning Christianity into a largely Gentile movement and moving it beyond its original sectarian character in terms of the nature of the com- munity and its organization apart from Judaism, but he cannot be accused of recreating or reinventing the image of Jesus.

What I have noted time and again in the concluding section of these chapters is that there is neither an evolutionary spiral of ideas about Jesus, nor a gap between the historical Jesus and the Christ of faith, for the very good reason that many of the members of the inner circle had known and certainly remembered what the historical Jesus was like, and they them- selves found the worship of Jesus as risen Lord, the praying to him as divine, the naming of him as God or Christ or Logos, to be perfectly natural. Unless one is prepared to say that the very earliest witnesses, some of Jesus's own companions and family, got it all wrong about a person they knew intimately, it is impossible to drive a wedge between the historical Jesus and the Christ of faith. We can talk about how some specific ideas—for example, Jesus as the heavenly high priest (Hebrews) or Jesus as the Lion of the tribe of Judah (Revelation)—arose as a result of later reflection on the meaning of Jesus and the Christ event. But central ideas such as Jesus being the Christ, being the Son of God, being the risen Lord, being the mysterious Son of Man of Daniel 7—these ideas were already in play at the outset of the Jesus movement; they were discussed both before and after the death of Jesus. There is no nonmessianic Jesus to be found at the bottom of the well of history. Nor does the inner circle let us think for a moment that there is a Jesus to be found who ought not to be the object of worship, prayer, devotion. Any quest for such a Jesus is bound to end in frustration or in wild conjectures not well tethered to the limited historical sources we have from the first century. The evidence that we have is that it was this same Jesus, who was both the man from Nazareth and the risen Lord.

The transformation of Jesus in the imagination of the inner circle is something that was not complete until each member encountered the risen Lord—every one of them. And the Jesus they encountered did not become a different person than he was before. Any apparent transformation of Jesus was partly a matter of the transformation of the understanding of this inner circle after Easter—they remembered what Jesus was like, but only after Easter did they understand the implications—and partly a matter of the new roles Jesus assumed after Easter (and the old ones he abandoned, such as being an earthly teacher). These changes in the disciples' understanding and Jesus's roles led to the explosion of Christological reflection about Jesus amongst the inner circle. All along the way Jesus had a face, a presence, a teaching, a character, a transformative power, an impact that was so compelling for these inner-circle members that they could come to say that this same man from Nazareth was also a Son of God and a savior and Lord who came back from the dead. Frederick Buechner speaks well of the indelible impact that the real historical Jesus left on the memories of his disciples from the earliest to the latest ones:

> *Ecce Homo* Pilate said—Behold the man—and yet whatever our religion or lack of it, we tend to shrink from beholding him. The risk with Jesus is too great; the risk that his face would be too much for us, if not enough, either a face like any other to see, pass by, forget,

or a face so unlike any other that we would have no choice but to remember it always and follow or flee it to the end of our days and beyond.

So once again, for the last time or the first time we face that face. ... Take it or leave it, if nothing else it is at least a face we would know anywhere—a face that belongs to us somehow, our age, our culture; a face we somehow belong to. Like the faces of the people we love, it has become so familiar that unless we take pains we hardly see it at all. Take pains. See it for what it is, and see it whole, see it too for what it is possible it will become.... He had a face [that was] not a front for him to live his life behind but a frontier, the outermost visible edge of his life itself in all its richness and multiplicity.... The *faces* of Jesus then—all the ways he had of being and being seen. The writers of the New Testament give no description of any of them because it was his life alive inside of them that was the news they hawked rather than the color of his eyes.[367]

Seared into the memories of the inner circle of Jesus was the indelible impression of what Jesus was really like, such that when you come to know these faithful followers in some degree of detail, you come to know Jesus himself. To be sure, each member of the inner circle brought something distinctive to the discussion of who Jesus was; each added something fresh and new. This should not be put down to their remarkable creativity, but rather to the complexity of Jesus himself. As Eduard Schweizer said so long ago, he was the man who fit no one formula.

There comes a point, after you have walked with the inner circle of Jesus for a while, that you must make a decision. Despite their foibles and flaws, these disciples were honest women and men—not merely sincere, but *honest*. Our culture has a hard time distinguishing between earnestness and honesty, but these disciples were characterized by both. One has to ask what led such a diverse group of disciples, from various backgrounds and social contexts, to believe wholeheartedly that Jesus was the Christ, the Son of God, the Lord, the Logos, and so on? Did they call a conclave and cook the whole thing up after the crucifixion? Was there some kind of "Passover plot"? Would they have given their lives to and for ideas about Jesus's divinity if they suspected that these ideas about Jesus weren't well grounded in the historical Jesus himself, but rather were the phantasms of their own overheated imagination?

I must say I find it hard to believe such a suggestion. The historical probabilities surely lie with the suggestion that these were honest witnesses, struggling mightily to explain the significance of a person they had encountered and who in the process had irrevocably changed their lives. One has to decide, then, whether the Jesus they remembered and tried to explain, grasping after terms and titles large enough to convey his importance, was the real Jesus, or not. Bear in mind that it is not a matter of trusting much later Christian testimony—say, from the Council of Nicea in the year 325, or even later councils. It is likewise not a matter of later conspiracies to concoct a Jesus-is-God theology. No, it is a matter of trusting the very earliest witnesses of the historical Jesus, some of those who knew him best.

It is true enough that we do not have the "Jesus papers," a literary residue that Jesus himself wrote down and left behind. What we do have, however, is something far more compelling—a living legacy, glimpses of the real Jesus in the lives of each of the members of Jesus's inner circle. As for me, as both a historian and a New Testament scholar, and also as a believing Christian, the answer is obvious. The Jesus these persons remembered is the real Jesus, and there is no other historical Jesus to be found at the bottom of the well of history or at the bottom of a *tel* at Nag Hammadi. The question then becomes, Will we accept the Jesus they knew, with all the limitations and possibilities that impinge on our lives with that acceptance? If we do so, we may just become less of a Jesus-haunted culture and more of a Jesus-shaped culture. At the least, those individuals who accept this will discover a Jesus they never knew before.

The Royal Line of Jesus?

For a moment when one reads the title of James Tabor's latest book, *The Jesus Dynasty* (New York: Simon & Schuster, 2006), one may be forgiven for thinking this is a book that grows out of the debacle surrounding Dan Brown's *Da Vinci Code,* with its claims about Jesus's marriage and descendants. But even a cursory glance at this study makes clear that this is a serious work written by a genuine archaeologist and historian, and its claims—for example, the brothers of Jesus were among the Twelve, the resurrection was a spiritual rather than physical event, and Jesus was a disciple of John—are meant to be taken seriously. This is far from fiction, though it involves no small amount of historical conjecture, as we shall see.

I must say at the outset that it is a pleasure to read such a well-written book, and one that takes so seriously the interface between the New Testament, history, archaeology, and the story of earliest Christianity. Absent from this study are wild theories about Gnostic gospels being our earliest and best sources about the life of Jesus, thank goodness. Equally refreshing is Tabor's willingness to take serious the historical data not just in the synoptics but also in the Gospel of John. Furthermore, Tabor is convinced that the James ossuary is indeed the ossuary of the brother of Jesus and has a genuine inscription on it. He is equally clear that both the canonical gospels and the James ossuary provide evidence for the fact that Mary and Joseph had other children besides Jesus. So far, so good. But unfortunately there are many flies in the ointment, however smoothly the ointment is sometimes applied in this book. I will deal with these problems under three headings—presuppositional problems, archaeological problems, and historical and exegetical problems.

PRESUPPOSITIONAL PROBLEMS

In the beginning of the second major part of his book, Tabor reminds us that we should not give much if any credence to later apocryphal stories about Jesus in the second-century document known as the Infancy Gospel of Thomas, much less even later legends about Jesus traveling to India or Great Britain! I quite agree. I wish he had taken his own advice and ignored much later traditions from the so-called Hebrew Gospel of Matthew, and even later Jewish traditions about Jesus on which he bases important conclusions in this study. Tabor rightly stresses: "Historians give such legendary material little credibility." We have to face the fact that thirty years of Jesus' life are simply missing and attempts to fill them in with legends and fables do nothing to advance our quest for the historical Jesus" (p. 87). Undaunted, however, since both nature and historians abhor a vacuum, Tabor proposes to fill in the gaps with the help of archaeological and later historical tidbits, using some gospel tales while dismissing various other parts of the gospel evidence. Let me give an example.

Tabor sternly reminds his audience, while discussing Jesus's burial, the empty tomb, and his "appearances," that "[h]istorians are bound by their discipline to work within the parameters of a scientific view of reality. Women do not get pregnant without a male—ever.... Dead bodies don't rise—not if one is clinically dead—as Jesus surely was after Roman crucifixion and three days in a tomb. So if the tomb was empty the historical conclusion is simple—Jesus' body was moved by someone and likely reburied in another location" (pp. 233–34). Tabor has come up with a location as well: in Galilee, outside the city of Tsfat. Who knew! This conclusion is based on the testimony of a sixteenth-century mystical rabbi named Isaac ben Luria, who had no independent knowledge of any early evidence about the death and burial of Jesus (p. 238).

Sadly, I have to say that Tabor has no right to lecture anyone about what is historically plausible if he is going to go chasing after these sorts of red herrings from a much later era. This is not the mark of a good historian who limits himself to the earliest and best evidence we have. Furthermore, one might ask, Which scientific view of reality does Tabor have in mind in the stern reminder cited above? There are actually quite a few such views, and many of them include the possibility of what we might call miracles. Does he really not know that there are plenty of good historians and scientists who do indeed believe in miracles, and who in no way see that as a violation of their critical judgment or commitments?

It is not a good historical principle to rule out causes of events in advance of examining the evidence, especially when none of us has an exhaustive knowledge of either historical or natural causation. The proverbial anti-supernatural bias is no more a good historical presupposition than the naïve assumption some people make that everything requires a miraculous explanation, as when someone talks about a demon or spirit causing him to catch a cold, and so on. All data needs to be critically analyzed, of course, but no one should rule out the miraculous from the outset.

Tabor's assertion that "the assumption of the historian is that all human beings have a biological mother and father, and that Jesus is no exception" (p. 59), suggests that this is some sort of monolithic credo of all modern or critical historians when it comes to the miraculous. This is simply false. I might add that the assumption "Miracles cannot happen and therefore do not happen" is a *faith* assumption, not something based on empirical evidence or a careful study of history. There are thousands of credible testimonies to miracles even in our own era. Though we like to pride ourselves on our open-mindedness in modernity, in fact ancient historians were far more open-minded when it came to the miraculous than some modern historians. One might ask, What happens, then, when one takes these sorts of skeptical assumptions, following the modern scholarly credo of "justification by doubt" (discussed in my Introduction), and applies them to the archaeological, historical, and literary evidence about Jesus and his earliest followers? What happens is the kind of presentations we find all too often in Tabor's book.

ARCHAEOLOGICAL PROBLEMS

Tabor's book begins with hard archaeological data and its analysis. He discusses, among other things, the so-called Talpiot tomb—a first-century tomb found in 1980 in the Jerusalem suburb of East Talpiot—which contained ossuaries that bear various names similar to or the same as the names in Jesus's family. The discussion is crisp and interesting, but all is not yet disclosed as to how this might be connected to the historical Jesus. I say this in part because the Talpiot tomb is not a recent discovery, and various archaeologists involved with it in the past have dismissed or denied the suggestion that it has any connection with Jesus's family. Furthermore, while there were ten ossuaries in the Talpiot tomb, one went missing, as the British say. The suggestion that the missing one is the James ossuary, found in a different location, does not make sense of all the data we have about the latter ossuary, which was found in the decade prior to the discovery of the Talpiot tomb. Nevertheless, the idea can't be entirely ruled out, for it is possible that the owner of the James box does not remember correctly when he bought that ossuary. But Tabor will also pique our curiosity with other archaeological evidence.

Tabor trots out for us the shop-worn tale of Mary being impregnated by a Roman soldier named Pantera (p. 64ff.). As he rightly notes, this story first appeared in a work written by a Greek philosopher named Celsus (circa A.D. 178) titled *On the True Doctrine,* which is a polemical document Origen was to take on. Tabor then points to rabbinic traditions, predicated on the word of Rabbi Eliezer ben Hyrcanus, which refer to Jesus as the "son of Panteri."

The problem with this evidence lies in its dating. The earliest Jewish text that includes this idea is the Palestinian document known as Tosephta t. Hullin 2.22–24. This is not a first-century text at all; indeed, it was written at a time when the polemics between early Christianity and early Judaism were in high gear. The same can be said about the text from Celsus, only in that case the debating partner was a pagan. As even John Dominic Crossan recently said on the CBS *48 Hours* "Mystery of Christmas" show we both appeared on in December of 2005, these stories about Pantera are later rebuttals to the claim that Jesus was born of a virgin. They are not the origins of the gospel stories, which are clearly earlier than such texts.

Tabor is right that all four gospels suggest Joseph was not Jesus's father. What he fails to say is that we need to consider the source and sort of the remarks we find in John 8:41 and Mark 6:3. They don't come from Jesus or from his disciples; rather, they come from skeptical outsiders or even opponents. Gospel of Thomas saying 105 is much too elliptical to support Tabor's reasoning at this juncture. In my view it may well be that the "son of Panteri" polemic is a rebuttal to the Christian "son of a parthenos" claim of the followers of Jesus. This is typical of the kind of punning and wordplay that went on in debates beginning with Jesus and the Pharisees and continuing with his followers and other Jews unpersuaded by the gospel.

Tabor's enthusiasm for the possible connection of a Roman soldier named Pantera with Jesus propels him to go on a trip to Bad Kreuznach in Germany, where there is a gravestone with this name on it. To be specific, we have the name Tiberius Julius Abdes Pantera, a soldier that the gravestone says was from Sidon. Tabor, with a great deal of creative imagination, links this fact with the story in Mark 7:24 where Jesus enters a house in Sidon and doesn't want anyone to know it. Could this have been the home of Jesus's actual father? Let's consider the evidence Tabor presents us with.

Tabor is right that the names Tiberius Julius suggest that this soldier was a slave who became a freedman and a soldier. Since Tiberius came to rule in A.D. 14, and since our man presumably received the name and the Roman citizenship for his service in the army, that service must have come after the year 14. The gravestone also mentions that this soldier's unit was the first cohort of archers and that the soldier served some forty years in the army, dying at the age of sixty-two. In all likelihood we are meant to think he died with his boots on. This in turn would mean he became a soldier at the age of twenty-two.

German theologian Adolph Deissmann concludes from this inscription that Pantera died in the middle of the first century. If this is correct, it follows that (1) Pantera was not a Roman soldier in 2–6 B.C., the period in which Jesus was born (as Tabor acknowledges); and (2) if indeed this cohort of archers went to Dalmatia in A.D. 6 and then on to the Rhine in A.D. 9, as Tabor avers (p. 69), then our man Pantera was not even yet with them, or if he was, he had only just become a soldier in the first decade of the current era, not in the period 2–6 B.C. In other words, the calculations are off by a least a decade. Thus, Tabor is wise in the end to back off and more weakly suggest that Jesus's father was "possibly" Pantera (p. 72).

Another troubling feature of the Pantera-as-father position is that it ignores the Mary we know from the gospels. She grew up in a strict honor-and-shame culture, and she was exceedingly young when she became betrothed and pregnant—probably, as Tabor suggests, barely a teenager. We then have to ask how such a girl would even have met Pantera of Sidon, a man who lived more than forty miles away in a different province and was not yet a soldier. Even more to the point, since young daughters were closely watched and protected in devout Jewish homes, she would never have been alone with any strange man at that age, much less a pagan. The historical implausibilities of this whole scenario suggested by Tabor and others are too great to be given real credence. I agree with Tabor's lament that we should not abstract Mary from her first-century Jewish milieu (p. 74), but unfortunately he is the one who opens the door to this particular implausible scenario.

What we learn from these archaeological discussions is that Tabor has a propensity to argue well beyond what the evidence suggests, and sometimes beyond what it allows. This is especially clear from Tabor's discussions of the recent finds at the Suba cave in the Judean hills, where a water installation and drawings suggesting Christian life and baptism were found. Interpreting one drawing as depicting John the Baptist, Tabor suggests that the cave may have been a place where John the Baptist, and perhaps later Jesus, practiced baptism on those who came to them. As Tabor admits, however, the drawing on the cave wall probably dates to the fifth century A.D. (p. 132).[1] And certainly we have no hard evidence that John the Baptist himself ever was in the cave or used it. What we have evidence of is that this was a pilgrimage spot for later Christians and that some sort of water and anointing rituals were likely performed here.

Tabor admits there is no hard evidence for his view, but his enthusiasm for what he has helped to uncover leads him to say, "I am convinced that the Suba cave is our earliest archaeological evidence related to John the Baptizer—and very possibly to Jesus himself" (p. 133). But what is the basis of this enthusiastic conclusion? Tabor makes the same mistake many of us do. His enthusiasm for something he has discovered or learned propels him to overreach, to draw conclusions that outstrip the historical evidence. As the British would say, "He over-eggs the pudding." Unfortunately, Tabor does it with such regularity that he piles one overly enthusiastic conclusion or idea on another, building uncertainty upon uncertainty, until we have an edifice with very shaky foundations at crucial points.

James Tabor has a very active imagination. He paints a scene for us on pages 151–52 of him sitting outside the Suba cave imagining Jesus himself baptizing people in this cave—perhaps even his own disciples and family. It is a nice bucolic picture not well grounded in any historical evidence. It is precisely this sort of material that will lead many to conclude that Tabor is simply eccentric, and unfortunately this will lead them to dismiss a good deal of material in this book that *should* be taken seriously. As another example of Tabor's eccentricity, he is a latter-day disciple of Albert Schweitzer's position that Jesus was trying to be an earthly messiah. This view continues to get a hearing in scholarly circles long after one would have rightly thought it had had its day. Let's see what Tabor says about Jesus's eschatology in general and Schweitzer's position in particular.

HISTORICAL AND EXEGETICAL PROBLEMS

Tabor gives us a helpful summary of where his speculative eschatological argument is going (p. 121). He takes the Schweitzerian point of view about Jesus (see his dedication on p. vii) with all its liabilities but also its possibilities. Here is his summary: "Jesus is best identified with what might be described as the Messianic Movement of 1st century Palestine. It was intensely apocalyptic, and though sharing certain ideas with the Essenes, it had a much broader appeal to rank-and-file Jews of all persuasions, united in their hope for God's deliverance[,]... who expected a radical change based on the messianic predictions of the Hebrew Prophets.... God would intervene to fulfill those messianic predictions" (p. 121).

Tabor avers, with Schweitzer, that Jesus was not a violent revolutionary or Zealot, but one who believed that God would soon and suddenly intervene in human history, and there would be a violent overthrow of the Roman Empire and its lackeys, and a reestablishment of the rule of Jews in the land of Israel. Given that belief, Jesus appointed twelve governors for the tribes (the disciples), trained them, and prepared for the end. When the end didn't come as soon as expected, Jesus went up to Jerusalem to throw himself on the rack of history in order to make it turn. This effort, alas, failed: the dominion of Rome was not suddenly displaced by the kingdom of God, with Jesus and the Twelve ruling over it.

Tabor also tells us that a mystical Paul who claimed to see the risen Lord in essence invented what later became Christianity, involving a view of Jesus as both divine and human. This conclusion then is leveraged so as to suggest that there was in the beginning another form of Jewish Christianity (less Christological, but tastes great) that Tabor wants to trace back to James. In fact he wants to argue that three or four of Jesus's brothers were amongst the Twelve originally chosen by Jesus, who was trying to set up a royal dynasty, and that after the death of Jesus it was the holy family who took over the movement. So much for the role of Peter as depicted in Acts 1–4 and Galatians 1–2.

For whatever reasons, scholars often seem to enjoy setting up contrasts between Jesus and his followers, particularly Paul. Tabor is one who fits this mold. Tabor states boldly: "There are two completely separate and distinct 'Christianities' embedded in the New Testament. One is quite familiar and became the version of the Christian faith known to billions over the past two millennia. Its main proponent was the apostle Paul. The other has been largely forgotten and by the turn of the 1st century A.D. had been effectively marginalized and suppressed by the other" (p. 261). This latter was of course the Christianity of James. One wonders why Tabor does not draw attention to the canonical documents called Hebrews, Jude, and Revelation, which also all reflect early Jewish apocalyptic thinking. Apparently it is not true that there was a move to marginalize this form of thinking when the canon was beginning to be drawn up.

Besides the fact that Tabor dramatically overplays the contrast between James and Paul as individual thinkers and apostles, he also portrays a picture of early Christianity as involving dueling banjos, which is also false, as I have shown in this study. The fact that this conclusion of Tabor's is familiar and not unique does not make it true. On the one hand, Tabor allows that Paul was accepted into the inner circle of Jesus's followers by the pillar apostles (p. 262). On the other hand, he thinks that what Paul preached radically distinguished him from the other apostles. Following Schweitzer, Tabor speaks of Paul's Christ mysticism and thinks that Paul promulgated an otherworldly gospel about a preexistent Christ who came to earth, died and rose, and returned to heaven in glory. But this is to stop the tale before the end of the story, for as Tabor admits, Paul believed that Jesus was coming back, perhaps in his own lifetime. Further, Paul believed that the kingdoms of this world were going to get a divine makeover when Jesus returned. In other words, the end of the story is not up there or out there somewhere; it is down here.

But we must consider some of the exegetical particulars of Tabor's argument, for the devil is in the details, as they say.

Proposition 1: Jesus the Baptist, Disciple of John?

Let us first consider Tabor's portrait of John the Baptist. In Tabor's view, John saw himself as carrying out the mission announced in Isaiah 40:3 and Malachi 3:1. While he may have spent some time at Qumran, and he used the same texts that those Essenes did to envision his mission, his approach to the coming conflagration was not to withdraw, purify, and thereby save oneself (as the Essenes' was) but rather to call the nation to repentance and baptism in preparation for what was to follow. John took a more extroverted, the Essenes a more introverted approach to the interpretation of those prophetic texts.

Tabor believes John began his mission in the spring or summer of A.D. 26 (p. 125). He also believes that John saw himself in the mold of Elijah, calling even the authorities and rulers to account as Elijah had done. He believes that John deliberately picked the location of Aenon near Salim, just south of the Sea of Galilee, as this was very near Tishbe, the home of Elijah. As Tabor says, it was also near the major thoroughfare used by Galilean Jews to go up to the festivals in Jerusalem, especially those who wanted to avoid going through Samaria.

Tabor then suggests that soon thereafter Jesus himself came to be baptized by John and heard the call of a different Isaianic text (Isa. 42:1). "By such a response he was publicly joining and endorsing the revival movement John had sparked.... [F]rom the time of Jesus' baptism he was ready to take his destined place alongside John as a full partner in the baptizing movement. Together they were prepared to face whatever lay ahead in the prophetic roles to which each believed he was called" (p. 129). But did Jesus actually join John's movement, or did he simply endorse it? Do we have any hard historical evidence that Jesus baptized people alongside John? And while we're at it, do we have any hard evidence that John saw himself, or that Jesus viewed John, as the priestly messiah spoken of at

Qumran? The answer to all these questions is probably no. John may well have, and Jesus more certainly did, see John as an Elijah-like prophet. This did not make him a priestly messiah figure.

I am wont to say, "A text without a context is just a pretext for what you want it to mean." It is not enough to know either the archaeological context or the general historical context or even the textual history of particular verses. One must deal in depth with the primary source of information we have about Jesus and his first followers—namely, the New Testament texts themselves. In Tabor's case, his love for archaeology leads him to see archaeology and historical context as primary sources and New Testament texts as secondary sources for his proposals. This is exactly the opposite of what should be attempted. The historical context and archaeology are important to an enterprise like studying the historical Jesus to the extent that they clarify, illuminate, or clearly refute what the New Testament says.

A good example of how this study is long on archaeological and historical context but weak on exegesis is Tabor's treatment of Luke 7:28: "I tell you among those born of women, none is greater than John, but the one who is least in the kingdom of God is greater than he." This is a particular type of wisdom saying known as a contrast saying, and it is a singular mistake not to deal with both halves of the contrast. Tabor unfortunately wants to deal only with the first half of the saying, which leads him to conclude, "It is clear in the Q source that Jesus is declaring John to be greater than he" (p. 136). Tabor considers the second phrase to be a later Christian addition to the text. But this interpretation will not do. Not only is there not a shred of textual evidence that the second clause was added later, but such a reading destroys the very form of a typical puzzling wisdom saying for which Jesus was so famous. There can be no doubt that Jesus had a very high estimation of John and his ministry. Tabor is right that this fact must not be obscured or neglected. It is equally clear that he did not see him as a messiah or as greater than himself. There is simply too much evidence in our earliest gospel sources to the contrary.[2]

On what basis does Tabor argue that Luke 7:28b is a later addition? Grasping at straws, he appeals to a fourteenth-century document alleged to preserve the more original Hebrew version of Matthew. This purported Hebrew Gospel of Matthew is found in a rabbinic document called Even Bohan, written by one Shem-Tob Ibn Shaprut of Aragon. This document was part of the ongoing border war between Jews and Christians in the attempt to claim the Jewish heritage for one or the other of these two communities. If we actually examine this Hebrew Matthew, we see that it is material that has been edited to serve the polemical purposes of its Jewish author, reflecting the dispute between Jews and Christians that he was involved in. There is no historical evidence whatsoever that this document existed, even in an earlier form, prior to the third century.

It simply won't do to take later evidence that has obviously been edited and shaped by a polemical controversy of a later era and proclaim it an earlier version of the Gospel of Matthew than what we have in our Greek text of Matthew! This is not merely an argument from silence, since we have no early evidence that the Hebrew Matthew even existed. It is an argument against the earliest and best evidence we do have. It violates all the basic historical principles about adhering to our earliest and best evidence in order to draw conclusions about a matter.

Let us take another example of how Tabor does not "look" before he takes exegetical leaps. On page 137 he deals with the Lord's Prayer as presented in Luke 11:1–4. Already there is a problem: he simply assumes that the conclusions of Q specialists are right that Luke preserves the more original form. A simple and systematic study of how Luke edits his Markan material and how Matthew edits the same Markan material would have told him that Luke is a freer editor of his source material and that Matthew is consistently more conservative. But for the sake of argument, let's just deal with the Lukan form here.

The text begins with the request of the disciples, "Teach us to pray, just as John taught his disciples to pray." Tabor takes this to mean, "Teach us to pray the same prayer John taught his disciples to pray." Tabor even says, "Jesus repeats to them the prayer that he had learned from his teacher John." But the Greek here surely does not mean this. The comparative term *kathōs* indicates that the disciples are not asking for Jesus to repeat the teaching he learned from John. Rather, they want to be taught to pray "just as" John's disciples had been taught to pray. The comparison has to do with the activity of praying, not the content of the prayer. Notice something else as well: John's disciples are distinguished from Jesus's here, but Jesus's disciples are comparing themselves to John's. This is interesting and understandable, since Jesus had some earlier associations with John and seems to have drawn some of his disciples from John's as well. But nowhere in any historical source do we even remotely hear about John teaching Jesus the Lord's Prayer.

While Jesus may well have learned much from listening to John, we have no historical evidence that Jesus was ever John's disciple. His baptism by John should not be interpreted as signifying discipleship. John baptized many people who did not become his disciples, and Jesus was probably one such person. In fact, the evidence suggests that John felt it would be more appropriate for Jesus to baptize *him*! John, as Jesus said, was more than a prophet. This does not mean Jesus saw him as either the messiah or his own teacher. Rather, he saw him as the final eschatological prophet, an Elijah figure who announced the coming of God's divine saving reign on earth. Jesus, by contrast, expected no singular successor, and he did not include himself amongst the Twelve. Both of these facts tell us something about Jesus's self-understanding.

Tabor, having gotten up a head of steam, is not only prepared to argue on the basis of questionable later evidence, and exegesis that is far from obvious. He is prepared to argue on the basis of silence itself. For example, he says, "It is no accident that the following year of A.D. 27 is largely blank in our records. That was the year of the joint work of the Two Messiahs— now lost to Christian history and memory" (p. 137). In this remark, Tabor is admitting to the fact that part of his most crucial and essential theory, that Jesus and John viewed themselves as the two messiahs mentioned at Qumran, is nearly entirely an argument from silence. One has to ask, Why should we think that either John or Jesus simply adopted the Essene view about two messianic figures? Nothing in their teachings suggests such a view. Indeed, nothing in the canonical gospels suggests that anyone saw John as the priestly messiah figure of Qumran at all, not even Jesus. This is pure conjecture.

It is Tabor's historical reconstruction that while John was baptizing in the north near the sea of Galilee in the year 27, a sabbatical year when people would have had more free time to listen to preachers like John and Jesus, Jesus was baptizing in the south in Judea (see pp. 141–42). There are several problems with this reconstruction. One moment Tabor is prepared to give the Gospel of John its due for providing us with an eyewitness testimony enriched by accurate historical and chronological details. The next moment he chooses not to deal with the hard evidence of John 4:1–2, which suggests that Jesus himself baptized no one; rather, his disciples did the baptizing. That text notes that the Pharisaic observers of both practices noticed that Jesus was gathering more disciples than John. Apparently not wanting to undercut John's ministry, Jesus stopped his activities and returned to Galilee through Samaria. Tabor dismisses John 4:2 as the work of a later editor (p. 149), though it's clear that the same hand, writing in the same style—that of the Beloved Disciple himself—is responsible for the discussion in John 3 about Jesus and John.

The material in John 3:27–30 is also important to this discussion, for it has a parallel in the synoptics in Mark 2:19–20. In both these texts Jesus is called the "bridegroom," while in John 3 John the Baptist declares himself to be the "friend of the bridegroom." This comports with the saying of John the Baptist that he knew someone greater than he would come after him, whose shoes he would not be fit to tie or untie. It seems clear that in both our earliest and latest gospel evidence (and evidence in between), John himself denies that he is the messianic one, but he believes he has a special relationship to the bridegroom: he is the best man, as it were, meant to announce the coming of the bridegroom. Tabor's partnership-of-equals idea about Jesus and John does not deal adequately with what evidence we do have on this matter. Even allowing for the gospel writers' desires to place John clearly in Jesus's shadow, there is still a clear pecking order in the earliest of these sayings, which indicates that neither Jesus nor John viewed the matter as Tabor suggests.

Proposition 2: James the Beloved Disciple?

The title of Tabor's book, *The Jesus Dynasty,* is based on the argument that Jesus set up a family dynasty, with his brothers among the disciples. But will the evidence support such a theory? Consider Luke 6:14–16, which Tabor cites (p. 164). Tabor says that the phrase "James of Alphaeus" means James son of Alphaeus, and this is likely correct. As we saw in the case of Simon bar Jonah, Jewish men were normally identified by such patronymics. But Tabor then wants to turn around and read the adjacent phrase "Judas of James" as meaning Jude *brother of* James. This will not do. The Greek construction is the same in both cases, and the original audience hearing this wording would have assumed that the genitive modifier had the same sense in both cases. Immediately prior to the verse in question, when Luke wanted to say someone was a brother of another disciple, he inserted the word *adelphos* (for instance, "Andrew the brother of Peter," v. 14). There is a good reason translations render the phrase "Judas of James" as referring to a son and a father. This is the natural and appropriate way to render the phrase if there is no further qualification, as in the case of Peter and Andrew. This in turn means that this Judas cannot be the one who was Jesus's brother. But then neither was Simon the Zealot or Jacob listed as one of Jesus's brothers. This logic cannot stand close scrutiny, and with its demise so also goes most of Tabor's theory about a Jesus dynasty.

Furthermore, where is Jesus's brother Joseph amongst the Twelve? In a desperate move Tabor suggests that Matthew/Levi son of Alphaeus is actually Joseph (p. 164), even though no gospel text or later source even remotely suggests this. But then no source suggests that Mary was married to Clopas who is really Alphaeus either, as Tabor argues. The facts

simply won't fit this theory, no matter how hard Tabor strains to accom-
modate them. The reason why the New Testament is silent about Jesus's
brothers being amongst the Twelve (something Tabor calls the best kept
secret in the New Testament) is that they weren't! Tabor suggests that
only John 7:5 ("Not even his brothers believed in him") argues against his
theory (p. 165), but of course we saw in Chapter 6 that Mark 3:21–35
(where Jesus's family wonders if he's lost his mind) is clear on this score as
well and cannot be dismissed. It is ironic that in the process of dismissing
such evidence Tabor then adds, "It is amazing what firm opinions have
been built upon such shaky foundations" (p. 165). Unfortunately, this
remark can more aptly be applied to his own argument.

Tabor also theorizes that James was the Beloved Disciple (pp. 206–7).
This will not do on several accounts, though Tabor apparently cannot
imagine Jesus bequeathing his mother to anyone else. But let's think
through the narrative logic of John's gospel for a minute:

- The only occasion we find Jesus's disciples and his family together is
  at the Cana wedding, but they in fact are not one group; they are
  mentioned separately (John 2:12).

- The first time thereafter that we hear about Jesus's brothers, they are
  egging him on and are said not to believe in him (John 7:5). This
  transpires prior to any mention whatsoever of the Beloved Disciple
  in this gospel. That reference does not occur until at least John 11 if
  not John 13. Those who were hearing this gospel, which would have
  been read aloud to the audience, would have had no way of associating James with the Beloved Disciple. Indeed, they would have drawn
  quite the opposite conclusion—that James was not a disciple, nor
  were the other brothers. The Beloved Disciple was called by this
  name because he was a disciple, not a relative of Jesus.

- The *coup de grâce* for this argument comes in John 19:25. Here Mary
  is bequeathed to the Beloved Disciple, who for the first time takes
  her into his own home, which is surely in Jerusalem. But the gospels
  tell us that the brothers lived in Galilee, not Jerusalem. Tabor apparently does not recognize that Jesus saw his eschatological family of
  faith as his primary family from the beginning of his ministry to the
  end. Thus Mary is joining the Jesus community; she is not going
  home with James. Furthermore, as Mary exits the scene with the
  Beloved Disciple in John, he is called simply "the disciple," not the
  brother of Jesus.

Lost altogether in the discussion is our earliest source for information about James—namely, Galatians 1–2, which encompasses Paul's account of his visits to Jerusalem. On the first occasion Paul goes up to Jerusalem in the mid to late 30s to see Peter, and he also sees James. Peter is mentioned first on that occasion. Fourteen years later Paul goes back with Barnabas and Titus and talks of seeing James, Peter, and John, in that order. Paul says these are the men reputed to be the "pillars" of the Jerusalem church, as we saw in earlier chapters. Then finally Paul reports that men were sent from James to Antioch to check out what was happening there.

These revealing narratives reflect the change in leadership amongst the inner circle in Jerusalem—from Peter first and also James; then James, Peter, and John; and finally James alone, because Peter has moved on as evangelist of Jews and is found in places like Antioch. It's clear, then, that by the late 40s James is the head of the Jerusalem church. There's no evidence whatsoever in Paul about a Jesus dynasty that was in place there from just after the death of Jesus.

Tabor has a very different reading of Galatians 1–2. He thinks that Paul had to consult with James on his first visit to Jerusalem, though the text says merely that Paul "saw" no other apostle except James the brother of Jesus. Galatians 1:18 is quite clear: Paul went to Jerusalem to spend time with Peter. The verb *historēsai* refers to his consulting and learning from and conveying information to this one person over the course of a fortnight. We may be sure the two men didn't spend all that time debating the weather. James he merely "saw"; Peter he consulted with. Why? Because Peter knew the whole Jesus story from stem to stern, whereas James had not been present for as much of the ministry. He was at home with the family in Galilee, and perhaps even in charge of the family.

Tabor also wants to argue that Galatians 2:9 suggests that only Peter and John are seen as pillars, supporting James on his right and left. But in fact Paul calls all three of these men pillars, including James. According to Paul, the head of the church is not James; it is the risen Jesus, with these three men as human leaders of the movement. And both Galatians and Acts agree that Peter is the first human leader of this church, serving until he is replaced by James after Peter goes on the road witnessing to Jews.

I quite agree with Tabor that James has been given short shrift, and it's my hope that this very book will help remedy that. But it will not do to displace Peter or Paul, who knows these eyewitnesses, with some "Jesus dynasty" argument. After all, we are talking about the leadership of the Jerusalem church, and only in a tenuous way about the rest of the movement, especially after the year 50. Tabor also wants to see James's decree, discussed in Part 5 above, as being about Noah's rules, but as we saw the decree is about eating in pagan temples and avoiding both the idolatry and the immorality that happen in such venues.

Tabor is certainly right that James was the overseer of the Jerusalem church from the late 40s until his death in 62. Various later sources, including Clement of Alexandria, even go so far as to suggest that Jesus chose James as overseer of the Jerusalem church (see Eusebius, *Hist. Eccl.* 2.1.3). If he did so, he must have done it by some extraordinary means after Easter, because Peter was clearly the one chosen as the head of the Twelve, and he stayed leader in Jerusalem until he became itinerant. The theory that James and the holy family were responsible from day one for the continuation of the Jesus movement simply does not comport with the earliest evidence we have from Paul, the gospels, and Acts 1–12.

Proposition 3: Who Do You Say That I Am?

We are not done with surprises yet. The ghost of Schweitzer is conjured up once more on pages 166–67, where Tabor tells us that the phrase "Son of Man," at least in future-oriented sayings, does not refer to Jesus. Indeed, it does not refer to a particular individual; rather, it stands collectively for the faithful people of God who will receive the rule from their messiah. Tabor thinks this is what Daniel 7 suggests. He maintains that the coming of the Son of Man refers to an event, not to a particular individual popping out of the clouds, and that Jesus thought his mission would lead right up to such a final event. There are too many problems with this scenario to deal with here, but I must list the most egregious mistakes involved:

- It is perfectly clear that Jesus used the phrase bar enasha ("Son of Man") to refer to himself throughout his ministry. (Identifying oneself in the third person was not uncommon in a collectivist culture like that of Israel.) This is one of the most well assured elements of New Testament scholarship in general. Clearly in the case of Jesus's own usage it refers to an individual, though scholars sometimes debate whether Jesus used it of himself and also of another individual in the future Son of Man sayings.

- In Daniel 7 there can be no question that an individual is involved. He is called "one like a son of man," not a group like a son of man.

He is seen as the human and humanizing figure that eclipses the previous beastly emperors and their empires referred to earlier in that same Old Testament chapter.

- Jesus's discussion of the Son of Man coming on the clouds (Mark 14:62) refers to a theophany event involving an individual. In that passage it is an individual who will come and judge Jesus's judges. It is this pronouncement that leads the high priest to claim that Jesus was committing blasphemy. The people understood perfectly well that Jesus was referring to himself! This is what prompted the handing of Jesus over to Pilate for execution: Jesus was claiming to be a ruler, indeed a judge over Israel, as Daniel 7 had predicted.

More could be said, but this must suffice. Tabor is right that Jesus had a messianic view of himself, but not the sort that Schweitzer thought he had, as is very clear from Mark 13:32, where Jesus disavows knowing when the end will come. Nor does Mark 9:1 suggest otherwise, which in the Markan outline is seen to refer to the transfiguration of Jesus, not the second coming or end of the world.

AND SO?

We must be careful about the beguiling nature of an argument such as Tabor's. His book is well written, with parts of it reading almost like a thriller. It has copious pictures of biblical sites with able commentary from Tabor. He is a good archaeologist and knows the various sites in and around the Holy Land well. However, his precise knowledge of the archaeological remains can lead one to think he also has precise knowledge about what is in and behind the biblical texts. This is not really the case in many instances. Many of the conclusions he presents in his book would be disputed by even the most liberal of New Testament scholars. Much of his analysis is pure conjecture. His hypotheses must be sifted with the same degree of rigor that Tabor uses in sifting the archaeological remains he digs up. When we do this, there are some fragments left, but not nearly as many as Tabor would allow.

By the time one gets to the close of *The Jesus Dynasty,* one realizes that Tabor is no dispassionate scholar, whose interest in Jesus, James, and Jude is merely academic. No, Tabor believes there is much at stake in studying the historical Jesus for Christianity today. He puts it this way: "If Christianity can give James his rightful place as successor to Jesus' movement, and begin to realize that his version of the faith represents a Christianity with claims to authenticity that *override those of Paul,* even more doors of understanding between Christians and Jews will be opened. But just as important, in terms of Christian mission and purpose in the world the unfinished agenda of John, Jesus, and James can find new life and relevance in modern times" (p. 315, emphasis added). He goes on to suggest that the view of Jesus in the Koran comports with this reconstructed image of Jesus, through the eyes of James and perhaps the Ebionites. Tabor is hopeful that this form of Christian belief may be resuscitated, if not fully revived.

A fair bit of what Tabor says about Jesus and James is true as far as it goes, but it leaves out far too much, and indeed much that is central and crucial. Everyone in the inner circle of Jesus had seen the risen Lord. The testimony of the earliest sources is clear about this. It is not just the sayings of Jesus as found in Q that can or should be the basis of Christian faith. Christianity must also be about who Jesus was and what he accomplished by means of his life, death, and resurrection. We do not need to pose an either/or dichotomy between what we learn from the sayings of Jesus and what we gain from other materials. A both/and approach is much nearer to the truth. And part of this both/and approach must include a recognition that our chronologically earliest canonical witness to Jesus—that is, Paul—is neither a distorter of the truth about Jesus, nor a liar, nor one who is radically at odds with James or Peter or others on crucial matters of Christology and eschatology. Such a reading would be simply false. The differences come, as they so often do, in the sticky matter of praxis and how Christians might be together, live together, have fellowship together, while still being Jews and Gentiles.

Yet I must say in the end that Tabor has done us a great service in trying hard to integrate his great wealth of knowledge about and love of archaeology with the New Testament text and other historical sources. Would that more scholars would take archaeology and history seriously when they interpret New Testament texts. Though Jesus may not have intended to found a family dynasty, he certainly left a legacy and a following, and Tabor has given us some glimpses of that legacy. For this we should be grateful.

Acknowledgments

At HarperSanFrancisco, a special thanks to Terri Leonard, Carolyn Allison-Holland, and Kathy Reigstad for your diligent and helpful copyediting and production efforts. To Helena Brantley for tirelessly promoting the book. To Kris Ashley for keeping me on track. And to my good friend and editor Roger Freet—thanks for your patience and wisdom on this project especially. I could not have done it without your help.

Notes

EPIGRAPHS

1. N. Dahl, *Jesus the Christ: The Historical Origins of Christological Doctrine* (Minneapolis: Fortress Press, 1991), p. 94.
2. R. L. Wilken, *The Spirit of Early Christian Thought* (New Haven: Yale Univ. Press, 2003), pp. xv, xiv, 46.

CHAPTERS 1–13 AND CONCLUSION

1. See the devastating and painstaking investigation in S. C. Calston, *The Gospel Hoax: Morton Smith's Invention of Secret Mark* (Waco: Baylor Univ. Press, 2005).
2. It is, of course, true that there were overzealous scribes in the postapostolic era who sometimes corrected the earlier manuscripts in a direction that they perceived would be more "orthodox" in character, but this is a marginal phenomenon that hardly changes the essence of the NT stories and their claims. "Orthodoxy" was not the creation of third- through fifth-
century scribes, much less of Constantine! It already existed in its nodal forms in the first century, as is perfectly clear from reading Paul's letters—our earliest NT documents.
3. For a critique of the Jesus Seminar, see B. Witherington, *The Jesus Quest* (Downers Grove: InterVarsity Press, 1995). I am thinking, of course, of Robert Funk, who recently passed away.
4. I do a good deal of work with the graduate chapters of InterVarsity Christian Fellowship, and it is interesting to see how overwhelmingly the people joining these fellowships are in the sciences, including the hard sciences. Could it be that the arts are less "liberal" (that is, open-minded) than they used to be?
5. See Fee's review of Ehrman's earlier work in the *Critical Review of Books in Religion* 8 (1993): 203–06.
6. See the introduction to my *Letters and Homilies of the New Testament*, vol. 1 (Downers Grove: InterVarsity Press, 2006).
7. See J. D. G. Dunn's massive and magisterial study, *Christianity in the Making*, vol. 1, *Jesus Remembered* (Grand Rapids: Eerdmans, 2003).
8. The term "Torah" refers to the Old Testament in general or, more specifically, to the Pentateuch (the first five books of the Bible, attributed to Moses) or even more narrowly to the Law within those books.
9. The wealth almost certainly wasn't her own, because in her society, women could not inherit or have money unless they were royalty or so rich they could find a way around the cultural norms and rules.
10. For Jesus's view on what makes a person unclean, see Mark 7:15; on male/female conversation, see John 4:27.

11. On all these Lukan stories, see A. J. Levine and B. Witherington, *The Gospel of Luke* (Cambridge: Cambridge Univ. Press, forthcoming 2007).

12. See E. J. Epp, *Junia: The First Woman Apostle* (Minneapolis: Fortress Press, 2005).

13. See, for example, 1 Cor. 9:1 and 15:7. On all this, see B. Witherington and D. Hyatt, *Paul's Letter to the Romans* (Grand Rapids: Eerdmans, 2004), pp. 387–90.

14. Compare B. Witherington, *The Paul Quest* (Downers Grove: InterVarsity Press, 1998), B. Witherington, *Women in the Ministry of Jesus* (Cambridge: Cambridge Univ. Press, 1984), and *Women and the Genesis of Christianity* (Cambridge: Cambridge Univ. Press, 1990).

15. I am indebted to the helpful study of my friend and colleague at St. Andrews, R. J. Bauckham, *Gospel Women* (Grand Rapids: Eerdmans, 2002), pp. 109–202, which was the inspiration for this brief study. He comes to the same conclusion.

16. See B. Witherington, *The Christology of Jesus* (Minneapolis: Fortress, 1990).

17. Notice that in the woes in Luke 10:13 both Bethsaida (just north of Migdal) and Chorazin (a bit further north of Migdal and east around the top of the lake) are anathematized, and we are told that miracles and other acts of Jesus happened in these little cities. If Jesus preached and healed in Bethsaida and in Chorazin, it is highly likely that he did in Migdal as well, since it is right on the same track that goes around the northern rim of the lake. Clearly there is much more we would like to know about Jesus's activity in the little towns on the north shore of the Sea of Galilee. Whatever else one can say, it attracted the attention of some women.

18. There are additional problems with amalgamating Miriam with the woman of John 7:53–8:11. First, John 7:53–8:11 is not a Lukan story; second, it was not even originally a part of the Gospel of John but was added later in several places. It is a text looking for a home.

19. The more detailed study of this text should be consulted. See B. Witherington, "On the Road with Mary Magdalene, Joanna, Susanna, and Other Disciples: Luke 8:1–3," first published in *Zeitschrift für Neutestamentliche Wissenschaft* 70, nos. 3–4 (1979): 242–48; now reprinted in A. J. Levine and others, eds., *A Feminist Companion to Luke* (Sheffield: Sheffield Univ. Press, 2002).

20. C. H. Dodd, *The Interpretation of the Fourth Gospel* (Cambridge: Cambridge Univ. Press, 1953).

21. There is absolutely nothing to the claim that *rabbouni* suggests an intimate or familial relationship between Jesus and Mary. It is the respectful Aramaic term a student would use of his teacher. Wives did sometimes call their husbands "master," of course, but that is a different word from *rabbi* or *rabbouni,* which literally means "my great one."

22. Compare Pagels's *The Gnostic Gospels* (New York: Vintage Books, 1981) to her recent work *Beyond Belief* (New York: Random House, 2003).

23. This is rather different from even Luke's "the Dominion is in your midst" (Luke 17:20–21—surely not an example of Jesus wishfully thinking the Dominion was already extant within his adversaries, the Pharisees).

24. See H. Shanks and B. Witherington, *The Brother of Jesus* (San Francisco: Harper, 2003), pp. 165–98, for later traditions about James being James the Just.

25. For example, Stephen Patterson and Marvin Meyer, apparently using Robert Miller's translation of the Gospel of Thomas, included this gospel in the Gnostic Society Library volume.

26. K. Snodgrass, "The Gospel of Thomas: A Secondary Gospel," *Second Century* 7 (1989–90): 19–38, and C. M. Tuckett, "Thomas and the Synoptics," *Novum Testamentum* 30 (1988): 132–57.

27. See the discussion in B. Witherington, *The Gospel Code* (Downers Grove: InterVarsity Press, 2004), pp. 102–4; see also Craig A. Evans, "Thomas, Gospel of," in *Dictionary of the Later New Testament and Its Developments,* ed. Ralph P. Martin and P. H. Davids (Downers Grove: InterVarsity Press, 1997), pp. 1175–77.

28. J. D. G. Dunn, *The Evidence for Jesus* (Philadelphia: Westminster Press, 1985), p. 98.
29. Especially interesting is the rhetoric of the compilers of the Gnostic Society Library, who say on their website in their introduction to Thomas:

> There is a growing consensus among scholars that the Gospel of Thomas—discovered over a half century ago in the Egyptian desert—dates to the very beginnings of the Christian era and may well have taken first form before any of the four traditional canonical Gospels. During the first few decades after its discovery several voices representing established orthodox biases argued that the Gospel of Thomas (abbreviated, GTh) was a late-second or third century Gnostic forgery. Scholars currently involved in Thomas studies now largely reject that view, though such arguments will still be heard from orthodox apologists and are encountered in some of the earlier publications about Thomas. Today most students would agree that the Gospel of Thomas has opened a new perspective on the first voice of the Christian tradition.

> It would be hard to describe how many things are wrong with this paragraph. Most scholars certainly do *not* think this gospel was compiled before all the canonical gospels, and even the Jesus Seminar thought that the Gospel of Thomas added only two or three authentic sayings of Jesus not found in the canonical gospels—sayings that do not really change the way we would view Jesus and his teachings. Furthermore, it is not merely "orthodox" biases that lead to the conclusion that Thomas is a second- or third-century document and probably Gnostic in origin (which is to say, arising after the beginning of the Gnostic movement in the middle of the second century). The character of the distinctive sayings of this gospel, when compared to documents like the Pistis Sophia from Nag Hammadi, suggest this conclusion—a conclusion that is also supported by various Jewish scholars, scholars of no Christian or Jewish faith, and the majority of Christian scholars.

30. Some of this material can be found in a slightly different form in Witherington, *The Gospel Code*.
31. See the detailed article by B. A. Pearson, "Nag Hammadi," in *Anchor Bible Dictionary*, ed. D. N. Freedman (New York: Doubleday, 1992), vol. 4, pp. 984–93.
32. All the Nag Hammadi translations that follow come from the standard work *The Nag Hammadi Library*, ed. J. M. Robinson (San Francisco: Harper, 1980). This particular document was translated by W. W. Isenburg.
33. See the discussion by P. Perkins, "Mary, Gospel of," in *Anchor Bible Dictionary*, ed. D. N. Freedman (New York: Doubleday, 1992), vol. 4, pp. 583–84.
34. See my *Women in the Earliest Churches* (Cambridge: Cambridge Univ. Press, 1988).
35. Pagels, *Beyond Belief*, p. 31.
36. F. Matthews-Green, "What Heresy?" *Books and Culture* (Nov.–Dec. 2003): 10.
37. See H. Clarke, *The Gospel of Matthew and Its Readers* (Bloomington: Indiana Univ. Press, 2003), pp. 205–7.
38. See the surveys of evidence in K. P. Donfried, "Peter," in *Anchor Bible Dictionary*, ed. D. N. Freedman (New York: Doubleday, 1992), vol. 5, pp. 251–63, and the volume Donfried wrote with R. E. Brown and J. Reumann, entitled *Peter in the New Testament* (Minneapolis: Augsburg Press, 1973). See also R. Pesch, *Simon-Petrus: Papste und Papsttum* (Stuttgart: Kaiser Verlag, 1980), and the literature cited in all these sources. It is, however, quite astonishing to me that there is no article on Peter in InterVarsity's *Dictionary of Jesus and the Gospels*.
39. While Peter seems originally to have been from the little fishing village north of Capernaum known as Bethsaida, by the time Jesus catches up with him and visits in his home, he is in Capernaum.
40. C. Myers, *Binding of the Strong Man* (Maryknoll, NY: Orbis Books, 1989), p. 132.

41. So, for example, Jerome, who says there must have been something divinely compelling in Jesus's face; otherwise, these men would not have acted so irrationally as to follow a man they had never seen before. His very countenance must have seemed irresistible (Homily 83). If this were actually the case, it is hard to explain the widespread rejection of Jesus even by his own hometown folks. Cf. J. Marcus, *Mark 1–8* (New York: Doubleday, 2002), p. 185, who stresses the overwhelming power of Jesus's word: "All human reticence has been washed away because *God* has arrived on the scene in the person of Jesus, and it is *his* compelling voice that speaks through Jesus' summons."

42. Myers, *Binding,* p. 133.

43. See the discussion in Witherington, *Christology of Jesus,* pp. 129–31.

44. See the discussion in B. Witherington, *John's Wisdom* (Louisville: Westminster/Knox, 1995), p. 70.

45. On the Matthean traditions about Peter, see B. Witherington, *The Gospel of Matthew* (Smyth and Helwys, 2006).

46. On the historicity of this passage, including the remarks to Peter by Jesus, see D. A. Hagner, *Matthew 14–28* (Nashville: Nelson, 1995), pp. 465–66.

47. God is called "the living God" in various places in the OT; see Deut. 5:26; Ps. 42:2; 84:2. That label is used in intertestamental literature in pagan contexts to distinguish the real God from pagan gods; see 2 Macc. 7:33; 15:4; 3 Macc. 6:28.

48. See H. Clarke, *Gospel of Matthew,* pp. 138–41.

49. It would also follow, if the saying is eschatological, that it has nothing to do with John 20:23 either—a saying about the inner circle of disciples forgiving sins or refusing to do so—which in any case is not directed to Peter in particular.

50. See the commentary in Witherington and Hyatt, *Paul's Letter to the Romans.*

51. S. Garrett, *The Temptation of Jesus in Mark's Gospel* (Grand Rapids: Eerdmans, 1998), p. 82.

52. *De sera numinis vindicta* 9.554b.

53. See my discussion in *Jesus the Seer* (Peabody: Hendrickson Press, 2000), pp. 1–100.

54. There was actually a watch of the night called "cockcrow"—between 12 and 3 A.M.

55. For more on the righteous sufferer, see Ps. 55:4–5; cf. Ps. 41:6–12; 42.5 LXX. Here *psuche,* which we translate as "spirit," refers to the inner life of the person. The phrase "sorrowful unto death" is like our phrase "sick to death." It means Jesus has reached the limit to which his sadness can go. Here surely there is an allusion to Ps. 42:6.

56. This conclusion is supported by the OT text to which Jesus here alludes—Isa. 31:3 and possibly Ps. 51:11–12.

57. Dan. 11:40, 45 LXX.

58. For a more detailed treatment of this story, see Witherington, *John's Wisdom,* pp. 353–58.

59. See Witherington, *John's Wisdom,* p. 405.

60. On Luke's use of sources in Acts, see B. Witherington, *The Acts of the Apostles* (Grand Rapids: Eerdmans, 1995), pp. 165–73.

61. See Witherington, *Acts of the Apostles,* pp. 81–82.

62. The term "Judaizers" refers to Jewish Christians who sought to "Judaize" Gentile Christians by requiring them to be circumcised and obey the entire Mosaic Law.

63. J. D. G. Dunn, *The Acts of the Apostles* (Harrisburg: Trinity Press, 1996), p. xiv.

64. Cf. 3:19; 10:43; 11:18; 17:30; 26:18–20.

65. A much more detailed exposition of all this can be found in Witherington, *Acts of the Apostles,* pp. 128–251.

66. See J. T. Squires, *The Plan of God in Luke-Acts* (Cambridge: Cambridge Univ. Press, 1993), pp. 68–71.

67. On Luke's use of sources, see Witherington, *Acts of the Apostles,* pp. 165ff. and 344–45.

68. See Witherington, *Acts of the Apostles,* p. 347.

69. Midrash on Ps. 146:4.

70. Jub. 22:16; Joseph and Aseneth 7:1.

71. It is sometimes objected that if Jesus himself had made this point clear, as Mark 7 suggests he did, then Peter would not be having this mental struggle. This is forgetting that there were many things Jesus taught the disciples that they did not understand during his ministry. Indeed, many things he taught took years for his followers to understand and implement. Furthermore, the drift of what Jesus says is only perfectly clear in Mark 7 because of Mark's own parenthetical comment that "thus he declared all foods clean."

72. We should hear echoes here of Luke 2:10-14.

73. For more on God's intervention, see 17:32; 22:22; 23:7; 26:24. For the other outpourings of the Spirit, see 2:1-4; 4:3; 8:17. In commenting on the Spirit's activity among Cornelius's family, Peter only remarks that they had received the Spirit "as also we did"; he does not say, "They spoke exactly as we did."

74. On the dating of Galatians, see B. Witherington, *Grace in Galatia* (Grand Rapids: Eerdmans, 1998).

75. The Beloved Disciple could have been one of the elders at this meeting, if that is what "elder" means in 2 and 3 John (rather than simply meaning the generic "old man"). On this, see Part 4, below.

76. Notice that Gal. 2:11 says "when Peter came to Antioch." From where? And what had he been doing before that? We cannot tell, but what this suggests is that he had not taken up residence in Antioch, but at the same time Paul knew of his pattern of living and fellowshipping with Gentiles until he came under pressure from the hard-liners in Jerusalem.

77. Cf. Matt. 11:30 to Sir. 51:26.

78. See Witherington, *Acts of the Apostles*, p. 454.

79. See B. Witherington, *Letters and Homilies of the New Testament*, vol. 1, the introduction (Downers Grove: InterVarsity Press, forthcoming 2006), and also especially T. L. Wilder, *Pseudonymity, the New Testament, and Deception* (Lanham, MD: University Press of America, 2004).

80. For example, in the second century Papias of Hierapolis states this view explicitly (see Eusebius, *Hist. Eccl.* 2.15.2, and also Irenaeus, *Adv. Haer.* 4.9.2; 4.16.5; 5.7.2).

81. Cf. 1 Pet. 4:13 to Col. 1:24.

82. There may in addition be an interesting connection between what is said in 1 Pet. 3.1-7 and 1 Tim. 2 in regard to women's behavior and apparel. It is possible that these two letters were written in close proximity to each other in both time and space—both from Rome and both in the period A.D. 64-66. Perhaps there was contact between Peter and Paul near the end of their lives. We could also point to the stress on future eschatological salvation in 1-2 Timothy and in what Peter says in 1 Pet. 1:3-12.

83. See M. Reasoner, "Persecution," in *Dictionary of the Later New Testament and Its Developments*, ed. R. P. Martin et al. (Downers Grove: InterVarsity Press, 1997), p. 908.

84. See J. R. Michaels, "1 Peter," *Dictionary of the Later New Testament*, pp. 914-23, here p. 915.

85. See the detailed and convincing study of R. J. Bauckham, *Jude, 2 Peter* (Waco: Word, 1983).

86. B. Witherington, "A Petrine Source in 2 Peter," *Society of Biblical Literature Seminar Papers 1985*, pp. 187-92.

87. Understandably, Origen tells us in his John commentary that there were serious doubts about 2 Peter being from Peter, whereas the attestation of 1 Peter was universally accepted (see Eusebius, *Hist. Eccl.* 6.25.8).

88. See the discussion in Witherington, *John's Wisdom*, p. 356.

89. See his 1 Corinthians.

90. Cf. Acts of Peter 37-39; Eusebius, *Hist. Eccl.* 3.1.

91. See B. Witherington, *New Testament History* (Grand Rapids: Baker, 2001).

92. See Witherington, *Acts of the Apostles*, pp. 1-40.

93. See at length my discussion of the virginal conception in B. Witherington, "Birth of Jesus," *Dictionary of Jesus and the Gospels*, ed. J. B. Green et al. (Downers Grove: InterVarsity Press, 1992), pp. 60-74.

94. In fact, this is precisely what it did suggest, as we see in the later debate between Origen and Celsus, where Celsus posits that the father was a Roman soldier, one Pantera.
95. On this story, see B. Witherington, *The Gospel of Mark* (Grand Rapids: Eerdmans, 2001).
96. Luke, in terms of the form of his work, presents himself as a Hellenistic historian in the mold of Polybius or Thucydides, and thus a serious historian. It is also quite clear that he presents himself as one whose subject matter is Jewish history, and more particularly the Jewish history that has to do with Jesus. There are some obvious similarities between what he is doing and what we find in Josephus's *Antiquities,* but Luke is concerned about *salvation* history, not just the history of the Jewish people in general, and thus the story of the inbreaking eschatological or saving reign of God. The eschatological flavor goes beyond Josephus's occasional interest in miracles.
97. On the date of Jesus's birth, see Witherington, "Birth of Jesus," pp. 66–68.
98. See the detailed discussion of J. Nolland, *Luke 1–9:20* (Waco: Word, 1989), pp. 99–103, and the bibliography there. It needs to be said that if Luke's veracity as a historian cannot be impugned on the basis of these verses, there are certainly no verses in the rest of the gospel that are more historically problematic and more debated than these.
99. The Greek here refers to not merely storing up ideas, but valuing and evaluating them, ruminating on them because their meaning is not immediately apparent. This is the opposite of the portrayal of someone who is hard-hearted and immediately rejects the message.
100. See the discussion in Witherington, *Women in the Ministry of Jesus*.
101. Nolland, *Luke 1–9:20*, p. 97.
102. See D. Bock, *Luke: The NIV Application Commentary* (Grand Rapids: Zondervan, 1996), p. 92.
103. See, for example, M. Niddah 5:1; cf. 2:5 and 1:3–5. The final thing of great interest is the way Luke characterizes the Law. It is called both the Law of Moses and the Law of the Lord. It seems reasonably clear that Luke had a very high view of the inspiration and divine authority of the scriptures, even though he seems only to have been able to read them in Greek, using the Septuagint. The holy family is portrayed as fulfilling God's will by acting according to the Law's requirements.
104. R. E. Brown and K. P. Donfried, eds., *Mary in the New Testament* (Philadelphia: Fortress, 1978), pp. 161–62.
105. Apparently Passover was the most popular and well-attended festival, not least because it was the primary festival apart from Yom Kippur where an animal sacrifice would be required—which is to say, where a priest and a temple or altar would be almost a necessity (hence the trip to Jerusalem).
106. See J. B. Green, *The Gospel of Luke* (Grand Rapids: Eerdmans, 1997), p. 153.
107. See M. D. Johnson, *The Purpose of the Biblical Genealogies with Special Reference to the Setting of the Genealogies of Jesus* (Cambridge: Cambridge Univ. Press, 1969).
108. See R. Brown, *The Birth of the Messiah* (London: Chapman, 1977), pp. 137–39.
109. Brown, *Birth of the Messiah*.
110. B. M. Metzger, *Textual Commentary* (New York: United Bible Societies, 1971), p. 7, is surely right that the reading *gennasis,* which has the narrower meaning of "birth" or "engendering," is later. The earlier and better witnesses of various text types have *genesis*. See J. D. Kingsbury on the import of this reading in "The Birth Narrative of Matthew," in *The Gospel of Matthew*, ed. D. E. Aune (Grand Rapids: Eerdmans, 2001), pp. 154–65.
111. Kingsbury, "Birth Narrative," pp. 156–57.
112. There is clear evidence from the papyri that *sunerkomai* means "to marry"—SEG 831. See *New Documents Illustrating Early Christianity,* vol. 3, ed. G. H. R. Horsley (Sidney: Macquarie University, 1982), p. 85.
113. On this entire matter, see Shanks and Witherington, *The Brother of Jesus*.
114. I. Broer, "Die Bedeutung der 'Jungfrauengeburt' im Mattausevangelium," *Bibel und Leben* 12, no. 4 (1971): 248–60.

115. Attempts to redefine these words to mean "while" or "without" are clearly special pleading, as is the attempt to see these words as unrelated to what comes before them. A. H. McNeile puts it this way: "In the New Testament, a negative followed by *heos ou* (e.g. 17.9) ... always implies that the negated action did, or will take place after the point in time indicated by the participle." The issue here is not what *heos* means without *ou* or what the phrase means in very different sorts of contexts. When this phrase is preceded by an aorist indicative as it is here ("gave birth") and follows the imperfect verb "he was not knowing," it is hard to escape the conclusion that Joseph "knew" Mary in the biblical sense after Jesus was born.

116. See the discussion of the brothers and sisters of Jesus in Shanks and Witherington, *The Brother of Jesus*, pp. 93–109.

117. It is quite clear that the reason the church fathers denied the obvious grammatical sense of the text is that they saw sexual relations with a man as something less than holy, or even as defiling. See Cromatius, *Tractate on Mat. 3.1;* Chrysostom, *Hom. Mat. 5.3;* and other citations in *The Ancient Christian Commentary on Scripture 1 a,* ed. M. Simonetti (Downers Grove: InterVarsity Press, 2001), pp. 19–20.

118. Clarke, *Gospel of Matthew,* p. 9.

119. On Jewish weddings of that era, see A. W. Argyle, "Wedding Customs at the Time of Jesus," *Expository Times* 86 (1974–75): 214–15, and J. Jeremias, *The Parables of Jesus* (New York: Scribner, 1972).

120. See Witherington, *John's Wisdom,* pp. 77–80.

121. Witherington, *Women in the Ministry of Jesus,* p. 84.

122. J. Ashton, *Understanding the Fourth Gospel* (Oxford: Oxford Univ. Press, 1993), pp. 269–70.

123. Anne Rice, *Christ the Lord: Out of Egypt* (New York: Knopf, 2005).

124. On all this, see Witherington, *Women in the Ministry of Jesus,* pp. 86–88.

125. Hooker, *Mark,* p. 115.

126. See B. Buby, "A Christology of Relationship in Mark," *BTB* 10, no. 4 (1980): 149–54; and especially D. M. May, "Mark 3:20–35 from the Perspective of Shame/Honor," *BTB* 17, no. 3 (1987): 83–87.

127. The contrast is made even more vivid in Matt. 12:49, where Jesus actually points to or places his hands upon his disciples and says they are his family.

128. Mark 6:1–6.

129. D. M. May, "Mark 3:20–35 from the Perspective of Shame/Honor," p. 86.

130. See my discussion in *Women in the Ministry of Jesus,* pp. 89–92.

131. R. H. Gundry, *Mark: A Commentary on His Apology for the Cross* (Grand Rapids: Eerdmans, 1993), p. 291.

132. Metzger, *Textual Commentary,* pp. 88–89. Interestingly, the Palestinian Syriac simply has "the son of Mary."

133. Given the later reverence for the holy family, it is not plausible that Christians would have invented this saying.

134. Myers, *Binding,* p. 212. See also Judg. 11:1–2.

135. See Painter, *Mark's Gospel,* p. 97.

136. I deal at length with the historicity of this story in *Women in the Ministry of Jesus,* pp. 92–96.

137. See my discussion in *Women in the Ministry of Jesus,* p. 187, n. 103. The example of Rabbi Eleazar ben Shimeon standing and weeping near a crucified man can be cited.

138. On all this, see Witherington, *Women in the Ministry of Jesus,* pp. 96–97.

139. See Witherington, *Acts of the Apostles,* pp. 113–14.

140. The word that I have as "sign" can sometimes be translated "constellation," but the action that follows makes it clear that we are talking about earthly activities involving beings, including human beings. The place where John sees these entities does not dictate their nature.

141. For pagan beliefs, see Cicero, *De Nat. Deor.* 2.15.39–40; Seneca, *Benef.* 4.23.4; 1 En. 80:7–8; for Jewish equating of stars with angels, see 1QM 10:11–12; 2 En. 4:1; 2 Bar. 51:10; Philo, *Plant.* 12–14; T. Sol. 2:2; 4:6; 5:4; 6:7; 7:6.

142. M. Reddish, *Revelation* (Macon: Smyth and Helwys, 2001), p. 235, is right that John is not interested in describing the origin of evil, but he is very interested in chronicling its demise. His eschatological focus is clear.

143. Reddish, *Revelation,* p. 233.

144. See E. Fiorenza, *Revelation: Vision* (Minneapolis: Fortress Press, 1991), p. 80: "A coin of Pergamum, for instance, shows the goddess Roma with the divine emperor. In the cities of Asia Minor Roma, the queen of heaven, was worshiped as the mother of the gods. Her oldest temple stood in Smyrna. Her imperial child was celebrated as the world's savior, incarnation of the sun-god, Apollo. John probably intends such an allusion to the imperial cult and the goddess Roma insofar as he pictures the woman clothed with the sun as the anti-image of Babylon, the symbol of world power of his day and its allies (chaps. 17–18)."

145. Furthermore, ignoring the birth requires that we interpret this text by a text that it likely has no relationship with: Rom. 1:3–4.

146. I have dealt at considerable length with the passage elsewhere. For the full discussion, see Witherington, *Letters and Homilies of the New Testament,* vol. 1.

147. It is true that wives sometimes dined with their husbands at such meals, but not usually, and no women are mentioned as present and dining at this particular meal.

148. A fuller form of this material can be found in Witherington, *Revelation.*

149. Cf. Rev. 2:2 to John 16:2; Rev. 20:6 to John 13:8; Rev. 22:15 to John 3:21; Rev. 22:17 to John 7:37.

150. See the discussion by S. E. Porter, "The Language of the Apocalypse in Recent Discussion," *New Testament Studies* 35 (1989): 582–603. On whether John is being deliberately idiosyncratic in his use of the Greek, perhaps in order to make a protest against the dominant culture, see A. D. Callahan, "The Language of the Apocalypse," *Harvard Theological Review* 88 (1995): 453–70.

151. Nor can this phenomenon be adequately explained by the numerous echoes and allusions to OT texts in Revelation.

152. See Eusebius, *Hist. Eccles.* 3.24.17; 3.25.2–3.

153. *Exposition on the Second Epistle of John.* See the discussion in J. Lieu, *The Second and Third Epistles of John* (Edinburgh: T&T Clark, 1986), pp. 5–7.

154. It should be noted that he is called "the other disciple" here, referring to the one other than Peter, and this is the same language used in 20:3. It is, however, relatively certain that this is a reference to the Beloved Disciple, because in John 20, as in John 21, he is portrayed as the spiritually insightful one.

155. For a fuller treatment of this subject, see Witherington, *John's Wisdom,* pp. 198–366.

156. It is my view that this document was not written primarily for the Johannine community itself, who already knew very well who the Beloved Disciple was, but for that community to use in evangelism with outsiders—hence all the asides in this gospel, like this one about Mary.

157. See the helpful discussion in A. Culpepper, *Anatomy of the Fourth Gospel* (Philadelphia: Fortress, 1983).

158. Possibly we have a clue in Mark 14:3 in the parallel account of Jesus being anointed by Mary of Bethany. There we are told that the anointing took place in the house of Simon the leper. Let's suppose for a moment that this family had the contagious disease of leprosy and that it had killed both the father, Simon, and Lazarus. This would explain two other facts the story presents us with. First, none of these three persons (Mary, Martha, Lazarus) seems to be married. If someone was perpetually unclean due to such a disease,

that person was exempt from the Jewish duty to marry and procreate. Second, these disciples did not travel with Jesus, but rather stayed at home.

159. Here as elsewhere in this gospel, the label "the Jews" refers to Jewish officials—in particular, those who are opposing Jesus. See John 10:31.

160. See R. E. Brown, *The Gospel according to St. John*, vol. 1 (Garden City: Doubleday, 1966), p. 424.

161. See particularly the accounts in Mark 14:3–9 (which is clearly the same as the one in Matthew 26:6–13) and Luke 7:36–50. I have dealt at length with the source and historical critical issues involved in *Women in the Ministry of Jesus*, pp. 53–55, 110–12.

162. See Witherington, *Women in the Ministry of Jesus*, p. 193.

163. See Witherington, *John's Wisdom*, p. 208.

164. Beasley-Murray, *John*, p. 238.

165. See C. K. Barrett, *The Gospel according to St. John* (Philadelphia: Westminster, 1978), pp. 556–57.

166. See Witherington, *John's Wisdom*, pp. 324–25.

167. Again suggesting that at least this disciple has a home nearby.

168. See M. Oberweis, "Das Papias-Zeugnis vom Tode des Johannes Zebedai," *Novum Testamentum* 38 (1996): 277–95, but see the discussion in E. Schnabel, *Early Christian Mission*, vol. 1 (Downers Grove: InterVarsity Press, 2005), pp. 820–21.

169. See Witherington, *Revelation*, pp. 1–40.

170. R. E. Brown, *The Epistles of John* (New York: Doubleday, 1982), pp. 14–35.

171. As C. H. Dodd, *Johannine Epistles* (London: Hodder & Stoughton, 1945), p. 10, points out, "we" is common in homilies of all periods as a rhetorical device to unite speaker with audience. It is important to note that Dodd (p. 15) also recognizes that we are dealing with an exordium in 1 John 1:1–4.

172. See J. Painter, *1, 2, and 3 John* (Collegeville: Liturgical Press, 2002), p. 138. Notice how our author almost always uses the first-person singular when referring to himself as the writer of this document (cf. 2:1–26; 4:20; 5:13), but when he refers to the eyewitness testimony he always uses the first-person *plural*, as he does when referring to the Christian experience that he shares with the audience. Thus C. Kruse is right, in *Letters of John* (Grand Rapids: Eerdmans, 2000), p. 61, that while this document is written by an individual, not a "school," it embodies a testimony that many eyewitnesses (of which our author is one) shared.

173. Very unconvincing is the argument that the "we" in the first few verses refers to those who have only heard the eyewitnesses and are passing on the tradition from them. Were this the case, we would not have expected the verbs "seen," "observed," and "handled" here. Furthermore, from a rhetorical point of view, it is both inept and deceptive to claim to be one of the eyewitnesses who handled and saw, when in fact one isn't such a person. This undermines the very function of this language, which serves to establish the authority and ethos of the speaker. But see Painter, *1, 2, and 3 John*, pp. 130–31.

174. See Kruse, *Letters of John*, p. 52.

175. On "word of life" referring to a person here, see J. E. Weir, "The Identity of the Logos in the First Epistle of John," *ET* 86 (1974–75): 118–20.

176. There is now a thorough and convincing refutation of the basis for Brown's claim that the sensory language here is used to refer to the Johannine school rather than to an actual eyewitness: Kruse, *Letters of John*, pp. 53–56, refuting R. E. Brown, *Johannine Epistles* (New York: Doubleday, 1982), pp. 158–61.

177. A. Plummer, *The Epistles of St. John* (Cambridge: Cambridge Univ. Press, 1884), p. 15.

178. Smith, *First, Second, and Third John*, p. 37.

179. See B. Witherington, "The Waters of Birth: John 3.5 and 1 John 5.6–8," *New Testament Studies* 35 (1989): 155–60.

180. See Witherington, *John's Wisdom*, p. 357.

181. Some of this material has appeared in another form in Shanks and Witherington, *The Brother of Jesus.*
182. See J. F. Strange, "Galilee," in *The Dictionary of New Testament Background,* ed. C. A. Evans and S. Porter (Downers Grove: InterVarsity Press, 2000), p. 394.
183. Jerusalem, Talmud Qam.6D.
184. I reject the more obscure view, based on later ascetical views and tendencies in the church, that 1 Cor. 9:5 refers to a sister-wife—that is, a sister who would travel with an apostle and look after him, serving in some ways as a wife surrogate.
185. See Gal. 1–2. On the bogus theory that Jesus was married to Mary Magdalene, see Witherington, *The Gospel Code.*
186. F. F. Bruce, *Peter, James, and John* (Grand Rapids: Eerdmans, 1979), p. 87.
187. See Matt. 27:57–61 and parallels.
188. See, for instance, the ongoing discussion on the *Biblical Archaeology Review* Web site.
189. This list dates to at least within twenty years of Jesus's death, while there were still eye-witnesses alive, for Paul wrote 1 Cor. in the early 50s.
190. Cited in Eusebius, *Hist. Eccl.* 4.22.4; cf. 2.23.4; 3.20.1.
191. Though the ossuary has been embroiled in controversy for the last two years, the IAA report attempting to discredit the authenticity of the inscription on this ossuary has now itself been thoroughly discredited by a variety of Aramaic experts and scientists. Further-more, those who originally authenticated the inscription such as Andre LeMaire and Edward Keall of the Toronto museum are standing by their findings. Clearly the IAA needs to release this ossuary for further testing. See the Web site of the *Biblical Archaeology Review* at bib-arch.org for updates.
192. The absence of the mention of the sisters probably suggests they were married by this time and thus were part of a different patriarchal family structure.
193. The vast majority of scholars are in agreement that Paul's letters are chronologically the earliest NT documents, even though the gospels generally record earlier events than the events mentioned in Paul's letters.
194. In Matt. 28:10 and John 20:17 Jesus is speaking about his disciples as "brothers," not about members of his physical family, in all likelihood. This is made clear in John by the reference to God as "our" Father, indicating that Jesus is using the family language in a spiritual way in this text. Matt. 28:10 refers forward to Matt. 28:16, where it is said that the disciples went to Galilee, obeying the command in 28:10.
195. One of the more helpful recent treatments of James is J. Painter's *Just James* (Minneapolis: Fortress, 1999).
196. This document seems to come from the late second century and from a Jewish Christian community that sees itself in continuity with James and the earliest Jewish Christians.
197. Asceticism is the practice of abstaining from certain things, chiefly food and drink but sometimes also sexual activity and even all contact with other human beings, in an effort to purify one's life.
198. Lest we think James is the only one who had such tendencies among the earliest Jewish followers of Jesus, Paul tells us that in Rome there were Jewish Christians who did not eat meat and abstained from wine as well. See Romans 14:2, 21.
199. This term derives from the term *perushim,* which probably means the "separated ones." The Pharisees were a particular sect of early Judaism who were noted for their concern with maintaining a clear sense of the boundary between Jewish and non-Jewish identity and practices. Because of that concern, they had an emphasis on circumcision, Sabbath-keeping, ritual purity, and the like.
200. This is an important text and not to be lightly dismissed. It shows that the later extremely ascetical portrait of James is likely to be an exaggeration.
201. The Qumran sect is the same as the Dead Sea sect, those who produced the Dead Sea Scrolls. They are also likely the same persons as those Josephus calls the Essenes. A sig-

nificant number of them lived at the Dead Sea apparently and sought to prepare for God's final intervention and judgment on the corruption in Israel.

202. C. A. Evans, "Comparing Judaisms: Qumranic, Rabbinic, and Jacobean Judaisms Compared," in *The Brother of Jesus*, ed. Bruce Chilton and Jacob Neusner (Louisville, KY: Westminster John Knox), pp. 161–83, here p. 182.

203. Acts 12:2 and 12:17, when compared, make very clear that one should never make the mistake of identifying James son of Zebedee and James the brother of Jesus. On the historical reliability of this and other traditions in Acts, see Witherington, *Acts of the Apostles*.

204. One could ask, Does he mean the other brothers of Jesus, or the other Christians? It is probably the latter, though the former can't be ruled out altogether.

205. Painter, *Just James*, p. 43.

206. Eusebius was a Christian writer who wrote around the turn of the fourth century.

207. See the discussion in Witherington, *Grace in Galatia*.

208. See the discussion in the appendix in Witherington, *The Paul Quest*.

209. Galatians appears to be chronologically the earliest NT document written (or one of the earliest documents). It is certainly the first to mention James, doing so in this significant way.

210. See the fine essay by R. J. Bauckham, "For What Offense Was James Put to Death?" in *James the Just and Christian Origins*, pp. 199–231.

211. Clement of Rome was a Christian leader in Rome in the late first century.

212. Cf. Ezek. 40–48; Jub. 1.17–28; 1 En. 90.28–29 11QTemple; Test. Ben. 9.2.

213. See R. J. Bauckham, "James and the Gentiles (Acts 15:13–21)," in *History, Literature, and Society in the Book of Acts*, ed. B. Witherington (Cambridge: Cambridge Univ. Press, 1996), pp. 154–84.

214. See Josephus, *Ant.* 18.328–29.

215. See the discussion in R. J. Bauckham, *Jude and the Relatives of Jesus in the Early Church* (Edinburgh: T&T Clark, 1990), pp. 71–72.

216. The vows of the Nazirite are discussed in Number 6. This text says that if someone wants to vow to be separate to the Lord in a special way they must abstain from wine and wine vinegar and grape juice and grapes or raisins. They must abstain from shaving the hair on their heads, and they must never go near a corpse. This vow is normally seen as a temporary one, for the same chapter specifies that when the vow is over they are to shave their head, and offer sacrifices.

217. On the theory of James being a Nazirite, see Bruce Chilton, "James in Relation to Peter, Paul, and the Remembrance of Jesus," in *The Brother of Jesus*, pp. 138–59, here pp. 146–47.

218. Some material in this chapter appears in another form in Shanks and Witherington, *The Brother of Jesus*.

219. See the discussion in Witherington, *Acts of the Apostles*, pp. 539–44.

220. In general, Romans tried to allow conquered peoples to maintain their native religion, simply adding to that religion the Roman cults—particularly, during the Roman Empire, the imperial cult. Jews were a special case since they were monotheists and would not accept the worship of additional deities. Romans tended to be accepting of ancient religions that had a long pedigree but not new ones, especially new ones that came from the east. When the Christian movement began to emerge from the shadow of Judaism, it was no longer perceived as an ancient and licit religion. It was therefore subject to close scrutiny and potential prohibitions, and its practitioners were expected to venerate the emperor as well. This problem became acute from the time of Nero's persecutions onward.

221. See Bauckham, "James and the Gentiles," pp. 154–84.

222. I have examined all 112 instances of this term, which occurs only in Christian sources and in two other sources influenced by Christians. The term always carries the overtones of idol worship and refers literally to the pollution or stuff of idols. See Acts 15:20,

which explains quite clearly that James is talking about food polluted by idols, something that was believed by some Jews to happen in temples when dining took place in the presence of idol statues. Paul in 1 Cor. 10:20–21 says that it is a matter of dining with demons if you eat in the presence of idols. Some Jews believed that while the pagan gods were not gods, they were nonetheless real spiritual beings—namely, demons—which could negatively affect a believer and his or her food.

223. See Witherington, *Conflict and Community in Corinth* (Grand Rapids: Eerdmans, 1995), pp. 186–232.

224. Cf. 1 Cor. 16; 2 Cor. 8–9.

225. It appears that Paul may have viewed the collection in an eschatological light, as a fulfillment of the prophecies about Gentiles going up to Jerusalem and making offerings.

226. Cf. the discussions by L. T. Johnson, *The Letter of James* (New York: Doubleday, 1995), and R. P. Martin, *James* (Waco: Word, 1988).

227. Rhetoric was the ancient art of persuasion involving polished speech and carefully crafted discourse.

228. James grew up in Nazareth, which as a small village was unlikely to have had a school where persons were trained to be scribes. A scribe was the ancient version of a secretary, and like modern secretaries scribes were given a varying range of freedom to compose things for the one dictating the correspondence, depending on how much they were trusted.

229. See R. J. Bauckham, *2 Peter, Jude* (Waco: Word, 1983).

230. It is interesting that this prescript to the letter of Jude bears a formal resemblance to the inscription on the James ossuary, in that Jude identifies himself in relationship to two different relatives, and the last clause is "brother of James," just as the last clause on the ossuary is "brother of Jesus." The other possible similarity is that in both the prescript in Jude and the ossuary the identifications are in relationship to persons one in someway is or was subordinate to.

231. The term "Diaspora" means literally "Dispersion," and it refers to the Jews living in any and all countries outside the Holy Land.

232. This Greek term *Christianoi* literally means those who are adherents of or belong to Christ.

233. R. J. Bauckham, *James* (London: Routledge, 1999), p. 16.

234. There are two forms of this seminal sermon material, with the Matthean form being clearly more Jewish in flavor. The other is found in Luke 6:17–49. As examples of that Jewishness, Matthew speaks of the kingdom of heaven as opposed to Luke's kingdom of God, and Matthew says, "Blessed are the poor in spirit" as opposed to Luke's "Blessed are the poor." See my Matthew commentary (Macon: Smyth and Helwys, 2006).

235. See my discussion of this list in *Jesus the Sage* (Minneapolis: Fortress, 1994), pp. 240–42.

236. See L. T. Johnson, *The Letter of James,* pp. 146–56, for various theories on how Christian a book James actually is.

237. P. J. Hartin, *James and the Q Sayings of Jesus* (Sheffield: Sheffield Academic Press, 1991), pp. 188–89.

238. As in the case of other NT documents, the audience is primarily hearers rather than readers; thus the text is written in a way appropriate for oral communication. For instance, wordplay (James. 1:1–2; 1:13; 3:17), alliteration (James 3:5), and other poetic devices are used to enhance the impact of the words on the audience.

239. The Wisdom of Solomon, like Sirach and the Wisdom of Jesus ben Sira, is an intertestamental Jewish text that focuses on giving sage advice.

240. The intertestamental period refers to the time between the writing of the latest composition found in the OT and the first composition found in the NT. The earliest NT documents are probably Paul's letters, the first of which was composed about A.D. 49. It is more difficult to say when the latest OT book was written, but it was probably before

the Maccabean era—which is to say, at least before the second century B.C. if not somewhat earlier.

241. Both 2 and 3 John are brief letters trying to solve internal community problems; 1 John is an exhortation trying to inculcate certain core ethical values, chiefly love, in order to help prevent the community from fragmenting, but also to help it discern and reject false teaching.

242. See Bauckham, *James*, p. 32.

243. By this I mean he was not for imposing Levitical Laws on all Jews, nor was he in favor of imposing the entire Mosaic Law on Gentile converts.

244. What Luther meant is that the epistle lacked substance; it lacked, in Luther's view, the gospel message about Jesus.

245. The term "eschatological" comes from the Greek *eschaton*, which means "end things." It is a reference to a belief that God's final saving and judging activity was already transpiring during the first century A.D.

246. See the discussion in Witherington, *Grace in Galatia*, pp. 216–40.

247. Bauckham, *James*, p. 140.

248. Bauckham, *James*, pp. 133–34.

249. Cf. 5:12 to Matt. 5:34–37.

250. In this section I am following the helpful treatment of Bauckham, "James and Jesus," pp. 100–137, here pp. 126–29.

251. Josephus, *Ant.* 20.199–203.

252. Josephus's works were in large measure preserved by Christian copyists through the centuries after the NT era, for Jews often saw Josephus as an ambiguous figure who himself collaborated with Rome. There was indeed some Christian editing of his work, as is usually recognized, for instance, in the passage that speaks about Jesus: *Ant.* 18.63–64. This is not thought to be the case about this present passage, however.

253. This was rightly emphasized in the helpful lecture given by Professor S. Mason, an expert in the interpretation of Josephus, at the Ossuary Panel Discussion at the Society for Biblical Literature (SBL) meeting Nov. 23, 2002, in Toronto.

254. Professor L. Feldman pointed out at the above-mentioned SBL meeting that the term "so-called" does not have to have a polemical edge. It can simply mean "the one *who was named or known as* the Christ."

255. Here the important essay by R. Bauckham, "For What Offense Was James Put to Death?" in *James the Just and Christian Origins*, pp. 199–231, must be consulted.

256. Nevertheless, there may be a historical memory behind the Christian account, for as Bauckham shows, it was the normal Jewish procedure in stoning to first push a person off of a high place and then stone him or her. (See Luke 4:29, where the practice was attempted on Jesus.) See Bauckham, "For What Offense," pp. 202–4.

257. In James's case, the ossuary is just long enough to contain the longest bone, as well as the smaller ones.

258. Since we have the example of Caiaphas being buried in an ossuary as well, and Caiaphas was a Sadducee, we cannot automatically assume that the person buried in the ossuary believed in bodily resurrection. It may merely suggest that he believed in some sort of viable form of afterlife. But in the case of James, it surely does comport with his belief in resurrection.

259. Greco-Roman inscriptions on sarcophagi could be quite extensive, in contrast to what we find on Jewish ossuaries, and they were often honorific, touting one's accomplishments in life. The James inscription is honorific only in the sense that it mentions James's more famous brother, which confers honor back on James.

260. The one parallel ossuary inscription mentions a brother who buries the deceased brother, which is clearly not the case here. But this other Jewish inscription mentions

that the brother is named Hanin or Hanina. It may in fact prove to be a close parallel
with the James ossuary, because it may be that this is a reference to another famous
rabbi, Hanina ben Dosa, who helped Judaism survive the fall of Jerusalem. The jury is
still out on this other inscription, but if it proves to be truly a reference to Hanina ben
Dosa, then we would have something very interesting here—the only two Jewish ossuary
inscriptions that mention brothers mention them because they were very famous Jewish
teachers.

261. Eusebius is quoting Hegesippus in *Hist. Eccl.* 4.22.4.

262. As my doctoral student Laura Ice has suggested, this may have been because of the Jewish tradition about the priesthood being passed down within a family line. For example,
one member or another of the family of Caiaphas was in power as high priest most of
the first century, until the destruction of the Temple in A.D. 70. This conjecture becomes
all the more plausible when we consider the fact that James was seen as one of the pillars of the new eschatological temple that God was building for his messianic people.

263. The so-called second Jewish revolt (really the third, if you count the Maccabean wars)
was in the early second century A.D. and was led by or centered on Simon bar Kokhba. It
was as ill-fated as the revolt in the 60s. Thereafter the Romans imposed severe restrictions in regard to Jews and especially their visitation to Jerusalem.

264. Bauckham, "For What Offense?" p. 228.

265. Sometimes in the hill country of Judea, with its more moderate climate and with the
burial of someone in a cave, it could take a considerable period of time, even over a year,
before only the bones of the deceased would remain.

266. We have examined the later Christian traditions about the burial of James in Jerusalem
in Shanks and Witherington, *The Brother of Jesus,* pp. 177–97.

267. R. Bauckham, "Jude, Epistle of," *Anchor Bible Dictionary,* ed. D. N. Freedman (New York:
Doubleday, 1992), vol. 3, pp. 1098–1103, here p. 1101.

268. W. Brosend, *James and Jude* (Cambridge: Cambridge Univ. Press, 2004), p. 6.

269. On 2 Peter as a composite document drawing on a variety of sources and attributed to
its most famous source, Peter, see Chapter 4.

270. See Bauckham, "The Letter of Jude: An Account of Research," *ANRW* 2/25/5 (1988):
3791–3826.

271. See Bauckham, "Jude," pp. 1099–1100.

272. See Brosend, *James and Jude,* pp. 183–87.

273. A different and much fuller form of some of the material found here can be found in
Witherington, *The Paul Quest.*

274. For the Jewish discussion, see J. Klausner, *From Jesus to Paul* (London: Allen & Unwin,
1943); C. G. Montefiore, *Judaism and St. Paul* (London: Goshen, 1914); H. J. Schoeps, *Paul:
The Theology of the Apostle in the Light of Jewish Religious History* (Philadelphia: Westminster,
1961); A. Segal, *Paul the Convert* (New Haven: Yale Univ. Press, 1992); and more recently,
D. Boyarin, *A Radical Jew* (Berkeley: Univ. of California Press, 1997).

275. Phil. 3:4–6; 2 Cor. 11:22.

276. 1 Cor. 9:20–23.

277. See the discussion in Witherington, *Grace in Galatia,* pp. 25–35.

278. On this, see the introduction to Witherington, *Grace in Galatia,* pp. 8–13.

279. See rightly G. Lyons, *Pauline Autobiography: Toward a New Understanding* (Atlanta: Scholars
Press, 1985), pp. 150–58.

280. 2 Macc. 2:21; 8:1; 14:38; 4 Macc. 4:26.

281. Gal. 1:14; 2:15.

282. Gal. 4 and 6. See my discussion of Paul's view of the Law in *Grace in Galatia,* pp. 341–55.

283. Cf. Gal. 3–4 and Rom. 9–11 to Heb. 11–12.

284. See J. Becker, *Paul: Apostle to the Gentiles* (Louisville: Westminster, 1993), p. 2.

285. See Segal, *Paul the Convert,* pp. 117–25.

286. 1 Cor. 15:9; Gal. 1:13, 23; Phil. 3:6.

287. See Gal. 6:12; 2 Cor. 11:24.

288. See N. T. Wright, "Paul, Arabia, and Elijah," *Journal of Biblical Literature* 115 (1996): 683–92.

289. See T. Donaldson, "Zealot and Convert: The Origin of Paul's Christ-Torah Antithesis," *Catholic Biblical Quarterly* 51 (1989): 655–82, whom I am following here.

290. Donaldson, "Zealot and Convert," p. 656.

291. See A. J. Saldarini, *Pharisee, Scribes and Sadducees in Palestinian Society* (Wilmington: Glazier, 1988).

292. See M. Hengel and A. M. Schwemer, *Paul: Between Damascus and Antioch* (Louisville: Westminster/Knox, 1997), pp. 7–10. See D. Daube, "Rabbinic Methods of Interpretation and Hellenistic Rhetoric," *Hebrew Union College Annual* 22 (1949): 239–62, for the influence on Hillel of Alexandrian rhetorical education.

293. Had Paul not seen a fundamental antithesis between what was appropriate now that Christ had come and what was appropriate during the reign of the Mosaic covenant, it is hard to understand why after his conversion he did not become like those referred to in Acts 21:20, zealous for the Law and believers in Christ, or like the Pharisaic Judaizers themselves (see Acts 15:5).

294. F. Craddock, *Philippians* (Atlanta: John Knox, 1985), p. 59.

295. Stendahl's enormously influential though now dated essay on this matter can be found in his *Paul among Jews and Gentiles* (Philadelphia: Fortress, 1978).

296. Cf. Gal. 1:13, 23; 1 Cor. 15:9; see 1 Tim. 1:13.

297. See the discussion of D. A. Carson, "Pauline Inconsistency: Reflections on 1 Cor. 9:1–23," *Churchman* 100 (1986): 6–45.

298. See the excursus in Witherington, *Grace in Galatia,* pp. 341–56. The literature on the subject is quite enormous, but some of the more helpful works are J. D. G. Dunn, ed., *Paul and the Mosaic Law* (Tubingen: Mohr, 1996), especially the detailed bibliography on pp. 335–41; F. Thielman, *Paul and the Law* (Downers Grove: InterVarsity Press, 1994); E. P. Sanders, *Paul, the Law, and the Jewish People* (Minneapolis: Fortress, 1983); S. Westerholm, *Israel's Law and the Church's Faith: Paul and His Recent Interpreters* (Grand Rapids: Eerdmans, 1988).

299. Rom. 3:19; 7:1; 1 Cor. 14:21.

300. 1 Cor. 9:8–9.

301. On this point, see R. B. Hays, *Echoes of Scripture in the Letters of Paul* (New Haven: Yale, 1989).

302. Gal. 3:23–4:7.

303. 2 Cor. 3:7–18.

304. See Gal. 2:11–14.

305. We can't simply contrast Paul's universalism with Judaism's particularism. Paul also believes in a form of particularism, though it is a universalistic particularism, if we may coin an apparent oxymoron. That is, Paul believes that salvation is in principle available for all, but only by grace and through faith in the particular person Jesus Christ. I fail to see how this is different in principle from the particularism of arguing that all may be saved or be part of God's people by submitting to the Mosaic Law. Even the Law has a place for Gentiles or *goyim* in the kingdom if they will but take up the yoke and keep the Law. Thus in the end this debate is not about universalism versus particularism, but between two forms of particularism that have the potential to include all but are at odds with one another.

306. Gal. 5:14; cf. Eph. 5:33.

307. Thielman, *Paul and the Law,* p. 140.

308. See the fuller discussion in Witherington, *Grace in Galatia,* pp. 341–55.

309. By definition a sect is an offshoot of or schism from a larger religious group that takes various elements of the mother religion into its own new community but often transforms those elements. There is generally no continuity of community between the parent group and the offshoot; the two have largely if not entirely different members. A cult, on the other hand, is by definition the founding of a new religious group, not a splitting off from an old one.

310. See my discussion in *Paul's Narrative Thought World* (Louisville: Westminster, 1994).

311. See my exegesis of this text in *Jesus, Paul, and the End of the World* (Downers Grove: InterVarsity Press, 1990).

312. See, for example, 1 Cor. 9; 2 Cor. 11:7. See also E. A. Judge, "Paul's Boasting in Relation to Contemporary Professional Practice," *ABR* 16 (1968): 37–50, his "St. Paul and Classical Society," *JAC* 15 (1972): 19–36, and his "The Social Identity of the First Christians," *JRH* 11 (1980): 201–17.

313. Acts 21:39.

314. On all these matters the more detailed discussion in my *Acts of the Apostles,* pp. 679–84, should be considered.

315. See T. J. Leary, "Paul's Improper Name," *New Testament Studies* 38 (1992): 467–69, and on the subject in general C. J. Hemer, "The Name of Paul," *Tyndale Bulletin* 36 (1986): 179–83.

316. Another form of this material has appeared in Witherington, *The Paul Quest.*

317. G. Lyons, *Pauline Autobiography* (Chico: Scholars Press, 1985), p. 171.

318. B. Malina and J. Neyrey, *Portraits of Paul* (Louisville: Westminster Press, 1996), p. 40.

319. See, for example, Malina and Neyrey, *Portraits,* p. 39, where these authors stress that Greco-Roman culture valued stability and the status quo and so "constancy of character. Hence 'change' of character was neither expected nor praiseworthy. Normally adult persons were portrayed as living out the manner of life that had always characterized them." The virtuous Stoic philosopher was one who "surmises nothing, repents of nothing, is never wrong, and never changes his opinion" (Cicero, *Pro Murena* 61).

320. See the classic study by A. D. Nock, *Conversion* (Oxford: Oxford Univ. Press, 1933).

321. Gal. 1:19–20.

322. A. Segal, "The Cost of Proselytism and Conversion," *Society for Biblical Literature 1988 Seminar Papers,* ed. D. J. Lull (Atlanta: Scholars Press, 1988), pp. 336–69, here p. 341.

323. That there was such a category of Gentile synagogue adherents is now demonstrable from the inscriptions. See the discussion in my *Acts of the Apostles,* pp. 341–44.

324. See rightly R. Kanter, *Commitment and Community* (Cambridge: Harvard Univ. Press, 1972), pp. 61–74.

325. See Gal. 3:2–8; 1 Cor. 1:13–17.

326. See K. Stendahl, *Paul among Jews and Gentiles.*

327. 2 Cor. 3; see also Gal. 4.

328. See S. Kim, *The Origin of Paul's Gospel* (Grand Rapids: Eerdmans, 1981), and more recently his "The Mystery of Rom. 11:25–6," a lecture given at the August 1996 Studiorum Novi Testamentum Societas meeting in Strasbourg, France.

329. For a fresh set of discussions of the ongoing impact of the Damascus road experience on Paul and his gospel, see R. N. Longenecker, ed., *The Road from Damascus: The Impact of Paul's Conversion on His Life, Thought, and Ministry* (Grand Rapids: Eerdmans, 1997).

330. See G. D. Fee, *God's Empowering Presence* (Peabody: Hendrickson, 1994).

331. See my discussion in *Conflict and Community,* pp. 459–65.

332. On the so-called hidden years, see M. Hengel and A. M. Schwemer, *Paul between Damascus and Antioch: The Unknown Years* (Louisville: Westminster, 1997).

333. See A. T. Lincoln, "Paul the Visionary," *New Testament Studies* 25 (1979): 204–220.

334. Cf. Luke 23:43; Rev. 2:7.

335. This is another term that supports the position that Paul was not suggesting in this text that such experiences were rare for him.

336. For confirmation from Acts, see for example not only the account of his conversion in Acts 9, but also Acts 16:6–10; 23:11. For confirmation from Paul himself, see 1 Cor. 2:1, 10, 16; 4:1; 15:51.

337. See Gal. 4:11–15.

338. See J. W. McCant, "Paul's Thorn of Rejected Apostleship," *New Testament Studies* 34 (1988): 550–72.

339. See, for example, Acts 13:11; 14:10; 16:18; 19:11; 28:3–6.

340. See 1 Cor. 11 on the former, and see both 1 Cor. 14:39 and my discussion of all this in *Conflict and Community*, pp. 276–80.

341. See the discussion in Fee, *God's Empowering Presence*, p. 583.

342. See the discussion in Fee, *God's Empowering Presence*, p. 586, and J. D. G. Dunn, *Romans 1–8* (Waco: Word, 1988), pp. 479–80.

343. See my discussion in *Friendship and Finances in Philippi* (Valley Forge: Trinity, 1994), pp. 71–72.

344. See my discussion in *Paul's Narrative Thought World* (Louisville: Westminster, 1994), pp. 245–49.

345. See Witherington, *Jesus, Paul and the End*, pp. 184–90.

346. 1 Cor. 9:27.

347. Phil. 3:14.

348. See Witherington, *Grace in Galatia*, pp. 389–405.

349. Such as 1QS 4:5.

350. 2 Cor. 6:6; 1 Tim. 4:12; 6:11; 2 Tim. 2:22; 2 Pet. 1:5–7.

351. See the discussion in Dunn, *The Epistle to the Galatians* (Peabody, MA: Hendrickson, 1993), p. 310, and Gal. 5:14.

352. See 2 Cor. 11:23–29.

353. 1 Cor. 11:1.

354. E. Castelli, *Imitating Paul* (Louisville: Westminster, 1991), makes the mistake of reading this appeal to imitation as a power move on Paul's part, not recognizing the pedagogical context. See Witherington, *Conflict and Community*, pp. 144–46.

355. See Quintilian, *Inst. Or.* 10.2.1–28.

356. See 1 Cor. 2:16.

357. See Witherington, *Conflict and Community*, pp. 145–46.

358. Hengel, *Paul: Between Damascus and Antioch*, p. 16.

359. See R. Bultmann, *Theology of the New Testament*, 2 vols. (New York: Scribner, 1951, 1955).

360. See L. Hurtado, *Lord Jesus Christ: Devotion to Jesus in Earliest Christianity* (Grand Rapids: Eerdmans, 2003).

361. My study of the church in Rome in the 50s (see Witherington and Hyatt, *Letter to the Romans*) pointed out that the Gentile and Jewish Christians in Rome were meeting separately, and one of the functions of Paul's message to the Romans was to try to get the Gentile Christian majority to do a better job of embracing the Jewish Christian minority. See especially Paul's imperatives in Rom. 16.

362. P. Trebilco, *The Early Christians in Ephesus from Paul to Ignatius* (Tubingen: Mohr-Siebeck, 2004), p. 99.

363. Trebilco, *Early Christians*, p. 593.

364. Trebilco, *Early Christians*, p. 382.

365. See Trebilco, *Early Christians*, pp. 614–19.

366. See Witherington, *The New Testament Story* (Grand Rapids: Eerdmans, 2004).

367. F. Buechner, *The Life of Jesus* (San Francisco: Harper, 1989), pp. 9–14, excerpted.

368. For more on all of this, see Witherington, *The Christology of Jesus,* and Witherington, *The Many Faces of the Christ* (New York: Continuum, 2005).

APPENDIX: THE ROYAL LINE OF JESUS?

1. See the review of this find in *Biblical Archeology Review* 2005 (May/June): 36–41, 58.

2. See my lengthy discussion of their relationship in *The Christology of Jesus,* pp. 34–56.

Subject Index

Scripture Index

OTHER SCRIPTURES